The discovery of humanity

THE DISCOVERY OF HUMANITY:
An introduction to anthropology

CHAD OLIVER
The University of Texas, Austin

1817

HARPER & ROW PUBLISHERS, New York
Cambridge, Hagerstown, Philadelphia, San Francisco,
London, Mexico City, São Paulo, Sydney

Sponsoring Editor: Alan M. Spiegel
Project Editor: Rhonda Roth
Designer: Michel Craig
Production Manager: Jeanie Berke
Photo Researcher: Myra Schachne
Compositor: The Clarinda Company
Printer and Binder: Halliday Lithograph Corporation
Art Studio: Vantage Art Inc.

The Discovery of Humanity: An Introduction to Anthropology

Library of Congress Cataloging in Publication Data

Oliver, Symmes Chadwick, 1928-
    The discovery of humanity.

    Includes bibliographies and index.
    1. Anthropology. I. Title.
GN25.046   301.2   79-26150
ISBN 0-397-47405-5

PHOTO CREDITS

To my daughter and son
Kim and Glen
with thanks, love, hope, and confidence

Contents

Preface: who needs a textbook?

Who needs a textbook, and what is it for?

There was a time when there were not many anthropologists, and courses in anthropology were basically restricted to the faithful few. The explosive growth of anthropology did not occur until after World War II. Times have decidedly changed. There are now thousands of anthropologists all over the world, and the American Anthropological Association alone has more than 10,000 members. Anthropology is no longer viewed as a somewhat exotic curiosity; it has become an integral part of a general education.

Whenever you multiply the practitioners of a given subject, you multiply the possible points of view. Anthropology is alive and it is a field in ferment. Anthropologists do not all agree on what the discipline is and where it should be going.

Writing a textbook today is not simply a matter of taking a series of ideas shared by all anthropologists and presenting it in an effective and readable way. Unless the text is so bland that it says nothing at all, the task involves difficult decisions about which approach to take, what to put in and what to leave out, and where the emphasis should be.

Clearly, there is no urgent need for "just another textbook." To put it mildly, there is no shortage of textbooks. If it is going to be useful—and in the final analysis that is what any good textbook should be—a text must do something different.

What is distinctive about this one?

This is an introductory text in cultural anthropology, but it stresses the unity of subfields of anthropology as a discipline. In our effort to understand the human animal, the divorce between physical (or biological) anthropology and cultural anthropology has not been a productive strategy.

Although I have given full weight to the importance of culture, I have placed more emphasis on biological considerations than is customary in a book devoted to cultural anthropology. The issue here goes far beyond such currently fashionable topics as sociobiology; it attempts to discover what kind of animals we are and why we function the way we do. Seen from this perspective, this is a book that can be used in courses on general anthropology as well as in courses with a more specific focus on cultural anthropology.

This is a text aimed at the audience we actually have. I hold the firm opinion that an introductory text is for introductory students. The aim of this book is to engage and inform those students, not to dazzle the instructor. Who are these students?

In any introductory anthropology class large enough to be statistically significant, many and probably most of the students are not anthropology majors. For most of them, this may be their only formal exposure to anthropology. The chance that *any* student in a particular introductory class will one day be a professional anthropologist is slim.

What does this mean? I think that it means that we must consider carefully what we are trying to do in introductory courses. We need to resist the trap of thinking of a first course in anthropology as the initial hurdle to be jumped on a track that leads ultimately to a Ph.D. degree. Our purpose is not to teach students how to ''do'' anthropology or to train them to ''be'' anthropologists. Rather, our goal should be to explain what anthropology is and why it matters to a variety of students. That is what this book seeks to do.

It is neither wise nor necessary to neglect the needs of students who may elect to do further work in anthropology. There can be no substitute for a solid foundation. At the same time, we must recognize our real priorities and speak to the audience that we actually have. Given the choice between clarity of presentation and the confusion that can result from including every possible example and shade of meaning, my vote has been for clarity.

This is a book that stresses the importance of field studies of the nonhuman primates. Perhaps the most fundamental question that anthropology can ask is this one: What does it mean to be human? If we are going to answer that question, it is essential that we understand both the degree to which human beings resemble other animals and the specific ways in which we are different. Our fellow primates are our closest living relatives in the animal world, and the chimpanzee in particular is very near to us in an evolutionary sense. I have spent a great deal of time discussing the ''natural'' behavior of chimpanzees for two primary reasons. First, somewhere in that shadowy area that spells out the differences between how chimpanzees do things and how human beings do them lies the essence of humanity. Second, the lifeways of wild chimpanzees pose some of the key questions about the human animal in a notably vivid way. It is always a mistake in teaching to offer complex answers to basic questions before the significance of the questions has been made clear. It has been my experience that it is virtually impossible to examine the behavior of chimpanzees without arriving at some appreciation of many of the problems with which anthropology concerns itself, including the phenomenon of culture.

This is a text that is designed to illustrate both the universals and the diversities that interpenetrate the human experience. It is surely crucial to understand the true range of cultural variability that has existed and still exists on this planet. One of the traditional lessons that anthropology has to teach is that "we"—whoever "we" happen to be—are not the models for all of mankind. However, the emphasis on the unique qualities of each and every cultural system should not blind us to another important anthropological lesson. You find human beings in all sociocultural settings; the people who live in other cultures are not aliens from another world. Moreover, there are ways in which cultures are much alike as well as ways in which they are different. I have tried to strike a balance between cultural universals and cultural distinctiveness, and I have attempted to avoid the habit of making people in various human societies seem to be more different than in fact they are.

In this book, ethnographic references are kept down to a workable number. Professional anthropologists are necessarily familiar with a great many human societies; in a sense, we deal with them on a daily basis. However, students who are encountering anthropology for the first time tend to be bewildered by the introduction of literally hundreds of different ethnographic examples. For this reason, I have been careful to utilize a minimum effective ethnographic universe rather than a maximum one. You will find many of the classics here—included because they are of proven teaching effectiveness—but you will also find that I have repeatedly used a small number of human societies, including our own, to illustrate my points. It seems to me that this approach has a double advantage. First, it enables the student to concentrate on the central arguments rather than bogging the student down in a maze of details. Second, it allows the instructor to introduce original examples or to utilize appropriate books of readings or selected case studies. In the same spirit, I have approached the study of prehistory in terms of major trends rather than through an analysis of lithic assemblages.

This is a text that provides a solid background in the history of anthropology. There is an unfortunate but understandable tendency in teaching anthropology to present materials as though "we've always known that." The plain fact is that we haven't. An important part of learning what anthropology is all about is getting to know some of the significant figures in the development of anthropology and understanding what sorts of problems they worked on and why. You will find that the two chapters devoted to the history of anthropology are not mere rehashes of familiar materials. I consider them basic to an understanding of where anthropology has been and where it may be going.

The goal of this book is to communicate. An introductory textbook that students can neither read nor understand is a waste of time for *everybody* concerned. The students would be better off without it, and the instructor is placed in the awkward position of attempting to explain what the author was trying to say.

Jargon has its uses—it is a convenient kind of shorthand when specialists talk to each other—but it has absolutely no place in an introductory textbook. I have avoided it like the plague.

If a text is going to communicate, it should be interesting. There can be no excuse for sensationalism in a book of this kind, but sensationalism is not necessary. The facts of the anthropological enterprise are intriguing in themselves. What is helpful, I think, is a prose style that does not cast the author in the role of an omniscient robot. I have relaxed where I felt that it was appropriate to do so, and I have occasionally tried to speak directly to the students as one human being to another. I have expressed some of my own opinions, but I have taken care to separate opinion from fact. A pinch of humility is a good ingredient in the anthropological stew.

The study of anthropology should be a fascinating thing. It is not a chore to be performed but an opening of the doors that lead to challenging new horizons. I would not presume to tell you how to teach your course, or even to determine what is of lasting importance in anthropology as opposed to what is ephemeral, but I do venture to hope that I have communicated something of the intellectual excitement of anthropology to you, who are my coworkers, and to the students, without whom anthropology as we know it could not continue to exist.

ACKNOWLEDGMENTS

It is not always easy to know where to stop in expressing appreciation to those who have helped in the creation of a textbook, but in this case I certainly know where to begin. Although in one sense he had nothing to do with writing this book, there is another sense in which this book could not have existed in its present form without the contributions of Walter Goldschmidt.

In the many years of our association, beginning when I was a graduate student at the University of California at Los Angeles, I have been profoundly influenced and stimulated by Walter Goldschmidt's creative approach to anthropology. While he would not agree with everything in this book and is not responsible for any of my errors of omission or commission, Goldschmidt's thinking permeates this work. It has not been possible to footnote all of his ideas, but I suspect that he will recognize his brainchildren. Thanks may be an inadequate tribute to a great teacher, but they are offered with sincerity and affection.

I owe a great debt to all of my teachers. I cannot single them all out for special mention, but I would like to name three of them. J. Gilbert McAllister made an anthropologist out of me in the first place and provided a model of integrity that I have never forgotten. Ralph L. Beals gave me wise counsel on many occasions. Joseph B. Birdsell nearly turned me into a physical anthropologist and left me with a lifelong interest in that aspect of anthropology.

My old friend, Edgar V. Winans, was instrumental in turning the idea for this book into a reality. Of the many reviewers of the manuscript, I would particularly like to thank Michael A. Little of the State University of New York at Binghamton. I learned something from each review, but Little's perceptive comments were helpful and very much appreciated.

I am indebted to all of my colleagues at the University of Texas at Austin, who have answered my many questions with care and patience. In particular, thanks are due to E. Mott Davis who endured countless queries as we consumed hamburgers together at the late, lamented Holiday House.

I wish to express my appreciation to the thousands of introductory students I have had the pleasure of teaching since 1955. Their support and enthusiasm have meant a great deal to me.

CHAD OLIVER

The discovery of humanity

1

A Point of View

Whatever else we human beings may or may not be, we are animals. This fact is hardly news, and most of us can rattle off certain salient points without thinking very much about them: we belong to the *animal* kingdom, we are *vertebrates* (because we have a backbone), we are *mammals* (because we have warm blood, hair, sweat glands, milk-producing devices, and the like), and we are *primates* (because we resemble other animals such as monkeys and apes more than we do animals like cows, horses, rats, or porcupines). Indeed, Bertram S. Kraus (1964) has suggested that all of us can tack a string of initials after our names simply by virtue of being what we are.

Thus: Sally Smith, A.K., S.K.M., P.C., S.P.V., C.M., O.P., S.O.A., S.F.H., F.H., G.H., S.S., S.S.S. The initials stand for:

Animal Kingdom
Subkingdom Metazoa
Phylum Chordata
Subphylum Vertebrata
Class Mammalia
Order Primates
Suborder Anthropoidea
Superfamily Hominoidea
Family Hominidae
Genus *Homo*
Species *sapiens*
Subspecies *sapiens*

This sort of thing is both fun and informative, but it remains an essentially sterile exercise in classification unless we go on to ask what would seem to be the obvious questions: So what? What difference does it make? What are the consequences of our being mammals and primates?

If we are interested in finding out why we are what we are and why we do some of things we do — which in one sense is what anthropology is all about — then it would seem logical to examine at least three elementary propositions.

1. Since we are mammals, we share some of the broad behavioral patterns of mammals generally. Growing hair, nursing our young, and being playful with our children are basic mammalian characteristics.

2. Since we are primates, we share some specific traits with other primates. Consider a few simple examples. You can climb a tree and so can I. (So can an Eskimo, even if the Eskimo has never seen a tree before.) This may not seem particularly remarkable, but have a horse try it. Moreover, we climb trees in a special kind of way: we grasp with our hands that have protective nails on the fingertips, rather than digging claws into the bark. When we climb a tree, or do almost anything else, we depend on our eyes to give us the information we need. Primates as a group have invested heavily in their eyes, just as they have developed grasping hands and feet. Observe a person hunting with a dog. The dog's first impulse is to get that nose down near the ground; the dog does not shade his eyes with his paws and peer about for prey. On the other side of the coin, you would find it decidedly unusual for a human hunter to drop down on all fours and sniff around for scent. On another level, we live our lives in social groups composed of both sexes and all ages; this too is a primate characteristic. You might think that all mammals do this, but they do not: There are many mammals in which the males remain separate from the females except at mating times and adults do not stay with their offspring after the young have reached puberty.

3. Since we are particular kinds of primates — we are not monkeys or apes, after all — there should be some aspects of our behavior that are uniquely human. Suppose you meet a man for the first time and are introduced to him. "Dear, this is your Uncle Joe. He just flew in from Saint Louis last week. You remember I told you about him — he's the one who wrote the book about ghosts." Here we have a small hatful of human attributes. You meet Uncle Joe with *words* — words that communicate about another time (last week) and another place (Saint Louis). He is your *Uncle* Joe; he is identified by putting him in a slot in a kinship system. You are told that he wrote a book, which other animals cannot do, and also that the book deals with ghosts — which is to say that it is concerned with the supernatural, a very human concept. Since Uncle Joe presumably does not have wings, we can assume that he flew in an airplane, which suggests a degree of technological complexity unique to the human species.

How do we know what is in fact unique to the human species and what is not? This is a critical question, and we will return to it shortly. Here, I would suggest that there is really just one way to find out for sure: we must examine the lifeways of nonhuman animals in order to determine both what we have in common with them and in what ways we are different. Until quite recently, our ignorance of the actual behavior of other animals was astonishing, and that ignorance was in part responsible for many of the *assumptions* we made about what was uniquely human.

It is now time to explain the reason for the preceding discussion, because the underlying rationale is crucial to understanding the point of view toward anthropology which this book seeks to develop. I would hope that you would find the three outlined propositions unexceptional and indeed more or less self-evident, but it is always a mistake to assume that what seems logical to one of us will necessarily seem logical to all of us.

UNDERSTANDING THE HUMAN ANIMAL

In order to make the problem clear, let us state two opposite and extreme ideas relating to the interpretation of the human animal.

The Superorganic Approach

The essence of this intellectual position may be stated as follows. What distinguishes mankind from other animals is the human possession of culture, which results in a special kind of learned behavior. Once it comes into existence, culture operates pretty much on its own; human beings are the *carriers* of culture, but otherwise they have little significant relationship to it. Any attempt to "explain" culture by reference to other kinds of phenomena — biological factors, say, or psychological considerations — is characterized as a "reductionist fallacy." Although the superorganic idea was first spelled out by A. L. Kroeber (1917), it received its clearest definition from Leslie A. White. In a characteristic passage, White argues:

> In short, it was discovered that culture may be considered, from the standpoint of scientific analysis and interpretation, as a thing *sui generis,* as a class of events and processes that behaves in terms of its own principles and laws and which consequently can be explained only in terms of its own elements and processes. Culture may thus be considered as a self-contained, self-determined process; one that can be explained only in terms of itself. (White 1949:xviii)

If we take the superorganic idea literally, several notions flow naturally from it. The business of anthropology is to study culture. Since all culture is learned, it is futile to try to find out anything about culture by searching for any innate behavior patterns in the human animal. Since culture can only be understood in terms of itself, culture alone is what we must study. Since human behavior is cultural behavior and cultural behavior is human behavior, there is really no other subject except culture that is relevant if we are investigating how and why human beings do the things they do. In a word: Everything is learned, and what is learned is culture.

The Exploding Bundle of Instincts

The conceptual opposite of the idea of the superorganic is the notion that human behavior can be explained without introducing cultural considerations at all. According to this view, the human animal is "programmed" with all sorts of biologically built-in urges, drives, and behavioral patterns. Just as with certain insects that are born as larvae, then spin cocoons around themselves, and finally emerge as adults equipped with everything they need in order to function, learning is of little or no importance. The basis of human behavior is instinctive — that is, innate — and we can be understood essentially as so many bipedal grasshoppers.

If we adopt this theoretical position, we can answer any fundamental question about human behavior by resorting to a few magic words and phrases. "Why do we fight wars?" "Because it's human nature to fight." "Why do we have family systems?" "Because we have an instinct to form pair bonds." "Why do males exercise political control in human societies?" "Because men have an urge to dominate women." And so on, and so on.

In point of fact, I know of no scientist who advocates such an extreme and simplistic "biological" theory of human behavior. Konrad Lorenz, who is often cited as representing such a position, in reality does nothing of the kind; his classic study of aggression by no means ignores culture, and Lorenz specifically states: "All the great dangers threatening humanity with extinction are direct consequences of conceptual thought and verbal speech" (Lorenz 1966:238). However, it is true that some scientists who stress the biological determinants of human behavior — including Lorenz in some passages — do tend to downgrade the cultural dimension. Thus we find zoologist Desmond Morris in *The Naked Ape* discussing primate evolution and contrasting "basic biological changes" with "mere cultural ones" (Morris 1967:39). If we were to sum up the instinctive view of human behavior, it would go like this: Nothing is learned, and everything is built-in genetically.

Now, what are we to make of all this? Traditional anthropology — and particularly cultural anthropology — has leaned very heavily toward the superorganic end of the spectrum. It may not have gone all the way in that direction, and it may have qualified its views to some extent, but it was clearly much closer to the superorganic viewpoint than to any other. As a matter of fact, this has been a characteristic of "social science" generally. The basic theoretical stance has been that what distinguishes human beings from other animals is learned behavior and that whatever there may be that is innate in mankind is of a fundamentally trivial nature. When I was a student, we were taught a kind of dogma: Other animals had instincts, but we had *culture*. The human animal had no instincts apart from a sucking reflex (to enable the infant to nurse) and perhaps a fear of falling. Moreover, it was at least implied that the cultures we learned were wholly arbitrary: A culture could take *any* form and there was no relationship worth mentioning between a cultural system and the psychobiological characteristics of human beings.

You do not have to take my word for this, and I will refrain from barraging you with quotations. I suggest that you check out almost any anthropology text-book written 15 or 20 years ago—and some a good deal more recently than that—and see for yourself. Do not be misled by the drawings of skeletons and the genetic diagrams: Those refer to the physical evolution of the human *body,* and you will find that there is no connection between this material and the discussions of culture.

There will come a time when a theoretical approach that takes into account *both* the importance of culture and what is biologically rooted in the human animal will be taken for granted and will require no special comment. We have not yet reached that point, however, and therefore some explanation is necessary.

Of course, what we are dealing with here is basically the old nature-versus-nurture controversy. Are we what we are because we are born that way or because of what happens to us after we are born? As with most troublesome questions that have plagued us for generations, there is probably some truth on both sides of the argument. By putting so much emphasis on the nurture side of the equation—quite understandably, because it is important—anthropologists have sometimes boxed themselves into theoretical positions that cannot be successfully defended. If we attempt to deny nature altogether we come face to face with a number of annoying facts that we cannot handle in our theoretical frameworks. That is one reason why a book like *The Naked Ape,* with its fascinating mixture of intriguing insights, dubious assumptions, and gratuitous potshots at anthropology, has raised so many hackles in anthropological circles. To refuse to consider valid evidence concerning the nature of the human animal is scientifically indefensible. Such a position forecloses our option and responsibility to present a balanced interpretation of human behavior.

Why have a number of anthropologists begun to question some of their own assumptions? What has been discovered that makes many of us uncomfortable with either the superorganic position or its opposite? Fundamentally, we have become aware of a few simple facts. They can be summarized this way: *All animals learn, and all animals have some innate behavior patterns. The thing that is unusual about the human animal is that it learns far more of its lifeway than any other animal. This human learning is special to some degree—it is cultural learning—but it is not entirely divorced from the kind of animal we are, and it has been influenced by the evolutionary processes that shaped us.*

What does this mean? Among other things, it means that it is not just the fact that human beings are capable of learning that distinguishes us. A worm can learn (not much, but something), a rat can learn, and a horse can learn. All of the higher mammals acquire some information from experience and by observing what their companions are doing. But it is now obvious that primates in general and some of the apes in particular have much greater learning capacities than was previously realized. This opens up an important question. Is all learned behavior culture, or is there something significantly different about what human beings learn and how they learn it? We cannot answer this question until we determine precisely what it is that we mean by culture. Since this problem is addressed directly in Chapters 7, 8, and 9, I will not go into it here. It is sufficient to say at this point that an understanding of the culture process remains central to the study of the human animal.

If all animals have some innate behavior patterns, that includes us. It may very well be true that human beings have relatively few *instincts* as that term is generally understood, and therefore a greater potential for behavioral flexibility than is found among other animals. Still, we should be cautious about being too dogmatic here. As Niko Tinbergen pointed out some time ago, instinctive behavior can be extremely subtle and complex, and different kinds of animals are equipped with different kinds of instincts (Tinbergen 1951). It is certainly true that possible innate behavior patterns in the human animal have seldom been investigated and are therefore poorly understood. Nevertheless, there is enough information available to make us wary of the old picture that presents the human organism as the proverbial blank slate, passively absorbing learning without contributing anything of its own.

By way of example, a newborn human infant has a strong grasping reflex. Observe what a father does when he first comes into contact with his child. Almost invariably, he will stick out his finger so the child can reach it, and the child will clutch the finger with its hand. If you support a newborn infant and put its feet on a level surface, the infant will begin to walk. We all speak of "teaching" our children how to walk, but this is a misconception — we may help them, but we don't teach them. Babies smile, yet are not taught to do so; infants who are born blind can and do smile quite well. It is misleading at best to say that the human animal has no instincts. Trivial? Well, if you do not think the infant's smile is important in the parent-child relationship, then I can state with confidence that you have never raised a baby in your home.

This does not mean that we should concentrate our efforts on trying to identify a large number of highly specific instincts that will "explain" human behavior, since it is apparent that most of what we do cannot be understood in so mechanical a fashion. We should, however, be alert to the possibility of general tendencies that have a basis in our characteristics as animals and in our evolutionary history. For example, is it possible, as Lionel Tiger and Robin Fox have suggested, that we have an innate propensity not only to learn but also to learn particular kinds of things? These anthropologists argue that:

> We behave culturally because it is in our nature to behave culturally, because natural selection has produced an animal that has to behave culturally, that has to invent rules, make myths, speak languages, and form men's clubs, in the same way that the hamadryas baboon has to form harems, adopt infants, and bite its wives on the neck. (Tiger and Fox 1971:20)

What are the consequences of the evolutionary crucible that formed us? What roles did aggression and territoriality play, and are they still factors that must be taken into account? How much of our behavior can be illuminated by the light of our primate heritage? If we lived for more than a million years by hunting wild animals and collecting wild plant foods, has this not left its mark upon us? To what degree do ecological considerations affect the kinds of societies we form? These are large questions, and they defy easy answers. The fact that they are being asked at all is an indication that anthropology is changing, and this awakening of new interests can be traced to a series of developments.

Ethology

The relatively new field of *ethology* is concerned with the study of animal behavior. The truly distinctive aspect of ethology is its emphasis on the study of animal populations living under natural conditions, as opposed to the study of captive animals in experimental situations. There are still many kinds of animals — in fact, most kinds of animals — that have never been studied by scientifically trained observers. Still, the contributions of ethology have been both important and influential. As we learn more and more about how other animals actually live, both the similarities and the differences between their lifeways and ours become more apparent. Ethologists are in a good position to formulate hypotheses about animal behavior that can be tested against what we know about the behavior of human populations. It cannot be stressed too strongly that we can never be certain about what may be uniquely human unless we have a reasonable knowledge of what other animals can and cannot do.

Field Studies of Nonhuman Primates

Incredible as it might seem, there was not a single nonhuman primate population scientifically studied in its natural habitat until after 1930. Jane Goodall did not begin her crucial investigation of wild chimpanzees until 1960. It is one thing to perform laboratory experiments on monkeys and apes — and they are not without value — but it is something else to observe the behavior of these animals as they live their normal lives. Whether we term these studies ethology or anthropology or primatology or zoology is of little moment; it is a matter of semantics and the particular training of the observer. What is important is the information that has been obtained. We too are primates, and the more we can discover about primates generally the better we can understand ourselves. The significance of these data is discussed in Chapters 4, 5, and 6.

The Study of Human
Hunting and Gathering Societies

A number of human groups that live by hunting wild animals and by gathering wild plant foods have survived into modern times. These small-scale societies have always interested anthropologists; indeed, some of the first cultures to be studied by anthropologists were of this type.

What is new, however, is the increasing sophistication of the field research, the recognition that these societies have much in common with one another, and an awareness that we were *all* hunters and gatherers for more than a million years before we were anything else. To put the matter simply, the human animal

An Arunta hunter. This Australian society of hunters and gatherers was among
the first of its kind to be studied by anthropologists.

evolved in this context, and it is only recently—within the last 10,000 years or
so—that we have been exposed to other kinds of lifeways. In one sense, there is
nothing novel about this approach except its quality; generations of anthropologists have known that mankind started out as a hunter and gatherer, although
they did not suspect the immense duration of that lifeway. In another sense, it
represents a new (or at least revived) way of looking at things; based on accurate data, it is considering the implications of the situation within which culture
began. For example, it was as late as 1968 that the influential book *Man the
Hunter* was published, a book described on its cover as "the first intensive survey of a single, crucial stage of human development—man's once universal
hunting way of life" (Lee and DeVore 1968). Some of the results of this approach are discussed in Chapters 10 and 17.

OTHER DEVELOPMENTS IN ANTHROPOLOGY

Over the years, as anthropologists have sought to clarify their understanding of
the human animal and the nature of cultural systems, there have been other
developments that have led us to formulate new kinds of questions. It is impossible to enumerate them all—they include data from fields as diverse as archeology and behavioral genetics—but in my judgment there have been several lines
of inquiry that are particularly important.

   First, there has been a growing recognition of the importance of *cultural
universals.* It is true that in some respects every human culture is unique; so is
every bird or every rabbit. For a long time, and for very good reasons, anthro-

pologists tended to stress the differences between one sociocultural system and another. However, it is also true that in some respects all cultures are much alike in the sense that they are built out of common elements. There is a close parallel here with the phenomenon of language. Obviously, German, Russian, Swahili, and Comanche are not the same; but equally obviously, these languages are constructed out of similar ingredients such as phonemes, morphemes, and the like (see Chapter 7).

It really depends, perhaps, on the conceptual level of the analysis being employed. Suppose we look at three cultures. In one we find a belief in a crocodile god, in another a belief in ancestral spirits, and in the third we find a belief in witchcraft. These are all different, but at the same time they all fit into a common category—they all involve supernatural concepts. There are many such elements, ranging from kinship systems to territorial groups, that are found in every sociocultural system. The differences between one culture and another have to be accounted for, but so do the similarities.

Second, there has been a revival of interest in the idea of *cultural evolution*. Cultural anthropology began with an evolutionary perspective, but it was largely abandoned for many years (see Chapters 11 and 12). The modern recognition that there is considerable validity to the general idea of cultural evolution has stimulated an interest in a number of basic problems. For example, what is the relationship between energy resources and the character of cultural systems? When farming is introduced into a society of food collectors, what happens to that society?

Third, there have been substantial contributions toward a theory of *cultural ecology* (see Chapter 12). Cultural ecology is not without strong evolutionary implications, since it treats human cultures in part as adaptive systems and implies a kind of "natural selection" that operates on the cultural level. However, the particular focus of cultural ecology is on specific human societies (or groups of societies) and the dynamic interrelationships between these societies and their total environmental settings. That is, cultural ecology deals not with a grand abstraction like "the culture of mankind," but rather with more precise kinds of units—the culture of the Kwakiutl, say, or the cultures of the Plains Indians. By "total environmental setting," I mean that it concerns itself not only with factors such as rainfall or soil types or game distribution but also with the presence of other competing human societies. By "dynamic interrelationships" I mean that a culture does not just passively "adjust" to a set of circumstances; it contributes something to the equation. For example, technological resources are obviously extremely important; a given chunk of land is one thing to a hunting society, something else to herders, and something else again to people who are planting crops. There are many facets to cultural ecology, but I want to emphasize just one point. By demonstrating that there is a relationship between a cultural system and its ecological matrix, cultural ecology has gotten away from the old idea that cultures "just happen" without rhyme or reason. It suggests that it is not true that *any* culture can assume *any* form; on the contrary, it asserts that cultures too are not immune from natural laws.

Finally, we may mention the development of what was once called the *new physical anthropology*. Exemplified by the work of such scientists as Joseph B. Birdsell and Sherwood L. Washburn, this has been characterized by a turn away from a curious fascination with the cephalic index (a measurement of the relation between the breadth and the length of the skull) toward a much more searching, probing, and imaginative inquiry into the nature and causes of human evolution. The impact of these studies has been profound, and it has led both physical and cultural anthropologists to rethink some of their basic assumptions.

If we may retrace some of our steps for a moment, it is important to make clear what such approaches as ethology and the field studies of nonhuman primates can and cannot do. They *can* direct us toward an appreciation of the qualities that are shared by all human beings everywhere — human universals, if you will. They can do this by suggesting leads or principles that can be checked out in human populations. They can direct our attention to some of the basic "building blocks" upon which all human sociocultural systems are built. They can also provide a kind of baseline that will enable us to determine what is truly unique about the human animal. They *cannot* be used to explain the differences between one human society and another, and the reason for this is simple. All human societies are populated by human beings. Since we are all human animals, it is understandable that our lifeways will have some things in common — things related to the kind of animals we are. By the same token, since we are all human animals, the shared characteristics of our species cannot account for cultural differences. That is a different kind of a problem. The information obtained from ethology and field studies of nonhuman primates can alert us to what does **not** vary, or varies only in detail, between one human population and another. It **is of** no value whatsoever in investigating cultural variables. If you want to know what is true of the human animal everywhere, these studies can be immensely helpful. If you want to know why Eskimos hunt seals with harpoons and Comanches hunt bison on horseback with bows and arrows, or why the Kamba have no chiefs and the Zulu do, it is obvious that these studies have no bearing on the question.

It is particularly unfortunate that there exists in some quarters the suspicion that any recognition of the importance of ethological studies is tinged with racist implications. In my view, the data of ethology point in exactly the opposite direction: they call our attention to what all human beings have in common. Nevertheless, the suspicion is there, and rather than ignore the matter, we must examine it directly.

RACE AND RACISM

For a number of reasons, it is a good deal easier to discuss racism than it is to explain "race." Racism is a simple (and simple-minded) phenomenon, while the problem of human "races" is considerably more complex. Stripped down to its unsavory essence, *racism* is the attribution of behavioral or cultural characteristics — usually negative ones — to people on the basis of what people look like. People are sorted into groups according to real or imagined visible physical traits, and then it is assumed that each group has different capacities or behaves in a different way.

The following statements are all racist:

"All blacks are lazy and stupid."
"All white people are cruel; you can never trust a white person."
"All American Indians are incapable of being civilized and yearn only to return to the warpath."
"All Orientals are inscrutable and like to work in laundries."

These statements are so clearly untrue that no thinking person could possibly take them seriously. The problem is that some forms of racism are more subtle and therefore not so obviously false.

What are they, really? Most of them boil down to two key ideas. The first is that there is some sort of a relationship between "race" and intelligence, which means that there is an inherent difference in intellectual ability between different "races." The second is that there is some sort of a relationship between "race" and cultural capacity, which means that some "races" are incapable of developing or participating in those complex cultural systems that are often called civilizations.

Let us look first at "race" and intelligence. Considered simply as a logical problem, it would seem likely that intelligence would be an evolutionary asset to any and all human populations — and this is true regardless of how we define either "race" or "intelligence." The ability to solve crucial problems would be a plus factor in any adaptive situation and therefore could be expected to appear in any developing human population. It is difficult even to imagine an evolutionary context in which natural selection would operate to enhance intellectual ability in one population and not in another.

Suppose, then, that we admit that there is no logical reason why one "race" should be brighter than another, but could such a situation "just happen"? Such evidence as there is — apart from prejudice, hearsay, and guesswork — involves so-called IQ tests. IQ stands for something called an intelligence quotient, but what precisely does that mean? Your IQ is a score that you get when you take a particular kind of test at a particular time. (The same individuals may get different scores at different times.) Does the IQ test truly measure intelligence? Strictly speaking, it does not. Rather, it measures your ability to take a specific test at a specific time. This is not without value, but it is not the same thing as measuring overall intelligence. Bearing this in mind, there are several things that need to be said about IQ tests. First, there is no such thing as a totally culture-free IQ test. Human beings cannot be tested "apart from" their cultural conditioning, since we are all cultural animals. This is true even on a level you may not have considered — the degree to which we are accustomed to taking tests in general, our motivations for doing well on tests, and the like. On another level, most IQ tests are largely verbal, and our performance on them is thus linked to our vocabulary skills. We *learn* the words we use, and what words we

Left, a Comanche Indian. *Top right,* one of the Hopi pueblos. *Bottom right,* a reconstruction of the Aztec city of Tenochtitlán.

learn depends in part on the cultures and subcultures in which we live. There is a difference not only between cultures but within cultures—it makes a difference to your vocabulary whether you grow up in a middle-class household or a ghetto.

To illustrate how important cultural differences can be in measuring "intelligence," test yourself on the following three questions:

1. If a man tells you that he has "eaten kithitu," what kind of food is he talking about?
2. If you hear a man addressed as "Number Ten," is this a compliment or a reference to his clothing size?
3. Which one of the following items does not belong in the series: (a) utumia, (b) a snake, (c) a forked stick, (d) a slaughtered goat?

I would be very surprised—indeed amazed—if you were not baffled by these simple questions. The reason has nothing at all to do with your intelligence or lack of it. The problem is that this is not a culture-free test. It has a built-in bias in that all of the questions require a knowledge of a particular cultural system. In this case, the culture involved is that of the Kamba. (The Kamba live in Kenya in East Africa, and we shall be meeting them again.) This may seem unduly tricky, but turn it around. If you devise a test involving electric lights, baseball, and a reference to Abraham Lincoln as a rail splitter, what chance would a Kamba have on that test? If no Kamba could pass the test, would you therefore conclude that the Kamba were stupid? (If you are interested, the correct answers to the three questions are given at the end of this chapter on page 17.)

There is a basic point to remember concerning "race" and "intelligence." Even when you make IQ tests as culture-free as possible, and regardless of which definition of race you choose, the differences in IQ *within* "racial" groups are greater than those *between* "racial" groups. This means that there are both very high and very low IQ scores in any large human population. It also means that there is no technique known to science by which we can predict the "intelligence" of any human being on the basis of that person's "racial" affiliation.

With regard to the question of a causal relationship between "race" and cultural capacity, any anthropologist knows from experience that such a relationship does not exist. It is not only that any normal human being can learn any cultural tradition (it is simply a matter of which one he or she is exposed to), but also that there is a very wide cultural range between societies in which the members all belong to the same "racial" group. This fact is obvious to anthropologists, but not all people share the familiarity of the anthropologist with different cultures in different parts of the world.

Again, it may be useful to take a specific example. Allow yourself a few minutes to study the pictures on page 12. All of the photos depict American Indians. The American Indians constitute a "racial" population by any meaningful use of the term. Their ancestors migrated to the New World from Asia at least 10,000 years ago (and quite possibly as much as 25,000 years ago) and then developed in relative isolation from other major human populations until comparatively recent times. They were, in fact, about as isolated as it is possible for a human population to get.

We are dealing, then, with a single human "race." But look at the cultural differences that are illustrated — and remember that these are only three examples out of many hundreds that might have been selected.

As you can see, the cultural variation between the Comanche, the Hopi, and the Aztecs is extensive. Of course, you cannot really *see* a cultural system, but you can get some indication of what a culture is like by looking at its visible manifestations; this problem is discussed in Chapter 8. Here we have a single "race," yet cultures that are obviously different. (It may be noted in passing that the Comanche, the Hopi, and the Aztecs also spoke languages that belong to the same linguistic family; it is called Uto-Aztecan. This does not mean that the languages were the same, but only that they were related in the same sense that English, French, and German belong to the Indo-European family of languages. The American Indians spoke more than 2000 different languages, which have been classified by linguists into approximately 125 language families.) If we tried to demonstrate some kind of racial causation for culture, we would have to argue that there were separate Comanche, Hopi, and Aztec "races," which is absurd.

This is only one example, but the same principle could easily be shown to apply elsewhere. Africa is a good case in point. If we confine ourselves to Africa south of the Sahara, it is a simple matter to demonstrate that traditional African cultures ranged from small-scale societies of hunters and gatherers to large and powerful state systems, together with just about everything in between.

There is nothing complicated about all this. For once, the evidence is clear and unequivocal: There is no connection between "race" and "culture," and assertions to the contrary are based not on facts but on ignorance.

You have probably noticed that throughout this discussion so far, I have used quotation marks around the words *race* and *racial*. The reason for this is bound up with the question of exactly what a race is. I mentioned earlier that it was easier to discuss racism than to explain race, and this is because the phenomenon of human races is complicated. The facts of the matter are something less than crystal clear, there is room for competent authorities to disagree, and the whole subject has become so emotional that it is difficult to subject it to scientific analysis.

To the racist—and to many people who are not racists at all but have not gone very deeply into the problem—the situation seems simple. Because people look different, they reason, they are different. You just assemble a list of visible physical characteristics—skin color, nose shape, hair form, and so forth—and assign people to categories on that basis. Those categories are races, and it is then assumed that various other things—character traits, mental abilities, and whatever—are associated with them. It cannot be stressed too strongly that race as a *social* problem (and racism generally) is based ultimately on what people see and believe. That is, it is based on what people look like and on the qualities that are supposedly linked to these external physical traits. It is not true that a real knowledge of human biology leads to either racism or a simplistic theory of pure racial "types."

If we strive to be as objective as possible and examine what is known about human races without preconceived ideas, the problem still resists easy solutions. A few anthropologists have attempted to "solve" the problem by declaring that human races do not exist. This is an attractive notion, but it is not very convincing. Races are real enough, and we will not get very far by pretending that they are only figments of our imaginations.

What, then, can we say about races? We can begin with a simple proposition. All living men and women belong to the same genus and the same species; we are all *Homo sapiens*. This means that whatever racial differences exist occur at the *subspecies* level. The practical effect of this is that we are all far more alike than we are different; the variations within the human population are relatively minor.

We can go on and point out a second basic fact: Race is inherited. Biological differences between one human group and another are the products of heredity; they are not something "tacked on" as a result of individual life experiences. This is important because there is only one way in which anybody can inherit anything in a biological sense, and that is genetically. If race is inherited, then the biological problem of race becomes essentially a problem of human genetics.

One might think that at this point the problem becomes simple, or at least a question of details. Instead of trying to sort out people on the basis of *phenotype* (external, physical characteristics) we can turn to an examination of the *genotype* (actual genetic makeups). Unfortunately, this approach has not yet solved the problem.

Part of the difficulty is that the human genetic code is immensely complex, and at present we can only identify fragments of the whole. As it happens, many of the major phenotypic expressions in the human animal—skin color, for example—are particularly complex genetically. However, even if we confine ourselves to genetic factors that are relatively simple and well understood, such as the inheritance of human blood groups like A, B, and O, we find that their distribution does not reveal nice and neat racial classifications. For instance, the A and O blood groups have what amounts to a worldwide distribution, with various populations differing only with regard to the *frequency* (rather than the presence or absence) of the blood types. Moreover, the frequencies themselves are puzzling; the highest known frequencies of A occur among the Blackfoot Indians of North America and the Lapps of Scandinavia! Where we do encounter a kind of presence-absence situation, it often does not seem to make sense in terms of other data. For example, B is virtually absent among American Indians, while its highest frequency occurs in Central Asia. At the same time, we know that the American Indians are the descendants of people who migrated to the New World from exactly that region—Asia (Kelso 1974:268).

If we add to this a recognition of the importance of DNA (deoxyribonucleic acid) in the regulation of human heredity, the complexity of the problem is multiplied several times over. All of this does not mean that there is no such thing as race, and it does not mean that race has no genetic basis. It does mean that at the present time races cannot be either identified or classified on a scientific level of analysis, and it does suggest that racial differences are a matter of degree. That is, they are generally relative rather than representative of absolute differences between human breeding populations. *Clinal analysis* (the plotting of the distribution of genetic traits through geographical zones) usually shows frequency gradients rather than fenced-in isolates, which suggests that one population tends to intergrade with another.

On the basis of such evidence as we now have, it seems reasonable to postulate that "all races originate as adaptive regional types" (Birdsell 1972:484). This simply means that no human population developed in a vacuum; natural selection is a process that operates under specific ecological conditions. Thus, darkly pigmented skin has a definite advantage in regions of high solar radiation; for one thing, it is more resistant to skin cancer. Similarly, it can be demonstrated that a compact body build is the most efficient form under extremely cold conditions, while a thinner or more linear structure is more efficient in a situation involving high heat. All of these adaptive principles—and there are a good many others that might be cited—have to do with mechanisms that assist the human body in coping with the stresses of the physical environment. Again, they have nothing to do with intelligence or cultural capacity.

There is probably no single definition of race that is acceptable to everyone. However, let us consider the implications of what we have been discussing. Since all living men and women belong to the same species, racial variation occurs below the species level. In other words, racial differences are a subspecies phenomenon. (A *species* may be regarded as a closed breeding unit. Under normal conditions, mating occurs only within the species. Thus, any human being can mate with any other human being, given the proper assortment of sexes, but a human being cannot mate with an elephant or a rat or a baboon and produce viable offspring. A *subspecies* is not a closed breeding unit. It is simply a population within a species, in which the members mate with one another more frequently than they do with people from other human populations. Thus, in the past, an Eskimo would be unlikely to mate with an African, even though he or she would have been biologically capable of doing so. Obviously, the greater the barriers between populations—whether these barriers are geographical distances or something else—the more distinct the breeding populations will become. Because of the presence of intermediate populations and the accelerating tendency of people to move around and to come into contact with one another, these differences cannot be absolute.) Even though we cannot yet spell out the genetic components with precision, we know that racial characteristics are inherited, which means that they have a genetic basis. Finally, it is likely that racial variations began as adaptive responses to particular ecological situations.

Putting all of this together, we can attempt a provisional definition of a race. *It is a population within a species that differs in degree from other populations on the basis of genetically transmitted physical characteristics which were originally adaptive in nature.*

In the final analysis, perhaps, the whole question of racial variation is important only in terms of itself; that is, it is of interest scientifically only if we wish to study races as a biological phenomenon at the subspecies level. If our interest is rather in the human population as a species and in why we do the things we do, then there is only one race that matters, and that is the human race.

The business of anthropology is to study the human animal from both a biological and a cultural point of view. Our most fundamental task is to try to understand and to explain both the similarities and the differences between one human group and another. It has been the premise of this chapter that biological and ethological factors can assist us in determining the universal characteristics of the human animal—the things that all of us share as a species. When we ask what it is that makes one sociocultural system different from another, we must turn to an examination of the culture process itself. Therefore, the study of culture remains central to any valid understanding of the human animal.

Here we are, all of us, as representatives of a life form that has become dominant on this planet. There can be no more crucial task before us than to find out as much as we can about ourselves. This is the discovery of mankind, and it is an exploration that is just beginning. How soon and how effectively we achieve that understanding may well determine what our fate as a species may ultimately be.

Answers to Questions on Page 12

1. He is not talking about any kind of food. The Kamba have an oath that is used in major legal disputes. A man swears on an object called a *kithitu* that his version of the case is true. (A woman cannot swear on the kithitu.) It is believed that if he lies the kithitu will kill—not the person doing the swearing but rather members of his family. The kithitu is either a wrapped bundle or a container of some other kind. Its ingredients are secret, but the kithitu always includes teeth from a snake or a meat-eating mammal such as a lion. "The kithitu has teeth," the people say. "It can kill." Possibly because of the involvement with teeth, the act of swearing on the kithitu is called "eating kithitu."

2. Neither. The Kamba have a saying that is applied to an unreliable man: "When you need nine men, he is Number Ten." Therefore, the reference is an insult.

3. The item that does not belong in the series is the snake. The utumia are the Kamba elders, the men who belong to the senior age grade. The symbol of their status is a long wooden staff which is forked at the upper end; the elders carry these sticks around with them. In order to attain the status of elderhood, a man must make a series of sacrifices. The sacrifices usually take the form of a goat which is slaughtered and presented to the existing elders for a feast.

SUMMARY

As human beings, we are both animals and particular kinds of animals. Since we are mammals, we share some behavioral characteristics with other mammals. Since we are primates, we share some more specific traits with other primates. Since we are human, some of what we are and what we do is uniquely human.

In interpreting the human animal, there are two extreme points of view. One is the *superorganic* position, which holds that we are totally different from other animals because we possess culture and that culture can be explained only in terms of itself. The other position can be termed the *exploding bundle of instincts* position, which argues that culture is irrelevant and that human behavior can be understood solely in terms of biologically built-in urges, drives, and behavioral patterns. The superorganic position maintains that for human beings everything is learned, and what is learned is culture. The other position maintains that nothing important is learned and that everything is implanted genetically. Neither one of these positions is acceptable; they are both demonstrably false.

All animals learn, and all animals have some innate behavior patterns. The thing that is unusual about the human animal is that it learns far more of its lifeway than any other animal. This human learning is special to some degree — it is cultural learning — but it is not entirely divorced from the kind of animal we are, and it has not been totally uninfluenced by the evolutionary processes that shaped us.

A number of different lines of inquiry have converged that have made anthropologists realize that we cannot simply say that everything is due to culture and let it go at that. *Ethology* is the study of animal behavior, and as we learn more about how other animals actually live (as opposed to how we thought they lived) both the similarities and the differences between their lifeways and ours have become more apparent. *Field studies of nonhuman primates* have led us to understand that we have some things in common with our near relatives in the animal world. The study of *surviving hunting and gathering* cultures has also contributed to our knowledge of the context within which the human animal developed; we were all hunters and gatherers until about 10,000 years ago. Other investigations — into an examination of cultural universals as well as cultural differences, into cultural evolution and cultural ecology, and into sophisticated physical or biological anthropology — have made it clear that the old notion of wholly arbitrary human cultures operating without rhyme or reason is very simplistic.

It is important to understand what these various approaches can and cannot do. Ethology and nonhuman primate studies and an examination of cultural universals can alert us to what is truly unique about the human animal and show us which characteristics are shared by all people everywhere. They cannot be used to explain the differences between one human society and another. That is a different kind of question. Since all living human beings in all societies belong to the same species, *Homo sapiens,* differences between one human lifeway and another cannot be attributed to the nature of the human animal. Such differences are cultural, and that is one reason why the concept of culture retains its importance in modern anthropology.

It is unfortunate that a recognition that culture cannot explain everything about the human animal is perceived in some quarters as racist. The true implications of these new lines of inquiry are the exact opposite of racism; they call attention to what all human beings have in common and stress that the differences between one human society and another are culturally determined and have nothing whatever to do with human biology. There is no connection at all between race and intelligence or race and culture. If our intention and our hope is to understand the human animal, there is only one race to consider, and that is the human race.

References

Birdsell, Joseph B. 1972. *Human Evolution: An Introduction to the New Physical Anthropology.* Chicago: Rand McNally.

Kelso, A. J. 1974. *Physical Anthropology,* 2d ed. Philadelphia: Lippincott.

Kraus, Bertram S. 1964. *The Basis of Human Evolution.* New York: Harper & Row.

Kroeber, A. L. 1917. "The Superorganic." *American Anthropologist* 19:163–213. (Reprinted in Kroeber, *The Nature of Culture,* 1952. University of Chicago Press.)

Lee, Richard B., and Irven DeVore (eds.). 1968. *Man the Hunter.* Chicago: Aldine.

Lorenz, Konrad. 1966. *On Aggression,* English trans. New York: Harcourt Brace Jovanovich.

Morris, Desmond. 1967. *The Naked Ape.* New York: McGraw-Hill.

Tiger, Lionel, and Robin Fox. 1971. *The Imperial Animal.* New York: Holt, Rinehart and Winston.

Tinbergen, Niko. 1951. *The Study of Instinct.* London: Oxford University Press.

White, Leslie A. 1949. *The Science of Culture.* New York: Farrar, Straus & Giroux.

Suggestions for Further Reading

Ashley-Montagu, M. F. (ed.). 1968. *Man and Aggression.* London: Oxford University Press. A collection of essays by distinguished authorities, most of them representing a different point of view from that expressed in this chapter.

Carrighar, Sally. 1965. *Wild Heritage.* Boston: Houghton Mifflin. A good and well-written popular introduction to ethology.

Chapple, Eliot D. 1970. *Culture and Biological Man.* New York: Holt, Rinehart and Winston. Not wholly successful, but a valuable pioneering attempt to put the major components of anthropology back together again.

Cohen, Yehudi A. (ed.). 1974. *Man in Adaptation: The Biosocial Background,* 2d ed. Chicago: Aldine. A very good collection of readings with perceptive comments by the editor.

Coon, Carleton S., Stanley M. Garn, and Joseph B. Birdsell. 1950. *Races: A Study of the Problems of Race Formation in Man.* Springfield, Ill.: Thomas. One of the most interesting studies of the subject, with particular emphasis on the adaptive nature of physical racial characteristics.

Eibl-Eibesfeldt, I. 1970. *Ethology: The Biology of Behavior.* New York: Holt, Rinehart and Winston. Fairly technical, but contains much useful information.

Garn, Stanley M. 1965. *Human Races,* 2d ed. Springfield, Ill.: Thomas. A lucid and helpful introduction to the subject.

Goldschmidt, Walter. 1966. *Comparative Functionalism.* Berkeley and Los Angeles: University of California Press. A consistently original and interesting essay in anthropological theory that addresses itself to some of the problems considered in this chapter.

Loehlin, John C., Gardner Lindzey, and J. N. Spuhler. 1975. *Race Differences in Intelligence.* San Francisco: Freeman. A reasonably balanced analysis of a highly controversial subject.

Spradley, James P., and David W. McCurdy. 1975. *Anthropology: The Cultural Perspective.* New York: Wiley. A good book that intelligently stresses the cultural point of view.

Swartz, Marc J., and David K. Jordan. 1976. *Anthropology: Perspective on Humanity.* New York: Wiley. A sound and interesting middle-of-the-road textbook.

Tiger, Lionel, and Robin Fox. 1966. "The Zoological Perspective in Social Science." *Man* (n.s.), 1(1):75–81. Less polemical in tone than *The Imperial Animal,* this seminal and tightly reasoned article is well worth looking up.

Wilson, Edward O. 1975. *Sociobiology: The New Synthesis.* Cambridge, Mass.: Harvard University Press. A complex, informed, and sometimes controversial attempt to relate population biology to the study of social systems.

———. 1978. *On Human Nature.* Cambridge, Mass.: Harvard University Press. A lively application of the principles of sociobiology to the human animal. Not altogether convincing and certainly debatable, this is, nevertheless, a thought-provoking book.

2

How to Recognize an Anthropologist

The literal meaning of *anthropology* is "the science of people" or "the study of people." The word is derived from the Greek *anthropos* ("mankind" in the generic sense of the term) and *logia,* which means either "science" or "study." Even if we confine ourselves to the first translation—the science of people or mankind—this definition does not get us very far. The problem is that the definition is so all-inclusive that it does not tell us what we need to know.

WHAT IS ANTHROPOLOGY?

Quite frankly, there is no single characteristic that will provide an adequate "definition" of anthropology. Rather, there are a series of characteristics that collectively can paint a recognizable portrait of what an anthropologist is and what is unique about anthropology. It is the combination of characteristics that really defines anthropology, not the presence or absence of any one factor.

My purpose here is to explore some of these major characteristics of anthropology. Although the emphasis will be on cultural anthropology, I believe that these features will apply to any kind of anthropologist, regardless of his or her specialized interests. In the next chapter, we will talk about the various subdivisions of anthropology. Here we will talk about anthropology in general.

A Biological and Social Science

The first characteristic of anthropology is that it is both a biological and a social science. This means that anthropology investigates the human animal both as an animal and as a particular kind of animal, the animal with culture. This dual focus is one of the major features of anthropology.

Suppose that we take a specific and commonplace example. We all know that human beings form family systems. For the moment, let us refrain from worrying about exactly what we mean by a family. Let us simply assume that we are talking about some sort of more or less permanent and socially sanctioned unit of males and females that produces children. If we find such "families" everywhere, in all human societies, what accounts for them? Why are they there at all?

There are several biological facts about the human animal that shed some light on the matter. Unlike most other animals, human beings do not have a breeding season. Both males and females are potentially sexually active throughout the year. As a species, it is fair to say that people have a pervasive and nearly continuous interest in sex. Check your local newsstand if you have any doubts on the matter, and remember that people everywhere have their stories and jokes with sexual motifs, their courtship patterns, their sexual folklore, and so forth. It would surely be an error to conclude that sex alone is responsible for the formation of long-lasting ties between males and females, but it is also an error to assume that sexual relationships have nothing to do with the situation.

There are consequences to sexual activities, and one of them is children. (Yes, we all know that it is possible to have sex without pregnancies, but generally speaking this is a fairly recent development. In any case, from the perspective of the species, it is only possible to avoid having children for a single generation. It is fairly difficult for a species to continue when all of its participants are dead. There is a word for it: extinction.) The human infant is a rather peculiar animal, and one of its peculiarities is the fact that it has a very slow maturation rate. It takes a human child an inordinately long time to grow up. At birth, a human baby is completely helpless. What is more important, the infant remains essentially helpless for a a very long period of time. Think about it for a moment. How old does a human being have to be before he or she can function more or less independently? Six months? Ridiculous. One year? Impossible. Two years? Three? Four? Whatever number you pick, you are necessarily talking about a very prolonged period during which the child is almost completely dependent on other people for survival. I am referring here to simple physical survival as an animal, without even considering at this point what the child must *learn* in order to participate in any human society. Consider how different this is from other animals. When a fish hatches from an egg, that fish is on its own. When a turtle hatches from an egg, it either lives or dies according to its own efforts. With mammals, some parental care is normally required; that is why female mammals produce milk. But compared to human beings, other mammals require only a brief period of care. A puppy or a kitten is not helpless for very long; as most of us have observed, after a year goes by they have become dogs and cats. When a horse has a foal, the "baby" horse can stand and walk a few hours after it is born; it can run and keep up with its mother in a matter of days.

Given this basic biological fact about human beings, it is easy to see that the human infant needs some sort of stable, caring unit. It must be fed, protected, and made to feel secure. At the very least, it must have the opportunity to learn what it needs to know, and it must have time to mature. (We are complicated animals physically, and much of our development necessarily occurs after birth. Consider our big brains, for example. A brain, after all, fits inside a skull. There is a limit to how big the skull can be and still pass through the human mother's birth canal.)

Theoretically, it is possible to combine these biological facts without a resulting family system of some kind. It is possible to have a sexual relationship without forming a family unit, and it is possible to care for infants outside the context of a family—in an orphanage, for example. Nevertheless, it is a fact that family units normally involve a sexual relationship between spouses, and it is also a fact that the family usually has the primary responsibility for caring for infants in all human societies. If this is the case in virtually all human societies, regardless of their cultural differences, it must mean that this is a system that makes sense in terms of the biological requirements of the species. To argue otherwise is to suggest that the species has repeatedly made some drastic and crucial mistakes, and such a species would not be around long enough to study.

Can we leave it at that and say that human family systems are simply the products of human biology? It won't work, and the reason why it won't work is that it leaves many facts about human families unexplained. It also will not work because there are roughly similar family systems—mated pairs with young—that occur among animals not equipped with the key human biological traits of year-round sexual activity and very slow maturation rates. Wolves are one such example, and gibbons (a type of ape) another.

When we examine human family systems in different cultures, we find considerable variation. In some societies, the rule is one spouse at a time— one man is married to one woman. In others, we find that the ideal form is for one man to be married simultaneously to several women; this is very common. In still others, the pattern is for one woman to be married simultaneously to several men; this is rare, but it does occur. When children are born, they may be considered to be related equally to both their father and their mother. Alternatively, descent may be reckoned through just the father's side of the family or just the mother's.

All human societies have rules about who is eligible to marry whom; human mating is never totally random. A common situation is one in which a man has two female cousins to each of whom he is equally related in a biological or genetic sense. One of the girls will be his preferred marriage partner—the girl he is supposed to marry. The other will be absolutely forbidden to him.

Mother-in-law jokes are a staple in many societies. In some societies a man and his mother-in-law are rigidly separated. In what is called an avoidance relationship, a man may not even speak directly to his mother-in-law. If he sees her coming down a path, he must hide in the bushes until she passes.

As soon as we consider variations such as these, it is apparent that we cannot explain them biologically. It is the culture that is different, not the biology. The same point can be made when we examine changes in family structures and attitudes through time. Our own culture provides a neat example. The ideal American family of the past was provided with a rather authoritarian father, a patient and long-suffering mother, and a host of children. My own grandfather used to summon his children into his upstairs office when there was a dispute, hold a trial, hear evidence, and hand down sentences for punishment. If I tried that today, my children would probably think that Daddy had gone off his rocker. It is clear that our attitudes are changing—attitudes toward the father as the "head" of the family, attitudes toward the "proper" conduct of the mother, and attitudes toward how many children we should have and what our relationships toward them should be. Whether these changes are "good" or "bad" can be endlessly debated; what is not arguable is the fact that it is not our biology that has changed but our culture.

This brief discussion of human family systems is designed to illustrate what we mean when we say that anthropology is both a biological and a social science. When we try to explain why people behave as they do, neither a biological nor a social (or cultural) theoretical framework provides a sufficient explanation by itself. We need to explore *both* theoretical dimensions and try to put them together in a meaningful way.

The Time Dimension of Anthropology

A second characteristic of anthropology involves the time span within which anthropologists attempt to examine the problems with which they deal. Anthropology takes as its temporal dimension *the total time that mankind has existed on this planet.* Obviously, not every individual anthropological study directly utilizes this immense time span, but it is always there as a frame of reference—a perspective against which to measure more limited investigations.

In theory, the problem here is a simple one. Written records do not go back very far; writing began about 3500 B.C. in Mesopotamia. Even this statement is somewhat misleading on several counts. The earliest written records are not very revealing, and for most parts of the world they do not have an antiquity that even approaches 5000 years. I do not know where you are as you are reading this, but the odds are that you are in the United States or Canada. There were no indigenous systems of true writing anywhere in the New World north of Mexico; therefore, if you go back beyond a few hundred years in your area you are effectively beyond the reach of written records. The human animal has been kicking around on this world of ours for a very long time—something on the order of three to four *million* years. Clearly, if you want to obtain some degree of perspective on mankind you cannot restrict yourself to the tiny fragment of time covered by written records. Anthropologists generally feel that trying to understand the human animal by studying written records alone is like trying to figure out the plot of a movie just by watching the final few seconds of the film. The problem, therefore, is to try to obtain nothing less than information that pertains to the vast *majority* of time that the human animal has spent on earth. Primarily, this is done through archeology, which is discussed in the next chapter. However, the basic principle to grasp here is the aim, not the technique. Unlike history, and unlike most other disciplines that study mankind, anthropology takes as its temporal frame of reference the total existence of the human animal.

A Comparative Science

The next point is related to this business about the total existence of the human animal. It is a characteristic of anthropology that it is a *comparative* science. Possibly the most basic procedure in anthropology is to compare one society or culture or population with another; anthropology is not just interested in one human group (or two or three or four) but in all human groups, regardless of when they lived or where they lived.

This is an ambitious undertaking—some would call it presumptuous—but there is a reason for it. Part of the reason has to do with the nature of science, and part of the reason concerns exactly what it is that anthropology is trying to do. Science can be defined in many ways, but any science must be generalizing rather than particularistic. This means that its goal is to arrive at statements of probability—laws, generalizations, principles—concerning the phenomena being studied. Mere fact collecting is not enough; you cannot just assemble a pile of facts and wait for principles to emerge by a process akin to spontaneous combustion. In the physical sciences, once you arrive at a reasonable hypothesis (or an educated guess) you can check it out by designing an appropriate experiment. The experiment does not necessarily prove or disprove the hypothesis, but it does render it either more or less probable. When dealing with human beings, it is usually impossible to conduct really meaningful experiments. For ethical reasons, you cannot treat people as though they were laboratory animals. What would happen, to take a far-fetched example, if you took human infants and transported them to the proverbial desert island and turned them loose? Assuming their survival—which would be highly unlikely—what sort of lifeway would they develop? We don't know. The experiment has never been performed, nor should it be.

How can we get around this ethical difficulty? Anthropology's answer is to investigate nature's own experiments. Every human lifeway represents one people's solution to the problems faced by all human societies. Here, in the world around us, we have a variety of "natural experiments"—lifeways that have developed in different situations and lifeways that involve many different variables. These various cultures are the laboratories within which anthropologists work; they provide us with the experiments against which we can check our data. It must be emphasized that these lifeways are not mere curiosities. Apart from the fact that they involve human beings, each of whom has value as a person, these cultures are all successful experiments. If they were not, they would not have survived to be studied. As such, each and every one of them can provide priceless information.

Anthropology seeks to determine what is truly universal about the human animal, as well as what varies from one culture to another. This can only be done by studying all cultures everywhere; otherwise, we run the risk of simply assuming that what is true of one culture (or two or three) is necessarily true of all. In practice, this may not be possible; there are not enough anthropologists to study every cultural variation in the world, and not a year goes by without some culture somewhere disappearing forever. Still, the larger our sample is, the more confident we can be in advancing generalizations about human lifeways. At the very least, when hypotheses suggest themselves from the study of a single cultural system, these hypotheses can be checked by investigating them in a variety of other cultural systems.

Whatever else anthropology may be, it is not ethnocentric. It does not project our own lifeway, or that of any other single group, as the model for all mankind. It is in this sense that we can say that one of the basic features of anthropology is the comparative method. An anthropology based on the study of a single culture or population is a contradiction in terms.

The Study of Primitive Cultures

The next major characteristic of anthropology is related to the principle we have just been discussing. The traditional orientation of anthropology has been toward the study of primitive societies and cultures. It is crucial to understand that the word ''primitive'' has nothing whatever to do with such concepts as ''good'' and ''bad'' or ''superior'' and ''inferior.'' As the term is used in anthropology, it merely refers to certain *types* of sociocultural systems that can be defined with regard to stated structural characteristics. It cannot be denied that there is an intrinsic fascination in such lifeways, and it is probably true that most anthropologists harbor an often concealed streak of romanticism in their personalities. It is also true that there is a certain amount of academic division of labor involved; anthropologists studied these lifeways in part because nobody else was doing so. However, this is not the theoretical reason for this concentration of effort on the investigation of primitive cultures. The theoretical justification for dealing with primitive cultures is that the majority of known human cultures are of this type.

This often comes as a surprise, but it is nonetheless true. If you count the number of different cultures that exist, rather than the number of people who follow a given lifeway, most human cultures fall into the primitive category. (Of course, if you go back in time a few thousand years, all human cultures were primitive.) If our goal is to obtain the largest possible example of human cultural systems, then we must study primitive cultures.

This does not mean that anthropologists study *only* primitive societies and cultures. Nonprimitive lifeways belong in the sample too, and many primitive cultures are changing almost before our eyes. For at least 40 years, anthropologists have been attempting to utilize their techniques of study and analysis in an examination of nonprimitive lifeways, including our own. There are anthropological studies of modern cities and small towns, studies of modern farming communities and counterculture communes. Indeed, there are specializations within anthropology—urban anthropology, for example—where the primary emphasis is not on primitive cultures at all.

Despite this, for anthropology as a whole the basic emphasis has been and still is on the study of primitive cultures and societies. Whether this involves an investigation of the genetic characteristics of a small-scale breeding population or an examination of the relationship between witchcraft accusations and stability of residence, the "laboratory" within which the anthropologist works is apt to be a primitive society. We must here repeat a point previously made. *Every* human sociocultural system represents one possible solution to the problems faced by human beings as a species. Whether our cultures are called primitive or civilized, the one is no less a culture than the other. It is absolutely necessary to learn as much as we can about all human cultures. If we fail in this task and do not accurately chart every primitive culture while it still exists to be studied, we will miss data that may ultimately prove to have been crucial to our understanding of the human animal.

The Investigation of Group Behavior

There is one final major characteristic of anthropology as a discipline. As a rule, the primary focus in anthropology is not on individual behavior as such, but rather on *group* behavior and the cultural guidelines that shape that behavior. The cultural anthropologist tends to work on the level of societies and cultures, while the physical anthropologist is usually concerned with populations. If an anthropologist tells you that the Masai herd cattle and have a particular kind of belief system, the anthropologist is not necessarily describing any individual Masai. The anthropologist is making a statement about what *most* Masai do and what *most* Masai believe. If we study deviant behavior of some kind—people who behave in statistically unusual ways—we must still ask, "Deviant from what?" This gets us right back to cultural norms and regularities.

In this sense, the approach of the anthropologist is different from that of the novelist. The novelist is interested in individual characters, such as Huck Finn, Elmer Gantry, and King Arthur. If John Q. Jones thinks he is a werewolf and goes trotting out to the graveyard to howl at the full moon, that is grist for the novelist's mill. The anthropologist by contrast is concerned with what most people in a society do—how they get their food, what sorts of family arrangements they have, what their attitudes are toward the world around them. If witchcraft is prevalent in a given culture, the anthropologist must deal with witchcraft as a part of the cultural analysis. If there is just one would-be werewolf, that is a subject for the novelist or a patient for a psychiatrist.

There is another aspect to this focus on group phenomena. Traditionally, anthropologists have worked in small-scale societies, and they have tried to find out everything they possibly could about the cultures they were studying; they were often in a position in which anything left unrecorded might be lost forever.

Partially for this reason, they became aware of how everything fitted together in a cultural system — how seemingly unrelated things such as magical practices and crop harvests made sense as parts of a larger whole. They tried to view everything in context, rather than considering each item as a separate entity. This is sometimes referred to as the *holistic* orientation of anthropology — always trying to take into account the total cultural context of the phenomena being investigated. Although this is obviously more difficult when dealing with large and complex cultural systems, it has persisted as a point of view wherever anthropologists have gone and whatever they have tried to study.

To sum up, it has been the argument of this chapter that there is no single feature that distinguishes anthropology as a scientific discipline. Instead, anthropology is characterized by a *combination* of features. They are:

1. Anthropology is *both* a biological and a social science.
2. It deals with the total time span of mankind on earth.
3. It is a comparative science.
4. Its traditional emphasis has been on the study of primitive societies and cultures, although it is not restricted to this.
5. Its focus is on group behavior and the cultural ideas that shape that behavior.

It must be stressed that this listing is not a complete one even when we confine our point of view to considering anthropology as a science. If we adopt a different slant, the basic characteristics would have to be modified accordingly. For example, there has always been a strong humanistic undercurrent in anthropology, and there are some anthropologists who prefer to regard anthropology academically as one of the humanities.

Be that as it may, most anthropologists treat anthropology as a science. As such, its primary characteristics are the ones outlined above. We can gain a better understanding of what anthropologists actually do by taking a look at the major subdivisions of anthropology, a topic considered in the next chapter.

SUMMARY

The literal meaning of *anthropology* is "the science of people" or "the study of people." There is no single feature which distinguishes anthropology from other disciplines, but rather a series of characteristics.

First, it is both a biological and a social science. It investigates the human animal both as an animal and as a particular kind of animal — the animal with culture. Second, it takes as its temporal dimension the total time that mankind has existed on earth. It does not confine itself to the period covered by written records. Third, it is a comparative science. The most basic procedure in anthropology is to compare one society or culture or population with another. Fourth, the traditional orientation of anthropology has been toward the study of primitive societies and cultures. Its goal is to obtain the largest possible sample of human cultural systems, and the majority of human cultures are of this type. Anthropology does not confine itself to the investigation of primitive lifeways, but that is where its primary emphasis has been. Finally, the major focus in anthropology has been on group rather than individual phenomena.

Suggestions for Further Reading

Jorgensen, Joseph G., and Marcello Truzzi. 1974. *Anthropology and American Life.* Englewood Cliffs. N.J.: Prentice-Hall. A collection of articles dealing with anthropological studies of American culture.

Kluckhohn, Clyde. 1949. *Mirror for Man.* New York: Whittlesey House. Still an effective and interesting presentation of the basic anthropological point of view.

Mowat, Farley. 1963. *Never Cry Wolf.* Boston: The Atlantic Monthly Press. An enchanting, wise, and amusing study of the social behavior of wolves.

Murdock, George P. 1949. *Social Structure.* New York: Macmillan. Not intended for the beginning student, this remains a classic example of one type of comparative approach in anthropology. It is based on data from 250 different cultures.

Pfeiffer, John E. 1978. *The Emergence of Man.* New York: Harper & Row. A well-written and consistently interesting account of the human animal that shows the importance of the time dimension to anthropology.

Service, Elman R. 1978. *Profiles in Ethnology,* 3rd. ed. New York: Harper & Row. These careful and vivid sketches of different cultures, most of them primitive, provide some idea of the range of cultural systems usually studied by anthropologists.

Spradley, James P., and George E. McDonough. 1973. *Anthropology Through Literature.* Boston: Little, Brown. A more humanistic approach to anthropology. Contains several selections by the author of this text, along with contributions by more distinguished writers.

Warner, W. Lloyd. 1953. *American Life: Dream and Reality.* University of Chicago Press. A kind of summary of the "Yankee City" series, representing one of the first attempts by an anthropologist to study a modern American city.

West, James. 1945. *Plainville, U.S.A.* New York: Columbia University Press. One of the first attempts at a modern "community study" by an anthropologist. This remains an interesting examination of small-town American life as it was several decades ago.

3

Cutting up the Pie:
The Subdivisions
of Anthropology

The ideal anthropologist, perhaps, would be a person who was equally expert in all areas of anthropology. Commanding a total knowledge of anthropology, such an individual could presumably tackle any anthropological problem from multiple points of view and tie it all together with a balanced judgment based on all the evidence that the discipline has to offer. Unhappily, these ideal anthropologists are found only in legends about the past; you will not find them in any anthropology department today.

This is unfortunate because much of what is uniquely valuable about anthropology requires an ability to interweave different lines of evidence and to employ a variety of different techniques in the investigation of a problem. It is unfortunate but it is also unavoidable. We are stuck with it for precisely the same reason that a single doctor cannot be equally competent in all branches of medicine; the general practitioner can know something about a lot of things, but what that individual *really* needs to know is when to call in a specialist. When things get complicated, either in practice or in research, you need all the expertise you can get — and that means a lifetime of training and experience directly related to the problem that confronts you.

It is simply impossible for one man or woman to be an authority on all the many facets of anthropology. There is too much to know, too much to read, too much to do, too much to digest. One cannot switch blithely from genetics to the supernatural, from baboons to stone artifacts, from folklore to anatomy, and pretend to be an expert on everything. About the best we can do is to try to keep up with major developments and cultivate our own special interests; at the very least we can be aware of our own ignorance. Like the general practitioner in medicine, we need to know when we are out of our depth and when to seek a specialist.

I am a strong believer in the unity of anthropology; I think that every student needs to know as much as possible about all aspects of the discipline. The broader the background, the better the anthropologist. At the same time, there comes a point at which the person must specialize. The alternative is to become a dabbler — jack of all trades and master of none. You would not want the same person to pull your teeth, build your house, fix your car, write your will, entertain you, and perform part-time brain surgery. Similarly, one kind of anthropologist is best equipped to identify ancient skeletal remains, another to study legal procedures among the Kikuyu, and a third to investigate how children acquire the languages they speak.

The advantages of specialized competence have to be experienced to be appreciated. When your car radiator boils over, it's helpful to have someone around who can seal a hose or replace a water pump. When I was working in Africa, I was fortunate to be able to turn for advice to a geographer and an anthropologist trained in psychology who were also members of the research team. Time and time again they would see things that I had missed, things that were quite obvious to them but had to be called to my attention. One of my closest friends is a geologist-archeologist. When we go fly fishing for trout together, I am continually amazed at what he notices — the different rock formations, the relationship between soils and vegetation, the reasons the river flows where it does. "Don't you *see* it?" he will ask with considerable patience. "Look — right *there*." Sometimes I can indeed see it when it is explained to me, but I can never see it with the depth of his vision.

So there are different kinds of anthropologists, trained to be specialists in different things; therefore, there are different kinds of anthropology. One way or another, we are all studying the same subject — the human animal — but we are doing it with different techniques and different perspectives.

I will let you in on a small secret. There is no absolutely "right" way of splitting anthropology up into precise fields and subdivisions. The boundary lines are not engraved on stone tablets anywhere, and there is considerable blurring and overlapping. Like a pie, it can be sliced in many different ways. What follows is no more correct than any other pie-slicing; it merely represents one reasonable way of viewing the problem.

The most basic division of anthropology is into two major fields: *physical anthropology* and *cultural anthropology*. Essentially, physical anthropology is concerned with the evolution and present nature of the bodily structure of the human animal. Cultural anthropology deals with the origins and history of culture, its evolution, and the structure and functioning of human sociocultural systems.

In ideal terms, physical anthropology investigates men and women in terms of how they are constructed as animals, while cultural anthropology studies how men and women live. Obviously, the two are interrelated, or should be; in part, human beings live the way they do because of the kinds of animals they are. Nevertheless, a study devoted to the dimensions of the femur (upper leg bone) in Neanderthal populations is pretty clearly physical anthropology, while a study dealing with witchcraft among the Kikuyu belongs in the realm of cultural anthropology.

This book has as its focus the field of cultural anthropology, and therefore I propose to discuss physical and cultural anthropology from somewhat different perspectives. I will be fairly general about physical anthropology, trying to communicate some sense of what the field is all about, without worrying about all the specializations within the field. When we discuss cultural anthropology, I will be more detailed and indicate at least the primary subdivisions of that field of study.

PHYSICAL ANTHROPOLOGY

When you get right down to it, the physical anthropologist is a human biologist with particular interests in human evolution and human variation. The physical anthropologist wants to know where we came from in a long-range biological sense and how we developed our present bodily structure. Therefore, the physical anthropologist is confronted with several basic tasks. In addition to studying living men and women, the physical anthropologist must *locate* the fossil evidence that bears on the development of the human animal and *interpret* that evidence when it is found.

Neither job is simple, but both can be fascinating. Consider this: When we first appeared on this earth, and for a long time afterwards, we were rare animals. We were by no means an overnight success. The early hominids (men rather than apes, but not necessarily men and women belonging to the same genus and species as ourselves; the term *hominid* refers to all mankind, living and extinct) were relatively few in number. Indeed, if we go back in time some three million years, there were probably fewer than 100,000 hominids on this entire planet — and of course there were none in the so-called New World of the Americas. Compare that with the situation today, when we number not only in the millions but in the billions. (As of 1970, there were an estimated four billion people on earth; by the year 2000 the projection is that this already huge number will double.)

In terms of searching for evidence of these early hominids, the problem would be complicated enough if all the physical evidence had survived to be found — rather like looking for the proverbial needle in a haystack. But the catch is that by no means all of the evidence is there, no matter how persistently you look. Early hominids did not bury their dead, and even if they had done so the odds against any particular hominid skeletal material surviving for three million years (or two million, or one million) are considerable. The truth is that it takes a fortunate series of accidents to permit bone to fossilize, and generally speaking if a skeleton (or a portion of a skeleton) does not fossilize it does not survive for very long. Out of the millions of our ancestors who once walked this earth, only a few thousand fell in such a way as to permit parts of their skeletons to persist through time.

I repeat that the task is difficult. The surviving evidence is not abundant, and what little there is must still be found. How do you go about searching for early hominid fossils? You cannot just poke about randomly, digging holes in the earth. There are no convenient signposts reading, "Here lies *Pithecanthropus erectus.*"

The Early Discoveries

In fact, many of the first early hominid fossils to be found were discovered by accident or by inspired guesswork. The first Neanderthal specimen turned up in 1856 when some workers were cleaning out a cave to prepare for blasting in a limestone quarry. (The site was located in a valley near the German village of Neander; *thal* means "valley" in German, hence the name.)

Eugene Dubois of Holland became convinced that the East Indies was the place to look for fossils and wangled an appointment as an army surgeon in the Netherlands Indies. After years of searching, he found part of a skull and a femur in Java; this was the first *Pithecanthropus erectus* specimen, described by Dubois in 1894. (The name means "erect ape-man," so named because the skull was too small for a modern man but to large for an ape; the femur — or thighbone — indicated that the hominid walked upright.)

A somewhat similar hominid from China, known as *Sinanthropus pekinensis* ("Chinese man of Peking"), was located by a chain of events that began with a fossil tooth found in a Peking drugstore. Raymond Dart found the first Australopithecine skull in a box of limestone fragments from a mine at Taung in South Africa; the skull was that of a juvenile, and Dart (in 1925) named it *Australopithecus africanus* ("the southern ape of Africa"). Even then — or particularly then — the Australopithecines were a source of controversey. Dart's description of *Australopithecus,* indicating a type of hominid intermediate between living apes and mankind, was not well received; for some years, the specimen was patronizingly referred to as "Dart's child." This was not an uncommon fate for the pioneers in the study of fossil hominids. Dubois was so stung by attacks on the authenticity of *Pithecanthropus erectus* that he buried the fossils in a box under the floor of his dining room and refused for years to produce them for inspection.

Today, the situation is different. We know far more about the distribution of early hominids during various periods of time, and we know something about the kinds of living places they favored. There is still an element of luck involved, but it is now possible to plan detailed excavations that can produce not only more hominid fossil specimens but also a wealth of information concerning the conditions under which these ancestors of ours lived.

Interpreting the Evidence

Locating the fossil evidence is one thing, and figuring out what it means is quite another. The interpretation of the hominid record is complex and requires highly specialized skills. Obviously, the *dating* of fossil materials is crucial — a known sequence through time is a necessary counterpart to the study of morphology or structure. It is not good enough to know that a given fossil is old; we

The search for hominid skeletal material is an important part of physical anthropology.

need to know *how* old it is and whether it precedes or follows other hominid forms.

It might be useful here to imagine an ideal site, one that does not occur in the real world. In this miraculous site, you would dig down into the earth — carefully, inch by inch — and find representatives of different fossil populations at different levels. Up near the top, you would uncover modern kinds of hominids — *Homo sapiens.* Further down, you would find skeletal material that was clearly different, skulls that were thick and heavy with great bony ridges over the eye sockets and a space for a brain considerably smaller than our own. This would be something like *Pithecanthropus erectus,* now usually classified (along with *Sinanthropus*) simply as *Homo erectus.* As you dug still deeper, you would find yet another fossil population — rather small hominids, erect in posture, with large molar teeth and brains roughly comparable in size to that of a gorilla. (Gorillas, of course, are much bigger animals than these small hominids — about three times bigger, in fact. Therefore, these fossil hominids have relatively large brains in proportion to the size of their bodies.) These are the Australopithecines —

hominids rather than apes, but hominids sufficiently primitive so that they cannot be placed in the same genus (Homo) as ourselves.

Now, if we had such an ideal site, what could we learn from it? At the very least, we could understand sequence and relative age. We know that, aside from special situations, the deeper down in a deposit the material is the older it is. (Take a freshly minted penny and drop it on the ground in some secluded place. Wait a year or so until it gets covered up by dust and mud and leaves. Take another newly minted penny and drop it in the same spot. Do this for 25 years. Then carefully excavate your little site. You should find your most recent penny at the top and your first penny on the bottom.) We are thus able to say that Australopithecine material is older than that pertaining to *Homo erectus,* and *Homo erectus* is older than *Homo sapiens.* The sequence is right there for us to see — first the Australopithecines, then *Homo erectus,* then *Homo sapiens.*

Dating There is no such ideal site, and yet in a sense there is something fairly close to it. After all, wherever we find these fossil hominids they are on the same planet. The geological history of the earth is rather well known, and it is possible to get an approximate date on a fossil from the geological deposit or layer in which it is found. This means in practice that even if fossil hominids are widely separated in space — say one from England and another from Africa — we know that they were roughly contemporaneous in time if they came from the same geological bed.

There are other approximate dating techniques that are useful. For example, fluorine analysis can assist in determining whether a fossil belongs in the layer in which it is found or whether it is intrusive. Fluorine in ground water gets deposited in buried bones at a fairly constant rate — the older the bone, the higher the fluorine content. There are too many variables to permit comparisons between widely separated specimens, but the technique will work in evaluating materials taken from the same area or nearby areas. It was largely through fluorine detective work that the famous Piltdown fossil was exposed as a hoax.

Dating by stratigraphy ("geological layers") or fluorine analysis, as well as by certain other techniques, is referred to as *relative dating* because these techniques yield only approximate dates — correct as far as they go, but not precise enough to enable us to say, "This fossil is exactly 1,522,444 years old."

Happily, there are also so-called absolute dating techniques available. They are not really absolute, because all of them have to allow for a margin of error, but they can provide reasonably precise dates. Willard Libby won the Nobel Prize in chemistry for developing *radiocarbon* (or carbon 14) *dating.* The process depends on the fact that all living things contain carbon. One form (isotope) of carbon, carbon 12, is stable, while the other form, carbon 14, is unstable and radioactive. While they are alive, plants and animals contain both forms of carbon in equilibrium. When death occurs, the carbon 14 begins to disintegrate at a known rate. By measuring the amount of carbon 14 left in a sample, it is possible to determine how long ago the plant or animal stopped living. It involves, in essence, a kind of atomic clock. Charcoal works best, but animal bones can also be dated in this manner. The catch with radiocarbon dating is that the relatively rapid disintegration rate of carbon 14 permits accurate dating only back as far as 30,000 to 40,000 years. In other words, it can provide a good date on any specimen that was alive within the past 40,000 years or so, but anything older than that cannot be dated by the technique.

For older fossils, the best known absolute dating method is called *potassium-argon dating*. This technique will not work directly on the fossils but can be used to date certain types of rock formations within which fossils are sometimes found. The method is similar to that discussed above; potassium 40 is an isotope of potassium that is radioactive and breaks down into a gas (argon) at a constant and known rate. The disintegration rate is fairly slow, and therefore igneous rocks (rocks of volcanic origin) can be dated as far back as three billion years. If fossils are found in such formations, or sandwiched between layers of volcanic deposits, it is possible to date them with some precision. This technique was used to date some of the fossil hominids from Olduvai Gorge in Tanzania (East Africa), one of the most important anthropological sites in the world.

There are other dating techniques available, some of them still in the experimental stage, but enough has been said to make the necessary point. When fossils are found, they *can* be dated in one way or another, and this is by no means a product of simple guesswork.

Assembling the puzzle Dating is crucial, but it is not the whole story. Even when sequences are known and can be nailed down with dates, the meaning of particular fossil specimens is not always apparent. The interpretation of fossil evidence can get very complicated indeed.

One reason for this is that with rare exceptions it is only in the movies or on TV that a scientist is lucky enough to uncover a complete early hominid skeleton, much less a series of such skeletons that will provide an adequate sample of a population. Most early hominid material is fragmentary and incomplete. In some cases, only the teeth have survived. In others, the teeth are still positioned in the mandible (lower jaw). Sometimes, portions of the rest of the skull are found but not the entire skull. If you are very fortunate, you may find some arm or leg bones. (The fleshy parts of the body, of course, do not fossilize. That is one reason why the size of the brain of a fossil hominid is given in terms of cranial capacity — the amount of brain that can be housed in a given skull.) To illustrate what this means, consider that the Australopithecines are among the best known of all fossil hominids. Here, where the record is good, we have the fragmentary remains of about 100 individuals. Of these, perhaps seven have skulls complete enough to permit an accurate estimate of cranial capacity. Such critical fossils as pelvic bones or foot bones are even rarer.

The physical anthropologist, then, is in a position not unlike that of a person trying to put together a jigsaw puzzle in which some of the pieces are missing and some of the pieces are incomplete. The puzzle is not easy, but it must be solved if we are ever to understand human origins.

I do not want to give the impression that physical anthropologists work only with fossil bones. Whether you are interested in evolutionary change or in the differences between modern populations, you must concern yourself with genetics. It is probably safe to say that most modern physical anthropologists are at least as familiar with gene frequencies and population genetics as they are with the analysis of skeletal materials.

The puzzle of hominid evolution necessarily involves the study of the antecedents of the human animal. We hominids did not pop into being out of nothing, and our development is one part of the more general evolution of the primates. Both extinct and living nonhuman primates are therefore a logical focus of study for physical anthropologists. Extinct nonhuman primates precede the appearance of hominids in time; they can tell us where we came from in a biological sense. Living nonhuman primates can provide information about our own structure and behavior because, although none of them are ancestral to the human animal, they are our closest living relatives in the animal world.

Inevitably, perhaps, an interest in the biology of nonhuman primates dovetails with an interest in the behavior patterns of these animals. We want to know not only how they are constructed but also how they live. In field studies of living nonhuman primate groups (as opposed, say, to a study centered on the comparative anatomy of the chimpanzee and the gorilla) the interests of the physical anthropologist and the cultural anthropologist often merge. It is essential to find out how these animals live under natural conditions. There is no other equally valid way of discovering what is truly unique about the human animal.

The problem, in a sense, is to understand how an animal moves from its lifeway to ours. This understanding leads to nothing less than a true appreciation of the significance of culture and the difference it makes in our lives.

I hope that I have succeeded in communicating something of the intellectual excitement of physical anthropology. It is alive, vital, stimulating, and important. I hope too that I have communicated my conviction that physical anthropology and cultural anthropology should never become entirely divorced one from the other. It is essential that we specialize, but it is also essential that we remember that our ultimate task is the same—to understand what the human animal is all about.

A SHORT SKETCH OF HUMAN EVOLUTION

Presenting a detailed and sophisticated outline of what is presently known about human evolution is beyond the scope of this book. Nevertheless, we need some degree of perspective, no matter how elementary.

Let us begin with a few basic facts. Geologists divide the history of the earth into a series of major segments called *eras*. The era in which we are now living, which has persisted for some 70 million years, is known as the *Cenozoic era*. (The Cenozoic era follows the Mesozoic era; the Mesozoic is popularly known as the "Age of the Dinosaurs.") There were no true primates until the beginning of the Cenozoic. *Therefore, all primate evolution, including human evolution, occurred within the Cenozoic era.* (The development of the nonhuman primates is discussed in Chapter 4.)

The Cenozoic era, in turn, is subdivided into a series of shorter segments

Epochs	Began (Millions of years before present)	
Recent (Last 10,000 years)	.01	*Homo sapiens* Modern type appears c. 40,000 years ago
Pleistocene	3	
Pliocene	5	
Miocene	25	*Ramapithecus*
Oligocene	40	
Eocene	60	
Paleocene	70	First primates

(Cenozoic era spans all epochs listed)

Figure 3.1 Key dates in the evolution of the hominids.

which are called *epochs*. The earliest generally accepted hominid, known as *Ramapithecus,* dates from rather late in the *Miocene epoch.* The Miocene began about 25 million years ago; its precise duration is uncertain. It depends upon where the dividing line is drawn between the Miocene and the next following epoch, the Pliocene. Most estimates place the end of the Miocene (or the beginning of the Pliocene) at around 5 million years ago. The *Ramapithecus* specimens are considered to be about 12 million years old. Therefore, specifically hominid evolution begins in late Miocene times, and all of it has occurred within approximately the last 12 million years. Figure 3.1 may help to clarify the general picture.

Viewed in this way, of course, the essential question is obvious. How do we get from a primitive hominid like *Ramapithecus* in the latter part of the Miocene to modern *Homo sapiens,* who appear toward the end of the Pleistocene epoch about 40,000 years ago? What comes in between?

The question may be obvious, but it is not an easy one to answer. The major problem, as we shall see, concerns the role played by the Australopithecines. Before we tackle that one, it is necessary to explain a crucial point. When we refer to a specific fossil form (*Ramapithecus* or whatever) we must think of it as a representative of a population. In the final analysis, the meaningful units of evolutionary change are breeding populations rather than specific individuals. When we say, for example, that *Ramapithecus* was the first hominid this is just a shorthand way of indicating that the population represented by *Ramapithecus* was composed of the earliest known hominids. In looking at any evolutionary diagram, regardless of the labels, remember that it is intended to represent successive breeding populations, populations that to some degree grade into one another, rather than a series of jumps from one isolated individual to another isolated individual.

With that in mind, suppose we have a look at our basic but abbreviated cast of characters.

In very broad and nontechnical fashion, we will characterize the major players in the drama of human evolution. (See Figure 3.2, p. 45.)

Ramapithecus

As the name suggests (Rama is a Hindu god), the first *Ramapithecus* specimen was found in India. Subsequent to that first find—made by G. Edward Lewis in 1934—*Ramapithecus* fossils have turned up elsewhere, most notably in Kenya, East Africa. Dates on various specimens range from 8 to 14 million years before the present.

The *Ramapithecus* fossils are quite fragmentary, consisting essentially of jaws and teeth. Their significance boils down to this: In both the *shape* of the jaws and the *structure* of the teeth, *Ramapithecus* more closely resembles a hominid than it does any type of ape, living or extinct. If you run your tongue over your teeth, or simply look in a mirror, you will find that your dental arch (the line of your jaw) is smoothly curved so that the teeth at the back of the jaw are further apart (from one side of the jaw to the other) than those at the front. This is a human trait; ape jaws are straight-sided with the back teeth forming parallel rows. *Ramapithecus* has a distinctly curved jaw. Moreover, *Ramapithecus* does not have the relatively large front teeth—canines and incisors—that are characteristic of apes.

Unfortunately, there is very little more that can be said with assurance

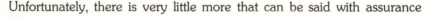
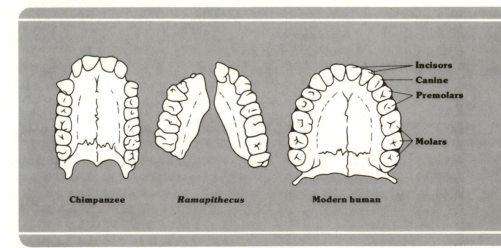

A comparison of the jaws and teeth of a chimpanzee, *Ramapithecus*, and *Homo sapiens*.

about *Ramapithecus.* No tools have been positively associated with the fossil specimens. The environmental conditions under which *Ramapithecus* lived are somewhat uncertain; the evidence suggests a mixture of forest and grassland habitats.

Ramapithecus, then, is the earliest known hominid. As such, unless and until still earlier hominid fossils are found, the *Ramapithecus* population must be considered as ancestral to all later hominids, including ourselves.

The Australopithecines

Australopithecine is a collective term which refers to several species of the genus *Australopithecus.* There are at least two species which are generally recognized. One is a small, gracile form — probably weighing around 60 pounds — that is known as *Australopithecus africanus.* The other is a larger, more heavily built form — possibly weighing as much as 100 pounds — that is referred to as *Australopithecus robustus.* The australopithecines were first discovered in South Africa; they have subsequently been found to be rather widely distributed in East Africa, extending at least as far north as Ethiopia. The time span for the australopithecines is considerable. The oldest specimens are more than five million years old, while the youngest check out at around one million years old. In other words, the australopithecines first appear in the Pliocene epoch, and they persisted well into the Pleistocene.

In terms of the amount of fossil material available and the number of sites excavated, the australopithecines are the best known of all the early hominids. They were rather small in stature, ranging between four and five feet in height. Physically, perhaps their most interesting characteristic is a combination of two traits: They were reasonably erect bipedal walkers with relatively small brains. Average cranial capacities are about 450 cc (cubic centimeters) for *africanus* and about 500 cc for *robustus.* Allowing for their comparatively small size, this still indicates that in the evolution of the hominids the erect posture came first and the explosive growth in the size of the brain came later. (The average cranial capacity for *Homo sapiens* is around 1400 cc — roughly three times as great as that of the australopithecines.)

The australopithecines were creatures of the savannas (relatively open grasslands) and the edges of forests. This is an extremely significant point, indicating that one of the major factors in hominid evolution was a movement out of the forests into more open country. The australopithecines were collectors of wild plant foods (roots, berries, and the like) and hunters of wild animals. They seem to have been fairly efficient hunters, killing small animals like lizards and rats and larger animals such as baboons and antelopes. They obviously lived and hunted in groups — a lone australopithecine would not have fared well against a male baboon — and as one might suspect they were equipped with crude tools and weapons. Indeed, the earliest known stone artifacts are associated with the australopithecines. These are of a type called *Oldowan,* a kind of chopper made by knocking a few flakes from a rock core to produce a cutting edge. (This is done by striking one rock directly against another, and is referred

Oldowan tools (upper left)
and other Paleolithic artifacts.

A reconstruction of what the australopithecines
might have looked like.

to as the *direct percussion* technique.) Undoubtedly, these choppers were employed to make other tools and weapons of wood and bone. It has been suggested that this is the primary advantage of the erect bipedal posture: It frees the
hands for tool using.

There are many intriguing puzzles concerning the australopithecines.
Among them is the seeming coexistence of two or more species and the remarkable stability of the genus over a very long period of time. Viewed structurally
and in terms of what can be reconstructed of their lifeways, the australopithecines seem to be logical links in the chain of human evolution. Whether or not
they in fact contributed genetically to later forms of hominids remains an open
question. What is beyond dispute is that the australopithecines were among the
descendants of the *Ramapithecus* population and clearly represent one of the
early hominid adaptations.

Homo erectus

So we come at last to our own genus, but not our own species. The best-
known examples of what is now referred to as *Homo erectus* are *Pithecanthropus erectus* (from Java) and *Sinanthropus pekinensis* (from China). Other
specimens have been found in Africa and the Middle East. So far as is known, all
Homo erectus fossils date within the Pleistocene epoch; most of them cluster
between one million years ago and about 400,000 years ago.

Physically, *Homo erectus* can be characterized as a rather large, heavy-

A restored skull and facial reconstruction of *Homo erectus*. This specimen is *Pithecanthropus erectus*.

boned hominid with a considerably bigger brain than that of the australopithe-cines: The average cranial capacity runs around 1000 cc. As their name suggests, they were erect bipedal walkers, but the skulls have a primitive appearance to them. The thick, jutting, bony brow ridges, the narrow receding forehead, the massive chinless jaws, the large teeth — all of these features mark *Homo erectus* as distinctively different from any modern representative of the genus *Homo*.

Culturally, we owe a considerable debt to these distant ancestors of ours. They discovered fire, one of the most significant of all hominid inventions, and they cooked their meat. Moreover, they had plenty of meat to cook: *Homo erectus* was probably the first reasonably successful hominid big-game hunter. They hunted small game like deer, of course, but included among the 90 or so mammals that they hunted were animals such as horses, rhinoceroses, and even a saber-toothed cat. They made tools of stone, bone, and antlers. Their most typical stone artifacts represented a considerable advance over the lithic tools of the australopithecines; known as *Acheulian* tools, the commonest type was a flint (or quartz) hand axe. These hand axes are bifacial; that is, they are worked on both sides, and some of them are beautifully made. The evidence suggests that the bulk of the hunting was done with wooden spears.

The spread of *Homo erectus* populations into a variety of habitats — some of them quite cold — indicates a cultural adaptation of no mean sort. For perhaps the first time, the human animal was venturing into ecological situations very different from the warm forests and grasslands where we first appeared on earth.

Homo sapiens

Although the dating is far from precise, modern types of hominids—the best known of which are the Cro-Magnon peoples of France—probably first developed about 40,000 years ago. Certainly, in the time period ranging from 30,000 years ago to 25,000 years ago, *Homo sapiens* occupied the whole of the inhabited world; it had replaced all other forms of hominids.

You may wonder what happened to our old friends the Neanderthals. At present, most physical anthropologists classify the various Neanderthals as an early subspecies of *Homo sapiens*. They are referred to as *Homo sapiens neanderthalensis*, as opposed to *Homo sapiens sapiens*. The inclusion of the Neanderthals in our own species is primarily based on the size of the Neanderthal brain; cranial capacities of Neanderthal skulls range from 1300 to 1600 cc, which means that some of them had bigger brains than we do. The Neanderthal subspecies has a considerable antiquity to it; some Neanderthaloid populations date back as far as 200,000 years ago. The Neanderthals persisted in time until they were replaced by *Homo sapiens sapiens*.

Returning to Cro-Magnon and related populations, there is little point in describing them physically: They were essentially similar to men and women living today. It was in the realm of culture that these peoples made their most dramatic advances. The Upper Paleolithic cultures—that is, those that flourished during the most recent part of the Old Stone Age—were remarkable in many ways. The surest index of this is in the area of population. We were no longer rare animals with an uncertain future. Two million years ago there were probably fewer than 150,000 hominids in all the world. By Cro-Magnon times, it has been estimated that the population had grown to more than three million people. Moreover, in terms of the total expanse of territory occupied, we had become the most successful of all the mammals.

The story of human evolution up to this point is basically the story of the development of big-brained hunters with hands that could shape and use tools and bodies that were versatile and capable of endurance. The Upper Paleolithic populations were among the most effective of all big-game hunters. Bison, reindeer, wild horses, mammoths—the Cro-Magnon peoples hunted them all. There is a single site in Europe containing the bones of more than 100 mammoths, and there is another one where an astonishing 10,000 horses were found at the base of a high cliff. Obviously, this quality of hunting takes more than a big brain; it requires good equipment. Stone-working technology had come a long way since the old days of crude direct-percussion artifacts; lithic techniques had become far more sophisticated. These people had spear throwers—shafts a foot or more long, with a handle at one end and a hook at the other to engage the butt end of a spear—that greatly enhanced the range and power of thrown spears. Barbed harpoonlike points multiplied the deadliness of these weapons.

I cannot in this brief sketch even begin to convey the richness of these cultures, a quality that may be sensed in the spectacular cave art of the period. Mention must be made, however, of yet another facet of late Upper Paleolithic life, and that is fishing. The Cro-Magnon peoples built elaborate traps called

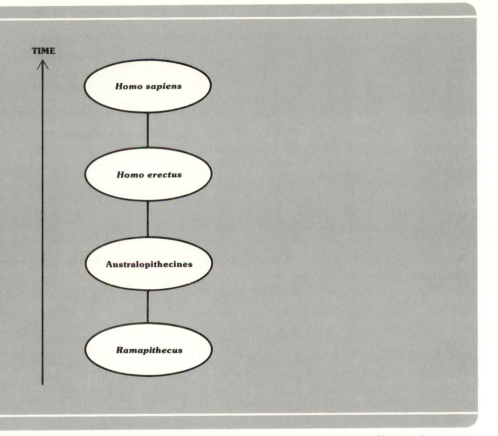

Figure 3.2 One view of the relationships among major populations of hominids.

weirs in which they caught salmon swimming upstream to spawn. They made special implements, like long forks, to impale the fish. They also had simple bone fishhooks in their arsenal, and it is intriguing to speculate that early forms of freshwater trout (the European or brown trout, *Salmo trutta*) were probably available in the inland streams.

This, then, is our basic cast of characters. One might say: So far, so good; the story that they seem to tell is both logical and consistent. If we were to diagram the relationships between them, without taking any such drawing with undue solemnity, it might look something like Figure 3.2.

New evidence has turned up, however, that is forcing us to revise some of our ideas about the evolution of the hominids. No matter how logical an interpretation may be, it cannot stand in the face of contradictory information. Thanks primarily to the work of two men, Richard Leakey and Donald Carl Johanson, we have been presented with an awkward series of facts.

In essence, Leakey (working in Kenya) and Johanson (working in Ethiopia) have come up with convincing evidence that the genus *Homo* is a

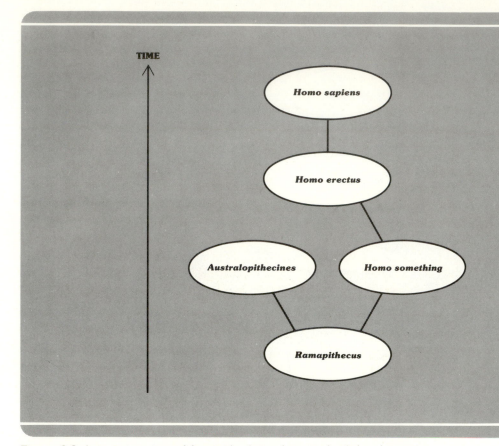

Figure 3.3 A tentative view of hominid relationships in the light of recent discoveries.

good deal older than was previously believed to be the case. Indeed, they have discovered fossil specimens of genus *Homo* that are reliably dated between two and three and a half million years ago. A moment's reflection will suggest what this does to the standard picture of hominid evolution: It places our own genus before *Homo erectus* and back in the time of the australopithecines.

These fossils are clearly not australopithecines; on the basis of cranial capacities (about 780 cc) and other morphological features, they appear to represent a very early population that must be assigned to the genus *Homo*. Wisely, the authorities have so far resisted the impulse to assign a species designation to these fossils. They are not *Homo erectus* and certainly not *Homo sapiens*. Until further evidence clarifies the situation, we must refer to them simply as *Homo something*.

It is still too soon to offer anything like a definitive interpretation of these fossils. They suggest two things of major significance. First, during this time period there were at least three kinds of hominids that coexisted—several varieties of australopithecines and one representative of genus *Homo*. Second, given the fact of their coexistence, it becomes difficult to derive *Homo erectus* from the australopithecines. In other words, it now seems reasonable to make *Homo something* ancestral to *Homo erectus*, which leaves the australopithecines as a side branch of the hominids that did not contribute genetically to later populations. If this is true, then our simplified picture of human evolution would look something like Figure 3.3.

We must now leave our tentative interpretation of the physical evolution of the hominids and move on to other matters.

CULTURAL ANTHROPOLOGY

As is true of physical anthropology, cultural anthropology is also going through a period of considerable change and self-examination. This is all to the good; it means that the discipline is alive and growing. However, the fresh orientations and divergent viewpoints do pose problems for anyone attempting to categorize cultural anthropology into a neat little series of taxonomic pigeonholes. Nevertheless, we do need at least a nodding acquaintance with the traditional fields (or subdivisions) of cultural anthropology. We must ask ourselves what cultural anthropology is all about and which kind of cultural anthropologist does what.

In the broadest possible terms, as we noted before, cultural anthropology is concerned with how people live: the ways in which people group themselves into societies and the cultures that provide the guidelines for their behavior. Cultural anthropologists are interested both in the universals of human existence and in the particular characteristics of specific sociocultural systems.

Basically, there are two major facets to cultural anthropology. One studies ongoing human societies — those that can be observed in operation or those that existed recently enough so that former participants can tell us about them. Whatever the focus of a given investigation — whether it deals with social groupings, political organizations, supernatural beliefs, economic systems, or ways of regulating sexual behavior — the cultural anthropologist is trying to find out how the system works. The other deals with cultures that no longer exist and which cannot be precisely remembered by living informants. It must reconstruct lifeways from clues left in the earth — cultural products such as stone tools or pottery or the remains of ancient campsites.

Archeology

The most distinctive branch of cultural anthropology, in the sense of being rather sharply different from the other subdivisions, is archeology. Insofar as it pertains to anthropology, archeology is essentially the study of prehistory.

History, by definition, requires written records. As we have seen, writing only goes back in time some 5000 years at most. The human animal is millions of years old on this planet. If anthropology is to deal with the total time span of human existence, the problem becomes self-evident. How can we come to grips with the millions of years of human activity and culture change that are not documented by writing?

The things that people make or use — stone axes and projectile points, pottery, old rock shelters that once housed a group of hunters, or the remains of ancient fires—last far longer than the people themselves. In fact, a stone tool, once it is made, is virtually indestructible. (Like a pot, it can be broken, but the pieces survive.) Moreover, we have a happy fact at our disposal. At any given time, there are many more artifacts than there are people. If we may paraphrase Shakespeare, one man in his time makes many artifacts, but he can only make one skeleton. Therefore, while early hominid skeletons are relatively rare, early tools and weapons are fairly common. In a sense, most of them are still there, waiting in the earth. For the great majority of time that hominids have existed, these are the only clues we have about how the human animal lived. The most basic task of the archeologist is to excavate these cultural products, interpret their significance, and arrange them into sequences.

There are two points that should be made right here. First, do not be confused by the fact that hominid bones and hominid artifacts are frequently found in the same site. An archeologist excavating a site will sometimes find hominid skeletal material. Similarly, a physical anthropologist searching for fossil bones often encounters artifacts such as stone tools. Even if they are found in the same site, the skeletal material is the major concern of the physical anthropologist, while the artifacts will be examined by an archeologist. Archeology is a branch of cultural anthropology because the tools are cultural products—things made by the human animal in response to cultural traditions. Skeletal materials are, of course, part of the biological make-up of the human animal and as such are the concern of physical anthropology. Thus, when an archeologist finds a burial site, the bones are turned over to a physical anthropologist for analysis. When the physical anthropologist finds artifacts, an archeologist is called upon for interpretation.

Second, it must be remembered that the archeologist is after information, not trophies. If artifacts are to tell their story, they must be meticulously excavated. The archeologist has to know exactly where everything came from, both the level within the site and the spatial location within the site. Otherwise, the archeologist cannot know what goes with what. Ideally, digging a site should be done in such a way that if necessary, every single item—every flint chip, every potsherd—could be replaced where it was found. Every archeological site, no matter how humble it may appear to be, is one part of the puzzle that we are trying to solve, the puzzle of what happened to the human animal on earth. Once it is destroyed, the information is lost forever. That is why archeologists tend to get a trifle impatient with amateurs who tear sites apart looking for decorative objects such as arrow points to cement into their fireplaces. It is not professional jealousy; it is dismay at the careless destruction of data. If you must dig, join your local archeological society and learn to do the job properly. It's more fun that way, and you just might be able to contribute something worthwhile.

In practice, archeology has become enormously complex. Nevertheless, what the archeologist is trying to do is not difficult to grasp. The archeologist is attempting to reconstruct extinct cultures in as much detail as possible from material remains left in the earth and, in addition, is trying to provide a chronology

A modern archeological excavation.

for human culture change. It is up to the archeologist to supply anthropology with the crucial time dimension it needs to operate.

There is another point that students sometimes find confusing. Archeology is one subdivision of cultural anthropology, but not all archeologists are anthropologists. To put the matter simply, there is more than one kind of archeology. For example, there is classical archeology, which is concerned with such Old World civilizations as Greece and Rome. There is biblical archeology, dealing with the locating and excavating of sites mentioned in the Bible. There is Egyptology, involving the study of "ancient" Egypt. And there is even historical archeology, which excavates old forts and settlements and other significant sites within the historic period. But all of the rest, including all of the really early materials and the entire prehistory of the New World, is technically a part of anthropology.

The other branches of cultural anthropology are all based on the study of living peoples.

Ethnography

Ethnography is really a highly specialized kind of reporting. We can define an ethnography as a descriptive account of a single human lifeway. Leaving aside certain modern developments, ethnography is very simple in theory and extremely difficult in practice. It is easy to explain what an ethnographer is trying to do, but actually doing it is something else again. That is why genuinely first-rate ethnographies are not conspicuous by their numbers.

The ethnographer selects a particular human society and goes out to find out everything possible about it. (This is called "going into the field," and it is a critical experience for most cultural anthropologists.) The ethnographer lives with the people being studied, participates in their lifeway to the extent feasible, tries to learn the language, and questions informants. What is being sought is nothing less than an understanding of the total culture of one human population.

Of course, you never get it all; cultural systems are too complex for that even if all goes well. Still, you get as much as you can.

The ethnographer records as much as possible, organizes the information, and writes a descriptive account of what the culture is like. An ethnography tells how the people in a given society get their food, how they reckon kinship, how they settle legal disputes, how they regard the supernatural, how they live. Everything is grist for the mill; ideally, we want to know everything there is to know about the society. (Actually, we must qualify that somewhat. Ethnographers do not report information that might prove harmful to the people concerned, and they do not use the real names of informants.) I use the term *descriptive* because the basic aim of ethnography is to supply objective information, not to theorize.

When you read an ethnography, it is essential that you understand the concept of the *ethnographic present*. This really has nothing to do with the tenses employed by the writer; it simply means that the account refers to the culture at the time it was studied, or to the culture that was remembered by informants. For example, if you read that the Comanche hunt bison on the Staked Plains and raid for horses deep into Mexico, this does not mean that they do these things now—it means that they once did them. The late semanticist (someone who deals with the problem of meaning in language) Alfred Korzybski once suggested that it would be a good idea to attach the date to all statements of known fact. The notion is rather too cumbersome to be generally employed, but it is a useful mental habit to get into when thinking about ethnographic materials. Thus, if we say that the Comanche (1850) hunted bison and raided for horses there is no doubt about what we mean.

Reliable, factual ethnographic studies are the building blocks for more ambitious or theoretical investigations; they are the foundations upon which most of cultural anthropology is built. It is impossible, after all, to compare anything until you have something to compare.

Ethnology

Ethnology is tougher to define largely because different anthropologists use the term in different ways. It seems to me that the word has at least three different meanings in anthropology, and about all they have in common is this: (1) like ethnography, ethnology is concerned essentially with living peoples as opposed to archeological remains, and (2) all ethnological studies are broader in some way than purely ethnographic accounts.

The first usage is what we might term *plural ethnography*. A descriptive account of more than one cultural system falls into this category. For example, suppose you choose to discuss not just the Comanche but also a number of other peoples who hunted the bison on horseback between 1600 and 1880: the Blackfoot, the Crow, the Cheyenne, the Kiowa, and others. This would be a descriptive account of the Plains Indians (plural) rather than a study of just one tribe, and therefore would be ethnology rather than ethnography. In similar fashion, we can speak of the ethnology of East Africa, or the ethnology of the Pacific, or for that matter the ethnology of the world.

The second usage can be called *historical ethnology*. This is a study of one or more cultures which attempts to account for present conditions in terms of the reconstructed past. As we have seen, ethnographies deal with the ethnographic present: a sort of this-is-the-way-it-is approach. In historical ethnology another dimension is introduced. It seeks to explain how things got to be that way by making reference to the historical development of the culture being discussed. Thus, to continue with the Plains Indians, we know that these people hunted bison on horseback only in comparatively recent times; the horse became extinct in the New World, and no Indians rode horses until after the horse was reintroduced to the New World by the Spanish in 1519. Exactly where did the Plains Indians get their horses? How did the horse change their way of life? What peoples were on the Plains before the horse arrived, and which peoples moved in afterward? As soon as we begin to ask questions of this sort, we are dealing with historical ethnology.

Finally, there is *scientific ethnology*. I use the term to refer to the theoretical or generalizing aspect of ethnology. This usage is rarely made explicit, but it certainly exists. The employment of ethnological data to construct principles or laws relating to sociocultural phenomena can be called scientific because it goes beyond the descriptive level and beyond historical (which is to say, particularistic) analysis.

Suppose, for example, that we survey all known cultures based on hunting wild animals and collecting wild plant foods and conclude that they all have certain features in common, characteristics that appear to be linked to their similar ecological bases. This results in a scientific ethnological statement. As long ago as 1889, E. B. Tylor examined data from a variety of different cultures and concluded that there was a strong correlation between *matrilocal residence* and the *mother-in-law tabu*. (Matrilocal residence means that when a man and a woman marry they go to live with the bride's family. A mother-in-law tabu is a custom according to which a man must avoid direct social interaction with his wife's mother.) This can be phrased as a law based on probable association: if X, then Y. It is a classic illustration of what is meant by scientific ethnology.

It must be admitted that in the real world these various usages of the term ethnology are not as clear-cut as I have here presented them; they tend to get mixed up, and the lines between them are often blurred in practice. Still, it is a handy way to think about the problem, and it is helpful in identifying the diverse materials included under the blanket term *ethnology*.

Social Anthropology

Social anthropology is somewhat similar to ethnology, with this major difference: Ideally, social anthropologists focus their attention on social structure rather than on the totality of a cultural system. Social anthropology primarily concentrates on how human societies are constructed and how they operate. It can be thought of as a kind of comparative sociology, and its approach is essentially nonhistorical.

There is a tendency to exaggerate the differences between social anthropology and ethnology. Social anthropology first came into vogue in England under the influence of anthropologists such as A. R. Radcliffe-Brown (1881–1955). There was a time when British anthropologists called themselves social anthropologists while American anthropologists referred to themselves as ethnologists, even though they were all doing much the same kind of thing. Gradually, the term *social anthropology* became fashionable, and the term *ethnology* came to have an old-fashioned ring to it. Today, ethnology seems to be staging something of a comeback, and some anthropologists vacillate between the two terms.

There *is* a difference between social anthropology and ethnology, as indicated above, but it is a difference that is sometimes hard to detect in practice. For instance, anthropological specialists in the study of folklore usually identify themselves as social anthropologists even though their interests clearly range far beyond the area of social structure. Similarly, practitioners of ethnoscience—who seek to find out how people in different cultures themselves categorize experience, as opposed to imposing anthropological constructs on the data—frequently consider themselves to be social anthropologists; they too do not confine themselves to anything resembling comparative sociology.

All this may seem to be nit-picking, and in a sense it is. Nevertheless, we cannot simply ignore labels. Learning to use words with precision is an important part of anthropology, and knowing what kind of cultural anthropologist someone is can at least provide some clues about that person's theoretical orientation.

Linguistics

Linguistics is the study of language. Not all linguists are anthropologists by any means, but some anthropologists are primarily linguists. It is a crucial field of study and an important part of cultural anthropology. There is no more critical problem in anthropology than the nature of language: how we speak, the underlying models or codes which produce meaningful speech, and how linguistic systems are interrelated with other dimensions of culture.

Beyond this, linguistics provides both techniques and data that are invaluable to the anthropologist. The relationships between languages supply essential clues to understanding the historical connections between peoples. The knowledge of what makes language tick tells us a great deal about how cultures work; the one (language) is a subsystem of the other.

Both in terms of theory and technique, linguistics has profoundly influenced anthropology. When an anthropologist struggles to learn the language of a population being studied, a bridge is being built that leads to an understanding of that society's culture. When language itself is finally understood as an attribute of mankind, we shall know far more about what it means to be human.

Applied Anthropology

The last division of cultural anthropology we will discuss here is usually referred to as *applied anthropology*. In some ways, it is not so much a specialized field as a product of anthropological expertise. What is to be done with the information that anthropologists have? To what extent should it be used, or can it be used, to contribute to the solution of modern problems? What are the responsibilities of the anthropologist to the people with whom the anthropologist works? What do *they* get out of the deal?

On a somewhat different level, what kinds of jobs should anthropologists seek? Should they all be employed as academics of some sort, or should they work in such areas as government, business, or social welfare? Clearly, this question has important implications with regard to the training of anthropologists. There is a common core of anthropological understandings that all anthropologists should share, but what additional approaches and techniques should be stressed? It seems likely that a fair percentage of the current generation of new anthropologists will be looking for jobs outside of the colleges and universities. There is nothing particularly controversial about this; it simply means that the training of anthropologists must take into account the practical aspects of what many anthropologists will actually be doing in the near future, whether this involves the analysis of urban groups or market surveys or the evaluation of data for government agencies.

Applied anthropology has had a checkered history and some anthropologists have had serious doubts about it. I suspect that this is a healthy thing. After all, applied anthropology *can* find itself in the position of tinkering with the life-ways of human beings, and noble motives notwithstanding, this is a serious matter. Politics and personalities enter into the equation, and what seems "right" to one person may seem "wrong" to another.

Consider this hypothetical situation. Suppose the government of Tanzania in East Africa decides that the Masai (who are cattle herders) should settle down and farm because Tanzania has a shortage of land and farming can support more people in a given area than herding can. The government approaches you, the anthropologist. Will you develop a strategy to persuade the Masai to give up their cattle and plant crops? This amounts to a planned destruction of the traditional Masai culture: The people love their cattle and they take immense pride in Masai ways of doing things. They don't *want* to be farmers. What should you do? Before you answer, remember that farmers are thicker on the land than herders are; the farmers have the votes. The Masai lifeway may be doomed whether you do anything or not. Would it be better to have a planned transition, just let it happen, or hope for a miracle?

There are no easy answers in this area. The problem is compounded by the fact that anthropologists too are human; we are neither all-wise nor all-knowing. However tempting it may be to play the oracle, it is well to remember that oracles are sometimes misunderstood—or just plain wrong.

It is probably safe to say that an increasing number of anthropologists will move into relatively noncontroversial applied fields. Some anthropologists seem determined to attempt to move society in the directions they consider to be appropriate. At the same time, most anthropological work still falls under the heading of basic research. Most anthropologists are trying to answer fundamental questions about the human animal because they believe that information about mankind is important in itself. If they can be of assistance to the peoples with whom they work, they will do what they can. Still, it is necessary to remember that there can be no adequate solutions to problems without accurate data—and even the most esoteric and theoretical study may turn out to have immense practical significance, as the history of science has demonstrated many times over.

SUMMARY

The most basic division of anthropology is into two major fields, *physical anthropology* and *cultural anthropology*. Physical anthropology deals with the evolution and present nature of the bodily structure of the human animal. Cultural anthropology deals with the origins and history of culture, its evolution, and the structure and functioning of human sociocultural systems.

Since the primary focus of this book is on cultural anthropology, the various specialized subfields of physical anthropology were not discussed. Although it does other things as well, it is the responsibility of physical anthropology to locate the fossil evidence that bears on the development of the human animal and to interpret that evidence when it is found.

The dating of the fossil evidence is crucial. This can be done by relative dating techniques, such as the use of stratigraphy of fluorine analysis, or in some cases by absolute dating techniques which allow some margin for error but still provide reasonably precise dates. Common absolute dating techniques include radioactive carbon dating, which works on organic materials no more than 40,000 years old, and potassium argon dating, which has a much greater range but can be applied only to certain types of rock formations.

The physical anthropologist does not work exclusively with bones—fossil or otherwise. Genetic analysis is a very important part of modern physical anthropology, and so is the study of the nonhuman primates.

Cultural anthropology is divided into a series of distinctive subdivisions. The most distinctive of these, in the sense of being rather sharply different from the other branches of cultural anthropology, is *archeology*. Insofar as it pertains to anthropology, archeology is essentially the study of prehistory. It is the job of the archeologist to reconstruct lifeways that no longer exist from clues left in the earth: cultural products such as stone tools or pottery or the remains of ancient campsites.

The other divisions of cultural anthropology are all based on the study of living peoples. *Ethnography* is really a highly specialized kind of reporting. An ethnography is a descriptive account of a single human lifeway. *Ethnology* is more difficult to define since the term is used in different ways by different anthropologists. It may be said that all ethnological studies are broader in scope than purely ethnographic accounts. Among the various usages, there are at least three kinds of ethnological investigations. First, there is *plural ethnography*. This is a descriptive account of two or more human lifeways. Second, there is *historical ethnology*. In addition to describing one or more cultures, it attempts to understand how they got to be that way in terms of historical development. Finally, there is *scientific ethnology*. This term is used to refer to the theoretical or generalizing aspect of ethnology: the attempt to employ ethnological data in the construction of principles or laws relating to sociocultural phenomena.

Social anthropology is somewhat similar to ethnology except that its focus is on social structure rather than on the totality of a cultural system. It concentrates on how human societies are put together and how they operate. *Linguistics* is the study of language. Not all linguists are anthropologists, but some cultural anthropologists are primarily linguists. There is no more critical question in anthropology than that of the nature of language. *Applied anthropology* deals with the question of how anthropological information and techniques can be put to use in attempting to find solutions for some of the difficult problems with which the modern world is faced.

Suggestions for Further Reading

Birdsell, Joseph B. 1975. *Human Evolution: An Introduction to the New Physical Anthropology,* 2d ed. Chicago: Rand McNally. A brilliant book covering everything from human genetics to the fossil hominids.

Blount, Ben G. 1974. *Language, Culture and Society: A Book of Readings.* Cambridge, Mass.: Winthrop. A useful collection of essays by various authors dealing with anthropological linguistics.

Bohannan, Paul. 1963. *Social Anthropology.* New York: Holt, Rinehart and Winston. A good general treatment of the subject.

Bowen, Elenore Smith. 1964. *Return to Laughter.* Garden City, N.Y.: Doubleday (Anchor Books). Elenore Smith Bowen is the pen name of anthropologist Laura Bohannan. Although called "an anthropological novel," this is really a slightly fictionalized account of what is actually involved in "doing" an ethnography. A rewarding and insightful book.

Burling, Robbins. 1970. *Man's Many Voices: Language in the Cultural Context.* New York: Holt, Rinehart and Winston. An introduction to anthropological linguistics.

Campbell, Bernard G. 1976. *Humankind Emerging.* Boston: Little, Brown. A beautifully illustrated and clearly written account of human evolution.

D'Andrade, R. G., E. A. Hammel, D. L. Adkins, and C. K. McDaniel. 1975. "Academic Opportunity in Anthropology 1974–90." *American Anthropologist* 77(4): 753–773. An important article which suggests that in the near future many anthropologists must seek employment outside the academic sector.

Fagan, Brian M. 1980. *People of the Earth: An Introduction to World Prehistory.* Boston: Little, Brown. An interesting and successful introduction to anthropological archeology.

Goldschmidt, Walter. 1976. *The Culture and Behavior of the Sebei.* Berkeley and Los Angeles: University of California Press. Not only a superb description of the lifeway of an East African tribe but also a penetrating discussion of some of the problems of ethnography.

Korzybski, Alfred. 1933. *Science and Sanity.* Lancaster, Pa.: Science Press. A difficult, original, and sometimes muddled study of semantics. Contains the suggestion for "dating" statements of fact.

Lowie, Robert H. 1935. *The Crow Indians.* New York: Holt, Rinehart and Winston. The first of three titles of Lowie, illustrating usages of the terms *ethnography* and *ethnology.* This is a classic ethnography.

————. 1937. *The History of Ethnological Theory.* New York: Holt, Rinehart and Winston. A pioneering study of theoretical ethnology.

————. 1954. *Indians of the Plains.* New York: McGraw-Hill. An example of what I have called *plural ethnography* and *historical ethnology.*

Plog, Fred, and Daniel C. Bates. 1976. *Cultural Anthropology.* New York:

Knopf. A good text, recommended particularly for chapter 4, "Ethics of Cultural Anthropology."

Washburn, S. L., and Ruth Moore. 1980. *Ape Into Human.* Boston: Little, Brown. A stimulating discussion of human evolution.

Weaver, Thomas (ed.). 1973. *To See Ourselves: Anthropology and Modern Social Issues.* Glenview, Ill.: Scott Forsman. The title pretty well speaks for itself, but note particularly the "Principles of Professional Responsibility" of the American Anthropological Association, together with the rejoinder by Anthony Leeds.

4

Primate, Meet Primate: Introducing the Chimpanzee

This chapter, logically enough, is a prelude to the next chapter. What I am leading up to is a discussion of field studies of chimpanzees, the subject of Chapter 5. Before that material can be meaningful, it must be placed in context. We need to know something about the chimpanzee prior to examining the ways in which chimpanzees live under natural conditions. In this chapter, I will try to provide the necessary background on the chimpanzee in as nontechnical a fashion as possible.

From the point of view of human beings, the most important single fact about the chimpanzee *(Pan troglodytes)* is simplicity itself: The chimpanzees are our closest living relatives in the animal world. The only true rival the chimpanzee has for this dubious distinction is the gorilla, and *every* test that scientists have been able to devise — ranging from gross anatomy to biochemistry — shows that the chimpanzee is biologically nearer to mankind than the gorilla. Most of us, when we look at a chimpanzee, feel an instant shock of recognition. This is no accident. Chimpanzees *are* very close to us; indeed, the more we find out about chimpanzees the closer the relationship appears to be.

As human beings, we are all vertebrates, mammals, and primates. So are chimpanzees. The primates are a fairly diverse lot, of course, but the chimpanzee is roughly the same sort of primate that we are; we are both *hominoids.* (Don't confuse the terms *hominoid* and *hominid.* Hominoid refers to a broad classification that includes both apes and mankind, while hominid refers just to mankind.)

The chimpanzee is the best living example that we have of an animal that is like ourselves in many ways but is nevertheless an ape rather than a hominid. This is a critically important point. A great deal of windy rhetoric has been devoted to the question of what it means to be human. Here nature has given us the opportunity to come up with at least one kind of answer to that most ancient of questions. If the chimpanzee is our closest living relative, then somewhere in the differences between the ways chimpanzees do things and the ways people do things lies the essence of being human. There can be no more significant problem than that. It is what anthropology is all about. More importantly, it goes to the heart of the questions that men and women have always asked about themselves.

What, then, is a chimpanzee, and exactly how are chimpanzees related to mankind? In order to answer these questions, we will have to spend a little time talking about the primates as a group. However, it will be useful to anticipate one of our major conclusions right now. *The chimpanzee is not ancestral to the human animal.* We are not descended (or ascended) from chimpanzees, nor from any other kind of living ape.

THE PROSIMIANS

The earliest known primates date from the beginning of the Cenozoic era. This places them in the Paleocene epoch, which began about 70 million years ago. These first primates belong to a group called the *prosimians.*

Long ago, the prosimians had the Primate Order to themselves; there were no other kinds of primates. They have suffered the fate common to pioneers, being generally replaced by their own more complex and efficient descendants. However, some prosimians have survived into the modern world. They are found today in parts of Africa, Southeast Asia, and the island of Madagascar. The best known of them are the lemurs (from Madagascar) and the tarsiers (from Southeast Asia). There are others; the galagos (known as "bush babies" in Africa), the lorises, the pottos, the aye-ayes, and the indris are all prosimians. These living animals are not identical to the first prosimians, of course, but they do resemble them in many ways.

The prosimians don't look much like other primates. They tend to be small, furry animals ranging in size from about that of a small rat to that of a medium house cat. Their brains are not particularly large, and they often have rather pronounced snouts and wet noses, indicating that they depend more on their sense of smell than do most primates.

Prosimians almost always live in the trees, although they do come down to the ground upon occasion. Many of them are nocturnal, which is why they are disappointing as zoo animals; they are asleep when the zoo is open. They feed on insects, fruits, flowers, and small lizards.

If you watch prosimians carefully, you will notice several things that stamp them as primates. For instance, they move through the branches by leaping and grasping, rather than scampering about and holding on with claws. One interesting characteristic of prosimians is that they have both nails and claws; most of the fingers and toes have nails, but a few of them have retained claws. The prehensile (grasping) grip is well developed in prosimians; indeed, the loris has the most opposable thumb of any primate. Again, if you look at a prosimian head on, you are bound to be impressed by its eyes. The eyes are positioned in front, rather than being on the sides of the face; this makes possible overlapping fields of vision in the two eyes, which is a primate characteristic. Moreover, the eyes are quite large relative to the size of the face; when you confront a tarsier, for example, there is a distinct sensation that the animal is all eyeballs. (The tarsier can even swivel its head around so that it can look straight back.)

The prosimians constitute their own *suborder* within the Primate Order. The suborder is called *Prosimii*. Intriguing as they are, the prosimians are only distant relatives of mankind. They are primarily of interest because they give us some understanding of what the first primates were like.

ANTHROPOIDEA

There are only two suborders of the primates. The other one is called *Anthropoidea*. It is a much larger grouping, and it includes all of the nonprosimian primates from monkeys to human beings.

Within *Anthropoidea*, there are essentially three major groupings of primates. These groupings are called *superfamilies*.

New World Monkeys

The first superfamily consists of the monkeys of the New World. These monkeys live in South America and Mexico. The proper name for this superfamily is *Ceboidea;* you can call them ceboids and nobody will mind. They include the only monkeys that can hang by their tails. They tend to have broad, flat noses; the technical term for this type of nose is *platyrrhine*. The New World monkeys include the little marmosets, which are quite different from the others, and such familiar monkeys as capuchins, howlers, and spider monkeys. The fossil record here is not good, but such evidence as there is suggests that the New World monkeys have evolved from prosimians by Miocene times, or roughly 25 million years ago.

Old World Monkeys

The second superfamily is made up of the monkeys of the Old World. They are found in Africa and southern Asia and have a kind of toehold in Europe at Gibraltar. Properly, they are the *Cercopithecoidea,* which is why they are usually just called Old World monkeys. They have tails, but they can't hang by them. They have *catarrhine* noses; that is, the nostrils face downward. The Old World monkeys have the same dental formula that we do: $2-1-2-3$. (This means two incisors, one canine, two premolars, and three molars on each side of the jaws. The New World monkeys have three premolars in their dental formula, which is a primitive trait.) There are many Old World monkeys. The superfamily includes the macaques, which are the most common zoo monkeys, the langurs, the baboons, the colobus monkey, and many others. Again, the fossil record is not all that one might desire. Perhaps the safest thing to say is that Old World monkeys were certainly present by Miocene times and probably go back well into the preceding epoch, the Oligocene, which began some 40 million years ago.

The Hominoids

We come now to the third superfamily of the Anthropoidea. This is the superfamily *Hominoidea,* or hominoids. There are two main groups (families) within the hominoids. One contains the apes *(pongids),* both living and extinct, and the other contains men and women *(hominids),* both living and extinct. You can spot a hominoid rather easily. Apart from looking in the mirror, if you find a primate that is relatively large in body size, has no external tail, and has a big complex brain, you have found a hominoid. As a group, the hominoids also show a movement away from a true quadrupedal stance. That is, they are not really four-footed animals like monkeys. In the trees, most apes tend to *brachiate,* or swing hand over hand from one branch to another. They often hang from one grasping hand and feed with the other. On the ground, most apes walk flat-footed but not flat-handed; they support themselves on the knuckles of their fingers rather than the palms of their hands. Men and women, of course, do not normally go about on all fours as adults.

There are four living genera of apes. Two of them live in Asia: the gibbon and the orang. (The orang is the same animal that is also called the orangutan or orangutang.) The other two apes are found in Africa. These are the gorilla and the chimpanzee. There is one living genus of the hominids, *Homo,* and one living species, *sapiens.*

The fossil record of the hominoids is fairly good. In the preceding chapter, we took a look at the development of the hominids. You will recall that the earliest known hominid population is represented by *Ramapithecus,* who lived in late Miocene times about 12 million years ago. One way or another, it appears that all later hominids are derived from the *Ramapithecus* population. Therefore, in seeking to understand the broader relationships between the hominoids, there are two obvious questions that must be asked. First, where did the *Ramapithecus* population come from? Second, what is the connection between the *Ramapithecus* branch of the hominoids, which leads to modern mankind, and the other branch or branches of the hominoids, which leads to modern apes?

The answer to both questions seems to be bound up with a population called *Dryopithecus.* Briefly, the dryopithecines were apes (not modern apes, but apes) who lived in the Old World in early Miocene times: 25 million years ago would be a reasonable estimate for their age. They share a number of specific features, notably dental characteristics, with both the later hominids and the later apes. For this reason, it appears likely that the dryopithecines are ancestral to both *Ramapithecus* (and thus to modern mankind) and to modern apes. In other words, we get a kind of fork in the superfamily tree at the beginning of the Miocene; one line leads to mankind and the other to still-living apes. (It may be noted that the ancestry of the relatively small gibbon is probably not that simple, but the statement holds for the orang, the gorilla, and the chimpanzee.)

OUR COMMON ANCESTOR

Now, what does all this mean? For our purposes, there are two major points that should emerge from this rather lengthy but necessary discussion. (Remember that what we are trying to do is to understand exactly what we mean when we say that the chimpanzee is our closest living relative.) First of all, the two suborders of the primates have been separated for a very long time. The prosimians lie at the base of primate evolution, but the prosimians and the anthropoids diverged into distinct groupings well before the Miocene epoch. This means that we are only distantly related to the prosimians. Moreover, the three superfamilies of the anthropoids have gone their separate ways at least since the beginning of the Miocene and probably well before that. This means that the hominoids as a group are not very close to the monkeys. It is within the hominoid superfamily that we must search for relatively close kin. In this connection — and this is the second major point — the last genetic link between living apes and mankind occurred with the dryopithecines at the beginning of the Miocene some 25 million years ago.

If we wish to indicate the nature of the relationship between ourselves and any living ape we cannot represent it with some kind of a vertical descent line. Taking the chimpanzee as an example, this is clearly impossible:

Homo sapiens

Chimpanzee

It is impossible because the chimpanzee has evolved in its direction away from the ancestral population (the dryopithecines) as long as we have evolved in our direction away from the same source. A vertical line won't do. Rather, schematically, we need something like a Y with the fork in the Y well back in the Miocene. In simplified form, it should look like this:

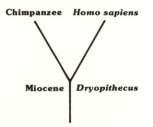

Chimpanzee *Homo sapiens*

Miocene *Dryopithecus*

To put it as simply as possible, we are related to the chimpanzee (or any other living ape) *not* because we are descended from them but because we

Top left, a tarsier—one type of prosimian. (Note the size of the eyes.) *Bottom left,* Old World monkey—baboon. *Top right,* New World monkey. (Note prehensile tail.) *Bottom right,* gorilla. (Note knuckle-walking stance.)

share a common ancestral population millions of years ago in our evolutionary past. How close is the relationship? Considering the time span involved, the biological kinship between ourselves and living apes is surprisingly solid. Indeed, it is probably fair to say that we are not as different as we look. Generally speaking, we seem to be closer biologically to the African apes (gorilla and chimpanzee) than to the Asiatic apes (orang and gibbon). Narrowing it down still further, the evidence is reasonably clear that the chimpanzee is more like us than the gorilla is.

The most impressive of modern tests designed to measure the relationship between living primates are biochemical in nature. A number of these tests, ranging from comparisons of DNA (deoxyribonucleic acid, the material from which genes are made) to hemoglobin (the oxygen-carrying protein of the blood), have been cogently explained and summarized by Washburn and Moore (1974). One example will suffice to show the kinds of results that have been obtained. If you introduce foreign substances into the bloodstream of an animal, that animal reacts by producing antibodies in its blood to combat the alien substances. If you inject human serum into a rabbit, the rabbit develops antihuman antibodies. After a rather long process, you can remove blood serum from the rabbit and use it to test other animals. Since this test serum is antihuman, the more humanlike the animal is the stronger a reaction you get. In other words, it is possible to measure the degree of biological relationship by the strength of the reaction. For convenience, the actual figures are converted into what are called *immunological distance units,* or ID units for short. Following the conversion, the "immunological distance" between one human and another is, of course, zero; there is no "distance" between them since they are the same. In terms of ID units, then, the primate order stacks up this way:

Man	0.0
Chimpanzee	0.2
Gorilla	1.0
Orangutan	2.2
Gibbon	3.4
Old World monkey	4.0 (average of several)
New World monkey	6.5 (average of several)
Prosimian	10.0 (average of several)
Tree shrew	13.0

Quoted in Washburn and Moore, the source of these figures may be found in a fascinating article by G. William Moore and Morris Goodman (1968). Several points are worth mentioning concerning these and other similar test results. First, the tree shrew *(Tupaia)* is a kind of borderline primate; usually classed as an *insectivore* (insect eater), it is a small mammal that is a living representative of a type of mammal that was ancestral to all other placental mammals, including the prosimians. Second, the varying "distance units" between mankind and different apes raise the possibility that the ancestors of living apes may have "split off" from the superfamily tree at different times; the time of separation between the chimpanzee and hominid lines may be more recent than is generally accepted. Finally, no matter how you slice it, it is apparent that the chimpanzee is much closer to mankind than any other animal. A moment's inspection of the figures on page 62 will show you that the chimpanzee in some respects is closer to us than to even the gorilla.

CHIMPANZEE ANATOMY

Now that we have the chimpanzee in focus, as it were, let us examine the animal in some detail. Most of us have a kind of mental picture of the chimpanzee that it is wise to abandon at the outset. We have seen chimps at the circus or on television or in the movies. We tend to think of them as cute little animals; *adorable* is the term that my beginning students often use. Well, chimps may be cute at times, and even adorable, but remember that the chimps you may have seen are apt to be immature females. The adult chimpanzee is a large, formidable animal.

An adult male chimpanzee will stand about 5 feet tall and weigh around 110 pounds; sometimes, they get bigger than that. (Females are somewhat smaller, weighing in at about 90 pounds.) More importantly, chimpanzees are immensely strong animals. In one early experiment, a chimp—pulling on a heavy rope attached to a device that measured the force of the pull—scored an astonishing two-handed pull of 1260 pounds. And that was by a female, albeit an unusually heavy one; her name was Suzette, and she weighed 135 pounds. There are one-handed pulls on record, by a male, of up to 847 pounds. These experiments have been subjected to criticism for their methodology, but careful evaluations have suggested that chimpanzees are roughly twice as strong as human beings when tested under comparable conditions (Edwards 1963:17). We do not know exactly how long chimpanzees live in the wild, but they have survived for more than 50 years in captivity.

As you might expect from their arm strength, chimpanzee arms are considerably longer than chimpanzee legs and are very powerfully muscled. (Try hanging from one of *your* arms while feeding with the other.) On the chimp's hand the fingers are relatively long while the thumb is somewhat short; this means that it is difficult for the chimpanzee to oppose its thumb to its fingers. On the chimp's foot the big toe is set more or less at a right angle to the other toes in the manner of the human thumb. This indicates that the chimpanzee foot is still a grasping foot, rather than being a specialized platform for standing like the human foot.

The chimpanzee spine forms a simple gentle curve; it lacks the so-called S-curve of the human spine. The effect of this is to throw the trunk of the body forward. If you examine a chimpanzee skull, you will find a big hole at the base. This allows the spinal cord to pass through to join the brain. The hole is called the *foramen magnum,* which is merely Latin for "large hole." In human skulls, the foramen magnum is located about in the center of the base of the skull. In the chimp, the foramen magnum is farther back, behind the center of the skull's base. Because of this, the chimpanzee's head hangs forward. Coupled with the spinal situation, this means that it is hard for a chimpanzee to stand fully erect. (see Figure 4.1).

Moving to the skull itself, the skull vault slopes rather sharply back from the brow ridges; there is no forehead to speak of. The cranial capacity, reflecting the size of the brain, averages around 400 cc. This compares with about 1400 cc for

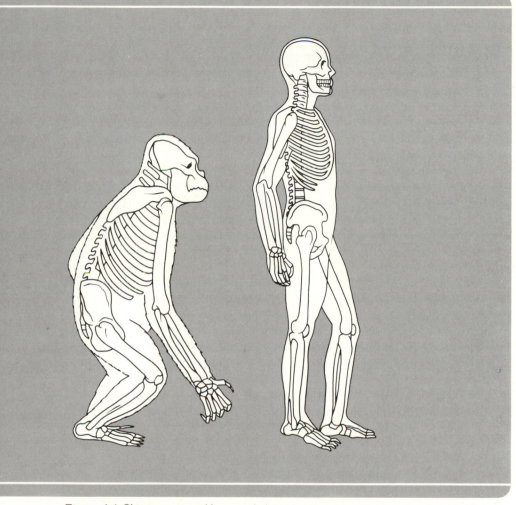

Figure 4.1 Chimpanzee and human skeletons.

the human brain. Although the chimpanzee brain is similar to the human brain in many respects, it should not be visualized as a kind of human brain in miniature. The chimpanzee brain is differently proportioned. The major difference concerns the forebrain, essentially the *cerebrum* or cerebral hemispheres. In humans, the cerebrum is far larger relative to total brain size than it is in the chimpanzee; it has increased in size until in effect it slops over to cover most of the rest of the brain.

The lower jaw *(mandible)* of the chimpanzee is quite heavy and lacks a chin eminence. The lips are thin and highly mobile; chimps are notoriously accurate water spitters, and they will often use their lips (rather than their hands) to pick up small objects. The impression that we sometimes have of the chimpanzee being very thick-lipped is due to the structure of the jaws, particularly the upper jaw, which projects forward. This forward projection of the upper jaw is called *alveolar prognathism*.

CHIMPANZEE INTELLIGENCE

This is not the place to review the extensive literature on problem-solving experiments carried out with captive chimpanzees. However, by this time a critical question will doubtless have occurred to you. Are chimpanzees intelligent? Can they think in such a way that they can come up with sensible solutions to the problems they confront?

One of the favorite early methods of testing chimpanzees involved hanging a desired object (a banana, for example) at a height the chimpanzee could not reach. If boxes are available, the chimp will stack the boxes, scramble up, and grab the object. If a stick is available, the chimp will seize the stick and use it as a bat to knock the object down. Note that the animal is not trained to do this; the chimpanzee figures it out on its own. This may not strike you as particularly amazing, but try it with your dog sometime.

Wolfgang Köhler devised a cunning variation on the above experiment. Working with a chimpanzee named Sultan, he placed a banana out of reach and presented Sultan with two hollow bamboo sticks. Sultan soon discovered to his considerable frustration that neither stick was long enough to reach the banana. He played around with the sticks for a time, and then he spotted something. He figured out how to insert the end of one stick into the hollow ''socket'' of the other. Having invented the longer stick that he needed, he promptly went fishing for his banana and got it.

Impressive? Yes, but consider what happened next. Köhler later repeated the experiment with the same animal, but he made it still more difficult. Sultan was provided with a hollow tube and a narrow wooden board. When Sultan attempted to insert the board in the tube, he found that it wouldn't fit—the board was too big. Sultan then proceeded to chew on the hard wood until the end of the board was smaller. He then fitted the board and the tube together and used the implement to rake in his banana (Köhler 1927:113–119).

Can chimpanzees think? Of course they can, unless one makes the definition of *thinking* so obscure as to be meaningless. They are not as intelligent as human beings, but they are bright animals by any standards.

One of my colleagues is fond of referring to what he calls ''the single primate fallacy.'' He means that you cannot take any one type of primate and generalize from that primate to all primates; the primates as a group are too variable for that. This is a caution worth remembering. We can use the chimpanzee as a kind of point of reference because the chimpanzee is the nonhuman primate most like ourselves. However, what holds for the chimpanzee will not necessarily apply to all primates, and the chimpanzee is not a perfect model for what the ancestral hominoids are like; the chimpanzee has developed away from the ancestral population just as we have done.

SUMMARY

The chimpanzee is the closest living relative that we have in the animal world, but it is important to understand that neither the chimpanzee nor any other living ape is ancestral to the human animal.

The earliest known representatives of the Primate Order of the mammals are called *prosimians*. They first appeared at the beginning of the Cenozoic era, about 70 million years ago. Surviving prosimians include the lemurs and the tarsiers, and they constitute a *suborder* of the primates.

The other suborder of the primates is called *Anthropoidea*. Within this suborder there are three groupings, which are referred to as *superfamilies*. One superfamily consists of the New World monkeys; it is called *Cebidea*. Another consists of the Old World Monkeys, called *Cercopithecoidea*. The remaining superfamily is called *Hominoidea,* or hominoids. There are two main groups *(families)* within the hominoids. One contains the apes *(pongids),* both living and extinct, and the other contains people *(hominids),* both living and extinct.

There are four living genera of apes. Two of them are Asiatic, the gibbon and the orang. Two of them are African, the gorilla and the chimpanzee. There is one living genus of the hominids, *Homo,* and one living species, *sapiens.*

The last genetic link between living apes and mankind probably occurred some 25 million years ago early in the Miocene epoch. In other words, there was a fork in the superfamily tree at the beginning of the Miocene; one line leads to mankind and the other to still-living apes. Therefore, we are related to the chimpanzee in the sense that we *share* a common ancestral population that lived millions of years ago. It has been established that we are closer biologically to the African apes than to the Asiatic ones. Between the African apes, the chimpanzee is more like us than the gorilla is.

The popular picture of the chimpanzee is somewhat wide of the mark. Adult chimpanzees are large animals, and they are roughly twice as strong as human beings. The cranial capacity of chimpanzees, reflecting the size of the brain, is around 400 cc. This compares with about 1400 cc for the human brain.

Chimpanzees are quite capable of solving rather complex problems. We can use the chimpanzee as a point of reference because the chimpanzee is the nonhuman primate most like ourselves. However, it must be remembered that what applies to chimpanzees does not necessarily apply to all nonhuman primates; there is considerable variation within the Primate Order. Moreover, the chimpanzee is not a perfect model of what early hominoids are like. Just as we have done, the chimpanzee has evolved through time.

References

Edwards, William E. 1963. *Study of Monkey, Ape and Human Morphology and Physiology Relating to Strength and Endurance. Phase III. The Testing of Chimpanzee Strength Prior to 1961.* United States Air Force Systems Command, Aerospace Medical Division, Technical Documentary Report No. ARL – TDR – 63 – 22. New Mexico: Holloman Air Force Base.

Köhler, Wolfgang. 1927. *The Mentality of Apes.* New York: Random House (Vintage Books).

Moore, G. William, and Morris Goodman. 1968. "Phylogeny and Taxonomy of the Catarrhine Primates," in B. Chiarelli (ed.). *Taxonomy and Phylogency of Old World Primates.* Turin: Rosenberg and Sellier.

Washburn, S. L., and Ruth Moore. 1974. *Ape into Man.* Boston: Little, Brown.

Suggestions for Further Reading

Beals, Ralph L., and Harry Hoijer. 1965. *An Introduction to Anthropology,* 3d ed. New York: Macmillan. There are later editions of this classic text, but this one contains (in chapter 2) much useful information about primates.

Birdsell, Joseph B. 1975. *Human Evolution: An Introduction to the New Physical Anthropology,* 2d ed. Chicago: Rand McNally. Previously recommended, this book has a fine section on the classification and evolution of the primates.

Bramblett, Claud A. 1976. *Patterns of Primate Behavior.* Palo Alto, Ca.: Mayfield. Although primarily devoted to field studies, this data-packed book offers a clear outline of primate taxonomy.

Pilbeam, David R. 1972. *The Ascent of Man.* New York: Macmillan. A good basic account of human evolution, including extensive primate materials, by a creative and thoughtful anthropologist.

Simpson, George Gaylord. 1950. *The Meaning of Evolution.* New Haven, Conn.: Yale University Press. A brilliant and supremely readable work by an eminent paleontologist; the chapter on primates is particularly outstanding and has been very influential.

5

The Other Side of the Mirror: Field Studies of Chimpanzees

It is a happy fact that we know more about the "natural" behavior of chimpanzees than we know about any other ape. Not only is the chimpanzee the animal that is closest biologically to ourselves, but it is the ape that has been most extensively studied in its native habitat. If you read through the available field studies on the various apes, you would rapidly conclude that the data on the chimpanzee are incomparably richer than those for other apes. I certainly do not intend to slight the important (and often extremely difficult) work that has been done on the gibbon, the orang, and the gorilla, but the fact remains that we have a much clearer picture of chimpanzee life in the wild. From either point of view — whether on the basis of closeness of relationship or simply on the basis of going where the information is most complete — we must turn to the chimpanzee in an attempt to understand the behavior of a nonhuman primate that resembles the hominids in many ways.

It is all too easy to take this information for granted, just something stuck in a textbook, but in fact we are extremely fortunate to possess these facts at all. It was a very real and chilling possibility that *nobody* would get around to doing a detailed field investigation of chimpanzees until there were no chimpanzees left except in zoos. One might think that the importance of field studies of the nonhuman primates was so obvious that we soon would be buried in a barrage of reports, but that is not the way it was. Apart from casual observations and uneven amateur studies, there was not a single successful long-term systematic field investigation of *any* nonhuman primate species until Clarence Ray Carpenter studied the howler monkey in 1931. At about the same time, two assistants of the psychologist Robert M. Yerkes, Harold Bingham and Henry W. Nissen, pioneered field studies of the African apes. Bingham attempted to study the wild

Jane Goodall in the field with a wild chimpanzee.

gorilla with indifferent success, but Nissen (although he was able to observe the animals for less than three months) reported valuable data on the chimpanzee. Carpenter himself later (1940) conducted a productive field investigation of the gibbon in what is now Thailand.

In retrospect, the remarkable thing is not so much that field studies were so late in coming but rather that they had so little impact. As Harvard's Irven De-Vore noted in 1965, after the initial flurry "the entire subject of primate field studies lay dormant for nearly twenty years" (DeVore 1965:vii). Now at last— and in the nick of time—we are beginning to get substantial field reports on the living primates, and the lifeways of all of the apes have been studied to some degree. It would certainly be misleading to pretend that "it's all been done" and there is nothing more to know, but at the very least a solid beginning has been made. In the case of the chimpanzee, following Nissen's initial study in 1931, there have been a series of valuable investigations. The best single study is the one carried out by Jane Goodall and her assistants. It is so good that it seems fair to say that one can no more discuss chimpanzees without reading Goodall than one can discuss evolution without reading Darwin. Jane Goodall began her work with chimpanzees in the Gombe Stream Reserve of Tanganyika (now Tanzania) in 1960. Encouraged by the late anthropologist L. S. B. Leakey, Goodall set up camp in the reserve — at first accompanied by her mother — and proceeded to observe chimpanzees in unparalleled detail. It was not easy, to put it mildly, and her persistence can only be described as heroic. After eight months in the field, she could not get closer to the wild chimpanzees than 50 yards, and even that was when the animals were secure in the trees. After 14 months, she could get as close as 30 feet, even when the chimpanzees were on the ground. Eventually, many of the chimpanzees were literally eating (bananas) out of her hand. The great advantage to the Goodall study, aside from her personal qualities as a sensitive observer, is its time dimension. Although political problems are now plaguing the project, the same chimpanzees have been kept under careful scrutiny since 1960. (Goodall has not been on the scene the entire time, of course, but her assistants have.) This has made it possible to know the animals as individuals and to trace details of social life — such as mother-child relationships — over a period of many years. Indeed, some of the major findings of the study only emerged after years of investigation. The moral seems clear: Useful as short-term studies may be, the only way to obtain in-depth information is through a prolonged and patient expenditure of time, effort, and money.

Mention must also be made of field studies of the chimpanzee carried out by Vernon and Frances Reynolds (1965) in Uganda, Adriaan Kortlandt (1962) in the Congo, and by several distinguished Japanese primatologists including Y. Sugiyama (1968, 1969) and A. Suzuki (1969). In addition, Geza Teleki, working with the Goodall team, has provided us with fascinating information on the hunting techniques of chimpanzees (Teleki 1973a, 1973b). Putting it all together, it can be seen that our knowledge of the chimpanzee is impressive, if by no means complete.

Since my purpose here is to provide a meaningful comparison between some aspects of human behavior and that of our closest living relative, I am not going to attempt to present anything resembling a complete "natural history" of the chimpanzee. Instead, I propose to focus on a series of critical questions that are designed to illuminate both the similarities and the differences between our own lifeways and those of chimpanzees.

The questions are as follows:

1. What kinds of groups do chimpanzees form under natural conditions, and how large are the groups? What level of population density are we dealing with?
2. What sort of leadership do we find in chimpanzee groups? How are the

groups organized, and how crucial is dominance and rank ordering?

3. What type of mating pattern exists among wild chimpanzees? Do they form stable family groups, mate at random, or what?
4. Are the chimpanzees territorial animals or aren't they?
5. How do chimpanzees obtain their food, and what do they eat?
6. Are chimpanzees basically arboreal or terrestrial animals? That is, do they live in the trees or on the ground or both? Do they ever walk erect on two legs under natural conditions?
7. Do wild chimpanzees either make or use tools?
8. How do chimpanzees communicate with one another? Under what circumstances do they vocalize, and what happens when they do?
9. When infants are born, what is their chance for survival and how much do they have to learn in order to function as adult chimpanzees? In short, how are the kids raised?

These are large questions, and not all of them can be answered completely. However, some of the areas of discussion are quite clear, and the others allow at least tentative conclusions. Where it seems pertinent, as we discuss each topic, I will offer some brief observations concerning other apes and human hunting and gathering societies. This will serve the double purpose of reminding you again that all apes are not alike — remember the single primate fallacy — and pointing up the significance of these data for understanding the kinds of human societies that chimpanzee groups most nearly approximate.

GROUPS

Chimpanzees, like human beings, are intensely social animals. A captive chimp in isolation is a pitiful creature, and chimpanzees under natural conditions are seldom alone. It is true that individual chimpanzees, usually males, may wander off by themselves for brief periods of time, but they always rejoin their companions shortly. It is most unusual for a chimpanzee to remain by himself for more than a single day. Chimpanzees seem to enjoy the companionship of fellow chimpanzees, and even a badly crippled animal will try to drag himself along to join in a session of mutual grooming. Indeed, a truly isolated chimp is either a sick or very disturbed animal and will not survive in the wild. Chimpanzees live in groups, find their identities in groups, and take pleasure in the social interactions within groups.

For want of a better term, it is possible to recognize a kind of *maximal group* of chimpanzees: all the chimpanzees in a given area who know one another. Goodall calls this maximal group a community and suggests that it contains about 50 animals. However, this rather large group is seldom if ever together at one place at one time. The groups that count in everyday living, ranging from temporary associations to clusters of animals that are usually together, are subdivisions of the ''community'' and therefore smaller in size.

These smaller groups vary in both size and composition. In his pioneering study, Nissen reported from 4 to 14 animals in groups, with an average of 8.5 chimpanzees per group. Adriaan Kortlandt saw as many as 30 animals in one group, and felt that there were two different kinds of groups among chimpanzees. He called one of them a *sexual group,* and reported that it was composed of adult males and females without children. This type of group, according to Kortlandt, moved frequently, was very noisy, and was more aggressive in its behavior than the other type of group. The second group he called a *nursery group,* and it was composed of immature animals, their mothers, and sometimes a few adult males. This kind of group was said to be quieter, on the shy side, and relatively slow in its movements.

Bearing in mind the fact that these groups are essentially just animals that happened to be together at the time of observation, Kortlandt (1962) stated: "Individuals were free to join or leave a group at will, and the groups themselves often merged or split up." This statement must be qualified; it is obvious that an infant could not switch over to a "sexual group," and moreover it is not always all that simple for an adult animal to change groups. Nevertheless, the statement does point up an important fact about chimpanzee groups: The groups tend to be relatively fluid as opposed to being completely fixed and closed.

Jane Goodall (1965) offers much more complete information about chimpanzee groups. As of that time, she had seen 498 temporary groups, that is, groups within the "community." The largest group contained 23 animals, and 91 percent of the groups contained 9 animals or less. On 350 occasions she was able to establish the age and sex compositions of the groups she observed. The results were:

Adult males and females with young: 30 percent
Males only: 28 percent
Adult females and young: 24 percent
Mature or adolescent males and females only: 18 percent

Vernon and Frances Reynolds (1965) obtained essentially similar counts among chimpanzees in Uganda.

We might conclude from this something like the following. Within a given area containing perhaps 50 chimpanzees, the animals move about in fairly fluid subgroups. The average size of these subgroups is around 8 or 9 animals, although some groups are larger than this and some are smaller. The groups tend to be composed of all possible age and sex combinations, with three major exceptions. The exceptions are:

1. Adult females do not form groups by themselves.
2. Juvenile animals do not form groups by themselves.
3. Adult males and young do not form groups by themselves.

For what it is worth, Goodall (1971) suggests that firm friendships between males are more common than those between females. She is able to demonstrate conclusively that juvenile chimpanzees cannot make it on their own without adults, and her evidence of the close ties that exist between mothers and their offspring is impressive. Even 4- and 5-year-old chimps seem lost without their mothers, and if the mother dies about the only possible substitute appears to be an older female sibling, that is, an older sister. Adult male chimpanzees either cannot or do not substitute for the mother.

Goodall estimates that her chimpanzees attained a population density of about 2.6 per square mile. Vernon and Frances Reynolds report an even higher density of about ten chimpanzees per square mile. These figures are really quite remarkable. Chimpanzees are at least roughly comparable to human beings in size and stature, and yet in terms of population density they are more successful than known human societies of hunters and gatherers. Such human societies have quite low population densities; it is often necessary to think of square miles to the person rather than persons per square mile. Of course, surviving human hunting and gathering societies have frequently been forced into areas where there is little competition for land, which means that they tend to occupy difficult habitats. However, this is not always the case; the Andamanese of the Bay of Bengal live in a reasonably bountiful environment, and yet have a population density of around 2.2 persons per square mile.

The chimpanzees do have one advantage: They can exploit the vertical dimension (the trees) more efficiently than any human society. Still, these figures should make us stop and think a bit. It has often been suggested that it was culture that enabled the early hominids to survive. The chimpanzees do not have a true culture, and yet they are doing better in terms of population density (a common criterion for evolutionary success) than some human societies with culture.

In my opinion, this suggests that the initial advantage of possessing cultural systems may have been that it allowed our remote ancestors to expand into radically different habitats. If we had remained in the tropical forests and adjacent savannas where we first developed, we might have done moderately well without culture. However, as soon as we tried to move into different ecological zones—semidesert country, say, or the frozen wastes of the Arctic—culture became not only a luxury but an absolute necessity. It should be pointed out, continuing this line of speculation, that after human cultural systems had evolved into the complex structures we know today, they would certainly have had an enormous advantage over any hypothetical cultureless society of hominids. Nevertheless, they were not that way in the beginning, which accounts for my suggestion above.

LEADERSHIP AND DOMINANCE

There is a persistent myth about apes in general and chimpanzees in particular, a myth with decidedly Freudian overtones. In essence, it is that ape societies are led by one big, powerful dictatorial male. This bruiser, it is alleged, keeps all the females for himself. All of the other adult males sit around in gloomy frustration and plot the overthrow of Big Daddy. Sound familiar?

Well, chimpanzee societies are not in fact organized in that fashion. Both group leadership—to the extent that there is any—and dominance relationships are somewhat complex and on the subtle side. We might begin by repeating the point that chimpanzee groups tend to be fluid rather than fixed. George B. Schaller (1965), in reviewing the chimpanzee data, refers to the groups as "highly unstable" with "daily changes in composition as subgroups join and part." It follows from this that these groups cannot have regular and permanent leaders, since the same animals are not always present. Vernon and Frances Reynolds are quite specific on this point:

> Although there was some evidence of differences in status between individuals, dominance interactions formed a minute fraction of the observed chimpanzee behavior. There was no evidence of a linear hierarchy of dominance among males or females; there were no observations of exclusive rights to receptive females; and there were no permanent leaders of groups.

The problem is not actually quite that simple, as we shall see in a moment. However, it does seem entirely correct to say that chimpanzee groups are not "bossed" by single dominant males. There is in truth very little sign of real leadership among chimpanzees.

What structure there is in chimpanzee groups is probably best viewed in the light of dominance relationships. A chimpanzee group is by no means totally amorphous, as Jane Goodall's data make abundantly clear. Goodall writes: "Mature males were always dominant to females, adolescents, and juveniles, and mature females always dominated adolescents." Here we must stress two points. When one animal is said to be dominant over another, it primarily means that in a conflict situation one animal backs down and is submissive and the other animal stands its ground. The animal that stands its ground is said to be dominant. It is not a matter of "ordering" subordinates about, but simply a statement of what happens when there is a conflict of interest—two chimpanzees and only one banana, for example. The other point, as noted earlier, is that dominance interactions among chimpanzees are not a pronounced characteristic of their behavior. As Goodall puts it, "aggressive and submissive interactions between individuals are infrequent." In other words, there is a dominance pattern according to which adult males tend to be dominant over all other animals and adult females are dominant over immature animals, but this dominance structure does not always reveal itself in everyday behavior.

It is there, however, and it can be pushed a bit further. Despite the Reynolds' observations in Uganda, Goodall's chimpanzees in Tanzania exhibited fairly clear rank ordering among males. That is, some adult males were dominant over other adult males. Apparently, each community (maximal group) contains one male that is dominant over all the other males. Early on in the Goodall study, the dominant male was an animal named Goliath. Goliath would express his dominance by charging displays: He would run at other males, hooting loudly, his hair erect, dragging branches and throwing objects. When this happened, the other males would either run away or make submissive gestures. Later, Goliath was displaced by a male named Mike. Mike learned to use two large kerosene cans—swiped from the Goodall camp—in his charging displays. The fearsome racket was too much for Goliath, and Mike remained as the dominant animal for six years. By that time, Mike was getting old, and he in turn was supplanted by a younger male named Humphrey. The situation is further complicated by a system of alliances. Thus, Goliath was particularly friendly with a wonderful chimpanzee named David Graybeard. Even after Goliath had lost his top ranking, he was not an easy animal to intimidate when David Graybeard was around. Away from David Graybeard, he was more vulnerable.

Dominance relationships between females are much less pronounced. However, it clearly makes a difference to a juvenile who its mother is, and conversely a mother's status can be affected by the status of her son.

It is interesting, as Goodall points out, that although an adult male is quick to threaten a subordinate, he is equally quick to calm his victim afterwards—by a touch, a pat on the back, or a hug of reassurance. Threat displays do not normally lead to actual fighting. The group remains cohesive, and the dominant animal does not in any meaningful sense plan and dictate the activities of others.

As compared with many other nonhuman primates, the "pecking order" among chimpanzees is pretty loose and easygoing. The rather rigid troop organization of baboons is well known, and gorilla groups are considerably more stable than those of chimpanzees with definite male leaders.

Human hunting and gathering societies are similar to those of chimpanzees in at least two respects. First, the local groups of people tend to be fairly fluid and loosely structured. Second, such societies do not have "chiefs" or dictatorial leaders. They have very informal headmen who lack the power to order anyone around.

MATING AND "FAMILY" LIFE

Chimpanzees are almost totally promiscuous in their mating behavior. The situation is simple. The female comes into heat—called estrus—midway between her menstrual periods, which occur about every 35 days. She remains in estrus about ten days per month. (This activity does not occur if the female is either pregnant or producing milk for a child.) When in estrus, the female's sexual skin of her genital area becomes pink and swollen. At this time—and only at this time—the female is sexually attractive to males. All available males will mate with her; none are excluded, and single males do not monopolize females in heat. Goodall once witnessed seven different males mating with one female within one hour. (Goodall never witnessed any homosexual behavior among wild chimpanzees.)

Obviously, neither the chimpanzees nor an observer can know who the father of a particular child is. The social relationship of a child to adult males is with all the males in the group, not to any particular male. Chimps do not form male-female pairs to care for the child. Adult males are generally quite tolerant toward infants; they will put up with considerable disturbance from them, even interference in mating, without asserting their strength.

The ties between a mother and her children are intense and persistent. We shall have more to say about this when we discuss child raising, but here it may be said that mother-child relationships lie at the very core of chimpanzee society. It is of considerable theoretical interest to note that mature males do not mate with their mothers, and sibling (brother-sister) matings are infrequent.

Although much remains to be learned in this area, chimpanzee mating habits appear to be fairly typical of apes generally. For instance, mating behavior has been seldom observed in the wild gorilla, but recorded instances did not involve the dominant male. In other words, in gorilla societies, too, the dominant male does not have exclusive right to receptive females. Gibbons, however, seem to form relatively permanent mating couples.

One hesitates to speak for the chimpanzees on this subject, but it is worth noting that the sex act does not appear to be as intense or as prolonged as it is among human beings. The whole thing is over within 30 seconds, and it does not seem to be a very profound emotional experience.

There is no human society of any kind that permits so nearly random mating behavior as that of chimpanzees. Indeed, it is characteristic of human societies that they tend to fence in sexual relationships with all manner of rules and regulations that are simply unknown among chimpanzees. Jane Lancaster (1975) speaks of the *matrifocal subunit* as being critical to the organization of nonhuman primate societies. She means by this that the ties between mother and child are extremely important. As she points out, one of the major differences between these societies and those of human beings is that nonhuman primates lack the sociological role of husband-father. Adult males are present in the group, but they neither act as fathers to specific children nor as mates to specific females. It seems reasonable to conclude from this that the mother role is very ancient among primates, while the sociological aspects of fatherhood represent more recent developments.

TERRITORIALITY

In one sense, of course, all animals are territorial; an animal must live somewhere. In the words of the old joke, "everybody got to be someplace." However, this is not what the ethologists have in mind when they speak of territorial behavior. In essence, what they are getting at is this question: Do the animals occupy an area on an exclusive basis, and will they defend that area against intruders? Naturally, this refers to "intruders" of the same or similar species; no mammal defends its territory against birds, insects, or worms.

The situation with the chimpanzee, in my opinion, is not clear-cut. Most authorities state that the chimpanzees are not territorial, and there is much to recommend this view. A community or maximal group of chimpanzees sticks pretty much to a home range, rather than wandering indiscriminately over the map, and it utilizes the same trails and pathways over and over again. On the other hand, the fluidity of the subgroups and the mobility from one group to another preclude the establishment of definite territories. When chimpanzees meet (even chimpanzees from different communities) the interactions are usually peaceful.

The problem is twofold. In the first place, when a chimpanzee moves from one group to another its acceptance is by no means automatic. There is a great deal of tension in the situation (which can be seen graphically on film), and the newcomer is sometimes violently rejected. In the second place, reports from Jane Goodall in 1976 and 1977 indicate that the chimpanzees in the Gombe Stream Reserve have divided into several distinct groups. They appear to have marked out territories, and fighting between groups has occurred. Both males and females have been killed in these conflicts. It is possible, but far from certain, that this unusual chimpanzee behavior has been triggered by a reduction in habitat, which has the effect of increasing the population density in the area.

I would conclude from this that chimpanzees are not ordinarily territorial animals but do have the potential to become territorial under certain conditions. This need not surprise us. There are other examples in which the same animal (species) is territorial in one ecological situation but not in another. The African antelopes are particularly instructive in this regard (Moss 1975).

Gibbons are definitely territorial and defend their territories against other gibbons by vocal threats, aggressive displays, and occasionally by serious fighting. The gorilla is more like the chimpanzee and does not appear to be a truly territorial animal.

It is difficult to make a useful comparison between chimpanzee territoriality and that of human hunters and gatherers. I suspect that we have much to learn about both. The most that can be said at this point is that there is some resemblance between the two. In general, strongly defended territories are more characteristic of other types of human societies—farmers and herders at the tribal level, and state systems—while hunters and gatherers are more variable in their territorial behavior. Australian hunters, for example, regularly speared uninvited strangers, while many other hunters and gatherers were considerably more relaxed about trespassers.

FOOD

Of all the questions that can be asked about a human society, none is more revealing than how the people obtain their food and how the food is distributed. The food quest affects a society in many ways and shows major organizational features of the lifeway. Much the same is true of the chimpanzee.

When Nissen conducted the first study of the wild chimpanzee, he collected a list of 34 foods eaten by chimpanzees. Most of the foods—28 out of the 34—were fruits. It was concluded from this that the chimpanzee was essentially a vegetarian animal.

Goodall has considerably extended Nissen's list, reporting 73 different

Left, chimpanzees hunting; *right,* a chimpanzee eating meat.

kinds of vegetable foods eaten by chimpanzees under natural conditions. She lists 37 fruits, 21 leaves or leaf buds, 6 blossoms, 4 seeds, 3 stems, and 2 barks. When chimpanzees eat this type of food—and it does constitute by far the major part of their diet—each animal essentially forages as an individual. There is no active sharing, apart from sporadic tidbits given by a mother to an infant. Chimpanzees spend as much as six or seven hours a day in active feeding.

Chimpanzees also eat other kinds of food, however. Insects (ants and termites) are seasonally important in their diet, and they will occasionally eat eggs. Far more important is Goodall's discovery that chimpanzees not only eat meat but also hunt and kill animals for food on a more or less regular basis. It turns out that chimpanzees are not exclusively vegetarian animals at all.

Chimpanzee predation (hunting) is fascinating not only because of the fact of its existence, unsuspected for so long, but also because of the way it is done. Geza Teleki (1973a, 1973b) has made a special study of this, and the following observations are based primarily on that research.

Left, chimpanzee ''fishing'' for termites. *Top right,* adult chimpanzee and child.
Bottom right, chimpanzees in the wild.

Chimpanzees hunt and kill nearly all the mammals that are available to them: baboons, colobus monkeys, bushpigs, and bushbucks. About the only limiting factor on their predation appears to be the size of the prey animal—they do not hunt animals that weigh more than approximately 20 pounds. This means, of course, that most of the animals they kill are very young or immature.

Hunting is done only by adults and almost exclusively by males. Sometimes the hunting is done by individuals, and sometimes it is done jointly by as many as four or five male chimpanzees who coordinate their activities. Weapons are not used. If the opportunity presents itself, a chimp may simply grab the prey animal and kill it by twisting its neck in both hands, biting it in the back of the neck, or smashing the head against the ground or the trunk of a tree. However, if necessary, the chimpanzees may chase an animal 100 yards or more, or engage in elaborate stalking for over an hour. If the prey animal is caught by more than one chimpanzee, it is torn apart.

The chimpanzees are silent while the actual hunt is taking place, although there is clear evidence of cooperation in moving and taking up favorable positions. Once the animal is brought down, there is an outburst of vocal cries. This is a signal that brings in other chimpanzees from as far as a mile away. The chimpanzees form what is called a *sharing cluster*, requesting meat from the hunters. Usually, everybody gets some, although not always. It is a mark of how "soft" the dominance pattern is among chimpanzees that if the dominant male in the community has not been one of the hunters he joins the sharing cluster with the rest. Sometimes he gets some meat and sometimes he doesn't.

It is not known for certain exactly what triggers chimpanzee predation. Males often hunt after they have eaten large quantities of fruit, so more than simple hunger is involved. Moreover, there are times when the hunter and the hunted—chimpanzees and baboons, for example—associate quite amicably.

The significant fact is that chimpanzee males engage in socially organized hunting and share the kill to some extent with the other chimpanzees in the community. It is true that the meat eating does not constitute the major part of the chimpanzee diet, but the hunting pattern is clearly present. Baboons also hunt for meat at times, but the chimpanzee is the only ape known to hunt and kill other animals. The other apes appear to be almost exclusively vegetarians, although the gorilla will readily eat meat in captivity.

The omnivorous diet of chimpanzees is strikingly reminiscent of that of human hunters and gatherers. They too exist on a mixture of meat and wild vegetable foods, and among surviving hunters and gatherers the wild plant foods gathered by the women often constitute a larger part of the diet than the meat killed by the male hunters. This may be due to the scarcity of game in the areas in which these societies now exist, but nevertheless that is the situation. The major difference seems to be that among human beings hunting is more regular and systematic and is carried out with weapons, and sharing is much more consistent with both wild plant foods and meat. The division of labor is also more pronounced among human beings: The adult males do not as a rule forage for wild plant foods if there are animals available to hunt.

ARBOREAL OR TERRESTRIAL?

At night, chimpanzees build nests in the trees for sleeping. They bend down small branches, tuck in the twigs, and sometimes line the nest with leaves. There is some interweaving of the branches. Except for young chimpanzees, who sleep with their mothers, each chimpanzee builds its own nest every night. Therefore, as far as nocturnal behavior is concerned, chimpanzees are clearly arboreal.

In the daytime, it is another story. The chimpanzees descend to the ground and spend at least part of each day as ground-dwelling (terrestrial) animals. They take to the trees when they are alarmed and often when they are feeding, but it is not unusual for chimpanzees to spend as much as 50 percent of their waking hours on the ground.

In the trees, they climb and brachiate, that is, swing hand over hand from branch to branch. On the ground, their usual mode of locomotion is to knuckle-walk. As noted earlier, this involves walking flat-footed but not flat-handed; the weight of the upper part of the body is supported on the knuckles (not the palms) of the hands. Significant as this may be, it is even more interesting to learn that wild chimpanzees often stand erect and walk or run on their two legs, freeing the hands for other activities. Kortlandt estimated that they assumed this stance as much as 15 percent of the time. They do so when they want a better view, when they are carrying something, and occasionally in threat displays. They sometimes run on two legs, and young chimpanzees frequently stand erect when they are playing. In fact, it is probably fair to say that chimpanzees assume an erect posture whenever they take a notion to do so, and this despite the features of the chimpanzee anatomy that would seem to make such a position difficult for them.

The human animal has often been defined as the erect bipedal biped — the animal that walks erect on two legs. Here again, the chimpanzee has forced us to revise our thinking. We will either have to abandon this shopworn definition or welcome the chimpanzees into the human family.

TOOLS

There is another familiar definition of the human animal. Supposedly, we are the animals that make and use tools. So we do, of course, but once again the wild chimpanzees have given us cause for reflection. One of Goodall's more remarkable discoveries was that chimpanzees both make and use tools under natural conditions.

Termites in Africa build large earth mounds, some of them taller than an adult human being. During the period between October and January, the worker termites extend the mound passages to the surface, preparing for the mating flight of the insects. At this time, the chimpanzees "fish" for termites. They pick grass stems or small twigs, bite them off to the proper length, and — in the case of twigs — strip off the leaves. Holding these "rods" in their hands, they poke them down the holes into the mound passages. The termites grab the rods and hold on. The chimpanzees then pull out the rods and pick off the clinging termites with their lips. The significant thing here is that the chimpanzees are not only using a tool but actually making a tool, since they are modifying the materials before employing them as artifacts.

Goodall also observed chimpanzees making a kind of sponge by crumpling up leaves. They lower the sponge into pockets of water they cannot otherwise reach, allow it to absorb the water, and then suck the water out. Other chimpanzees have been seen using rocks as hammers to break open nuts and also inserting sticks into the nests of bees to obtain honey. In addition, chimpanzees frequently hurl objects — stones, branches, anything that is handy — in threat displays.

It is essential to realize that these are not "trick" or trained chimpanzees, nor are they animals in contrived experimental situations. These are wild chimpanzees, and they have learned these techniques for themselves.

It must be admitted that the chimpanzee manufacture and use of tools is very elementary by human standards. Any human hunting and gathering society would put the chimpanzees to shame with the skill and variety of its tool-making techniques. Still, the amazing thing about the chimpanzee artifacts is not their quality but the simple fact that they make and use tools at all. This behavior has not been reported for any other nonhuman primate.

COMMUNICATION AND VOCALIZATION

Chimpanzees express themselves and communicate by means of vocal calls, gestures, facial expressions, and body postures. So do we. It is possible to exaggerate the similarities, particularly with regard to vocalizations, but we can understand many of their signals without undue difficulty. Thus, when an adult gently pats a child on the back we know what is going on. When one chimpanzee extends its hand to another, or the animals meet in a friendly embrace, this is not very mysterious. When a chimp puts on what Goodall refers to as a "play face" and grunts and laughs, we can share the fun. When a chimpanzee stands erect and puffs out its body hair, baring its canines and screaming, we can understand enough to get out of the way.

It is in the area of vocal cries and sounds that chimpanzees differ most notably from human beings. Wild chimpanzees are very noisy animals. Nissen found their sound production "almost unbelievable," and Vernon and Frances Reynolds reported that the chimpanzees were the noisiest animals in the forest. In short, they make a lot of vocal racket. This perhaps is not so different from the behavior of some human beings, but what *is* different is the kind of vocal noise it is.

Chimpanzees do not have a true language. Instead, they have a call system that is apparently innate in the species. They can and do communicate certain types of information with vocal cries, but we must not confuse simple communication — even vocal communication — with language. Think about it for a moment. When a dog barks at an intruder, the dog is communicating something. When a cat rubs up against your leg at feeding time and gives a plaintive meow, the cat is communicating. We need not belabor the point here. For the present, just remember that vocal communication and language are not synonyms.

Chimpanzee vocalizations have been extensively studied. Different observers classify the sounds somewhat differently, but all agree on their general characteristics. Jane Goodall lists 23 vocalizations produced by wild chimpanzees, gives the usual context of the call, and notes the response of other chimpanzees (Goodall 1965:462–464). Let us examine four such calls as representative examples.

1. The first is described as a series of low panting grunts. It is often referred to as "food barking" or "food muttering." The vocalization is made in three situations: when two chimpanzees are greeting, when two chim-

panzees start to groom one another, or when they approach and start to eat desirable food. The response? If it is a greeting situation, the other chimpanzee makes a similar sound. If it is a grooming situation, the other chimpanzee makes a similar sound. If it is a feeding situation, other chimpanzees hurry toward the food.

2. Another call is described as a fairly loud, low-pitched "hoo." It is a type of chimpanzee hooting. It is given by a male when he moves off from the group and looks back at others. The response is that the others look toward the male and usually move off after him.

3. The third is described as a single loud scream. It is given by a male before chasing after another chimpanzee. The response is that the other animal either rushes away with a similar scream or makes appeasement gestures.

4. The last call is described as a series of loud panting hoots ending with panting roars. It is given by a male when he crosses a ridge where he cannot be seen by the other chimpanzees; it is accompanied by ground slapping or branch hitting. The response is that the chimpanzees beyond the ridge usually call out.

Now, what is going on here? Clearly, the chimpanzees are communicating by the use of vocal cries. What is it that is being communicated?

If you won't take this too literally, we will attempt some translations.

1. "Hello!" Or: "Let's groom." Or: "Here is good food."
2. "Come on!"
3. "Look out for me!"
4. "Here I am!"

Of course, we cannot really translate chimpanzee cries into human language equivalents. However, for purposes of discussion, it is not unreasonable to suggest that the vocalizations signal something like the foregoing. Proceeding on that assumption, note how limited these calls are. They are all immediate responses to ongoing situations. They all "refer" to right here and right now.

Consider what a chimpanzee *cannot* do with a call system of this sort. The animal cannot store information with words. ("Look, the way you build a nest is to proceed through the following five steps. . . .") The animal cannot communicate about another time and another place. ("Day before yesterday, I saw a leopard over on the Kenya border, and I resolved in no uncertain terms . . . .") It is impossible to "tell stories"—whether factual or invented—with such a vocal inventory. ("Once upon a time, there was this baboon out looking for trouble, and . . . .")

Probably, these calls are not learned anymore than a cat must learn to purr or a dog learn to bark. Certainly, captive chimpanzees that have been raised apart from other chimpanzees produce many of the calls in appropriate situations.

Other apes appear to have roughly similar call systems, but they do not usually produce as much vocal noise as chimpanzees. Gorillas, for example, are described as generally silent when undisturbed. Clearly, in the area of vocal communication, there is a substantial difference between chimpanzees and human beings. Here we may have an important clue about what is truly distinctive about our own species.

CHILD RAISING

One of the most interesting things about the Goodall study, based on keeping track of individual chimpanzees through time, was the strength of the ties between a mother and her offspring. Surprisingly old chimpanzee children — in the 3- to 5-year bracket — are very close to their mothers, and even 18-year-old mature males spend a good deal of time with their aging mothers. It is not too much to say that the mother-child relationship lies at the very core of chimpanzee society.

Chimpanzee females differ in their abilities as mothers. Some of this may be due to temperament, but in general chimpanzee mothers seem to improve with experience. As a rule, they welcome children and are very protective of them. Indeed, the whole group, including the males, shows lively curiosity when an infant is born. Females other than the mother often try to pick up the infant and hold it.

It cannot be too strongly stressed how much the child depends on its mother. It is not merely that the mother physically protects the infant, nurses it, and carries it about. The mother is crucial psychologically as well; the child needs the mother for security and a sense of well-being. A young chimpanzee past the suckling age that loses its mother shows definite signs of abnormal and disturbed behavior. Even when all goes well, the life is not an easy one. Goodall estimates that 50 percent of chimpanzee infants do not survive to maturity.

The story of what happens to a developing chimpanzee is essentially the story of how a young animal becomes more and more independent of its mother. Despite the lasting ties between mother and child, the young chimpanzee moves from a position of total dependence to a position in which it can function on its own and develop social relationships with other animals.

At first, the infant is in total physical contact with its mother. The baby clings to its mother, generally onto her belly, and the mother supports it when necessary with one arm. The mother will not allow other chimpanzees to touch the infant. She nurses the child and sometimes will allow it to take food from her mouth. The child sleeps with its mother in her nest.

After about six months, the youngster shifts its position and begins to ride piggyback; the mother assists in this transformation, simply picking the child up and setting it on her back. After that, it is literally a matter of hanging on for dear life. At about this time, the child begins to eat some solid foods. The mother plays with the infant occasionally, tickling it to make it laugh or hanging it on a branch and gently pushing it back and forth like a swing. Gradually, the child is permitted to move away from the mother for short distances, although it is always kept in sight. After a year or so, the child may be physically separated from its mother about 25 percent of the time during the day. It begins to play with other infants and juveniles — wrestling, having tugs-of-war over twigs, and so forth. By the time the chimpanzee is 16 months old, it will run at and strike another infant aggressively — and then reassure the other with gestures. At 18 months, it can groom another animal with correct technique. (Grooming involves picking through the hair of a companion, searching for bugs and dirt. It is a very important social interaction and helps to keep the animals in good condition.)

When the young chimpanzee is around 2 years old, it can feed independently of its mother. The time it spends away from direct physical contact with its mother increases to about 90 percent of the daylight hours. The child is extremely active, a trait not unknown in human children, and it plays constantly — preferably with other infants or juveniles, though it will even pester adults if nothing better is available. Older animals are quite gentle and indulgent toward the younger generation, helping them up and down trees and the like.

At approximately 4 years of age, the chimpanzee begins to construct its own nest for sleeping. Puberty arrives between 7 and 9, and a chimpanzee is full-grown physically at 10 years old. Females generally bear their first infant between 11 and 12; a male is fully mature socially at around 15 years. It is worth noting that this whole cycle is somewhat compressed by human standards; chimpanzees have a faster maturation rate than we do. A 10-year-old chimpanzee is comparable to a human teenager.

What does a chimpanzee learn in the process of growing up? Quite possibly more than we can specify. To some extent, different chimpanzees learn different things. It is a mistake to assume that the behavior of one group of chimpanzees is identical to that of another group. The variations may not be great, but they do exist. For example, "fishing" for termites has been reported only for the chimpanzees in the Gombe Stream Reserve; it has not been witnessed elsewhere.

Chimpanzees must learn what foods to eat and which ones to avoid. They learn how to construct nests by watching their mothers. They observe mating behavior very closely; captive chimpanzees raised in isolation from other chimpanzees have great difficulty in mating when they are sexually mature. Grooming and, probably, correct responses to vocal calls are learned. A chimpanzee must learn to socialize before it can interact successfully with other chimpanzees. The intense play activities of the young and the constant testing of one animal against another are obvious forerunners of the dominance patterns that figure in adult lives.

Still, observers consistently report that chimpanzee mothers protect, reassure, and comfort their children; they do not *instruct* them. A young chimpanzee learns mostly by doing, and to some degree by imitating what other animals are doing. As far as we can tell, adult chimpanzees do not attempt to teach the young. Rather, they offer them security, and they affectionately tolerate their presence. In other words, they provide the opportunity for the developing chimpanzee to learn for itself.

I repeat that any chimpanzee must learn some things in the process of growing up—it is not all "instinctive." Moreover, it is certainly true that most chimpanzees are capable of learning far more than they actually do. Despite this, one of the most striking things about the lifeways of chimpanzees is that they do not appear to change in really fundamental ways through time. There is some innovation, but the changes are not cumulative from generation to generation. There is no reason to believe that chimpanzee societies 10,000 years ago were much different from what they are today. There is no reason to believe that chimpanzee societies 10,000 years in the future—if there are any—will be notably different from those studied by Jane Goodall or Adriaan Kortlandt.

Here again, we seem to be dealing with a major difference between chimpanzees and human beings. Any human being in any human society must learn almost infinitely more than a chimpanzee in order to function as a human being. Beyond this, what we learn does not stop with us—it provides a foundation for future generations, so that human cultures have at least the potential for dramatic changes through time.

What, then, have we learned from our chimpanzee friends? We have learned that in some ways we are not as different as we used to think. Indeed, it can be argued that in some specific respects—their intensely social life, their rudimentary tool use, the cooperative hunting by males, their ability to walk erect, their diet, even their population densities—the similarities are too close to be entirely accidental.

We have also learned that there are crucial differences between the societies of chimpanzees and those of human beings. Outstanding among them are their nearly random mating patterns, the absence of the social role of husband-father, the lack of true language, and the failure to develop complex, cumulative cultural traditions.

Almost certainly, the last two items are interconnected. If chimpanzees had developed a true language, it is difficult to see why they would not also have produced cultures that were at least roughly comparable to those of human beings. We are smarter than chimpanzees, to be sure, but not *that* much smarter. Viewed from the human perspective, the problem of the chimpanzees is not so much their "intelligence" but their inability to communicate complex ideas across generational lines.

Clearly, this sheds new light on just how important the phenomenon of language is to human beings. Like all major discoveries, it suggests some new questions. Why is it that chimpanzees, bright animals that they are, do not have a true language? Is there a complete break between human beings and chimpanzees in this area, or is there only a difference in degree? This is the problem we will consider in the next chapter.

SUMMARY

Despite their obvious importance, there were no successful field studies of nonhuman primates until C. R. Carpenter studied the howler monkey in 1931. Shortly thereafter, Henry Nissen undertook the first field investigation of the chimpanzee. After Nissen, there were a series of chimpanzee field studies. The most important was carried out by Jane Goodall, who began working with chimpanzees in Tanzania in 1960.

Chimpanzees are intensely social animals and they live in groups. Chimpanzee "communities" — animals in a given area who know one another — comprise about 50 animals, but this large group is seldom if ever together as a functioning group. Goodall reported that the largest group she saw contained 23 animals and that most of the groups she encountered contained 9 animals or less. The groups were composed of all possible age and sex combinations, with three major exceptions. Adult females did not form groups by themselves, juvenile animals did not form groups by themselves, and adult males and young did not form groups by themselves.

Both group leadership and dominance relationships are subtle and complex among chimpanzees. Groups tend to be unstable and lack true leaders. However, adult males are dominant over all other animals, and adult females are dominant over immature animals. There is some rank ordering among males; each community has one male that is dominant over all the other males. However, these dominant males do not boss the others around, and in general dominance interactions among chimpanzees are relatively relaxed and easygoing.

Mating among chimpanzees is promiscuous. When a female comes into heat, all available adult males will mate with her. Chimpanzees do not form regular mating couples. The ties between a mother and her children are intense and persistent. Apparently, mature males do not mate with their mothers, and siblings matings are infrequent. Socially speaking, adult males do not act as fathers to specific children or as mates to specific females.

Chimpanzees are not ordinarily territorial animals, but they clearly have the potential to become territorial under certain conditions.

The bulk of the chimpanzee diet is vegetarian, consisting primarily of fruits. However, they also eat insects and occasionally eggs. More importantly, we now know that chimpanzees hunt and kill animals for food on a fairly regular basis. In fact, they hunt and kill nearly all the mammals that are available to them. Although foraging for wild plant foods is done by both males and females on an individual basis, hunting is basically a male activity and is engaged in by as many as four or five males who coordinate their actions. The results of the hunt are shared.

At night chimpanzees build nests in the trees for sleeping. During the daylight hours, they spend much of their time on the ground. Although their usual method of locomotion on the ground is knuckle-walking, they do stand erect and walk and run on two legs part of the time.

Chimpanzees are now known to both make and use simple tools. They construct stripped-down twigs in order to "fish" for termites, they make sponges out of crumpled leaves, and they use unmodified stones to crack open nuts.

Chimpanzees express themselves and communicate by means of vocal calls, gestures, facial expressions, and body postures. However, the vocal calls are quite different from true language. The call system is innate and limited to immediate responses to ongoing situations.

Chimpanzee mothers protect, reassure, and comfort their children, but they do not instruct them. A young chimpanzee learns mostly by doing and to some extent by imitation. Chimpanzees do learn some things in the process of growing up. They are clearly capable of learning far more than they actually do. Nevertheless, there is very little change from one generation to the next. The learning does not seem to be cumulative across generational lines, and therefore the chimpanzee has not developed complex cultural traditions.

References

Bingham, H. C. 1932. "Gorillas in a Native Habitat." Washington, D.C.: *Carnegie Institution Publication* 426:1–66.

Carpenter, C. R. 1934. "A Field Study of the Behavior and Social Relations of Howling Monkeys." *Comparative Psychology Monographs* 10(48): 1–168.

———. 1940. "A Field Study in Siam of the Behavior and Social Relations of the Gibbon." *Comparative Psychology Monographs* 16(5): 1–212.

DeVore, Irven (ed.). 1965. *Primate Behavior: Field Studies of Monkeys and Apes.* New York: Holt, Rinehart and Winston.

Goodall, Jane. 1965. "Chimpanzees of the Gombe Stream Reserve," in DeVore 1965. See also Lawick-Goodall, 1971.

Kortlandt, Adriaan. 1962. "Chimpanzees in the Wild." *Scientific American* 206: 128–138.

Lancaster, Jane B. 1975. *Primate Behavior and the Emergence of Human Culture.* New York: Holt, Rinehart and Winston.

Lawick-Goodall, Jane van. 1971. *In the Shadow of Man.* Boston: Houghton Mifflin. (This was Jane Goodall's married name.)

Moss, Cynthia. 1975. *Portraits in the Wild: Behavior Studies of East African Mammals.* Boston: Houghton Mifflin.

Nissen, H. W. 1931. "A Field Study of the Chimpanzee." *Comparative Psychology Monographs* 8 (1):1–122.

Reynolds, Vernon, and Frances Reynolds. 1965. "Chimpanzees of the Budongo Forest," in DeVore 1965.

Schaller, George B. 1965. "Behavioral Comparisons of the Apes," in DeVore 1965.

Sugiyama, Y. 1968. "Social Organization of Chimpanzees in the Budongo Forest, Uganda." *Primates* 9:225–258.

———. 1969. "Social Behavior of Chimpanzees in the Budongo Forest, Uganda." *Primates* 10:197–225.

Suzuki, A. 1969. "An Ecological Study of Chimpanzees in a Savanna Woodland." *Primates* 10:103–148.

Teleki, Geza. 1973a. "The Omnivorous Chimpanzee." *Scientific American* 228:32–42.

———. 1973b. *The Predatory Behavior of Wild Chimpanzees.* Lewisburg, Pa.: Bucknell University Press.

Suggestions for Further Reading

Bramblett, Claud A. 1976. *Patterns of Primate Behavior.* Palo Alto, Ca.: Mayfield. Contains descriptions of 15 nonhuman primates in their natural habitats, including reliable summaries of all the field investigations of chimpanzees.

Goodall, Jane. 1979. "Life and Death at Gombe." *National Geographic* 155: 592–620. One of Goodall's most fascinating articles, this report on the Gombe Stream chimpanzees provides the latest available information on fighting and territoriality.

Jay, Phyllis (ed.). 1968. *Primates: Studies in Adaptation and Variability.* New York: Holt, Rinehart and Winston. A good book to read in conjuction with DeVore 1965, previously cited.

Kortlandt, Adriaan. 1967. "Experimentation with Chimpanzees in the Wild," in D. Starck, R. Schneider, and H. J. Kuhn (eds.), *Neue Ergebnisse der Primatologie.* Stuttgart: Fischer. Contains some interesting information on such subjects as the reactions of chimpanzees to stuffed leopards.

Lawick-Goodall, Jane van. 1967. *My Friends the Wild Chimpanzees.* Washington, D.C.: National Geographic Society. Those seriously interested in the chimpanzee should read *In the Shadow of Man,* previously cited. However, this one is well worth looking into.

MacKinnon, John. 1974. *In Search of the Red Ape.* New York: Holt, Rinehart and Winston. Probably the best available book on the least known of the apes, the orang. Among other things, provides a graphic picture of the difficulties involved in studying this animal in the wild.

Reynolds, Vernon. 1965. *Budongo: An African Forest and Its Chimpanzees.* Garden City, N.Y.: Natural History Press. Contains a fuller account of these chimpanzees than the article previously cited.

Schaller, George B. 1963. *The Mountain Gorilla.* University of Chicago Press. By far the best single book dealing with the gorilla in the wild.

——. 1964. *The Year of the Gorilla.* University of Chicago Press. A less technical account than the preceding. This is a delightful book which should be read by anyone interested in field studies of primates. Particularly valuable in providing some perspective on the chimpanzee data.

6

Communicating with Chimpanzees: A Dialogue Begins

Along about 1930, a psychologist named W. N. Kellogg had an interesting idea. What would happen, he wondered, if you took an infant chimpanzee and placed it in a completely human environment? If you raised a chimpanzee exactly as you would raise a human child, what would that ape be like?

Dr. Kellogg realized that in order for the experiment to be successful, halfway measures would not be sufficient. You could not treat the animal as an ape part of the time and as a human being part of the time. You must give the chimp an opportunity to learn only human ways of doing things. The infant chimp must be dressed in diapers, fed with a bottle, and given the same love and affection that a human child would experience. Most importantly, the chimpanzee must be treated as a member of the family. Dr. Kellogg was going to be Daddy, Mrs. Kellogg was going to be Mommy, and the Kellogg's own baby son was going to be the chimpanzee's brother.

The idea was that the chimpanzee would never be treated as a pet. They would not teach it stunts and attempt to make a trick animal out of the chimpanzee. Instead, they would try to raise the chimpanzee exactly as they raised their own son. Their son was to serve as both a playmate and as the control subject in the experiment. Dr. Kellogg reasoned that if he treated them both the same, then the differences between the two at the end of the experiment would reveal some of the basic differences between human beings and chimpanzees.

The Kelloggs got a young female chimpanzee from the Yale Anthropoid Experiment Station. Her name was Gua, and she was 7½ months old. At that time, the Kelloggs' son Donald was 10 months old. Note that throughout the experiment, Donald is older than Gua.

In their report of the experiment (Kellogg and Kellogg 1933) the Kelloggs treat their subject matter by topic, rather than providing a month-by-month narrative. I will follow that plan here, briefly indicating some of their findings, and then give a more detailed account of the attempts that were made to teach Gua to speak.

Donald was clearly superior to Gua in what the Kelloggs called manual dexterity—skill in the use of the hands. In general, Gua would use her lips rather than her hands in such tests as picking up a small object from a flat surface. Obviously, this was due to the structure of the chimpanzee hand, which makes it difficult to oppose the thumb to the other fingers. From that point on the chimpanzee did surprisingly—almost alarmingly—well.

Donald first walked unassisted at 12 months. He could walk backwards at 18 months. He never did run in the period covered by the experiment. Gua could knuckle-walk when she arrived at the Kellogg household. She could walk erect at that time ($7^1/_2$ months) if her hands were held. She practiced walking by getting between Dr. Kellogg's legs and holding onto his trousers; the two of them took strolls through the neighborhood in this fashion. At $8^1/_2$ months, she could walk backwards in this manner. She could walk erect and without assistance at 9 months. She could run on two legs when she was $12^1/_2$ months old—about the time that Donald was taking his first staggering steps.

Gua had sharper vision than Donald and better hearing. She also had a better sense of balance. The Kelloggs would test their two subjects by putting them in a spinning chair. Donald held on for dear life, got red in the face, and cried. Gua leaned back, relaxed, and held out her hand to catch the breeze.

Both Donald and Gua liked to play, and they played together well. For some reason, Gua liked to put her fingers in Donald's mouth. Donald liked to chew fingers. They soon became quite a team. Gua would point her finger, and Donald would promptly lean over and chew it. Perhaps the most interesting thing about their play activities involved imitative play. The chimp has quite a popular reputation as a behavioral mimic; that is what the English verb *to ape* means. Nonetheless, imitative behavior in Gua was markedly less pronounced than it was in Donald. Donald constantly imitated Gua, but Gua seldom imitated Donald. Gua tended to be the leader in new games, with Donald tagging along and trying to do what he saw Gua doing. This capacity to imitate on the part of the human subject may be significant in cultural learning. (There are, however, other factors to consider in this particular experiment. Despite their chronological ages, it must be remembered that Gua's maturational rate is faster than Donald's.)

According to the Kelloggs—and, after all, they are evaluating a chimpanzee against their own child—Gua was both more affectionate and more cooperative than Donald. Moreover, in most respects Gua learned faster than Donald did. For example, consider the "hand in loop" experiment. A string was tied to a stake and the other end of the string was tied around the wrist of either Donald or Gua. The idea was to see if the subjects could untie the string around the wrist within a specified period of time. Donald made a surprise solution on his first trial. (He was then 14 months old.) However, his next eight trials were all failures. Gua flunked her first trial (11½ months old), solved it on the second attempt (in 35 seconds), and then made 28 successful trials with only one error. The exception to this general trend was that Donald was superior in learning situations that involved imitation.

Again with one exception, Gua had a consistently better memory than Donald did. The exception was significant: Donald was slightly better at remembering words (responses to spoken commands) than Gua was.

When we come to the area of communication and language, it is a dramatically different story. Let us quote the Kelloggs directly on this point:

> It was in the development of articulate sounds in which Donald significantly outshone the ape. There was no attempt on Gua's part to use her lips, tongue, teeth, and mouth cavity in the production of new utterances, while in the case of the human subject a continuous vocalized play was apparent from the earliest months. It was as if the child, like other normal humans of similar age, was *practicing* the formation of new vowels and consonants. . . . Although Gua in her turn could form several vowels and although she seemed to be able to manipulate her lips and tongue with perhaps greater facility than the boy, *no additional sounds were ever observed beyond those which she already possessed when we first made her acquaintance.* There were no "random" noises to compare with the baby's prattle. On the whole, it may be said that she never vocalized without some definite provocation, that is, without a clearly discernible external stimulus or cause. The superiority of the child in vocal imitation stands also as a striking difference between the two subjects. [Donald picked up a number of sounds from Gua, including her food bark at mealtimes; Gua picked up no sounds at all from Donald.] (Kellogg and Kellogg 1933)

Recognizing the importance of the language factor, Dr. Kellogg decided to make a special effort to teach Gua to speak. He selected the word *papa*, reasoning that the sounds involved should not be difficult for a chimpanzee. Every day, he would seat Gua on his lap, peer at her, and say *papa* slowly and distinctly. Gua seemed alert and interested, but she did not do anything. This went on for weeks. Finally, Dr. Kellogg tried to manipulate Gua's lips as he pronounced the word *papa*. Gua liked this fine. After months of effort, Dr. Kellogg was rewarded after a fashion. He said *papa*, over and over again, and moved Gua's lips. Gua slowly and carefully reached out—and stuck her finger in Dr. Kellogg's mouth.

Gua never made the slightest progress in learning to say any words whatsoever. It is of interest to note that at first Gua was superior to Donald in responding to spoken words. (Instructions such as "come here," "sit down," and so forth.) Even at the end of the experiment, which was terminated after nine months, Donald knew 68 correct responses to words and Gua knew 58 — not a very dramatic difference. But Gua could never learn to say anything.

It appeared, on the basis of the Kellogg experiment, that there was a complete ''break'' between human beings and chimpanzees in the area of language. The difference seemed to be a qualitative one: Donald had the capacity for language and Gua did not. Gua had something else — an apparently innate set of vocal calls.

Two questions might occur to you at this point. How would it affect the experiment if you started it when the chimpanzee was younger and continued it for a longer period of time? Insofar as the development of language is concerned, it does not seem to change the results very much.

VIKI

In 1947, Cathy Hayes and her husband took a baby chimpanzee into their home immediately after the chimpanzee was born (Hayes 1952). The chimp's name was Viki, and they kept her for several years. The end result was that Viki, with great difficulty, managed to say three words: *mama, papa,* and *cup.* They were not very clear, but let us give Viki the benefit of the doubt.

Here we must ask another question. If Viki could say three words, however imperfectly, would this constitute evidence that Viki had a language? The answer is clearly negative, for reasons that will be explained in this chapter and the next. After all, a parrot can do better than that, and parrots do not have languages. To understand the problem, imagine that you have a child of your own. After years of effort, your child can say only three words and does not progress beyond that point. You would correctly assume that something was wrong.

For some years, there the matter rested. It appeared to be impossible to teach language to a chimpanzee. Something was wrong — something was lacking — and the problem was to find out what that something was. Basically, there were two schools of thought. One was that the chimpanzee vocal apparatus was simply inadequate to produce the necessary sounds. (If you watch Viki on film, you can see that she is having severe articulation problems.) The other was that the chimpanzee brain lacked something vital to language. It was not so much that the chimpanzee was not ''smart'' enough, but rather that the crucial language-producing areas of the brain were missing or undeveloped.

In either case, the linguistic gulf between human beings and all other animals remained. We had languages and they did not. It was a comfortable assumption, and it was a useful one as well. It showed in a dramatic way just how essential language was in the mix that makes us human.

WASHOE

Then, in 1966, Washoe arrived on the scene. Washoe, a female chimpanzee like Gua and Viki, had been captured in Africa. She was about one year old when she came under the care of two psychologists, R. Allen Gardner and Beatrice Gardner. The Gardners placed Washoe in a very special learning environment—a large trailer in their backyard equipped with all sorts of toys and games. They decided to try again to teach language to a chimpanzee. However, they went about it in a new way. Instead of trying to teach Washoe to speak (vocally), they taught her the American Sign Language, the means of communication employed by many deaf persons. To put it simply, they gave Washoe the opportunity to talk with her hands rather than with her mouth.

Using a variety of teaching techniques, including showing Washoe a sign and rewarding her when she used it correctly, the Gardners and their chief assistant, Roger Fouts, proceeded with their task. It is no exaggeration to say that the results were amazing.

After five years, when Washoe was taken from her Nevada home to Oklahoma, she knew approximately 160 sign words. Moreover, she could use them—one at a time, in combinations, and in what amounted to simple conversations with her human companions. Her first word was *more.* Her first word combination, ten months after her training began, was *gimme* (give me) *sweet.*

While Washoe was with the Gardners, she never saw another chimpanzee. She thought of herself as human. (Viki felt the same way. When sorting photographs into two piles, animal and human, she put her own picture on the human pile on top of a photograph of Eleanor Roosevelt. She put a picture of her own father in the pile with horses and elephants.) Washoe knew who she was, too. When asked "Who you?" she would reply, "Me Washoe." (This was all done with signs, of course. The Gardners communicated only with sign language when Washoe was present.) Sometimes, her understanding was truly remarkable. When outside observers were called in to witness her signs, there were occasions when the observers were not really fluent in sign language. Washoe would obligingly slow down her signs so they could understand.

Washoe was capable of stringing signs together in meaningful sequences. For example, she signed *Key open please blanket.* This meant that she wanted the locked cupboard in which blankets were kept opened (Fouts 1974:478). She could transfer the meaning of a sign to new situations. After learning *open* to refer to the opening of particular doors, she extended it to other doors, such as cupboard doors (as indicated above) and refrigerator doors. She then extended it to all containers, such as boxes, briefcases, jars, and bottles. She even used it to request the turning on of water faucets (Gardner and Gardner 1975:247). On several occasions, she invented simple signs of her own. One of these was a sign for *bib,* made by drawing an outline of a bib on her chest, and another was for a game of *peekaboo,* made by covering her eyes with her hand. Even more intriguing was her novel use of known signs in unfamiliar situations. The most impressive example of this was when she was shown a picture of a duck. Never having been taught the sign for *duck,* Washoe signed *water bird* (Fouts 1974:479).

The idea of trying to teach language to a chimpanzee through nonvocal techniques represented a conceptual breakthrough. Other scientists have tried variants of the technique with similar success. David Premack has taught a chimpanzee named Sarah "to read and write with various shaped and colored pieces of plastic, each representing a word" (Premack and Premack 1972:92). That is, they can communicate with each other by arranging plastic tokens. Yet another chimpanzee, Lana, has learned to communicate by typing on special keys plugged into a computer (Rumbaugh, Gill, and von Glaserfeld 1973). These special keys pressed by Lana stand for words and concepts, not letters. Essentially, Lana is required to complete displayed "sentences" that are in "correct" word order and to press a "reject" key when shown an incorrect or invalid sentence. Like Sarah's plastic tokens, Lana's "language" is an invented one to some extent; it is called Yerkish, after the Yerkes Regional Primate Center in Georgia.

LANGUAGE AND THE CHIMPANZEE

No one would deny, I think, that the abilities shown by the chimpanzees in these experiments are remarkable. At the very least, they indicate that many of the problems that chimpanzees have with language are rooted in their vocal apparatus rather than in their brains. Still, the most basic question has not been answered to everyone's satisfaction. Do chimpanzees have the capacity to learn a true language, or don't they?

It is a question that has profound implications for the origin of language, the nature of language, and the possible uniqueness of the human animal. Obviously, it cannot be answered until we know for certain exactly what a language is. There are nearly as many definitions as there are linguists. If the matter were not so serious, it would be amusing to witness the scramble to redefine language in such a way as to exclude Washoe. About the most that can be said at this point is that the authorities disagree.

Instead of choosing between definitions and quoting the experts, let us take note of some salient facts:

1. The "languages" taught to chimpanzees are not part of the natural behavior of chimpanzees. As far as is known, wild chimpanzees have nothing really comparable to these systems of communication. They do have barks and hoots and gestures, but these are far more limited than the signs that Washoe learned.
2. All of the "languages" taught to chimpanzees were created by human beings. It is not a matter of learning to interpret "chimpanzee language" but rather a matter of teaching a chimpanzee to communicate with a human technique.
3. Chimpanzees like Washoe were placed in very special learning situations that were devised by human experimenters. Whether they learned readily or with great difficulty, it would be hard to argue that the situations were comparable to those faced by normal human children.
4. At the present time, it would appear that the "languages" taught to chimpanzees are different in some respects from ordinary human lan-

Koko signing "sleep."

guages. Aside from the vocal aspects, they do not seem to be truly phonemic, and there may be some problems with syntax. (These terms will be explained in the next chapter.)

On the other hand, it would be a harsh critic indeed who would claim that chimpanzees have demonstrated no linguistic abilities at all. Washoe in particular has shown positive evidence of language capacity. If it cannot be maintained that chimpanzees have zero linguistic ability, then we have to conclude that the differences between human beings and chimpanzees in this regard are a matter of degree rather than a qualitative (presence-absence) difference. The quantitative difference may be very large, as it almost certainly is, but it is still a difference in degree rather than in kind. In brief, we have vastly more linguistic ability than chimpanzees, and all normal human beings use languages. Chimpanzees have some latent linguistic capacity, which they do not put to use under natural conditions.

It must be emphasized that major disagreements exist concerning the meaning of the "language" experiments with chimpanzees. At least some of the questions that have been raised may be answered by further research. The Gardners are now working with chimpanzees that have been exposed to sign language from birth. (You will recall that Washoe was about a year old when they got her.) In addition, some of their trainers are deaf or were raised by deaf parents; they are more proficient in Ameslan (American Sign Language) than Washoe's instructors were. Indications are that these chimpanzees are learning signs faster than Washoe did.

It is now apparent that the chimpanzee is not the only ape capable of learning sign language. In a fascinating experiment that began in 1972, a female gorilla named Koko has been taught to use approximately 375 signs (Patterson 1978:453).

Meanwhile, what of Washoe herself? Washoe is in Oklahoma at the Institute for Primate Studies. On an artificial island, she is interacting with other chimpanzees. She is being closely watched. To what extent will the chimpanzees use signs to communicate with each other? How will the use of sign language develop over the years? Will Washoe teach signs to her children?

The story at present is a sad one. Late in 1976, Washoe gave birth to a son. After birth complications, the infant died. Washoe wept profusely and repeatedly tried to get the dead child to respond to her by making the sign *baby*. Washoe gave birth to a second son in March, 1979. The infant lived only a few days and perished from a respiratory ailment.

It is still too early to say with assurance what chimpanzees can and cannot do. They have surprised us before. We will just have to wait and see.

SUMMARY

Since one of the crucial areas of difference between human beings and chimpanzees is language, scientists have been interested for a long time in the possible linguistic potential of chimpanzees. Early experiments concentrated on attempting to teach a chimpanzee to speak. Two psychologists named Kellogg took an infant chimpanzee, Gua, into their home and tried to treat her in the same way as they did their own young son, Donald. Although Gua was superior to Donald in many ways, she made zero progress in language. The chimpanzee was unable to produce any human vocalizations. On the basis of this and other similar experiments, the conclusion was reached that there was a complete gulf between human beings and chimpanzees with regard to language.

Then, in 1966, two psychologists named Gardner tried a different approach. Working with a young chimpanzee named Washoe, they tried to teach her the American Sign Language known as Ameslan. They succeeded beyond expectations. After five years, Washoe knew and could use about 160 sign words. Moreover, she did not simply ''parrot'' the signs. She knew what she was saying, she employed correct sequences of signs, she invented several simple signs of her own, and she produced novel combinations such as signing *water bird* for *duck*.

Variations on this experiment have confirmed the findings of the Gardners: Many of the problems that chimpanzees have with language are rooted in their vocal apparatus rather than their brains.

Although the matter has not been settled to the satisfaction of everyone, many scientists have had to modify their views concerning the linguistic abilities of chimpanzees. The differences between human beings and chimpanzees in the area of language now appear to be differences in degree rather than in kind.

References

Fouts, Roger S. 1974. "Language: Origins, Definitions, and Chimpanzees." *Journal of Human Evolution* 3:475–482.

Gardner, Beatrice T., and R. Allen Gardner. 1975. "Evidence for Sentence Constituents in the Early Utterances of Child and Chimpanzee." *Journal of Experimental Psychology* 104(3):244–267.

Hayes, C. 1952. *The Ape in Our House.* New York: Harper & Row.

Kellogg, W. N., and L. A. Kellogg. 1933. *The Ape and the Child.* New York: McGraw-Hill.

Patterson, Francine. 1978. "Conversations with a Gorilla." *National Geographic* 154: 438–465.

Premack, A. J., and D. Premack. 1972. "Teaching Language to an Ape." *Scientific American* 227:92–99.

Rumbaugh, D. M., T. V. Gill, and E. von Gaserfeld. 1973. "Reading and Sentence Completion by a Chimpanzee." *Science* 182:731–733.

Suggestions for Further Reading

Brown, Roger. 1970. "The First Sentences of Child and Chimpanzee," in Roger Brown (ed.). *Psycholinguistics: Selected Papers.* New York: Free Press. A thoughtful critique of the Washoe data by a distinguished linguist.

Linden, Eugene. 1974. *Apes, Men, and Language.* New York: Saturday Review Press. E. P. Dutton. A good popular book on the subject that ably summarizes both the data and opposing views on the meaning of the chimpanzee experiments.

Temerlin, Maurice K. 1975. *Lucy: Growing Up Human, A Chimpanzee Daughter in a Psychotherapist's Family.* Palo Alto, Ca.: Science and Behavior Books. A fascinating account of a chimpanzee that lived with a human family for ten years. Includes information on both sexual development and the use of sign language.

7

The Talking Animal: Language and Why It Matters

Many of us in this culture have gone to school for a very long time. Many of us feel that there is nothing quite so ordinary—and perhaps boring—as attending a class. And yet, stop a moment. The next time you go to class, whether it be anthropology or something else, reflect a bit about what is going on. It is really a profoundly unique experience. Someone is talking to you, explaining the cumulative thoughts and experiences of generations, suggesting ideas, exploring alternatives. You may not agree with everything you hear, you may ask questions, you may have a different point of view; still, you have the opportunity to learn what other human beings have said and done at various times and in diverse places. That mundane class in mathematics or physics or history or philosophy has no parallel in the animal world. It is one of the things that makes us different.

Of course, the basic situation is by no means confined to a formal classroom. Stories told around a campfire, sacred lore passed on in initiation ceremonies, the whispered advice of an experienced hunter, the reassurances of a midwife to a new mother, the legends that are chanted about the earth and the forest and the sky—all of these things have the same characteristics. We would not be human without them, and we could not do these things without language.

We live in a world of words. They are our almost constant companions. From the time we are born until the time we die we probably spend more time listening and talking than in any other activity. Even when we think, we tend to think in words.

Whatever language is, it is more than just communication. It is obviously possible to communicate certain types of information without language; we can do it by means of actions, and so can other animals, for example, when one animal becomes alarmed and its companions react to its disturbed behavior. Whatever language is, it is more than just vocal communication. Dogs bark and birds call and porpoises whistle and chimpanzees hoot. All of them are communicating vocally, and yet it seems clear that language involves more than this.

At the outset, in trying to come to grips with the phenomenon of language, it is important to separate language from writing. They are not the same. Writing is a relatively recent invention, going back only some 5000 years in those areas in which it was first developed. There were languages for untold thousands of years before there was any writing on this planet. Even today, there are many languages that are not written down. Beyond this, in cultures that do possess systems of writing, all normal human children — meaning those without hearing or speech disabilities — learn to speak and understand before they learn to read and write. To put it simply, the language comes first. Neither the capacity for language nor the quality of language has anything to do with writing. Writing is essentially a set of graphic techniques to represent speech in a visible medium. It is the speaking itself that is basic to understanding what language is and how it works. As Robert Hall once put it, "Writing is a set of marks you make with your fist, whereas speech is a set of noises you make with your face" (Hall 1950: 35).

If speech — the articulation of vocal sounds — alone constituted language, the problem would be fairly simple. One could describe the "sending" mechanism (the vocal cords, the palate, the tongue, the lips, and so forth) and the "receiving" mechanism (the ears) and let it go at that. Unfortunately, that won't get the job done. In theory, a person could produce almost an infinite series of vocal sounds which could be heard by another person and there would still be no language. It would merely be vocal noise, communicating nothing at all.

A language has to work, or else it isn't a language. At a bare minimum, this means two things. First, the vocal noises that we produce cannot be random; they must somehow be controlled and patterned. Second, the vocal noises must be deciphered by someone other than the speaker; the listener must understand what the speaker is saying. If you put it this way, it seems easy, and perhaps in one sense it is. After all, any child can do it. It is when you try to explain exactly how all this takes place that the problem becomes complicated.

LANGUAGE AND THE BRAIN

The capacity for language is somehow rooted in the structure of the human brain (see Figure 7.1). To be sure, the ability to produce sounds and to hear them is likewise essential, but without what happens in the brain there could be no language. It is the brain that imposes the pattern on our speech and enables us to "translate" what we hear into meaningful information.

It is difficult to be more specific than this. Clinical data suggest that three areas of the brain are crucial to language. These areas are parts of the cerebral cortex, the convoluted outer layer of the brain. Usually, they are located in the left hemisphere of the brain. Damage to *Broca's area* (toward the front of the

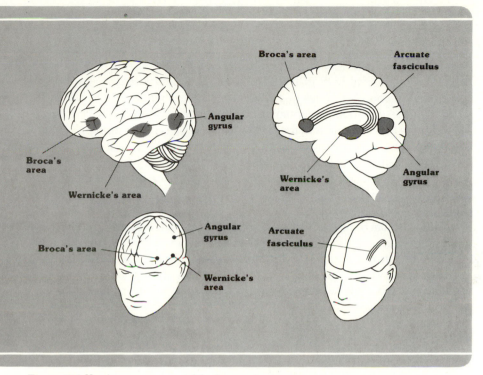

Figure 7.1 Key language areas of the human brain.

brain) produces an impairment of speech. Damage to *Wernicke's area* (further back) produces a loss of comprehension. Damage to the *arcuate fasiculus,* a bundle of nerve fibers connecting Broca's area with Wernicke's area, produces further complications — abnormal speech and an ability to understand words but not repeat them. Other data indicate that the *angular gyrus,* adjacent to and behind Wernicke's area, functions as a critical switching center, making it possible to associate one type of incoming signal with others. It has been suggested that the angular gyrus permits the linkage between the sight of an object, its feel, and its name.

Unfortunately for this attempt to pinpoint precise parts of the brain responsible for language, serious problems remain to be solved. For example, the known "language centers" of the brain are located in the left hemisphere of the brain in right-handed people but usually in the right hemisphere in left-handed people. Moreover, if serious brain damage occurs in the left hemisphere before a child is 2 years old, this does not prevent normal language development. The implication of this is that there appears to be at least some flexibility in the functions performed by various parts of the brain. We are dealing here with complex interactions, and about the only thing that can be said with assurance is that the capacity for language is situated in the cerebral cortex of the human brain.

THE USE OF SYMBOLS

In part, language depends on the human ability to create and manipulate *symbols*. Indeed, as Leslie A. White has cogently argued (1949), the ability to symbolize is fundamental both to language and to culture generally. A symbol is something—a sound or series of sounds, an object, a gesture—that stands for something else. Any normal human being can create symbols at will. (For example, I can say that the sounds in the word *glug* will represent "dinosaurs." When I say "glug" you think "dinosaurs." You may find this peculiar, but you will have no difficulty with it. Similarly, I can let my pipe stand for "virtue," or say that when I touch my ear with my finger this signals a coffee break.) As far as we know, no other animal can do this. It seems easy and natural for us simply because we are human beings.

It is essential to realize that the connection between a symbol and its referent is entirely arbitrary; it is just a matter of mutual agreement. There is nothing in the sounds in the word *house* that forces us to connect the sounds with the building. White states that once a symbol has been created it can be used as what he terms a *sign* and that other animals can be taught or conditioned to some degree to respond to signs. Obvious examples of this would be a hunting dog responding to spoken commands or a seeing-eye dog reacting to changing traffic signals. It is the human being who devises the commands or sets up the traffic signals, not the dogs. It is true that when a child learns a language the child does not invent (or create) the word symbols. However, the human species did create them—every word in every language, and all the signs as well. It is also true that children (and adults) can and do invent new words; the problem is not in creating them but in getting them accepted by others. It is of interest to note that the gestures created by Washoe—holding her hand over her eyes, drawing an outline of a bib on her chest—did not have arbitrary referents. There is an obvious connection between the bib outline and the bib or the eye shielding and a game of peekaboo.

THE NOVEL YET APPROPRIATE RESPONSE

Roger Brown (1958), in a fascinating book called *Words and Things*, pointed out the importance of what he called the novel but appropriate response. He meant that one of the characteristics of language is that we do not simply repeat back or "parrot" what has been said to us. More is involved than just learning a set of responses and using them in the correct situations. Rather, the flexibility of language is such that we can all say things that have never been said before. Even the simple paragraph that you are now reading is unique; you will not find it anywhere else. If you kept an accurate record of everything that you said in a single day it is highly unlikely that anyone else in the world said exactly the same thing in the same order. All of us can create novel sentences that make sense in the context in which they are spoken. When we are explaining something, we often say: "In other words . . . ." This matter of the novel but appropriate response underscores the significance of Washoe's use of the signs for *water bird*. By combining the signs in a meaningful way that she had not been taught, she was showing in a limited form one of the basic characteristics of language.

LEARNING A LANGUAGE SYSTEM

When a child learns a language, the child does not just record like a reel of tape. The child does not simply repeat back what has been said. This is not language, no matter how many words the child learns and regurgitates. It may be a necessary step, but it is certainly not the end of the road. The essence of learning a language is learning a system, a model, that shapes and controls speaking. We do not know precisely how this is done. It is not accomplished by the conscious learning of a set of formal rules. Most parents cannot themselves explain the principles of the language they speak, let alone teach them to a child.

By the time a child goes to what we often call a grammar school, the child is already speaking. The language exists and is used long before grammarians come along to tell us what is "right" and "proper." Indeed, there were languages for countless thousands of years before there was any analysis of language—and yet somehow the children learned. In some way that is not fully understood, the child internalizes the principles—sets up a model of how the language works—and proceeds to use it in speaking. When an English-speaking child says "Here come three mans" or "I throwed the ball" the child is correct; that is, the child is using the model for forming the plural of a noun or the past tense of a verb. It is the language that is "wrong," that is, irregular; and the child must then learn the exceptions to the rules. When my son was 3 years old, he once said something moderately startling and profane. "Where did you get that?" I asked him. "It just came out of my mouth," he replied. He was right, too, except that the critical thing is what happened *before* it came out of his mouth—the mental blueprint that determines what he will say and how he will say it.

It is exactly this thorny question—how in fact do we speak, and how do we get from the underlying code or model in our minds to the torrent of speech that pours from our mouths?—that has led to the development of *transformational linguistics,* pioneered by Noam Chomsky and others (Chomsky 1957, 1968). It can be argued that we do not really "teach" a child to speak at all; instead, we barrage a child with vocal examples from which the child *constructs* a model that enables the child to speak. (Indeed, you cannot stop a child from speaking unless you raise the child in an isolated cell. The situation is the opposite of that for chimpanzees, who must be encouraged to "talk" with signs. Every parent finds out soon enough that once the child starts talking there is no end to it.)

Chomsky has suggested that a child could not possibly devise a "theory of speaking" with the correct overall design just from the sounds the child hears unless in a sense the child knew what he or she was looking for—that is, unless the child already had an abstract model programmed in the brain so that the child simply had to fill in the design with the specifics of the particular language the child hears. Chomsky has stated that at birth a child knows language (a general plan) but not a particular language (such as French or Kamba or Kiowa). Utilizing comparative data on speech acquisition in different cultures, Eric Lenneberg has made much the same point (Lenneberg 1964, 1967). The development of speech, he says, is a maturational phenomenon; cultural differences have little or no effect on the age of the beginning and mastery of speaking. All children, he suggests, go through identical phases in acquiring speech. As he puts it, "The appearance of language is due to an innately mapped-in program for behavior, the exact realization of the program being dependent upon the peculiarities of the speech environment" (Lenneberg 1964). Again, nobody is suggesting that a child is born knowing a specific language like English or Kwakiutl; the suggestion is that we are born with a rather detailed capacity or model for language in general.

By no means all linguists agree with this proposition. It represents a radical departure from more traditional views in which the focus was largely on the mechanics of sound production and reception with the brain hardly mentioned at all. However, if scholars such as Chomsky and Lenneberg are right, or even partially correct, their ideas will have a profound influence on our understanding of how language—and culture itself—operates.

A language is not like the call systems of nonhuman animals. It is not limited to the communication of simple emotional states or here-and-now situations: *Danger! Food! Play!* It is something quite different. With language, we can talk about other times and other places. We can explain complex ideas. The languages we speak serve as a kind of storehouse for cumulative human knowledge. Language is usually regarded as a part of culture, but it is a very special part. Language is the primary vehicle of culture. Most of what we learn comes to us through the medium of language and is interconnected with language. Without language our cultures—which are permeated with symbols—would be quite rudimentary if they existed at all. When a child first begins to understand and to produce language, the child has taken a giant step toward becoming a functioning human being; that is, the child has started to acquire the culture of the group in which the child lives. A human being without culture, apart from a newborn infant, is a contradiction in terms. (I am speaking of normal human beings, of course. People with severe pathological disorders present a different kind of problem.)

Language, which enables us to recreate experiences in words—to tell stories both factual and invented—is closely linked to the rest of cultural systems. It follows that some knowledge of what makes language tick should shed light on the culture process in general. Even a cursory study of language shows that languages are never chaotic, disorganized things. All languages have structure; they are systems of interrelated parts. They are not all the same by any means, but they do all have certain basic principles in common—just as all cultures do.

UNIVERSAL ELEMENTS OF LANGUAGE

Let us examine some of the universal elements of language.

First of all, no language makes use of *all* the possible sounds that human beings can create. We can all make a variety of vocal noises that do not count in the particular language that we speak. Instead, a cultural selection is always made so that only a limited number of possible sounds are actually used in any given language. (The selection is not a conscious one. Except in the case of artificial languages, nobody calls a conference to decide which sounds will count and which ones will not. Nevertheless, through time, the selection occurs.) The number of distinctive sounds employed in a language is rather small. Few languages use more than 40.

Phonemes

The distinctive, significant sounds used in a language are called *phonemes*. A phoneme is a sound that makes a difference, a sound that counts.

Consider the English word *cat*. Think of it in terms of the sounds that are employed rather than the letters used in writing the word. (Ideally, of course, an alphabet would have a one-to-one relationship with the sounds used in a language. Each letter would stand for a single sound. In the real world this does not happen. For example, there are 26 letters in the English alphabet, but many of the letters can stand for more than one sound, depending on context. This is true even if we disregard the sometimes bizarre vagaries of English spelling. Even specialized systems of transcription, such as the International Phonetic Alphabet, cannot fully cope with all the sounds in all the languages; there are too many subtle variations, and human beings can produce a staggering number of different vocal noises.)

Unless we get very pedantic about it, the word *cat* is composed of three phonemes: *c-a-t*. (Say the sounds to yourself.)

The way to find out if a sound makes a difference is to change it. Suppose we alter the first phoneme. Instead of *c-a-t* we have *b-a-t*. Obviously, this does make a difference; it has phonemic value, it *does* something. Or we can switch the middle phoneme and *c-a-t* becomes *c-u-t*. Similarly, we can replace the final phoneme and *c-a-t* becomes *c-a-p*.

Note that the phoneme by itself has no specific meaning attached to it—it only signals a change in meaning. To understand this, refer again to the above example. Consider the first sounds (phonemes) in this series of words:

c-a-t
c-u-t
c-a-p

The sound represented by the letter *c* has no common referent in the three words. It does not "mean" anything by itself; there is nothing similar about *cat*, *cut*, and *cap* except for the partial overlap of sounds. In the same way, the sound represented by the letter *a* has no common referent in *cat* and *cap,* and the same applies to the sound represented by the letter *t* in *cat* and *cut.*

The phonemes used in a language can only be sequenced in certain ways. Different languages have different "rules" concerning the ordering of phonemes, but all languages embody such principles. For example, consider the sounds *p-a-s* in English. We can combine them in that order: *pas.* We can combine them this way: *asp.* We can reverse them: *sap.* We can put them in this order: *spa* (as in *spatula*). What we cannot do in standard English is to use them this way: *psa.* (How about the word *psalm?* Remember that we are talking about sounds, not spelling. Pronounce the word and you will see what I mean.) Remember that other languages have other rules. There are no English words that begin with the sounds *n-g.* However, in Swahili (an African Bantu language that contains some borrowings from Arabic and English) such words are common. Examples are *ngoja* ("wait for") or *ngombe* ("cow"). Such unfamiliar sound combinations are trouble spots when outsiders learn a foreign language; native English speakers tend to butcher Swahili by using constructions like *gombes* for "cows." *All known languages are built ultimately out of phonemes.*

Morphemes

As we have seen, phonemes by themselves do not have specific meanings attached to them; they only signal a change in meaning. When phonemes are combined so as to form meaningful sound units, these units are called *morphemes.* Morphemes are most easily thought of as words and parts of words. They are sound units with specific meanings attached. The use of the plural here is intentional; many morphemes have more than one possible meaning. Examine the usages of the word *dog* in the following sentences:

"My dog is a cocker spaniel."
"My dogs are killing me!" (That is, my feet hurt.)
"I ate a hot dog for lunch."
"That novel of yours is a real dog."
"Red dog!" (In football, the linebacker is rushing the quarterback.)

Basically, there are two kinds of morphemes. One is termed a *free* morpheme, meaning that it can stand alone. *Dog* is an example. The other type is called a *bound* morpheme, meaning that it must be used in combination with other morphemes in order to function as a morpheme. For example, in the word *dogs* the final *s* sound is a bound morpheme. It is a morpheme because in that position it carries a particular meaning; it converts the singular to the plural. It is a bound morpheme because it cannot stand alone; it must be hooked onto the end of a word to retain its meaning.

Bound morphemes too must be used in particular ways in particular languages. In English, certain forms always precede the words to which they are attached, for example, *re-* and *un-.* Others must follow the words to which they are linked: *-s* and *-er* (as in the pair *work-worker*).

In English, we call these forms *prefixes* and *suffixes*. Other languages have *infixes*, and the forms can occur at other points in the words. Languages also differ in terms of how many morphemes can be combined in a single word. Languages such as German or Eskimo tend to string together more morphemes in one word than is common in English. However, the essential point is that all languages employ morphemes in regular ways; the "rules" vary from language to language, but all languages have morphemic principles.

Syntax

All languages have *syntax* as one of their basic features. Syntax is simply meaningful word order. The importance of word order varies from one language to another, but in no language does one merely spout out words at random. The English sentences "John hits Fred" and "Fred hits John" employ exactly the same words, but it makes a difference where the words are—particularly if you happen to be Fred or John. Either construction is "acceptable" English, but not this one: "Fred John hits." (This one, of course, might be okay in another language—German, for example. You may recall Mark Twain's famous description of a German sentence as resembling a man diving underwater, swimming a long distance, and finally emerging with the verb in his mouth.)

The problem of syntax is actually more complex than I have presented it here. There is much variation from one language to another, and apparently simple questions of word order can lead into more subtle linguistic areas. For example, take this English sentence, "Bob hits the ball." In some ways, this is a very "typical" English sentence. The framework of it is *subject-verb-object*. In it, something (or someone) *does* something to something else. It implies a situation in which an agent produces an action—it is the agent (Bob) that is primary and is responsible for whatever takes place. This seems natural to us perhaps because we speak English. In other languages, what is going on might be reported in a very different form. Translated, it would look like this: "Ball hitting is taking place with Bob." The Navaho language is something like this, and here we have quite a different emphasis. It is an *event* or type of action (ball hitting) that is primary, and the person (Bob) is secondary. This implies a situation in which activities are central and people are linked rather loosely to what is happening. Does this suggest a different view of the world? Are these different views about "reality" conditioned by the languages we speak? We will return to this problem shortly.

Lexicons

Every language has a *lexicon*. A lexicon is the total number of words in the language. If you write down a lexicon and arrange the words alphabetically, you have an unabridged dictionary. The lexicons of different languages are not identical. In part, this is due to the fact that lexicons have a close relationship with the rest of the cultural systems of which they are a part; people only have words for what they need or wish to talk about. One would not expect hunters and gatherers to have words like *cyclotron* or *transistor* or *skyscraper*. On the other hand, languages in primitive societies may have words and make distinctions that do not occur in English. In Eskimo there are many words for *snow* and *ice* because variations that are not usually significant for us can be crucial for the Eskimo. There is no connection between the size of the lexicon and the quality of the language. You will search in vain for the word *automobile* in the works of Shakespeare, but you would not conclude that Shakespeare's English was therefore inferior to our own. In any language, new words can be invented or borrowed as they are needed.

It should also be noted that personal lexicons vary among the speakers of the same language. Nobody really uses the total inventory of words in a language. The words we use depend upon the subcultures of which we are a part. English is not entirely the same in New York and Texas, in the ghetto of an inner city and in an affluent part of suburbia. A heated discussion between two biochemists may be meaningless to a poet. The same principle applies to the use of language in primitive societies; a shaman (doctor) or a priest may employ specialized vocabularies not shared by the rest of the population, and there may be differences between one class and another, between the sexes, or between one type of artisan and another.

All languages change through time. No language is ever wholly static as long as the language continues to be used by a population. If you doubt this, check out a copy of Chaucer's *Canterbury Tales* in the original English and try to read it. Languages change not only in vocabulary but in syntax and phonemic structure as well. It is quite futile to attempt to ''freeze'' a language unless the language is already dead — that is, unless the language has no native speakers left.

Finally, in terms of the universal characteristics of language, all specific languages are learned. Whether or not there may be some ''deep structure'' or generalized language model built into the human brain, we all must learn the specific languages we speak. Certainly, no one is born knowing how to speak Kikuyu or English or Kiowa or Japanese. Any human child can learn any language; it depends entirely on which language the child is exposed to in the process of growing up.

LANGUAGE AND OUR PERCEPTIONS OF THE WORLD

When we were discussing syntax, we raised the possibility that speakers of different languages might view the world around them in somewhat different ways. This notion goes back to an idea proposed by the anthropological linguist Edward Sapir in 1929. Sapir wrote:

> Language is a guide to ''social reality.'' . . . Human beings do not live in the objective world alone, nor alone in the world of social activity as ordinarily understood, but are very much at the mercy of the particular language which has become the medium of expression for their society. It is quite an illusion to imagine that one adjusts to reality essentially

without the use of language and that language is merely an incidental means of solving specific problems of communication or reflection. The fact of the matter is that the "real world" is to a large extent unconsciously built up on the language habits of the group. No two languages are ever sufficiently similar to be considered as representing the same social reality. The worlds in which different societies live are distinct worlds, not merely the same world with different labels attached. (Sapir 1929:209)

Sapir was suggesting that language is much more than a kind of neutral code for transmitting information. Rather, he argued, the languages we speak affect the ways in which we see, interpret, and think about the universe in which we live.

This insight of Sapir's was developed further by Benjamin Lee Whorf. Whorf's career was unusual. Trained in chemical engineering at M.I.T., he was employed for most of his professional life as a fire prevention expert by an insurance company. (The story goes that Whorf was the person who substituted the word *flammable* for *inflammable* on petroleum containers, having discovered that many people thought that an *inflammable* substance was one that could not be set on fire.) For Whorf, linguistics was a kind of hobby. As is true for many persons, his "hobby" was what really interested Whorf. He studied under Sapir, lectured at Yale for a time, and made highly original analyses of various languages, notably Hopi.

In 1941, Whorf published an article he had written two years earlier. Its title precisely indicates the subject of the paper: "The Relation of Habitual Thought and Behavior to Language" (Whorf 1941:75–93). In it Whorf offered an extensive comparison between Hopi and what he called SAE, or Standard Average European, the latter group of languages including English. Among other things, he noted that SAE languages basically have three distinct tenses for verbs: past, present, and future. He suggests that this linguistic feature leads SAE speakers to think of time as a series of "points on a line." Time can be visualized as something like a row of separate boxes. Thus, in English, we say: "Tomorrow is another day." In Hopi, there are no such verb tenses; there are, instead, modifiers that indicate a kind of progressive "getting laterness." Tomorrow is *not* another day in Hopi; it is the same day, only a little older.

Whorf further suggests that these and other characteristics of the two languages may be linked to additional cultural features. Thus, the emphasis on cyclical ceremonies and dances in Hopi culture may reflect the Hopi view of time; the careful preparation and meticulous performance of these rituals animates the time continuum, affecting the whole span of Hopi existence. In SAE cultures, there is no corresponding emphasis on the value of unvarying repetition. If one thinks of time as a row of boxes, what happens in one box has little or no effect on another box "down the line." We divide time into a series of linear chunks — seconds, minutes, hours, days, weeks, years. Indeed, we regulate our lives by these divisions of time. When we turn the page of a desk calendar, we are "turning over a new leaf" in more ways than one. Above all, we are told not to "waste time" (leave a box unfilled with useful activity) and to "get things done on time" (as though missing a specific point in the series were the equivalent of not doing it at all).

Consider the time machine, a fictional device "invented" by H. G. Wells in 1895. Don't worry about whether or not such a gadget is possible outside the pages of science fiction. Imagine an eccentric billionaire who dies and specifies in his or her will that $50 million will be given to the person who builds the first successful time machine. Suppose a Hopi and an SAE speaker both decided to compete for the prize. Would they be trying to build the same kind of machine at all? Would it be designed to do the same sorts of things? If not, does this have some relationship to the languages they speak and in which they think? In English, we can say "I'm going to the future" in exactly the same way that we say "I'm going to Detroit." The Hopi cannot say that; the Hopi is already *in* the future, so to speak, which is a different problem. This is the sort of linguistic puzzle that fascinated Whorf.

Whorf believed that the participants in a cultural system tend to share what he called a *thought world*, and that this thought world is shaped not only by linguistic patterns but by all the analogies and suggestive values that are *implied* by the linguistic patterns. The thought world, according to Whorf, "is the microcosm that each man carries about within himself, by which he measures and understands what he can of the macrocosm." In other words, the universe is not the same to all observers, because the universe is perceived and interpreted through a kind of cultural filter or lens; it is this filter or lens, intimately connected to language, that Whorf terms a thought world.

The idea that each culture tends to view and interpret reality along the lines supplied by its own linguistic categories is known as the *Sapir-Whorf hypothesis*. It has been neither proved nor disproved by experimental evidence. In part, this is because the hypothesis presents a kind of chicken-or-the-egg problem. Does the language influence the rest of culture, or is it the culture that is affecting the language?

Most anthropologists would probably agree that there is some sort of "fit" or congruence between language and the rest of culture. On the other hand, many would question both the extreme differences between languages suggested by Sapir and Whorf and the idea that specific languages are the primary determinants of particular cultures.

The possibility of an innate general plan or model for language as a species characteristic and the presence of elements common to all languages would seem to negate at least some of the power of the Sapir-Whorf hypothesis. As Joseph B. Casagrande has noted, "It may well turn out that what is universal in language functions much more powerfully, and in a more fundamental way, to shape men's thoughts than what is different" (Casagrande 1963).

OTHER AREAS OF LANGUAGE STUDY

Complex as all this may seem, there is far more to the study of language and human communication than I have touched upon here. Relatively recent areas of investigation include *kinesics* (body movements used to communicate, such as nodding the head or making eye contact) and *proxemics* (how people perceive and use social space). We shall encounter an example of the latter phenomenon in the next chapter. There are important techniques such as *glottochronology* (also known as *lexicostatistics*), which is a means of dating the approximate time of separation between related pairs of languages. There is the perplexing problem of precisely how language originated. There is a whole field of *ethnosemantics*, which is a sophisticated approach to the analysis and understanding of how people categorize experience. In ethnosemantics, anthropologists try to discover how the speakers of a language themselves group certain kinds of things together, rather than imposing the anthropologist's own categories on the data. Ethnosemantics has emphasized the distinction between the *emic* viewpoint, the framework used by the people themselves, and the *etic* viewpoint, which is supplied by an outside observer.

When you stop and think about it, it is apparent that linguistic activities do not occur in a vacuum. Language performance is an intensely *social* activity. It is all very well to discuss the mechanics of word and sentence production, but in fact what we say and how we say it is profoundly affected by the context in which speaking takes place. This is what *sociolinguistics* is all about. What is really going on in a speech community? Who is talking to whom? Does the speaking involve greeting behavior, is a joke being told, are instructions being given? Language is so flexible that it is even possible to say one thing and mean quite another. For example: "I'd really love to stay but I just remembered I left the water running in my bathtub." Translation: "This party is a bore and I want to go home." It is obvious that the relationships between speakers affect what is being said. If I meet a distinguished scholar I do not know personally, I might say: "Dr. Jones, it's a real honor to have a chance to talk to you." If I run into an equally distinguished scholar who happens to be a close friend, I would never say such a thing. I might say: "Joe, you old horse thief, what the devil are you up to now?" All of us in any culture adjust our style of speaking to the social situation. If we didn't, the results would be comical or even dangerous.

Recent developments in the ethnography of speaking hold forth the promise of shedding considerable light on many aspects of language. As a refinement of the sociolinguistic approach to language, this represents an attempt to go beyond the "laws of grammar" and to find precise linkages between the ways we speak and the sociocultural domains within which speaking occurs. As Richard Bauman and Joel Sherzer put it, "the task of the ethnographer of speaking . . . is to identify and analyze the dynamic interrelationships among the elements which go to make up performance, toward the construction of a descriptive theory of speaking as a cultural system in a particular society" (Bauman and Sherzer 1974:7).

All anthropologists would agree, I think, that the phenomenon of language is central to an understanding of the human animal. At the same time, most anthropologists would agree that we do not yet know exactly what language is and how it works. We can list many of the characteristics of language, but there is no single definition of language — to say nothing of a comprehensive theory of language — that is acceptable to everyone.

It is not necessary that we choose a definition of language to be memorized and regurgitated. The important thing is to understand *why* language is so critical for the lifeways of human beings. The symbol systems that constitute our languages make cultures possible. It is not only that we learn much of our cultures through the medium of language but also that linguistic systems *interpenetrate* cultural systems. All cultural systems are permeated with symbols, and the symbols are intimately linked to language. We do not know exactly what the situation was when the hominids first emerged as a distinct form of life. It is entirely possible, based on anatomical evidence, that the forerunners of *Homo sapiens* had considerably less linguistic ability than we do (Lieberman, Crelin, and Klatt 1972). We *do* know that no culture in the world today could function in its present form without language.

Therefore, all the complexity of detail can be resolved on one level into a simple proposition. Without language, cultures as we know them could not exist; and without culture the human animal would be a very different sort of creature.

It is popular in some quarters to refer to human beings as "naked apes." We are not apes, of course, and neither are we wholly naked. We do share some anatomical and behavioral characteristics with our primate kin. In trying to understand ourselves, we must recognize both similarities and differences between hominids and other primates. It seems to me that it might be useful to turn the reference around. Think of Washoe and the first tentative steps she has taken in the human direction. Think of all the other apes who have not taken even those beginning steps. We are not the naked ones; we are wrapped in the fabrics of our cultures — fabrics that are largely woven out of linguistic strands. Naked apes? No, *they* are the naked ones: remarkable animals who must face the problems of existence without the tremendous advantages of adaptive cultural systems made possible by the miracle of language.

SUMMARY

So far as is known, only human beings acquire and utilize vocal language under natural conditions. The capacity for language is somehow rooted in the structure of the human brain. Of course, the ability to produce sounds and to hear them is likewise essential, but without what happens in the brain there could be no language.

In part, language depends on the human ability to create and manipulate *symbols.* The connection between a symbol and its referent is entirely arbitrary. (The signs invented by Washoe had a clear connection with what they stood for; they were not arbitrary.) Another characteristic of language is the ability to produce *the novel but appropriate response.* That is, we can all say things that have never been said before; much more is involved than simply learning a set of responses and using them in the correct situations. (Washoe's utilization of the *water bird* signs was one aspect of true language ability.)

The essence of learning a language is learning a system, a model, that shapes and controls speaking. We do not know precisely how this is accomplished. Some linguists, such as Noam Chomsky and Eric Lenneberg, have argued that the basis for language is innate. The human child has an abstract language model programmed in the brain and merely has to learn the specifics of the particular language to which it is exposed.

No language makes use of all the possible sounds that human beings can create. A cultural selection is always made, so that some sounds count and some do not. The distinctive, significant sounds used in a language are called *phonemes.* Phonemes in themselves have no specific meanings attached; they only signal changes in meaning. When meaningful sound units are produced — particular combinations of phonemes — they are called *morphemes.* Morphemes are most easily thought of as words and parts of words.

All languages have *syntax* as one of their basic features. Syntax is simply meaningful word order. On all of these levels — phonemes, morphemes, and syntax — languages are not random but operate according to rules and principles. Every language has a *lexicon,* which is the total number of words in the language. New words can be invented or borrowed as they are needed. All languages also change through time, and all specific languages are learned.

The *Sapir-Whorf hypothesis* holds that our perceptions of the world around us are strongly influenced by the particular languages we speak. Implicit in this idea is the notion that there are great differences between languages. As Sapir said, "No two languages are ever sufficiently similar to be considered as representing the same social reality." Modern thinking about language, which tends to stress linguistic universals, casts doubt on this assumption.

Language performance is an intensely social activity. What we say and how we say it is strongly affected by the context within which speaking takes place. The study of the sociocultural contest of language activities is known as *sociolinguistics.*

Without language, cultures as we know them could not exist. It is for this reason that an understanding of language is fundamental to an understanding of how the human animal operates.

References

Bauman, Richard, and Joel Sherzer (eds.). 1974. *Explorations in the Ethnography of Speaking.* London and New York: Cambridge University Press.

Brown, Roger W. 1958. *Words and Things.* Glencoe, Ill.: Free Press.

Casagrande, Joseph B. 1963. "Language Universals in Anthropological Perspective," in

Joseph H. Greenberg (ed.), *Universals of Language.* Cambridge, Mass.: The M.I.T. Press.

Chomsky, Noam. 1957. *Syntactic Structures.* The Hague: Mouton.

———. 1968. *Language and Mind.* New York: Harcourt Brace Jovanovich.

Hall, Robert A. 1950. *Linguistics and Your Language.* New York: Doubleday (Anchor Books).

Lenneberg, Eric H. 1964. "The Capacity for Language Acquisition," in J. J. Fodor and J. A. Katz (eds.), *The Structure of Language.* Englewood Cliffs, N.J.: Prentice-Hall.

———. 1967. *The Biological Foundations of Language.* New York: Wiley.

Lieberman, Philip, Edmund S. Crelin, and Dennis H. Klatt. 1972. "Phonetic Ability and Related Anatomy of the Newborn and Adult Human, Neanderthal Man, and the Chimpanzee." *American Anthropologist* 74(3):287 – 307.

Sapir, Edward. 1929. "The Status of Linguistics as a Science." *Language* 5:207 – 214.

White, Leslie A. 1949. *The Science of Culture.* New York: Farrar, Straus and Giroux.

Whorf, Benjamin Lee. 1941. "The Relation of Habitual Thought and Behavior to Language," in Leslie Spier, A. I. Hallowell, and S. S. Newman (eds.), *Language, Culture, and Personality.* Menasha, Wis.: Banta.

Suggestions for Further Reading

Blount, Ben G. (ed.). 1974. *Language, Culture and Society.* Cambridge, Mass.: Winthrop. A well-organized and selected book of readings; includes Harry Hoijer's discussion of the Sapir-Whorf hypothesis and Whorf's article, "The Relation of Habitual Thought and Behavior to Language."

Burling, Robbins. 1970. *Man's Many Voices.* New York: Holt, Rinehart and Winston. A provocative discussion of the cultural context of language, including a succinct summary of the work by Brent Berlin and Paul Kay on color perception.

Greenberg, Joseph H. 1968. *Anthropological Linguistics.* New York: Random House. A good, clear introduction to the field.

Hall, Edward T. 1959. *The Silent Language.* New York: Doubleday. A fascinating and well-written analysis of some of the more subtle aspects of communication, including social space. Hall's more recent work, *The Hidden Dimension* (1966), is also of considerable interest.

Haugen, Einar, and Morton Bloomfield (eds.). 1974. *Language as a Human Problem.* New York: Norton. A fairly technical collection of papers, including Eric Lenneberg's article on "The Neurology of Language."

Hockett, C. F. 1973. *Man's Place in Nature.* New York: McGraw-Hill. An unusual introductory text by an anthropological linguist containing an excellent discussion of language.

Hymes, Dell (ed.). 1964. *Language in Culture and Society.* New York: Harper & Row. A classic in its field with an extensive bibliography. Contains Harry Hoijer's article, "Cultural Implications of Some Navaho Linguistic Categories," which influenced some of the ideas presented in my discussion in this book.

Lenneberg, Eric H. 1967. *The Biological Foundations of Language.* New York: Wiley. An important book that should be read by anyone seriously interested in the subject.

Whorf, Benjamin Lee. 1956. *Language, Thought, and Reality: Selected Writings of Benjamin Lee Whorf,* edited by John B. Carroll. New York: Wiley. A collection of Whorf's major publications, almost all of which are of exceptional interest.

8

Culture: What We Learn and Why

For as long as anthropology has existed, the concept of culture has been its major focus of interest. Perhaps because of this sustained examination, culture has been defined and redefined almost to the point of total mystification. The extended analysis of culture has been both useful and necessary, but it has served to obscure a fundamental point: The idea of culture is not bewilderingly complex but is instead elegantly simple.

Look at it this way. When a human infant is born, that infant is helpless in several different senses. The child cannot physically survive on its own, of course; at a bare minimum, it must be fed, protected, and cared for. But suppose — just as an exercise in imagination — that little Cuthbert or Mary Sue *could* survive physically. Let us assume that the child matures biologically into an adult but does so in complete social isolation. Why could he or she not participate in a human society — any human society? Why could the male not become a Polynesian fisherman, a Cheyenne warrior, or a Bushman hunter? Why could the female not become a Kamba farmer, a Pueblo potter, or a United States senator? Obviously, the answer is that Cuthbert and Mary Sue do not know what they have to know. They have had no opportunity to learn the ropes that would enable them to operate in a human society.

The human infant at birth may not be a blank slate upon which literally anything can be imposed; I personally do not believe that it is. The infant certainly has some built-in drives and may be programmed genetically to learn certain kinds of things. Nevertheless, every child must learn the specifics of the lifeway in which he or she finds himself or herself. There is no other way a human being can function. The problem of culture, then, is precisely this: What does Cuthbert or Mary Sue have to acquire that transforms him or her from an animal that does

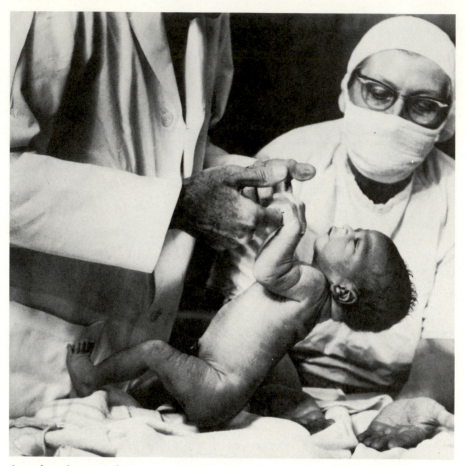

A newborn human infant.

not know what to do into an animal that knows what is expected of a Kwakiutl, a Hopi, or a Masai? What the person acquires — what he or she learns from other human beings in the society — is culture.

Anthropologically speaking, culture does not refer to some hypothetical level of nice manners and refinement. There is no distinction between "cultured" and "uncultured" unless one is referring to the difference between human beings and other animals. The critical thing about human beings is that we learn vastly more of our lifeways than do other animals; what we learn about how to live in a particular society is our culture, whether this involves headhunting, writing poetry, or strangling a goat for a sacrifice.

Obviously, it is culture — what we learn — that accounts for the differences between one human society and another. We are all essentially the same biologically: just plain old *Homo sapiens*. The differences between one human society and another may be neither as vast nor as whimsical as they are sometimes por-

Human adults.

trayed, but they are clearly considerable. These differences are learned, whether one is an Eskimo seal hunter or a German automobile mechanic. Any human being can learn any culture; it depends entirely on which cultural context a person is exposed to in the process of growing up. The process of learning a culture is known as *enculturation*.

We all start out like the infant in the picture on page 118. Enculturation and physical growth transform us into the adults shown above.

Definitions of culture are a dime a dozen — or perhaps a dollar a dozen at today's prices. There is an entire book devoted to such definitions (Kroeber and Kluckhohn 1952) and enough new entries since the book was first published to make possible a new book of similar length. For the most part, the various definitions are addressed to a real problem — different ways of looking at the same animal, different points of view that affect research and the analysis of cultural questions. However, it hopelessly confuses the issue to begin with competing and sometimes contradictory definitions. Our purpose here is to try to understand the phenomenon of culture, and this requires a reasonably consistent theoretical position.

A DEFINITION

A good definition is not an end but a beginning. It points the way toward significant issues; it makes you think rather than presenting a kind of handy-dandy item to commit to memory. In this spirit, let us examine a definition of culture and see where it leads us. In a well-known discussion of the subject, Clyde Kluckhohn and William Kelly argued that culture consists of all the "historically created designs for living, explicit and implicit, rational, irrational, and nonrational, which exist at any given time as potential guides for the behavior of men." (Kluckhohn and Kelly 1945:97)

Before we tackle this definition on an item-by-item basis, let us be specific about what this point of view implies. This thing we call culture is essentially *a set of ideas* that people carry around in their heads. In Kluckhohn's phrase, it is a *design* for living — a model of connected ideas that is shared to some extent by the members of a human society. A culture is a loose kind of mental blueprint that tells people what they can do or are supposed to do. In other words, the true locus of culture is in the human mind.

THE CUMULATIVE ASPECT OF CULTURE

Now, suppose we zero in on the definition. What does "historically created" mean? It means that to some extent cultures are handed down to us from the past; we *learn* a culture rather than just make it up as we go along, which is why we do not have to reinvent fire with each new generation. A culture has continuity to it and it is cumulative in nature; each generation builds on the ideas which have preceded it. Our own culture is changing so rapidly that we speak of a "generation gap" and even a gap within generations. This raises an important point because it suggests that you cannot treat culture simply as a static precipitate of history; it is not like a football tossed from one generation to another. If cultures are cumulative, this means that innovation is possible; if there were no innovations there would be nothing to accumulate, and we would all still be living in caves.

Still, there are two ideas to bear in mind. First, innovation does not come out of nowhere — it is conditioned by what has gone before. There is no cultural eraser, and traditional and deep-rooted ideas have a way of popping up in rather superficial disguises. Second, although all cultures change through time, most cultures throughout most of our existence as a species have not changed with anything like the speed of our own. The notion of cultures being historically created is much more obvious in most cultures in which the changes from one generation to the next tend to be slight; statistically speaking, we are the peculiar ones.

We have already talked about cultures being "designs for living," but there is an additional point that should be made. A design has unity to it; it has organization and patterning. A culture is not just a random grab-bag of unrelated ideas. The components of a culture tend to be interconnected; the parts have to fit and work together. It is this characteristic of culture that makes it both possible and necessary to speak of cultural *systems*.

IMPLICIT CULTURE

Some of culture is explicit and operates on a conscious level. When we instruct our children on rules for behavior or teach someone how to chip flint to make a stone axe, we are communicating explicit cultural ideas. It is easy to fall into the habit of thinking that *all* culture involves this sort of thing, but it is a false assumption. A great deal of any cultural system is implicit. Rather than being overt and conscious, it is covert and unconscious. It has been said that perhaps the most important things you can find out about any culture are the things that people never talk about—the ideas that go so deep that they are taken for granted and are seldom if ever verbalized.

Consider touching and embracing between males, for example. In our culture, biologically mature males cannot touch and fondle one another without an implication of homosexuality; a rather brisk handshake is about all that is usually permitted. But note that this is not true in situations that are highly charged emotionally. Watch football players in a key game, for instance. If a player scores an important touchdown, he is mobbed by the team—patted on the butt, hugged, even kissed. Now, no football coach ever communicates this explicitly. He does not say, "Okay, gang, we all know that we are not to embrace one another except under the following 14 conditions." Nevertheless, it *is* communicated. Other cultures do things differently, and again what is "right" is not formally taught. There are Indian cultures in Brazil in which the men sleep together around the fires. The hearty embrace between males is a standard form of greeting in much of Latin America. Young Kamba men in Kenya often stroll about holding hands.

Consider some of our curious ideas about bodily functions. If the proverbial man from Mars listened to our television advertising about toilet paper, he would not have the faintest idea of what the stuff was actually used for. We call it "bathroom tissue" and are seemingly enchanted with the cute floral designs, the aroma of perfume, and whether we can squeeze it or not.

Consider what Edward T. Hall calls "proper conversational zones." This is a fascinating example of the social usages of space. Hall points out that *every* culture has what amounts to a "comfortable" distance between the participants in a conversation. In an average chat—neither whispering in the ear of a lover nor bellowing at a class from a lecture stage—we stand between 20 and 36 inches apart. In other cultures—Mexico, for example—the "proper" distance is much shorter. The result is that when a person from the United States talks to a citizen of Mexico, the Mexican keeps moving forward to close the gap and the American keeps backing away to reach a "comfortable" distance. Such a conversation can cover considerable territory in quite a literal sense (Hall 1959: 160–164). Note again that this is never communicated to our children in an explicit way. Indeed, it cannot be, since we are not consciously aware that "proper conversational zones" exist.

CULTURE AND RATIONALITY

Kluckhohn characterizes culture as being "rational, irrational, and non-rational." The precise shades of meaning intended here are not particularly crucial. The important idea is that cultures are not wholly rational, no matter whose definition of "rational" you choose. If a cultural system represents one people's solution to the problems of living, it is apparent that no culture can be entirely irrational. Such a culture would not work and the society would perish. On the other hand, it is difficult to maintain that *all* the ideas in a cultural matrix serve rational purposes. The notion that human beings are rational animals is deeply embedded in the American culture, but surely it would take a confirmed optimist to argue that everything we do has a rational basis.

People are emotional creatures as well as reasoning ones, and in any culture we tend to juggle symbols in strange ways. A culture can tolerate a certain number of nonrational ideas; it is one of the things that makes us interesting. It is possible to analyze seemingly bizarre customs so that they do indeed make sense in their cultural context; we should certainly not assume that something is nonrational just because it seems odd to us. This is one of the cogent points made by Marvin Harris in an engaging book called *Cows, Pigs, Wars, and Witches* (Harris 1974). Nevertheless, all cultures probably include at least some nonrational elements. The Maya, for instance, happened to admire cross-eyed people. Parents would tie a ball of resin to a baby's hair so that it would hang between the eyes and cause the infant to focus on it. That may be trivial, but it is hard to call it rational. More critically, all cultures change through time. An idea that may have been quite rational in one situation may be retained in a situation in which it is no longer appropriate.

I am making these points at some length because they have important implications. If cultures are not entirely conscious, rational systems, and if cultures are always to some degree conditioned by past experience, this suggests that the invention of ideal cultures by well-intentioned people may be a decidedly formidable task.

Kluckhohn concludes his definition with the thought that designs for living are "potential guides for the behavior of men." Here, I would like to stress the word *potential*. The ideas that comprise a cultural system provide guidelines for behavior. A culture is not a monolithic strait-jacket that allows no room to maneuver. While all cultures include some compulsory injunctions—things you must do or must not do—all cultures also include ideas that permit considerably more latitude. They are, so to speak, suggestions rather than orders. Just as there is no such thing as a culture so flexible that there are no rules at all, there is also no such thing as a culture so rigid that *every* action in *every* possible situation is culturally prescribed. We will return to this problem in the next chapter.

It may be noted that the idea of culture as a design for living has been retained in a widely quoted definition by Ward H. Goodenough. As he phrases it, "a society's culture consists of whatever it is one has to know or believe in order to operate in a manner acceptable to its members, and do so in any role that they accept for any one of themselves" (1957:167).

STUDYING A CULTURE

If culture is a set of ideas, this poses problems for an anthropologist—or anyone else—who wishes to study a cultural system. It also creates problems for a student who is trying to understand what the anthropologist means when he or she talks about the culture of a particular human group. The issue here is not whether or not cultures are "real." The issue concerns how the anthropologist comes to grips with culture and what it is that the anthropologist winds up with.

You cannot study culture directly, no matter how clever you are and no matter what sophisticated testing techniques you may employ. You cannot go out into the field and *see* a culture and bring it triumphantly home in a sack. What you are after is a set of ideas. What you *see* are people doing things— hunting elephants, dancing, engaging in legal disputes—and the things that people have made: houses, spears, granaries, television sets. These things, which we can call actions and artifacts, are not culture. Rather, they are the *products* of culture. They are what people do and the things (artifacts) that people make in response to the ideas they have in their heads. This is what Robert Redfield was getting at when he argued that culture is "manifest in act and artifact"—it does not consist of acts and artifacts but reveals itself in the actions that people perform and in the things they make.

If we were limited in our investigations to what was visible, we would have to *infer* the culture from acts and artifacts. We would have to guess at the motivating ideas, and in part that is what we do. Fortunately, there is something else that we can do. What it boils down to is asking questions. We can ask people to explain why they are doing what they do. It would be essentially correct to define an anthropologist in the field as a person who goes around asking questions. Some of the questions are elementary—things that any child would know. (Anthropologists at work often convey the impression that they are stupid beyond belief.) Some of the questions are complex, requiring specialized knowledge for an answer. However, asking questions is not the end of the road. Even if you had an absolutely ideal informant who was willing and eager to tell you everything, you still could not "get" a culture just by asking questions. In the first place, no single informant knows *everything*. A man, for example, might know next to nothing about birth practices. A woman might have very vague ideas about how raiding parties operate. A smith (ironworker) could not tell you how a shaman (doctor) achieved a cure. Even if you had unlimited time and complete cooperation from everybody — a fantasy situation — you could not get it all.

The problem is that much of culture is covert and cannot be verbalized. The "reasons" that people give for their behavior may be quite truthful as far as they go and still be wrong. Put yourself in the position of an informant. Why are you going to school? Why do you wear the clothes you have on? Why do you eat the foods you eat? How important are grades, and why? How representative of the total culture are your answers?

We must remember that conversations, too, are acts. A question-and-answer session is a type of behavior, and it is conditioned by many factors the participants may not be aware of — the status positions of the speakers, the desire to create a certain impression, the families we come from, the hidden values that lie deep within us. In this sense, the answers we get to our questions are themselves cultural products. Before we can "reach" the culture itself, we must go beyond what people tell us.

THE CULTURAL MODEL

To be candid about it, the cultures that anthropologists describe are always approximations of the real thing. You cannot split open skulls and extract the culture. Therefore, cultural descriptions are always *abstractions from behavior*. They are models or constructs which are intended to *represent* the cultural system under investigation. On the basis of what the anthropologist sees and hears, the anthropologist puts together a set of ideas that represents the actual "design for living." He or she hopes the model will be reasonably accurate; there will be a tolerably close correspondence between the model and the reality. However, the model is not and cannot be the culture itself.

A cultural model can be checked out to some degree. The anthropologist can use it to predict what people will do in certain situations. (Remember that cultural statements are normative statements. They refer to what most people will usually do. Even if the model makes allowances for special groups of people within a society, it cannot pretend to predict individual behavior.) For example, I can predict what kind of house the Kamba will build and who will do the construction. I can predict how legal disputes will be handled. I can predict how the Kamba will conduct a particular kind of ceremony at the Sacred Tree. If I am right — if they really do it that way — then the chances are that my model of Kamba culture is fairly good. If I am wrong and they proceed to do things differently, then it's back to the old drawing board. The model must be modified or even rejected altogether.

Unfortunately, even the most careful anthropologist cannot check everything in this way. For one thing, the model may not take final shape until all the data are analyzed, and by then the anthropologist is no longer in the field. For another, the anthropologist may not have the opportunity to witness everything that goes on. One must sleep occasionally; it is notoriously difficult to be in two or more places at the same time; there are situations in which your presence is not welcome; and some events take so long that they are not completed in the year or two the anthropologist spends among the people being studied.

Much of this has to do with how cultures are studied and described, rather than with culture itself. It is important, I think, because it should inculcate an element of caution in the beginning student. When you read about "the culture of the Hopi" or "the culture of the Kamba," remember that these descriptions are abstractions from behavior; they are models, and they are usually both neater and simpler than the sometimes rather messy and confusing "designs for living" out there in the real world. Take them for what they are—honest attempts—but don't hesitate to take them with a grain or two of salt on occasion.

THE IMPORTANCE OF CULTURE

Let us return to the basic question of why culture is so important to the human animal. Among other things, culture is our fundamental technique for adaptation. All animals must adapt to the circumstances under which they live, and all animals must be able to adapt to changing situations. The alternative—not being able to cope—is extinction. Nonhuman animals primarily adapt biologically: They develop gills or fur or specialized digestive systems or whatever. They are certainly capable of some learning and can vary their lifeways to some extent, and this is particularly true of the higher mammals, such as the nonhuman primates. Nevertheless, in the long run, they depend upon bodily adjustments for survival. As animals, we too must adapt. We have some capacity for biological change; if we did not, we would all look like Australopithecines or Neanderthals. However, we can also alter our lifeways by changing our culture, and this is what we usually do. Instead of growing fur, we put on clothing. Instead of sprouting wings, we invent aircraft. Instead of changing our stomachs, we develop and process new kinds of food. This technique of cultural adaptation gives us a critical advantage; without it we might survive, but we would not dominate the planet as we do. We have a kind of built-in flexibility. Difficult as cultural change can sometimes be, it is both faster and easier than long-term biological changes.

A culture is a cumulative set of ideas that provides one society's answers to the basic problems of living. How do we obtain and distribute food? How do we ensure the survival of our children? How do we resolve conflicts within the group and between different groups? How do we know what to aim for in life? If the answers will not work, or if we can come up with better answers, we have the potential to change our cultures within a relatively brief period of time. This potential is probably not unlimited; we are primates, after all, and it is doubtful whether we can redesign our cultures in a wholly arbitrary fashion. Still, it is beyond dispute that we have a remarkable capacity for change. Our potential in this regard is greater than that of any other animal, and this is due to our cultural ways of living.

When we are enculturated—when we learn a culture—what exactly do we learn, and how do we learn it? We learn all of the specifics of the lifeway in which we participate. These may all be variations on a finite number of themes or basic principles, but the specific content of any particular cultural system must be learned. We have already seen that the human animal is equipped with a rather detailed program for the acquisition of language, but we still must learn the specifics of Kiowa or English or Kamba or whatever language we speak. Similarly, we all have kinship systems, but the details vary from one culture to another. All peoples have supernatural beliefs, but whether you get involved with a crocodile god or an ancestral spirit that lives in a tree depends on the culture you learn.

As far as the specifics are concerned—the things that make one culture different from another—we learn everything. We learn what kind of clothing to wear, what kind of shelters to live in, what kind of tools to make, and what kind of food to eat. We learn how we are expected to behave toward other people. The list is a long one, of course; a complete list would amount to nothing less than a total inventory of a cultural system. What needs to be stressed is that we learn many things that are not obvious.

Erich Fromm has said that one of the most important tasks undertaken by any culture is to make the people *want* to be what they *have* to be (Fromm 1941:252–253). That is, a culture inculcates values so that those who participate in a cultural system will desire to act in ways that are necessary or appropriate in that cultural context. Our very personalities and some of our deepest drives are to some degree taught to us by our cultures. These values and our orientation to the world we live in are integral parts of cultural systems.

All cultures include "customs" in the usual sense of the term. All cultures include a body of technical know-how. But no culture is simply a collection of rules about who tips a hat to whom and recipes about how to make a bow and arrow. Cultures are complex wholes, and part of their complexity involves the "juices" that make cultures go—the attitudes and beliefs that lie at the core of human motivational systems.

If we have so much to learn, how do we go about learning it? We learn some things through formal or conscious instruction. ("Look, son, *this* is the way you skin an antelope or throw a spear or grip a football.") We learn a tremendous amount through the medium of language. ("Listen carefully, daughter. Once upon a time there were two squirrels. Winter was coming on, and one squirrel. . . .") But we learn in many other ways as well. We learn by observation, by trial and error, by imitation, and by soaking up subtle nuances of the behavior we see around us.

Every parent knows that a child is a remarkably sensitive recording instrument. Children everywhere have a way of learning things that their parents don't want them to know. By no means all of this learning takes place on a conscious level, as we saw in connection with social space. A child—or an adult, for that matter—is surrounded by people doing things. From the cradle to the grave, we are influenced by what is going on around us. We learn from experience in the broadest possible sense, and the experiences we have are culturally conditioned. A Kamba child, for example, would be unlikely to learn anything from baseball for the simple reason that the Kamba don't play baseball. An American child, on the other hand, would not be apt to encounter a Masai warrior on the way to the waterhole.

Let us return to where we began. A culture is a design for living, a set of interconnected ideas that provides the guidelines for how people are going to live in a human society. We all must learn the cultures in which we are going to participate, and one of the most characteristic things about the human animal is that we learn far more of our lifeways than do other animals. An adult human being without culture is virtually a contradiction in terms; such a person could not function in any human society.

Every culture provides a kind of road map that tells us how to get to the local equivalent of the happy hunting ground. It tells us what we must do — and indeed what we must be — in order to operate effectively in the society of which we are a part.

SUMMARY

As far as anthropology is concerned, culture does not refer to nice manners and refinement. There is no distinction between "cultured" and "uncultured" unless one is referring to the difference between human beings and other animals. We learn vastly more of our lifeways than do other animals, and what we learn about how to live in a particular society is our culture. The process of learning a culture is called *enculturation*.

Clyde Kluckhohn has defined culture as "a design for living." It is a model of connected ideas that is shared to some extent by the members of a human society. A culture is a loose kind of mental blueprint that tells people what they can do or what they are supposed to do. In other words, the true locus of culture is in the human mind.

Cultures are not random grab bags of unrelated ideas. The components of a culture tend to be interconnected, which is why it is necessary to speak of cultural *systems*. It is important to remember that not all of culture operates on an overt and conscious level; much of it is covert and unconscious. Many ideas go so deep and are so taken for granted that they are seldom if ever verbalized.

It is impossible to study culture directly. A culture is a set of ideas, and the anthropologist cannot "see" ideas. You can observe people doing things — actions — and you can see the things that people have made. However, these actions and artifacts are not in themselves culture: They are the *products* of culture, or what people do in response to the ideas they have in their heads. This is what Robert Redfield meant when he said that culture was "manifest in act and artifact." Culture does not consist of acts and artifacts but shows itself in the actions that people perform and in the things they make.

To some extent, the anthropologist must try to infer the culture from what can be seen. However, asking questions is an essential part of finding out about culture. People can be asked to explain why they are doing what they do. This too can be tricky. People do not always know the reasons for their actions, and different people control different spheres of information.

In the final analysis, cultural descriptions are always abstractions from behavior. (After all, question-and-answer sessions are a kind of behavior also.) They are models which are intended to represent the cultural systems under investigation. A good model will be reasonably accurate, but the model is not and cannot be the culture itself.

Culture is our fundamental technique for adaptation. A culture is a cumulative set of ideas that provides one society's answers to the basic problems of living.

We learn all of the specifics of the lifeway in which we participate. This includes not only customs and technical skills but also values and an orientation toward the world we live in. We learn a great deal through formal instruction, and much cultural learning comes through the medium of language. However, we also learn in other ways: by observation, by trial and error, by imitation, and by soaking up subtle nuances of the behavior we see around us. We learn from experience, and the experiences we have are culturally conditioned.

References

Fromm, Erich. 1941. *Escape from Freedom.* New York: Holt, Rinehart and Winston.

Goodenough, Ward H. 1957. "Cultural Anthropology and Linguistics." *Georgetown University Monograph Series on Language and Linguistics* 9:167–173.

Hall, Edward T. 1959. *The Silent Language.* New York: Doubleday.

Harris, Marvin. 1974. *Cows, Pigs, Wars, and Witches.* New York: Random House.

Kluckhohn, Clyde, and William H. Kelly. 1945. "The Concept of Culture," in Ralph Linton (ed.), *The Science of Man in the World Crisis.* New York: Columbia University Press.

Kroeber, A. L., and Clyde Kluckhohn. 1952. *Culture: A Critical Review of Concepts and Definitions.* Peabody Museum Papers 47, 1. Cambridge, Mass.: Harvard University Press.

Suggestions for Further Reading

Beals, Ralph L., and Harry Hoijer. *An Introduction to Anthropology,* 4th ed. New York: Macmillan. One of the standard texts in the field, with a lucid chapter on culture.

Geertz, Clifford. 1965. "The Impact of the Concept of Culture on the Concept of Man," in John R. Platt (ed.), *New Views of Man.* University of Chicago Press. A somewhat different slant on culture treating culture as a symbolic system. Original and stimulating.

Goldschmidt, Walter. 1977. *Exploring the Ways of Mankind,* 3d ed. New York: Holt, Rinehart and Winston. A well-selected book of readings with extensive introductory sections by Goldschmidt. The discussion of culture is both clear and insightful.

Harris, Marvin. 1974. "Why a Perfect Knowledge of All the Rules One Must Know to Act Like a Native Cannot Lead to the Knowledge of How Natives Act." *Journal of Anthropological Research* 30(4):242–251. A provocative article that challenges some basic anthropological assumptions about culture and how it should be studied.

Keesing, Roger M. 1976. *Cultural Anthropology: A Contemporary Perspective.* New York: Holt, Rinehart and Winston. One of the more recent texts, this one is consistently interesting and the treatment of culture is particularly good.

White, Leslie A. 1949. *The Science of Culture.* New York: Farrar, Straus and Giroux. A challenging interpretation of culture as a superorganic phenomenon. Extreme in its views, but White is an excellent writer, and this book should make you think.

9

How It Works: Some Characteristics of Cultural Systems

Walter Goldschmidt once observed that "cultures differ more than people" (Goldschmidt 1956:98). He meant that there is more variation between cultural systems than there is in the actual behavior of the peoples who participate in different cultures. He might have added—although he didn't—that it is a commonplace of anthropology for a field investigator to encounter people in a different culture who remind one very strongly of people back home, wherever home might be. The details and the costumes and the nuances vary, but human beings are never totally alien. There, in a different cultural setting, one can spot the clever operator, the hasty man of impulse, the flirt, the homemaker who tries to hold everything together, the dreamer, the intellectual, the suspicious, the trusting, the loner, and so on. This should perhaps not be very startling—we are all human beings, after all—but it sometimes comes as a bit of a surprise because of another point made by Goldschmidt:

> It seems as if the culture tends often to fix on extremes, though I sometimes suspect that it is the ethnographer who fixes on the extreme and not the culture. . . . We have not entirely dissipated what one of my colleagues calls the "Oh-how-quaint School of Anthropology" in our literary emphasis upon the unusual. (Goldschmidt 1956:100)

It is possible that the traditional anthropological insistence on the total distinctiveness of each and every human lifeway has served to obscure an important fact: There are similarities as well as differences between the human lifeways of this earth. It is true that in one sense every culture is unique; no single cultural system is exactly like any other. It is also true that there are cultural universals:

things that are characteristic of *all* cultural systems. To some degree, it depends upon the level of the analysis. Are we to be more impressed by the variation between one kinship system and another (see Chapters 14, 15, and 16), or by the fact that all human societies have kinship systems? Are we to stress the differences between one human language and another, or the fact that all human beings have language? It seems to me that both viewpoints are demonstrably correct, and therefore both must be taken into account in trying to understand cultural systems and how they work.

Eventually, we may have to revise Goldschmidt's observation to read: "Cultures differ more than people—and cultures themselves may not be as radically different as we have been led to believe."

There are some aspects of cultural systems that are probably species-specific—directly related to the kind of animal that we are. This is not a new idea in anthropology, although until recently it has not received the attention it deserves. As long ago as 1923, Clark Wissler was outlining what he called "the universal culture pattern" (Wissler 1923:74). In 1945, George Peter Murdock published an important article entitled "The Common Denominator of Cultures" (Murdock 1945:123–142). In it, Murdock listed over 70 items common to all known cultures, including such things as age grading, athletic sports, cosmology, courtship, dancing, divination, food taboos, hairstyles, inheritance rules, magic, marriage, soul concepts, status differentiation, and so on. Necessarily, these are broad categories; it goes without saying that the specific content varies from one culture to another. Nevertheless, Murdock argued that there was something more involved here than a mere artifact of classification. He concluded that the basis of the "universal pattern" was substantial and could "only be sought, therefore, in the fundamental biological and psychological nature of man and in the universal conditions of human existence."

By 1949 we find Clyde Kluckhohn stating:

> The very fact that certain of the same institutions are found in all known societies indicates that at bottom all human beings are very much alike. . . . The biological potentialities of the species are the blocks with which cultures are built. Some patterns of every culture crystallize around focuses provided by the inevitables of biology: the difference between the sexes, the presence of persons of different ages, the varying physical strength and skill of individuals. The facts of nature also limit culture forms. No culture provides patterns for jumping over trees or for eating iron ore. There is thus no "either-or" between nature and that special form of nurture called culture. Culture determinism is as one-sided as biological determinism. The two factors are interdependent. Culture arises out of human nature, and its forms are restricted both by man's biology and by natural laws. It is equally true that culture channels biological processes. (Kluckhohn 1949:20–21)

A minority of modern anthropologists would argue that all major cultural features have their roots in the biology of the species. Again, they are not speaking of the specific content of cultural systems but rather of broad outlines and ingredients. They sometimes employ the image of a rubber sheet. It can be stretched and poked and twisted in a variety of ways, but still the sheet is the same, and there are limits to how far it can be pulled.

Two anthropologists with the rather unlikely names of Lionel Tiger and Robin Fox have advocated this general point of view. After discussing the relationship between the human "language-acquisition device" and the variety of particular human languages it makes possible, they state:

> In the same way, *all* the rest of human culture lies in the biology of the species. We have a *culture-acquisition device* constraining us to produce recognizable and analyzable human cultures, just as we must produce recognizable human languages, however varied the local manifestations may be. Just as a child can learn only a language that follows the "normal" rules of grammar for human languages, he can learn only a grammar of behavior that follows the parallel rules of the biogrammar. Of course, in either case, a departure from normal grammar may be tried, but the likelihood is that it will end only in gibberish. (Tiger and Fox 1971:13)

This is an extreme but provocative way of looking at it. It should neither be dismissed out of hand nor swallowed whole without further proof. Ideally, it should be a problem to be investigated rather than a position to be violently attacked or defended.

I believe that there are three propositions about this aspect of cultural systems that merit serious consideration. They are:

1. Despite the obvious differences between one culture and another, there are cultural universals. Since these are species-specific, they are probably related to the kind of animal that we are.
2. In their fascination with detailed cultural differences, anthropologists have probably suffered from what Robin Fox has aptly termed "ethnographic dazzle" (Fox 1971). This merely means that we have sometimes failed to see the forest for the trees: The preoccupation with surface detail has obscured the deeper similarities between one culture and another.
3. In discussing what he calls "the psychobiological character of man," Walter Goldschmidt has called attention to a fundamental fact: "We cannot create a model of society without consideration of the nature of the elements out of which it is made, and certainly one of these elements is mankind itself" (Goldschmidt 1966:33–34). At the same time, Goldschmidt stresses a crucial cautionary note: "Nothing that is biological in man is *ever* *merely* biological. All creature characteristics that enter into human action are involved in man's symbolic system; i.e., in cultural interpretation" (Goldschmidt 1966:48).

It is this latter point which now requires discussion.

THE CULTURAL CONTEXT

As far as the human animal is concerned, there is seldom if ever a direct and unmodified interaction between the biological organism on the one hand and the nonhuman environment on the other. We are not like cows grazing on a field of grass. There is almost always a third factor in the human equation, and that factor is culture.

No matter how basic the human activity is, its expression can be and usually is influenced by cultural considerations. Indeed, it is difficult to imagine any action performed by human beings that cannot be affected by the cultural context in which it occurs. Take a tough one like breathing, for example. The rate at which we breathe obviously depends on what we are doing—running, sitting, climbing a tree, swimming, embracing a lover—and all of these activities have a cultural component. We can even stop breathing. We can hold our breath so as not to reveal our position; we can hold it longer until we faint, a technique employed in some cultures to induce visions. We can foul the air we breathe until it is a threat to human life. We can carry oxygen underwater and breathe it in a controlled way. We can create mixtures of gasses different from those we normally breathe, as in the artificial atmospheres in a space capsule. We can check the breathing rate of a sick person and then treat that person according to some theory of disease.

Nothing is more basic than eating, but nobody just eats. What we eat, how we eat, and when we eat are all profoundly influenced by our cultures. The chances are excellent that you will never get hungry for cattle blood mixed with milk and seasoned with a little urine or that you will hunger for a raw chunk of seal blubber. These foods are eaten and relished by the Masai of East Africa and the Eskimo, respectively. Conversely, many peoples would regard such things as spaghetti out of a can or a hamburger as inedible. How we eat is more than a matter of what utensils we use, if any. Do men and women eat together, or separately? (In the Trobriand Islands, it is perfectly proper for an unmarried man and an unmarried woman to spend the night together and have sexual relations, but it is unthinkable for them to share a meal.) What about the children? Do they eat with their parents, or are they fed apart from the adults? In many parts of Europe, the American custom of having the kids join the adults at the dinner table is regarded as downright uncivilized. In this culture, we usually have three meals a day. If we miss one of them, we figure that we are in danger of starving to death. Every American professor who teaches a class at noon knows where the minds of the students are: You can sometimes hear the stomachs grumbling clear across the lecture hall. Other cultures do it differently: There may be two meals a day or one or catch-as-catch-can. Hunting peoples often go for days without a substantial meal and then gorge themselves; they may eat astonishing amounts of meat at a single sitting and then regurgitate and eat some more.

Of course, what we eat must sustain life, but beyond that almost anything goes. (Note that we can even refuse to eat for cultural reasons. A man or woman can go on a hunger strike to make a political point; it is quite possible to starve yourself to death. On a less extreme level, we have cultural ideals of what is physically attractive and what is not. If the ideal is to be buxom, we stuff ourselves. If it is to be slim, we torture ourselves with bizarre eating habits called diets.) What is acceptable as food and what is not often has little or nothing to do with nutrition. All cultures have some food tabus, denying foods that others find perfectly palatable. These tabus have considerable psychological force: A clan member forced to eat the totem animal of the clan will become violently ill, just as a confirmed vegetarian might if force-fed a slab of roast beef. Consider human flesh, for instance. Nobody doubts that human meat will support life as well as pork, to pick just one example. (In fact, human flesh was called ''long pig'' in certain parts of the Pacific when cannibalism was practiced; it is said to taste rather like pork.) Take the classic story of the desperate Arctic explorers trying to make it back to the base camp. They are starving and out of food. One of them dies. Should the survivors eat the meat and survive, or should they refrain and perish? Whatever answer you give — or they gave — it has nothing to do with nutrition. It depends on what you have been taught and what you believe, which is another way of saying that it depends on your culture.

I find accounts of extreme survival situations — shipwrecks, people adrift in a lifeboat, people lost in the desert, survivors of air crashes in remote areas — very revealing in this regard. People don't just get hungry: They get hungry for very specific kinds of food. Read the records; they are a gourmet's fantasy, with the particular fantasy depending on the person's cultural background. There was a fascinating event of this kind in 1972. A plane took off from Uruguay for Chile carrying a rugby team. It crashed high in the snows of the Andes. There were 45 people on board. Some 10 weeks later, 16 survivors were finally rescued. They had survived by eating the flesh of their dead companions, but what is much more interesting involves their thoughts of food. Understandably, they thought of it nearly all the time. They began by remembering the meals they had eaten at home, and then they made a list of all the restaurants they knew. They reconstructed menus of their favorite dishes, and they ordered elaborate imaginary meals item by item. The meals were specific to the last detail, even to the proper wine to serve with each feast. They could not get away from it even when they slept: Strawberry milkshakes invaded their dreams (Read 1974:159–162).

Much of the same point can be made about sex. Sexual drives are innate, of course, but their expression is shaped by cultural considerations. There is no need to spell this out in explicit detail, but a moment's reflection will show you how much cultural pressure there is in this area. Attitudes toward sex vary a good deal from culture to culture, and it is a mistake — although a very common one — to imagine that all primitive societies have an ideal of sexual freedom. The Yurok of California believed that sex was unclean (Goldschmidt 1951). The Cheyenne are described as sexually repressed (Hoebel 1960:20). The Kamba stated that it was irrelevant whether or not a woman enjoyed sex, and they thought it was funny when we asked whether a man ever tried to give his wife sexual pleasure. It is not only attitudes and techniques that are welcomed or frowned upon. Everywhere, people have strong feelings about when sex is appropriate, and where, and with whom. It may also be noted that sexual urges may be denied for cultural reasons: A person can choose to remain celibate, for example. It is difficult to think of any other animal that would behave in this manner.

Most of what we do in our lives we do as cultural beings. Regardless of the ultimate origins of culture and regardless of the linkages between some aspects of culture and the biology of the species, the way culture works is to shape and condition the actions and beliefs of human beings. We are culture-bearing animals, and as such there is little that we can do that is not subjected to cultural pressure and cultural interpretation.

The Cultural Triangle

In the last half century or so, one of the most important contributions of anthropology has been the discovery and documentation of the fact that cultures are not mere random assortments of unrelated ideas. In any culture, the design for living has a kind of unity to it: The major parts must all fit together and work together. We touched on this idea in the preceding chapter, and now it is time to examine it more closely.

The analogy is sometimes made that a culture is like an organism. It is not a bad analogy if you do not take it too literally. It suggests that you cannot take the head of a horse, the wings of a fly, and the body of a rat and combine them into a workable animal even if your name is Dr. Frankenstein and you have a singularly well-equipped laboratory. The components of a cultural system are interrelated and must function together. No matter how you slice up the cultural pie, there are connections between one part of a culture and another.

The fact that cultures are systems implies that what affects one part of a culture is likely to affect the rest of the culture as well. Simply for convenience, it is useful to think of the major components of culture as being arranged in a triangular shape (Titiev 1954).

Think of this cultural triangle (see Figure 9.1) as having some degree of flexibility to it: It is not static and frozen. Imagine that there are spring joints where the lines meet and that the lines themselves have some capacity to shrink or elongate. Without getting overly literal about it, remember that if one side of the triangle changes this will produce changes in the other sides as well: The angles will change and so will the lengths of the lines. The triangle represents a system, and the interactions within the system result in accommodations throughout the system whenever a basic alteration is introduced in a major cultural component. To spell it out in plain English, for example, one would expect that a fundamental change in values would change the character of both technology and sociopolitical organization. In theory, it does not matter where you start: A change in one part of the system produces changes in the other parts.

The most dramatic demonstration of this point involves a people called the

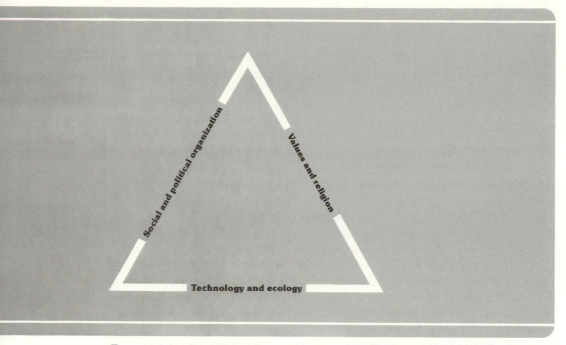

Figure 9.1 A cultural triangle.

Yir Yoront. This discussion is based on a classic article by Lauriston Sharp entitled "Steel Axes for Stone-Age Australians" (Sharp 1952).

The Yir Yoront were a hunting and gathering group who lived on the Cape York Peninsula of Australia. They had no domesticated animals except the dog, and metal tools were unknown to them. One of their most important artifacts was a polished stone axe hafted on a short wooden handle.

Only an elder male could make or own one of these stone axes. This principle was established by Yir Yoront supernatural beliefs: The idea of the "maleness" of the stone axes had been handed down from the mythical sacred world of the ancestors. The stone axes were symbols of mature masculinity, rather like the six-shooter in the old American West or the forked wooden staffs carried by Kamba elders. Anyone, including women and children, could use a stone axe — the women and children were just prohibited from making or owning them. In order to use a stone axe, a woman or a child had to borrow one from an adult male. Essentially, the borrowing followed kinship lines: A woman would borrow from her husband, a younger brother from an older brother, and so on.

Everything needed to make a stone axe was available in the territory of the Yir Yoront with one major exception. They had the wood for the handle, the bark which was rolled into cord for binding, and the gum which served as a kind of glue. What they did not have was the proper stone used for the axe head itself. The stone came from quarries located some 400 miles inland. In order to get the stones, the Yir Yoront males depended on a rather elaborate trading network. There were long lines of trading partners extending between the Yir Yoront and the stone quarries. Virtually all adult males had a male trading partner in the groups on both sides of him. These men regarded one another as brothers, and the relationship was critical both in maintaining good relations between neighboring groups and in bringing people together in large-scale multigroup ceremonies. (Trading networks of this sort are by no means unusual among primitive peoples, by the way. Objects were often exchanged over great distances, passing through many hands and many peoples before reaching their final destination. As a rule, items from remote areas arrived through trading between contiguous groups rather than as a result of prolonged expeditions.)

Anyone could use the stone axe for secular, everyday activities such as cutting firewood or chopping wild roots. However, in a sacred or ceremonial context only men from one particular clan could exhibit the stone axe. In the mythology of the Yir Yoront, the stone axes were intimately connected to the clan ancestors, and in important ceremonies the stone axe represented the clan.

Into this basic situation there was introduced a strange new item: Missionaries arrived upon the scene with modern steel axes. While it would be misleading to suggest that the steel axes were the only disruptive force acting on the Yir Yoront culture, they were certainly a major factor. Technologically speaking, the new steel axes were an improvement — they worked better and they lasted longer than the stone axes. To the missionaries, the steel axes represented "progress." The missionaries handed out the steel axes as gifts to those who visited the missions or who worked for the missions. Among the Yir Yoront as elsewhere, old men tend to be conservative. The elder males would have nothing to do with the missions and hence received no steel axes. Nearly everyone else got them: young men, women, even children. Moreover, the new steel axes *belonged* to these people: A child or a woman could *own* a steel axe, which would have been unthinkable with the stone axes that were owned and controlled by the older men.

In time, the effects of this were profound. The authority of males was generally undermined. (Recall that the old stone axes were symbols of masculinity, and now even a woman could own a steel axe that was demonstrably better.) The prestige of age was diminished; young men had the steel axes and old men did not. Family life was disrupted. A wife no longer had to defer to her husband to use an axe, and the father lost much of his leverage over his sons; there were cases in which sons refused to undergo the painful initiation ceremonies by which they became — socially — adult men.

Whether these changes were "good" or "bad" depends on your point of view, which is itself a cultural product. The point is that the changes did in fact occur. The old trading network between elder men was weakened. Stone axes no longer mattered very much, and the network tended to fade away as old men died and were not replaced. These trade relationships between "brothers" had been important in keeping up friendly relationships between neighboring groups. With confusing new patterns of ownership, theft became more common. The clan lost its sacred symbol. More critically, there was a break between the Yir Yoront and their mythological past—the ancestors had no steel axes. With the collapse of their ideological system, the Yir Yoront became an apathetic people.

Let us glance back at our cultural triangle. In the case of the Yir Yoront, we can see how a well-intentioned alteration in one part of the cultural system—the technology—reverberated throughout the culture. Values and religion were shattered. Social relations, as in the structure of family life, were strained to the breaking point. Even the politics of dealing with neighboring groups—foreign policy, if you will—were called into question.

The interconnections between the parts of a cultural system are perhaps most obvious in the case of a small-scale culture like that of the Yir Yoront. However, the same principle applies to all cultures. Reflect for a moment on what has happened to the culture of the United States since the introduction of the automobile. It is difficult to think of an area of our lifeway that has not been affected by the automobile. It is no accident that most American youngsters know the difference between a Ford, a Chevrolet, and a Plymouth even if they do not have a clue about the names of the congressional representatives from their state.

Our living patterns are shaped by cars: A city like Los Angeles could not exist without automobiles. We eat in cars, go to movies in cars, make love in cars. Think of the influence the automobile has had on dating behavior. It is one thing for a boy to "court" a girl in the parlor of her home with her parents lurking in the background; it is something else to pick her up in a car and be 50 miles away in less than an hour. The tourist industry runs on cars, and it is the major industry in some of our states. The whole economy rises or falls with the sale of automobiles. The automobile is a status marker and reveals much about its owner. If you are thumbing on the highway, are your chances of catching a ride better with the driver of Lincoln Continental or a VW bus? We discussed the foreign policy of the Yir Yoront. Consider our own. How much influence has the sources and prices of oil had on how we deal with other nations? What would happen to our culture if the oil stopped and the cars could not run?

In thinking about cultures, it is essential to bear in mind that cultures are systems. The design for living is not composed of unrelated oddments of belief and custom. The whole thing must work together, and when change occurs in one sector it may have unanticipated consequences in another.

"Ideal" versus "Real" Culture

As a teacher of anthropology, it has been my experience that when students first encounter the concept of culture they have a tendency to think of cultures as being much more rigid and monolithic than in fact they are. The design for living becomes a kind of straitjacket that dictates every action and every attitude. The image that comes to mind is very much like a formula: Given situation X, you will perform activity 44–B and feel emotion 72–D. Human beings become nothing but puppets jerked around on all-powerful cultural wires.

Frequently, this notion persists until a student actually does fieldwork and experiences the reality of a different cultural system. Although not usually discussed in this context, this expectation is one of the causes of what has been termed "culture shock." (Stripped of its baggage of jargon, culture shock is basically the feeling of unease or anxiety a person experiences when new cultural surroundings do not seem to make sense. You do not know why the people around you are acting as they do, and consequently you do not know how to behave yourself.) Confronted with the often messy and confusing realities of actual cultural systems, we search for the magic key that will make everything neat and simple and predictable. If we do not find that magic key, we interpret this as a failure on our part. (You would be surprised to learn how many budding anthropologists have turned back in despair after just such an experience. They were the honest ones, of course.) We need to remember, always, that the "cultures" we read about in ethnographies are models, abstractions from behavior, and as such they are invariably neater and more understandable than real cultural systems. In a word, the models are necessarily simplified; they tend to leave out the blurred edges, the contradictions, the fuzzy areas, and the sometimes bewildering performances of individual human beings.

In the first place, there is always the distinction that must be made between the rules of the game and the way the game is actually played. The rules of the game are normative statements of what people in a given cultural system are supposed to do. Some anthropologists refer to this as "ideal" culture. To discover how the game is actually played, you must observe what people in fact do in particular situations. Some anthropologists call this "real" culture. In my opinion, there is no such thing as a human society with a perfect fit between what people say they do and what they really do. Usually, this has little or nothing to do with dishonesty. Rather, it involves the way cultures work. The guidelines are there, but they cannot be totally rigid. No culture can anticipate every conceivable permutation of every possible situation, to say nothing of the peculiarities of individual human beings.

"It is very hard to be a real Kamba," I was often told. "Nobody follows all the rules." Consider the "rule" of residence, for example. (A rule of residence concerns where people are supposed to live after they marry.) In ideal terms, this was simple enough for the Kamba. At the time of marriage, the bride left her household and moved into the household of her husband's family. The Kamba even had a saying about it. "A son is like the center-post of a house," they stated. "He stays put. A daughter is like a bird—she flies away." So far, so good. It soon became apparent, in constructing census maps of several Kamba communities and figuring out who lived where, that this ideal pattern was often violated. Not all sons remained at home—they could not because of the amount and location of available land. Sometimes, a new residence was established in a different community. Sometimes, the man would have a job in a city like Nairobi and his wife remained with her parents. The "rule" of residence turned out to be a general statement of reasonable expectation: It's a good thing if it works out that way, other things being equal, but in fact other things are not always equal, and it is not always possible or even desirable. It is a guideline, not an inflexible command.

The analogy here between the rules of the game and the way the game is actually played is a useful one. Whether the game involved is poker, chess, or football, we all know that the likelihood of two actual games being identical is remote. Moreover, the more players there are and the more room to maneuver, the less the chances are that any two contests will be the same. I doubt very much that any football game has ever been played that was exactly like another, despite the fact that the rules are the same. This is one thing that makes games, like life itself, interesting. What makes one game different from another is not that the rules are broken, although they sometimes are, but rather that actual performance cannot be completely predicted by the rules. Weather conditions, injuries, the abilities of various players, training, and motivation can all affect the outcome. Culture is like that: The rules of the game are there and set broad outlines, but the way people live their lives is something else again.

For another thing, cultural injunctions or rules are not all of the same type. To use Clyde Kluckhohn's terminology (Kluckhohn 1941), some rules are indeed *compulsory* for all the participants in a cultural system. In our culture, murder is wrong, incest is wrong, and child abuse is wrong. Other cultural dictates, however, allow more latitude. They may simply be *preferred* — several courses of action are acceptable, but one is more highly valued than the rest. They may be *typical* — several ways of behaving are okay, but one is more often chosen than the others. There may be *alternative* rules — there is more than one "right" way to do things, and there is no detectable differences either in value or in frequency of expression. Finally, there can be *restricted* rules which apply only to certain segments of a society. For example, there are codes of conduct appropriate for children but not for adults, and there are particular clubs or religious groups which have expectations not shared by the total society.

Culture and Subculture

Primitive cultures are not always as uniform and homogeneous as they are sometimes pictured. There may be considerable variation between one group and another even though they have the "same" general culture. However, it is true that this problem becomes more acute when societies become larger and more complex. In state-organized societies like the Inca of Peru or the Baganda of Uganda there were distinct differences between the lifeways of the rulers and the peasant farmers or between one group of specialists and another. In the culture of the United States, it is obvious that there are cultural differences between rich and poor, between city dwellers and rural people, between one part of the country and another, between one ethnic group and another. If you move, say, from the inner city of Chicago to a small town in Texas you will find that the cultures are by no means identical.

Anthropologists call these variations within a larger cultural system *subcultures*. The much discussed and highly visible counterculture in the United States can be interpreted as a kind of subculture: it is restricted to a segment of the population, it is largely centered within certain age brackets, and it is distinguished by characteristic dress styles, occupations, and values. The term *subculture,* of course, carries with it no connotation of good or bad, superior or inferior.

It merely refers to a particular manifestation of cultural attributes within a larger cultural system.

Finally, on this matter of variation within cultures, I would suggest that "cultures may differ significantly with respect to tightness of organization, flexibility, and capacity and readiness for change" (Oliver 1965:422). That is, some cultures permit or encourage more alternative ways of doing things than do others. No culture can be so rigid that alternatives within the system do not exist, and no culture can be so fluid that there is no structure at all. However, within the realm of the culturally possible, some cultures are relatively elastic, some are relatively rigid, and many others are somewhere in between. This means that it is probably an error to expect that all participants in a given cultural system will behave in precisely the same way, and it is also a mistake to assume that there is no flexibility in a culture. Apart from the difference between the rules of the game and the way the game is actually played—and apart from subcultural variation—the culture itself may suggest or require a good deal of individual interpretation and choice. This does not mean that a person is ever independent of his or her culture; indeed, the very idea of "free will" is profoundly culture bound. Rather, it means that there is more latitude within cultural systems than is commonly believed. There are cultural limits, and no human being can function in a wholly spontaneous cultural vacuum this side of never-never land; but people are not entirely puppets—there is always room to maneuver.

Cultural Relativism

No discussion of the concept of culture, I suppose, can avoid the problem of *cultural relativism.* Indeed, many people regard the idea of cultural relativity as the major contribution of anthropology to human thought.

Definitions vary, as usual, but Walter Goldschmidt put it this way:

> In naive form, cultural relativism asserts that all peoples, all cultures, are equally good: if they be cannibals, well, that's not for me, but *de gustibus.* . . . In more sophisticated form it asserts that each culture must be valued in its own terms: does it satisfy the people themselves? If they are cannibals, what satisfactions does eating human flesh supply in terms of native values? (Goldschmidt 1959:225)

The doctrine of cultural relativism was developed to combat the thesis of *ethnocentrism,* the belief that one's own lifeway was superior to all others and that different cultures could be "judged" according to the ethical standards of the observer. Obviously, an ethnocentric viewpoint has no place in anthropology—if other cultures have little or no value, there is not much point in studying them. Trying to understand a culture in its own terms is an essential part of the anthropological enterprise.

On one level, the idea of cultural relativism—or something like it—is both useful and perhaps necessary. An anthropologist in the field cannot go about exclaiming, "How monstrous! How awful! Why, you people are *terrible.*" Moreover, the anthropologist cannot think this way either. There is no hope of understanding how a culture works if it is approached with contempt or loathing. At the very least, a suspension of judgment is required. With few exceptions, anthropologists have tended to err on the positive side if neutrality was impossible. The cultures they studied were "remarkable," "brilliant," and "wonderful" if they were characterized at all. The essence of the idea goes far beyond anthropology, of course. Whenever people travel — even into the household across the street — they may encounter ways of doing things different from their own. Certainly, in these situations, one would be well advised to treat other people and other ideas with respect.

Why, then, is there a problem? The problem occurs on another level. One of the most articulate supporters of the doctrine of cultural relativity, Melville J. Herskovits, argued that cultural relativism was a *philosophy* and that it asserted "the validity of *every* set of norms for the people whose lives are guided by them, and the values these represent" (Herskovits 1951:76).

Carried to its logical conclusion, this is a chilling philosophy, and it makes many anthropologists distinctly uncomfortable. As a philosophy, it holds that one way of doing things is always as good as another way and that there is no basis for ethical choice. Walter Goldschmidt, whose characterization of cultural relativism was cited above, was one of the first anthropologists to call attention to this problem.

It is one thing to try to understand a culture in its own terms and recognize its values. It is quite another thing to stand idly by and watch Nazis stacking human beings in gas ovens, saying only: "Well, that's the way they do things in that culture." There is no easy solution. On the one hand, cultural relativism leads ultimately to moral impotence. On the other hand, it is axiomatic that we can make value judgments only in the context of the values in which we believe.

Perhaps Roger M. Keesing has best summed up the current status of the problem. He wrote:

> Here then lies a dilemma. For much of the conflict and injustice in the modern world has been caused precisely by the powerful seeking to impose their values and ideologies on one another and on the weak — to spread their particular vision of the good life. How then can we transcend ethical relativism without committing the obverse, ethical imperialism?
>
> There is no simple answer. Many anthropologists would urge that cultural relativism is not a position one can ultimately live with — but that it is a position one needs to pass through in search of a clearer vision. By wandering in a desert of relativism, one can sort the profound from the trivial, examine one's motives and conscience and one's customs and beliefs. Like all vision quests, it can be lonely and dangerous; but it can lead to heightened perceptions of ourselves, of what it is to be human, and of what humans could be if they would. In a world where people foist their political dogmas and religious faiths on one another,

where modern ideological inquisitions save souls by dispatching them
with flame and lead, we sorely need such wisdom. (Keesing 1976:179)

SUMMARY

There is a sense in which *every* culture is unique: No individual culture is
exactly like any other. It is also true that there are *cultural universals* characteristic of all cultural systems. There are some aspects of cultural systems that are
probably species-specific, related to the kind of animal that we are.

No matter how basic the human activity is, its expression can be and usually is influenced by cultural considerations. It is difficult to find any action performed by human beings—breathing, eating, mating—that is not affected by the
cultural context within which it occurs.

One of the most important discoveries made by anthropology has been
the fact that the components of a cultural system are interrelated and must function together. This idea is sometimes illustrated by means of a *cultural triangle*. If
the sides of the triangle are designated to represent technology and ecology (on
one side), social and political organization (on another side), and values and religion (on the third side), then it is apparent that a fundamental change on one
side will produce changes in the rest of the triangle as well. This is simply another
way of saying that the parts of a cultural system are interconnected.

A well-known study by Lauriston Sharp demonstrates this point. When
steel axes were introduced to the Yir Yoront—an Australian people who had
previously used only stone axes—this triggered a series of cultural changes that
involved the relationship between males and females, the supernatural, and the
interactions between the Yir Yoront and neighboring groups.

There is a tendency to think of cultures as being more rigid and monolithic
than they actually are. There is some degree of flexibility in any cultural system,
and there is always a distinction between the rules of the game and the way the
game is actually played. Moreover, cultural rules or injunctions are not all of the
same type. As Clyde Kluckhohn has pointed out, they range from compulsory
rules to others that may be merely preferred or alternative.

Cultural systems are not always as uniform as they are sometimes pictured.
Even among participants in the "same" general culture, there may be considerable variation between one group and another. Anthropologists refer to these
variations within a cultural system as *subcultures*.

The doctrine of *cultural relativism* asserts that each culture must be understood in its own terms: Cultures cannot be "judged" according to the ethical
standards of an outside observer. As an attitude toward fieldwork or as a point of
view in trying to find out how a given culture works, this is not only acceptable
but probably necessary. However, as a philosophy of life, cultural relativism
poses some serious problems. If one way of doing things is as good as another
and there is no basis for ethical choice, this can only lead to a kind of moral impotence. Conversely, we can only make value judgments in the context of the
values in which we happen to believe. There is no easy way out of this dilemma.

Perhaps the best provisional hope is that we will at least recognize the standards that we are using in particular situations and understand why we are using them.

References

Fox, Robin. 1971. "The Cultural Animal," in John F. Eisenberg and Wilton S. Dillon (eds.), *Man and Beast: Comparative Social Behavior.* Washington, D.C.: The Smithsonian Institution Press.

Goldschmidt, Walter. 1951. "Ethics and the Structure of Society." *American Anthropologist* 53(4):506–524.

———. 1956. "Culture and Human Behavior," in Anthony F. C. Wallace (ed.), *Selected Papers of the Fifth International Congress of Anthropological and Ethnological Sciences.* Philadelphia: University of Pennsylvania Press.

———. 1959. *Man's Way.* New York: Holt, Rinehart and Winston.

———. 1966. *Comparative Functionalism.* Berkeley and Los Angeles: University of California Press.

Herskovits, Melville J. 1951. *Man and His Works.* New York: Knopf.

Hoebel, E. Adamson. 1960. *The Cheyennes.* New York: Holt, Rinehart and Winston.

Keesing, Roger M. 1976. *Cultural Anthropology: A Contemporary Perspective.* New York: Holt, Rinehart and Winston.

Kluckhohn, Clyde. 1941. "Patterning in Navaho Culture," in Leslie Spier (ed.), *Language, Culture, and Personality.* Menasha, Wis.: Sapir Publication Memorial Fund.

———. 1949. *Mirror for Man.* New York: Whittlesey House.

Murdock, George Peter. 1945. "The Common Denominator of Cultures," in Ralph Linton (ed.), *The Science of Man in the World Crisis.* New York: Columbia University Press.

Oliver, Symmes C. 1965. "Individuality, Freedom of Choice, and Cultural Flexibility of the Kamba." *American Anthropologist* 67(2):421–428.

Read, Piers Paul. 1974. *Alive: The Story of the Andes Survivors.* Philadelphia: Lippincott.

Sharp, Lauriston. 1952. "Steel Axes for Stone-Age Australians." *Human Organization* 11(No. 1):17–22.

Tiger, Lionel, and Robin Fox. 1971. *The Imperial Animal.* New York: Holt, Rinehart and Winston.

Titiev, Mischa. 1954. *The Science of Man.* New York: Holt, Rinehart and Winston.

Wissler, Clark. 1923. *Man and Culture.* New York: Crowell.

10

Prehistory:
The Roads Behind Us

It is not my purpose here to present a chronology of artifact types or to explore the details of the archeological record of the human animal. This cannot be done within the confines of a single chapter; indeed, it would be a challenging assignment to try to accomplish it in a single book. My aim is different, if not necessarily more modest. I want to characterize in very general terms the major features of our collective past. I want to give one answer to a basic question: What is it that is *essential* to know about the pathways behind us in order to arrive at a glimmer of understanding about the modern conditions of mankind?

This in itself is no small undertaking. It is not offered as dogma but rather for what it is: one view of the lessons that can be learned from a study of the anthropological record. Other viewpoints are most certainly possible, and I have deliberately avoided direct entanglements with the conflicting theories of assorted experts. At the same time, by confining myself to broad features that are generally agreed upon, I hope that I have not falsified the record in any way. After all, this is *our* past that we are talking about — yours as well as mine — and it is important that we get our facts straight.

We would not be human if we had no opinions of our own, no matter how general the materials. In looking back upon where we have been, I have not hesitated to express some of mine. In all cases, I have sought to make clear what is fact and what is interpretation or commentary. The roads behind us are very long. Let us retrace our steps together.

MANKIND BEFORE CULTURE?

Millions of years ago, in the sunshine of the savannas and the shadows of the warm forests, our remote ancestors made the transition from primitive apes to primitive hominids. We know that this occurred somewhere in the tropical areas of the Old World, and we know that it happened sometime in the Miocene epoch, which began some 25 million years ago.

We have a name for this earliest known population of hominids: *Ramapithecus*. But we should not delude ourselves by confusing a few fragmentary fossils and a fancy name with detailed factual knowledge. The truth of the matter is that *Ramapithecus* does not speak to us very clearly down the long corridors of time, and most of what it says is composed of large question marks.

Did these animals have a culture in any meaningful sense of the term? Were they capable of language? Did they use tools? Were they erect or semierect bipedal walkers, leaving their hands free for other activities? How complex were their brains?

We do not know, and we may never know. We have a few clues to work on, and that is all. We know something about their dentition, we know what their descendants were like, and we know a good deal about the behavior of modern apes. (If we ourselves are closely related biologically to the chimpanzee and the gorilla, it would seem logical to assume that *Ramapithecus* was as close or even closer.)

Two basic facts demand our attention. First, these populations can be distinguished anatomically from early ape populations. They are hominids, not apes. Second, they do not have the large projecting canine teeth that are characteristic of apes.

With these facts in mind, the rest is conjecture. It seems to me highly unlikely that these populations had truly cultural lifeways. We can grant them at best a kind of embryonic culture or protoculture. Even when we realize that the biological changes which produced these first hominids could not have been swift or sudden, there must have been a time when these populations were hominids physically but did not yet possess true cultures.

It is pointless to ask whether or not such animals could have survived; they obviously did or we would not be here today. Culture by its very nature cannot appear overnight. It is a cumulative thing, and judging by the cultures that existed even millions of years later, its initial development must have been very slow. The conclusion seems inescapable that these first hominids must have made a go of it essentially without culture.

This idea goes directly counter to much traditional wisdom. One of the great cliches of the modern world is that the human animal would not have a chance without culture. How often we hear the familiar phrases: "Physically, we are nothing much. Human beings are relatively small, weak, and helpless animals. We don't have the eye of the eagle, the strength of the elephant, the claws of the lion, the speed of the antelope, and so on and so forth. All we have is culture, and that has made the difference."

Well, there is no doubt that it is the possession of culture that has made us the *dominant* life form on this planet. There is also no doubt that we owe to culture our ability to adapt to an amazing variety of environmental situations ranging from the heat of the desert to the cold of the polar ice. Still, it is curious how we insist on downgrading our physical attributes.

Are we really all that pitiful, or is it simply that most of us no longer participate in lifeways that require us to demonstrate our physical abilities? Look at a
team of professional football players sometime. They are human beings. Would
you call them weak and helpless? Of course, such people are exceptional. Nevertheless, perfectly ordinary men and women have repeatedly demonstrated
that they are capable of impressive physical action when the situation demands
it. In primitive hunting and gathering cultures, both males and females routinely
exhibit difficult and sustained physical skills.

As William S. Laughlin has put it:

Pound for pound, man is a tough, durable, strong, and versatile animal.
To the extent that comparisons between species have validity, he is
superior in overall physical performance to all or most other mammals.
This physical superiority is intimately related to his hunting habit. . . .
A man can run down a horse in two or three days, and then decide
whether to eat it, ride it, pull a load with it, wear it, or worship it.
(Laughlin 1968:311–313)

Bernard G. Campbell phrased it this way:

When compared with the sleek grace of a jungle cat, the streamlined
strength of a 1,800-pound tuna, or the regal bearing of a horse, what is
man's puny body? The answer to that rhetorical question, as a careful
examination of our physical adaptations will illustrate, is: everything.
Among the physical traits that, added together, separate all humans
from all other animals, there are three of overwhelming significance: a
skeleton built for walking upright; eyes capable of sharp, three-
dimensional vision in color; and hands that provide both a powerful
grip and nimble manipulations. These features are found in some
degree in many primates; it is the elaboration of them in special
combination with one another which characterizes us. . . . Using his
two legs, a human has the endurance to outrun a deer. He can carry
heavier loads, pound for pound of body weight, than a donkey. . . .
No terrain is totally impassable to a man. He can reach an eagle's nest
or a pearl oyster's bed. Only a human, the British scientist J. B. S.
Haldane noted, can swim a mile, walk twenty miles, and then climb a
tree. (Campbell 1976:15–16)

The key to our physical characteristics is our versatility and our endurance.
We can do many things reasonably well, and we can do them for long periods of
time. I think that there is no need to exaggerate our physical prowess; there are
indeed some stronger and faster animals. On the other hand, it is a chronic error
to fall into the trap of thinking of human beings as essentially weak and helpless.
What does all of this have to do with our remote ancestors, the first hominids? They were not human beings in the modern sense, and they were probably

somewhat smaller than the average dimensions for *Homo sapiens*. I believe that the answer boils down to this: the hominids are relatively powerful animals now, and they probably always have been. In other words, we are dealing with a population that would not just fold up and collapse at the first hint of adversity.

If there is one thing that we know about virtually all the higher primates, it is that they are intensely social animals. They live in groups. Therefore, in imagining the conditions under which the first hominids lived, it is wrong to think in terms of some hypothetical lone hominid sallying forth to do battle with assorted beasts. Instead, we should focus on a different problem. Given a reasonably well-organized *pack* of hominids, would they be easy prey? I think not. If we endow them with little more than the capabilities of chimpanzees—the ability to hurl objects and to brandish sticks—I suspect that they would constitute a rather formidable population. And we must not forget the developing complexity of their brains. It is not necessary to have culture in order to be clever, and there is every reason to believe that the early hominids could outthink the competition.

The reduction in the size of the canine teeth, of course, suggests that the first hominids had developed alternative ways of doing what they had to do; they could not depend on tooth displays to frighten off predators, and they would have some difficulty in shredding coarse vegetation. Although we cannot be certain until more evidence is available, this would seem to imply a greater reliance on the grasping hand, which in turn suggests the development of a more or less erect posture and a bipedal stance. Judging by their usual habitat, which tends to have been fairly open country, it is likely that these hominids were hunters of small game animals as well as collectors of soft plant foods. The success of chimpanzees in hunting would seem to strengthen this possibility. More importantly, the emphasis on hunting in the *descendants* of these first hominids clearly points in the same direction.

Speculation is fun, and it is sometimes illuminating, but it is probably unwise to proceed further without solid evidence. The first hominids did appear on this earth millions of years ago, and they did survive. When we look in again at our less remote ancestors, we have considerably more information at our disposal.

THE PALEOLITHIC: THE OPENING OF THE WAY

Paleolithic means "Old Stone Age." When the major divisions of the prehistory of mankind were established, this was done primarily on the basis of differences between the characteristic ways of making tools in various periods of time. For the earlier periods, comprising by far the longest portion of our prehistory, this meant that attention was concentrated on lithic technology: the ways that stone tools were made. The reason for this was simplicity itself. By and large, it was the stone tools that survived. Artifacts made of other materials—wood, for example—did not last long enough to be studied.

The designations of the major prehistoric periods, to say nothing of the subdivisions within them, can be confusing. Without worrying too much about the precise dates involved, it is helpful to get one basic idea firmly in mind. Terms such as *Paleolithic* are *archeological* designations. They refer to *cultural* characteristics as reflected (or manifested) in lithic technologies. As such, they do not correlate exactly with geological divisions, which are based upon the characteristics of the earth itself. As a practical matter, all of hominid prehistory involving known tool sequences is confined to the last two epochs of the Cenozoic era—the Pliocene, which lasted from around five million years ago until about two million years ago and from which we have relatively scant evidence of tool use, and the Pleistocene, which began roughly two million years ago and from which we have abundant evidence of hominid tools. (Some geologists set aside the last 10,000 years or so as the Holocene.) Of course, cultural adaptations are by no means unrelated to such phenomena as the advances and retreats of the glacial ice, but nevertheless it is important to remember that two different dating schemes are being used, one archeological and the other geological, and one must be cautious about skipping back and forth between them.

The Paleolithic lasted for a very long time. Its beginnings are shadowy, and it is probably impossible to assign a fixed date for the origin of the Paleolithic. It may be said to have begun when the Old World hominids first made recognizable stone tools. A conservative estimate is that the Paleolithic started about two million years ago, although there is a strong possibility that it is older than that. It continued—again, with reference to the Old World—until approximately 10,000 years ago.

It is very difficult for the human mind to grasp just how immense a span of time this is. We tend to be glib in playing with large numbers, but the implications are slow to sink in. Try to think back from the present. It was just a little over 100 years ago—1876—that the Seventh Cavalry and George Armstrong Custer collided with the Dakota and the Cheyenne at the Little Big Horn. We think of someone like George Washington as having lived a long time ago; he died in 1799. Christopher Columbus seems a figure out of the remote past; he died in 1506. Christ was born less than 2000 years ago. Julius Caesar was assassinated 44 years before that. Already, with a short time frame of much less than 3000 years, it takes an effort of the imagination to comprehend the meaning of the dates. When we go back 50,000 years or 150,000 years or a million years— well, we are lost. It was not the world we know, and the people who lived in it quite literally belonged to a different species.

It is essential to try to understand just how critical the Paleolithic was in both the biological and the cultural evolution of the hominids. When it began, *Homo sapiens* did not exist. When it was over, men and women everywhere were indistinguishable physically from ourselves. When it began, our ancestors were few in numbers, equipped with crude stone tools and weapons, and confined to relatively few parts of the Old World. When it ended, mankind numbered in the millions, although the real population explosion had not yet occurred, tools and weapons were sophisticated enough to permit systematic big-game hunting, and the human animal had expanded its range throughout the Old World and across the land bridge between Siberia and Alaska into the New World of the Americas.

The most graphic way I know to show how important the Paleolithic was is by means of a device called a *culture clock*. Imagine the face of a clock or watch marked off into minutes and seconds. Postulate a scale in which one hour of time equals one million years of culture history. (Note that this scale will not allow for all of the Paleolithic, but it does include that portion of the Paleolithic that contained the most significant cultural developments.) On this scale, one minute of clock time stands for 16,666 years. One second of clock time works out to about 277 years. Therefore, let us pose the question. On this scale, how long did the Paleolithic last? With today marked at the end of the hour, the Paleolithic takes up an astonishing 59 minutes and 24 seconds. See Figure 10.1.

Viewed in this way, it is easy to see that the vast majority of our time on earth was spent in the Paleolithic. Indeed, everything else—the first cultivated fields, the first cities, all the empires, the eyewink of time between the invention of the airplane and journeys to the moon—occurs in the final 36 seconds of our imaginary hour.

The Paleolithic was not changeless, of course. It witnessed the discovery and control of fire, which goes back at least as far as *Homo erectus* in China (Choukoutien) some 400,000 years ago. It saw developments in lithic technologies from simple tools made by striking one rock directly against another to elegant artifacts made by complex stone-working techniques. Undoubtedly, there were social changes as well. By late Paleolithic times—archeologists call it the Upper Paleolithic—we have the great cave paintings of France and Spain, and we can sense lifeways that were not dramatically different from those of such historic peoples as the Eskimo.

Still, two facts stand out from any examination of Paleolithic times. First, compared to what we are used to in our own lives, change was very slow. Culture is a cumulative thing, and there is a kind of snowball effect in its growth. The longer it continues, the faster it goes. You may very well see more fundamental changes in your lifetime than occurred in 100,000 years of Paleolithic existence. Second, all men and women everywhere throughout the whole of the Paleolithic lived by hunting wild animals and gathering wild plant foods. No other lifeway had yet been invented.

The Paleolithic was the crucible that shaped us. It was in the context of the Paleolithic lifeways that the human animal evolved both biologically and culturally. The story told by the Paleolithic evidence is, in all probability, the story of the evolution of a hunting animal.

The central question must be whether or not all this has left its mark upon us. Is the fact that virtually our entire time on earth was spent in hunting and gathering societies without relevance in the modern world? Are we somehow immune from the principles of natural selection?

Physically, the legacy of our hunting heritage is plain to see. Our complex brains capable of devising cunning strategies, our grasping hands so adapted to

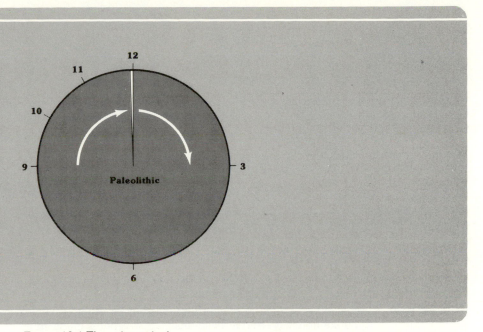

Figure 10.1 The culture clock.

the use of tools and weapons, our abilities to follow trails with our eyes and run and throw and carry and endure—these are the hallmarks of a supremely efficient hunting animal.

Culturally and psychologically, the evidence is less clear. Many authorities believe that our lifeways have changed so profoundly in the last few thousand years that the requirements of living in a hunting and gathering society have been totally lost. There is no doubt, of course, that the lifeways of most of us have changed drastically; hunting and gathering as a primary cultural adaptation is approaching extinction. The question is whether or not the *participants* in these new lifeways have been marked by the past in ways other than in their muscles and bones. It may be that the situation is as Jane B. Lancaster has expressed it:

> Nevertheless, although the physical and social reality of the world has changed radically in the past century, human beings are still virtually the same, equipped with the mind and emotions of the gatherer-hunter. Solutions to modern problems will only work as long as they take into account both realities—the rapidly changing nature of the physical and social world and the more slowly adapting nature of the human species. (Lancaster 1975:88)

If we were hunters and gatherers for millions of years, it is logical to assume that human beings evolved who found those activities rewarding as well as nec-

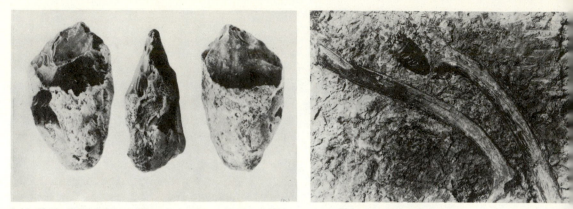

Left, Early Paleolithic artifacts from Java. *Right,* A Folsom projectile point embedded in the rib cage of an extinct type of bison. (From New Mexico; about 10,000 years old.)

essary. Primitive hunting, in particular, is both demanding and dangerous. A person must be motivated to hunt successfully—the activity ought to be satisfying psychologically. Ideally, it ought even to be fun.

Let us look briefly at some of the characteristics of primitive hunting. There is no need here to invoke nonsense about "killer instincts." What is involved is the total situation, and the actual killing of an animal is a very small part of it. (That's where the meat comes from, of course. But if you watch primitive hunters, or go along on one of their hunting expeditions, it is easy to see that the killing itself is not a happy occasion. Indeed, it is often done either with regret or without visible emotion. It is the planning and the execution of the hunt that is fun—and the feast that comes afterwards.) What is the essence of the experience?

First, it is done outdoors and away from camp. In other words, it is not done "at home." Second, it is done in the context of a small group of males who are separated temporarily from both females and young children. (In all known hunting and gathering societies, the men are responsible for the hunting.) Third, it requires cooperation between men who know each other well. It also requires intelligence and specific physical skills.

Fourth, it is a situation that calls for a sense of humor. Unless hunters are desperately tired or hungry, the camaraderie of the group manifests itself in jokes and good spirits. A sulker or a chronic complainer is a burden for everybody. Fifth, hunting is a contest with clear-cut winners and losers. It is not just the matter of who gets credit for the kill, for the meat will be shared by all including the women and children, but whether or not the hunt itself is a success. Either you get meat or you don't.

Does this total syndrome have any implications for the social worlds we live in today? On one level—a fairly literal one—you might ask yourself two questions. Do you see any parallels between all this and team sports? What in fact do males often do when they are "on vacation" from their work routines?

On another level, do we prefer to interact with small intimate groups or large anonymous groups? Do we feel pressure when we are penned up indoors for long periods of time? Do we find psychological satisfaction in the jobs we do, and if we don't why don't we?

The basic characteristics of hunting and gathering societies will be discussed in Chapter 17. I do not mean to suggest that such societies are utopias. They have their problems, and a life in such a context can be short, tough, and unpleasant. I also do not intend to imply that human beings are somehow equipped with "instincts" to hunt wild animals and to gather wild plant foods. Rather, I an raising the possibility that as animals we were designed to live in small-scale societies and to find psychological satisfactions in certain kinds of activities that are associated with small groups of people who know one another well.

The hunting and gathering option is not a viable one for the modern world, of course. At the very least, it would require the extinction of more than 99 percent of the world's population; it is not a lifeway that can support really large populations. Still, it had some things going for it. To mention just one, there was no alienation from the land upon which the people lived. Indeed, one often finds in such societies a feeling of literal kinship with the world around them. Consider this passage from Colin Turnbull's lovely book, *The Forest People.* The book is about the Pygmies of Central Africa, who are a hunting and gathering people. The reference to "the village people" concerns the Bantu-speaking farmers who also live in the area. A Pygmy named Moke is speaking to Turnbull:

> "The forest is a father and mother to us," he said, "and like a father or mother it gives us everything we need—food, clothing, shelter, warmth . . . and affection. Normally everything goes well, because the forest is good to its children, but when things go wrong there must be a reason."
>
> I wondered what he would say now, because I knew that the village people, in times of crisis, believe that they have been cursed either by some evil spirit or by a witch or sorcerer. But not the Pygmies; their logic is simpler and their faith stronger, because their world is kinder.
>
> Moke showed me this when he said, "Normally everything goes well in our world. But at night when we are sleeping, sometimes things go wrong, because we are not awake to stop them from going wrong. Army ants invade the camp; leopards may come in and steal a hunting dog or even a child. If we were awake these things would not happen. So when something big goes wrong, like illness or bad hunting or death, it must be because the forest is sleeping and not looking after its children. So what do we do? We wake it up. We wake it up by singing to it, and we do this because we want it to awaken happy. Then everything will be well and good again. So when our world is going well then also we sing to the forest because we want it to share our happiness." (Turnbull 1962:89–90)

TWO CHEERS FOR THE NEOLITHIC

Some 10,000 years ago, in that part of the Old World known as the Near East (roughly Syria, Iraq, Iran, Turkey, and adjacent regions), mankind made what were probably its most significant discoveries and embarked on a new and different series of lifeways. Originally, the Neolithic, or "New Stone Age," was identified by the introduction of new kinds of tools made of ground and polished stone. However, the changes in stone-working technology were not the really important aspects of what happened in Neolithic times. The critical developments can be simply stated: Mankind invented farming and began to domesticate economically useful animals. (The first crops were wheat and barley. A domesticated animal is one that lives and breeds in captivity or under human control. With the exception of the dog, who is our oldest companion, all of the important domesticated animals — sheep, goats, cattle, pigs, and perhaps horses — were domesticated in Neolithic times.)

The late British archeologist V. Gordon Childe was fond of referring to what happened as the "Neolithic revolution." When all is said and done, it does make sense to think of the Neolithic as revolutionary — revolutionary in that Neolithic developments made possible and even necessary distinctively different human lifeways. This was something new on the face of the earth. It had never happened before, and its implications are still very much with us.

Of course, the Neolithic did not happen overnight. Nobody blew a horn 10,000 years ago and announced, "Okay, we're in the Neolithic! No more hunting and gathering!" There are still hunting and gathering societies on this planet. The Neolithic complex of farming, domesticated animals, and pottery appeared in different places at different times, and its effects were gradual. Neolithic peoples continued to hunt wild animals and collect wild plant foods, as tribal farmers do to this day. Nevertheless, 10,000 years is not a very long time when measured against the total time span of mankind on earth, and there is no getting away from the fact that Neolithic kinds of societies and those built upon a Neolithic base have steadily expanded and replaced almost all hunting and gathering lifeways. The basic reason is not hard to fathom: In terms of population and organizational resources the hunting and gathering societies simply cannot compete, and they have been pushed back into areas nobody else wants — essentially land that is unsuitable for primitive farming, such as the Arctic or semiarid deserts.

We do not, in fact, know exactly what triggered the Neolithic. In retrospect, it is easy to see the enormous advantages of food production. However, these advantages were certainly less apparent at the time that farming began. In any event, even granting the clarity of hindsight, it is difficult to understand why the essential techniques took so long to develop. When we remember that people had over a million years of experience with the habits of wild animals and the characteristics of wild plants, the puzzle becomes troublesome indeed.

It is possible that population increases in ecologically rich zones caused a "spillover" of people into marginal areas and that this in turn stimulated the search for new sources of food. This hypothesis has been suggested by Lewis Binford, and it gains some degree of support from the fact that farming did begin in relatively difficult (as opposed to lush) regions (Binford 1968). Kent V. Flannery has suggested that intensive plant collecting was very widespread in the Near East and that one key factor leading to farming involved the "interchange of resources" between groups living in different ecological situations. In other words, plants were moved from one area to another, and this led to the development of new strains that required human care (Flannery 1965). It is also possible that changing climatic conditions made food production imperative. Beyond this, one cannot totally dismiss the notion that curiosity is one attribute of the human animal: Although it is extremely unlikely, the whole thing may have been the result of chance experimentation with the environment.

Whatever the "causes" may have been, the consequences of Neolithic developments were enormous. It is true that if you could somehow go back in time and look at an early Neolithic village you might not be unduly impressed. You would see several hundred people living in mud-walled houses surrounded by small fields—gardens, really—of cultivated plants. You would see animals such as goats or sheep poking about or herded away from the growing crops. You would see flint sickles and stone axes and grinding stones and pottery vessels. In itself, nothing very awe inspiring. But as a base to build on, that simple Neolithic village had almost unlimited potential. To understand this, we need only to recall that all of what we think of as the world's great civilizations— Greece, Rome, the United States, the Soviet Union, take your pick—were built on Neolithic foundations. They would have been impossible without agriculture and domesticated animals.

The characteristics of tribal societies—those based on simple farming or herding or on a combination of the two—will be discussed in Chapter 18. Here, it is only necessary to indicate a few obvious points. First, food production makes possible far higher population densities than are ever found in hunting and gathering societies. The same land that will support perhaps 50 people in a hunting and gathering situation will sustain thousands of people in a farming situation. Hunters and gatherers tend to have population densities of around one person per square mile; it is by no means unusual to find population densities of 100 persons per square mile among farmers. Second, farming makes a more sedentary (settled) lifeway both possible and necessary. You cannot farm on a finders-keepers basis; you have to stay put in order to cultivate and harvest your crop. Third, you have a real investment in both land and stock: these things are *owned* (whether by individuals or groups) in a way that wild resources never are. This makes possible the accumulation of property, and it also provides a strong incentive for raiding warfare; for virtually the first time, groups of people had something worth raiding for. Finally, new organizational techniques were required. The problems faced by relatively large numbers of people who must

Left, tourists visiting Neolithic site of Pan P'o in China. *Top right,* excavation of
Neolithic levels at Jericho. *Bottom right,* painted plaster relief from Çatal Hüyük,
a Neolithic site in Turkey.

interact on a fairly permanent basis are different from those encountered in a
small group of wandering hunters and gatherers. The old informal social controls
are difficult to maintain.

It may be noted in passing that Neolithic sequences differ somewhat in
the Old World and the New World. The general picture is similar—a relatively
gradual transition from hunting and gathering to food production—but the details are different. Farming is later in the New World; the earliest evidence dates
from around 5000 B.C. in Mexico. Different plants were cultivated, notably
maize (corn), beans, and squash. Largely because of a lack of suitable native
animals, animal domestication was much less important than in the Old World. It
is not known for certain whether or not there was any connection between the
inventions of farming in the Old World and the New World. Most authorities
treat the two developments as independent of one another, despite the rather
curious parallels in time. (Only some 3000 years separate the earliest appearances of farming in the two areas.)

Neolithic cultures were successful in themselves; they spread at the ex-
pense of hunting and gathering cultures, and many Neolithic kinds of lifeways
have survived into the modern world. In a sense, Neolithic cultures were somewhat like amphibians: They made possible new and different lifeways, and then
they in turn were threatened by their own descendants. Just as the amphibians

had to cope with more efficient land animals such as reptiles and mammals, the cultures of the Neolithic eventually were confronted with the development of nation states. The world around us today is the setting for the final acts in this great drama as the villagers who have retained Neolithic types of culture are more and more absorbed into and transformed by the spread of national state systems.

The innovations of the Neolithic made the modern world possible. If there had been no Neolithic, there would have been no later cities and writing and symphonies and science. This is the side of the Neolithic that is usually emphasized. There is another side to the coin. Just as our accomplishments had their remote origins in the changes of the Neolithic, many of our problems likewise have their roots in Neolithic soil. With good reason, we worry about overpopulation, alienation from the land and from each other, class conflicts, powerful leaders who are not always responsive to the will of the people, pollution, and destructive wars. All of these problems can be traced to Neolithic beginnings — they did not exist in any real sense in hunting and gathering societies. Hunting and gathering cultures certainly had their problems too, but they are not our problems. From this perspective, one is sometimes tempted to reach back in time, shake hands with our Neolithic brethren, and say, "Thanks a lot."

ALMOST MODERN TIMES

It is difficult to assign a precise date for the "end" of the Neolithic, and, as cultural developments increased in both speed and complexity, it is equally difficult — if not impossible — to find an all-inclusive label that will adequately represent the sweeping changes that transformed the post-Neolithic world.

In the Near East (Mesopotamia) between 3500 B.C. and 3000 B.C., the first cities appeared and writing was invented. What has been termed the "urban revolution" had begun. Cities such as Ur, with monumental temples and wheeled war chariots and sophisticated irrigation farming in the surrounding areas, represented something new on the human horizon. Technological changes came fast. Metal tools began to replace the age-old stone: first copper, then bronze, and eventually (by 1500 B.C.) artifacts of smelted iron. By 2900 B.C., ox-drawn plows were being used. If substantial numbers of people are going to live in cities, this requires efficient food production: The farmers outside the cities have to produce enough food to feed both themselves and the urban (city) dwellers.

In general, the rise of city life went along with a shift from simple horticulture (small-scale farming without the use of extensive systems of irrigation and plows) to high-yield agriculture. The social changes were equally profound. Urban centers must control the surrounding hinterland where the food is grown: This is one of the things that led to the development of state systems of political organization (see Chapter 18). Empires are essentially conquest states, and they are both established and maintained by organized warfare that is quite different

Teotihuacań restored.

from the hit-and-run raiding characteristic of earlier types of human societies. It takes specialists to operate a city: tax collectors and soldiers, craft guilds, priests and rulers, market officials, legal experts, a host of officials to run the machinery of government. Class divisions are very common, and it is a very long social distance from the rulers and their cohorts at the top of the social pyramid to the "commoners" and slaves at the bottom.

Whether one calls it an "urban revolution" or not, the early cities — to say nothing of the later ones — were vastly different from anything the human animal had experienced before. In a few thousand years, we had moved from the small wandering face-to-face groups of the hunting and gathering world to the big settled anthills of virtual social strangers that we call cities. (Not everyone lived in the cities, of course. Even if we restrict ourselves to the emerging states, the peasant or rural food producers continued to follow lifeways that in many respects had more in common with Neolithic villagers than with the townspeople.)

In the Old World, the hallmarks of civilization — cities and writing — spread rapidly, notably throughout the Near East, in Egypt, in India, and in China. In the New World, there were parallel developments, although, as was the case with the introduction of farming, they were somewhat later in time. By around 300 B.C. the Olmec of Mexico had developed a system of writing and complex calendrical calculations. The brilliant civilization of the Maya was flourishing by 300 A.D. Shortly thereafter (c. 600 A.D.) there were urban centers surrounded by terraced and irrigated agriculture in Peru. At about the same time, the city of Teotihuacán, northeast of modern Mexico City, covered 8 square miles and had a population estimated at 100,000 persons.

There were differences between the early civilizations of the Old World and the New World. The most important of these differences concerned the lack of plows in the New World and the less extensive development of metallurgy. Nevertheless, New World irrigation systems were so elaborate — comprising virtual floating gardens in some areas — that when the Spanish arrived in the New World in 1519 they found cities like Tenochtitlan, the main urban center of the

Aztecs in Mexico, which they judged to be as fine as any cities in Spain. We do not know for sure what connections, if any, there were between the developments of civilizations in the Old World and the New World. About the most that can be said at present is that the possibility of such contacts is fairly high but that the effects of such contacts are very uncertain (Riley, Kelley, Pennington, and Rands 1971). In other words, the rise of civilization in the New World appears to have been largely an independent development, but an increasing body of evidence suggests that there may have been sporadic influences from Old World sources.

It would take presumption bordering on insanity to attempt to trace in a few pages everything that has happened between the dawn of civilizations and the world of today. After all, the period involved, brief as it is compared to the total time span of the human animal on earth, includes all of recorded history. Instead, I would like to discuss a study that I think sheds some light on the contrasts between urban lifeways and other kinds of human societies.

Back in the 1930s, an anthropologist named Robert Redfield (1897–1957) began a series of studies on the peninsula of Yucatan, one of the states of modern Mexico. Redfield and his associates worked in four communities in Yucatan: Tusik, Chan Kom, Dzitas, and Merida. It is only about 150 miles from Tusik to Merida in linear distance. In terms of the kinds of communities they represent, it might be said that the distance between them is considerably greater.

In essence, Tusik was a small village with a population of around 100 persons. Merida was a modern city with a population at that time of about 100,000 people. Chan Kom and Dzitas were intermediate points in several senses: Chan Kom a large village and Dzitas a town. Interesting as they are—Chan Kom in particular being one of the best described "folk societies" in anthropology—Chan Kom and Dzitas are not necessary in understanding what Redfield discovered. Basically, he documented the fact that as he moved from the little village of Tusik to the city of Merida the outlook and the values—the world views—of the people changed in a dramatic way. The discovery was nothing new, of course. It has been made countless times in human history, and it is still made whenever a rural person moves to the city or vice versa. Redfield's accomplishment was to document the changes and to spell out exactly what they were. He discussed his findings in one of the more important—and most readable—books in anthropology, *The Folk Culture of Yucatan* (Redfield 1941).

In Tusik everyone belonged to the same ethnic group. All were Indians, and that was how they identified themselves. (They were, in fact, descendants of the classic Maya.) They recognized only two categories of people: us—the villagers—and them—the outsiders, foreigners, townspeople, and city folks. (They were aware that outsiders looked down on them as "poor Indians," but they were proud of their ways. They did not accept the authority of the Mexican government at that time.)

The people of Tusik were farmers, and maize was their chief crop. It was grown in *milpas,* fields prepared by the old slash-and-burn technique of primitive cultivation. (The term refers to the fact that the fields were first cleared of brush by cutting, and then the debris was fired before the maize was planted.) The fields were owned by families, not by individuals. Maize was regarded as sacred and could not be sold. Family life was very stable, and divorce was almost literally unthinkable. Kinship ties were elaborate and important; much of the old Maya kinship system had been retained. Tusik was a very small place; everyone knew everyone else, and knew them well.

Religion was central to the life in Tusik, and all the villagers shared the same religious beliefs. As Redfield put it, the people lived in a *sacred* world: The gods were felt to be very close, the entire village participated in religious ceremonies with every family contributing food, and the year was marked by a series of holy days.

Tusik was quite isolated. Only one person spoke Spanish at all. Only two were literate — tribal priests who could read Maya. Only one man was not a farmer, and he was the head priest. The people never ventured outside their own area if they could help it. They did allow a few trusted merchants to come to them. (They grew some chicle as a cash crop.) In those days, no roads led to Tusik. There were only pathways, and these were deliberately concealed to discourage intruders.

The city of Merida, to put it mildly, represented a very different ball game. As was once said of Rome, the people were fond of saying, "All roads lead to Merida." Merida contained one-quarter of the entire population of Yucatan. It was a center of trade and finance. It had banks, importers, exporters, wholesale houses, department stores, automobile agencies, hotels, businesses, power plants, and factories. It had institutions of higher learning, theaters, and a newspaper. Merida was much concerned with "progress." Three-quarters of all the doctors in Yucatan, and 80 percent of all the large hacienda owners, lived in Merida.

There were people from everywhere: people from every state in Mexico and from 56 foreign countries. There was no longer just one ethnic group; Merida contained people identified as Indians, whites, blacks, and Chinese. In Merida nobody farmed. Anything could be bought and sold, including maize and land, which was individually owned. The population was very diversified in terms of what people did for a living; the city directory listed over 100 different occupations just for persons whose last name began with the letter A.

Family life was quite unstable, and kinship ties were unimportant beyond the nuclear family level. Divorce was not only "thinkable" but simple — an easy divorce law had been passed in 1923, and Merida was something of a divorce mill. In Merida, of course, most people did not know one another. Housing in neighborhoods tended to be segregated, with Syrians in one place, old Spanish families in another, Indians in still another, and so forth.

Commercial dealings were the most important activities in Merida. Secular values were far more important than religious ones. Everyone did not believe in the same things — there were Catholics and Protestants and Theosophists and Communists and whatnot. As Redfield put it, "One is a member of a competing church or philosophy, rather than a participant in a common society and culture." The old holy days were no more; they had become holidays, fiestas which were business enterprises staged for profit.

Redfield drew on his Yucatan experience to formulate what has become known as the "folk-urban hypothesis." It is most clearly set forth in his provocative book, *The Primitive World and Its Transformations* (1953). Before examining it directly, we must make a brief side excursion into the forest of terminology. As the term is used in anthropology today, a "folk society" refers to the relatively isolated rural portions of national state systems: the peasant villagers as opposed to the people living in city centers. Thus, villages such as Tusik or Chan Kom represent kinds of folk societies. However, Redfield called Tusik a "tribal village," and therein lies the confusion. When he developed his folk-urban hypothesis, Redfield used "folk" as the equivalent of "primitive." Without getting into the details of the argument—for folk societies are like primitive societies in some respects—just remember what the referent is in the following discussion. Redfield is extrapolating from his Yucatan data, and when he refers to a "typical" folk society he means a "typical" primitive society. Think of it as a Neolithic kind of society, or a society of hunters and gatherers.

Redfield suggested that cultures could be thought of as ranging along a continuum—a line or an arc—with a typical "folk society" at one end and a typical urban society at the other end. (Societies that were neither the most primitive nor the most urban types occupied intermediate positions along the continuum.) These were intended to represent ideal types or models rather than any actual societies. According to this idea, the folk (primitive) society and the urban society were contrasting polar types: They were at opposite ends of the continuum and in some respects they represented opposite kinds of societies.

The ideal folk (primitive) society was isolated, homogeneous in race and culture, kin-based, and sacred. Relationships were personal and face to face. The people lived in what Redfield called a *moral order.* That is, everyone believed in the same things, humanity saw itself as one with nature, and the universe was felt to be morally significant. The world cared what people did, and everything—the gods, the animals, the rains, the land, the human beings—were all bound up together in a great drama of experience. Finally, people lived in a society of continually realized ethical conceptions. Everyone had the same standards of right and wrong, and these concepts were validated by experience. (For example, it was wrong not to share food. Failure to do so resulted in hunger for all, and the wrongdoer was expelled from the group.)

The urban society, in ideal terms, was cosmopolitan—that is, not isolated and provincial—and heterogeneous in race and culture. (There were different kinds of people, and they came from diverse cultural backgrounds.) Kin ties were largely supplanted by occupational ties: A person was placed on the basis of the job slot occupied, rather than by a position in an elaborate kinship network. (For instance, it was more crucial to know what a person did for a living than it was to know who that person's relatives were.) Secular values replaced sacred ones. Relationships were impersonal; the people in a city cannot possibly all know one another. The people lived in what Redfield called a *technical order.* That is to say, the organization was built on mutual usefulness, on coercion, or on the necessity to utilize the same *things*. As Redfield put it, "In the technical order men are bound by things or are themselves things. They are organized by necessity or expediency." A good example would be the way that cars move in response to traffic signals, or the way a factory is organized to produce television sets. The order no longer rests on convictions about the "good life." Indeed, people are no longer one with nature; they see themselves as opposed to the environment or else use a morally neutral nature for their own ends. (If a tree is in the way, cut it down. If the river floods, throw a dam across it.)

Now, there are several things that must be said about this folk-urban hypothesis. First of all, it is quite clear that Redfield himself had a distinct preference for the "folk" end of the continuum; his ideal primitive society has been somewhat romanticized, and perhaps his ideal urban society is rather more grim than necessary. His characterizations should not be accepted without question. Second, primitive societies are what they are in part because of their ecological situations, including their level of technological development. It is not just "isolation" that makes a sociocultural system primitive, and in fact the degree of isolation of most primitive societies has been exaggerated. Finally, it is noteworthy that the hypothesis has obvious implications in terms of cultural evolution; primitive societies preceded urban ones in time. When Redfield did his basic work in Yucatan, it was not fashionable to phrase cultural theories in evolutionary terms, as we shall see in the next chapter.

Granted their imperfections, however, Redfield's ideas do illuminate what has happened to our world. They provide the shock of recognition that comes from concepts that are essentially sound and original. The human animal has come a very long way from the small groups of Paleolithic hunters and gatherers to the teeming millions that throng our cities. The major changes have come fast, postdating the Neolithic. Whatever theoretical stance one assumes, it must be admitted that a modern city is a strange place in which to find a tropical primate.

The journey is not over yet, and stranger things by far are waiting for us beyond distant horizons. Is the story of mankind a tragedy, or will there be a happier ending? We do not know how it will all turn out. How well we understand our current problems and how effectively we deal with them are the pivots upon which our future will turn.

Certainly, we cannot hope to know where we are going until we understand where we have been and what we are. That is one reason why anthropology is so critically important—not as a collection of esoteric information but as a beacon that shines, however imperfectly, into the shadows that surround us.

SUMMARY

Culture by its very nature cannot appear overnight. It is a cumulative thing, and its initial development must have been very slow. The conclusion seems inescapable that the first hominids must have survived essentially without culture. Contrary to popular belief, the hominids as a group are both powerful and versatile animals.

As far as we know, the first true cultures appeared in the *Paleolithic,* or "Old Stone Age." The Paleolithic probably began about two million years ago in the Old World and persisted until around 10,000 years ago. It was during the Paleolithic that the hominids evolved into *Homo sapiens.*

The vast majority of the time that people have been on this planet was spent in the Paleolithic. There were cultural changes that took place in that immense span of time, but the rate of cultural change was very slow. All Paleolithic cultures were built on a base of hunting wild animals and collecting wild plant foods. If we were hunters and gatherers for millions of years, it is logical to assume that human beings evolved who found these activities rewarding as well as necessary.

Some 10,000 years ago in the Near East the *Neolithic,* or "New Stone Age," began. Although new stone-working technologies were introduced at this time—hence the name—the truly significant inventions of the Neolithic were farming and the domestication of economically useful animals. V. Gordon Childe employed the phrase "Neolithic revolution" to indicate the significance of these developments. Agriculture and domesticated animals made possible types of lifeways that the human animal had never before experienced. Population densities increased dramatically and people became more sedentary. New organizational techniques were required; the problems faced by relatively large numbers of people interacting on a fairly permanent basis are different from those encountered in a small group of wandering hunters and gatherers. The innovations of the Neolithic made the modern world possible. Both our modern accomplishments and our modern problems have their roots in Neolithic soil.

After the Neolithic, the rate of general culture change increased rapidly. Between 3500 and 3000 B.C., the first cities appeared in the Old World and writing was invented. There are differences between what happened in the Old World and in the New World, but there are parallels as well.

As Robert Redfield suggested in his *folk-urban hypothesis,* the human animal in a few thousand years had moved from a primitive ("folk" in Redfield's terminology) type of society—isolated, homogeneous in race and culture, kin-based, and sacred—to an urban type of society, characterized as cosmopolitan, heterogeneous in race and culture, job-based, and secular. One need not accept all the specifics of Redfield's proposition to appreciate that cultural transformations have indeed taken place. There is a very great difference between the small groups of Paleolithic hunters and gatherers and the teeming millions that crowd our cities. We are animals that evolved in one cultural context and now must learn to live in another. That is one reason for the importance of anthropology; we cannot hope to know where we are going until we understand where we have been and what we are.

References

Binford, Lewis R. 1968. "Post-Pleistocene Adaptations," in Sally R. Binford and Lewis R. Binford (eds.), *New Perspectives in Archaeology.* Chicago: Aldine.

Campbell, Bernard G. 1976. *Humankind Emerging.* Boston: Little, Brown.

Flannery, Kent V. 1965. "The Ecology of Early Food Production in Mesopotamia." *Science* 147:1247–1256.

Lancaster, Jane B. 1975. *Primate Behavior and the Emergence of Human Culture.* New York: Holt, Rinehart and Winston.

Laughlin, William S. 1968. "Hunting: An Integrating Biobehavior System and Its Evolutionary Importance," in Richard B. Lee and Irven DeVore (eds.), *Man the Hunter.* Chicago: Aldine.

Redfield, Robert. 1941. *The Folk Culture of Yucatan.* Chicago: University of Chicago Press.

————. 1953. *The Primitive World and Its Transformations.* Ithaca, N.Y.: Cornell University Press.

Riley, C. L., J. C. Kelley, C. W. Pennington, and R. L. Rands (eds.). 1971. *Man Across the Sea: Problems of Pre-Columbian Contacts.* Austin: University of Texas Press.

Turnbull, Colin M. 1962. *The Forest People.* Garden City, N.Y.: The Natural History Library (Anchor Books).

Suggestions for Further Reading

Adams, Robert McC. 1966. *The Evolution of Urban Society: Early Mesopotamia and Prehispanic Mexico.* Chicago: Aldine. The title tells the story; this is an excellent study of the problem.

Braidwood, Robert J., and Gordon R. Willey (eds). 1962. *Courses Toward Urban Life.* Chicago: Aldine. An authority on the Old World (Braidwood) and one on the New World (Willey) provide an illuminating discussion of the subject.

Childe, V. Gordon. 1951. *Man Makes Himself.* New York: Mentor Books. First published in 1936, this was perhaps the most influential of Childe's many books. Eminently readable, the work contains a seminal chapter on the "Neolithic revolution."

Clark, Grahame. 1969. *World Prehistory: A New Outline.* Cambridge England: Cambridge University Press. Much more than an "outline," this is an ambitious attempt by a distinguished archeologist to view the prehistory of mankind against a worldwide perspective.

Davidson, Basil. 1959. *The Lost Cities of Africa.* Boston: Little, Brown. A "popular" book in the best sense of the term, this is an exciting introduction to the civilizations of Africa written by a man who both knows his subject and is passionately involved in it. An excellent antidote to the widespread notion that there were only "savages" in Africa.

Diaz, Bernal. 1963. *The Conquest of New Spain,* translated with an Introduction by J. M. Cohen. Baltimore: Penguin Books. This is a unique book. Bernal Diaz del Castillo was one of the soldiers with Cortes in the conquest of Mexico, which began in 1519. Late in his life (he was past 70 when he began the book) he set out to set the record straight about what happened when a handful of Spaniards invaded the Aztec Empire of Montezuma. His intention was to write a "true history," and his credentials were the best: He was there. Here you will find, among many other things, a vivid eyewitness description of what the Aztec city of Tenochtitlan was like. Over the years, this book has been published in many different editions and under many different titles. There is nothing quite like it in world literature. Read it.

Fagan, Brian M. 1974. *Men of the Earth: An Introduction to World Prehistory.* Boston: Little, Brown. A remarkably successful attempt to tell the story of mankind on this planet, from the origins of the hominids to the rise of civilization. Accurate, readable, and stimulating.

Goldschmidt, Walter. 1959. *Man's Way.* New York: Holt, Rinehart and Winston. A richly rewarding book by one of the outstanding thinkers in anthropology. Much broader in scope than the study of prehistory alone, the reader will find here many valuable insights into the sociocultural evolution of mankind.

Howells, William. 1963. *Back of History,* rev. ed. Garden City, N.Y.: Doubleday (Anchor Books). Perhaps a trifle dated, but prehistory has not changed all *that* much. Howells is one of the best writers in anthropology, and the book is a joy to read.

Jennings, Jesse D. 1974. *Prehistory of North America,* 2d ed. New York: McGraw-Hill. A solid, concise introduction to the subject.

Miner, Horace. 1965. *The Primitive City of Timbuctoo,* rev. ed. Garden City, N.Y.: Doubleday (Anchor Books). A fascinating study of an ancient African city. Of particular interest to those intrigued by the ideas about urbanism put forth by Robert Redfield.

11

The Early Development of Anthropology

As a professional discipline, anthropology is very young. There were no professional (academic) anthropologists until E. B. Tylor began teaching at Oxford in 1884. (Tylor was appointed keeper of the University Museum in 1883, began to lecture on a regular basis with the title of reader in 1884, and became a professor at Oxford in 1896.) Indeed, anthropology was once half-seriously referred to as "Mr. Tylor's Science."

Now this does not mean that there was no serious anthropological work done prior to 1884, and it does not mean that Tylor single-handedly invented anthropology in a creative spasm on that date. It does mean, simply by definition, that anthropology before 1884 was something done by amateurs; a person could not be trained as an anthropologist when no center for training existed, and a person could not get a job as an anthropologist when there were no such jobs.

Obviously, when Tylor began to lecture on anthropology he had to have something to lecture about: He didn't just make it up as he went along. Therefore, it is safe to say that anthropology must have taken shape as a recognizable field of investigation before 1884. It is not realistic to try to assign a precise date for the emergence of anthropology; its roots can be traced back to the classical Greeks and even beyond. It is better to say that anthropology in something like its modern form was a product of the nineteenth century and that the second half of the nineteenth century (1850–1899) was particularly crucial to its development.

We all have a tendency to take current knowledge for granted, and it is sometimes difficult for us to realize how recent so much of our understanding of ourselves and the planet we live on really is. There has been a virtual explosion of scientific knowledge within the past century or so, and if we are to grasp the true contributions of anthropology — and the problems that the first anthropologists had to wrestle with — we must take a quick look at what the world was like while anthropology was struggling to be born.

Suppose we go back in time to the pivotal date of 1859, the year that Charles Darwin published *The Origin of Species.* At that time, it would not be much of an exaggeration to say that the very subject matter of anthropology hardly existed. We knew practically nothing about the prehistory of mankind on this planet, and we did not have even a reasonable guess about the antiquity of the hominids. Most people then still believed that mankind had been created in the year 4004 B.C. There was exactly one well-known fossil hominid; the first Neanderthal skull had been discovered in 1856, and its significance was unappreciated: It had been suggested that it was the skull of an idiot. The very concept of culture did not exist in a meaningful way; it was first defined by Tylor in 1871. We knew nothing about the mechanisms of heredity; the monk Gregor Mendel did not publish his pioneering work in genetics until 1866, and his discoveries were ignored until 1900. In 1859 not a single field study of any nonhuman primate had been conducted, and there would not be any such study for another 70 years!

Vast areas of the world were simply unknown in a scientific sense. Large portions of Africa, for example, had not even been explored, let alone studied. Mount Kilimanjaro, which is hardly an inconspicuous feature of the African landscape, was unknown to Europeans until it was reported by two missionaries, Krapf and Rebmann, who spotted it on their travels into the interior of East Africa between 1847 and 1849. (Krapf, by the way, was the first outside observer of record to visit the Kamba of Kenya.) It was 1871 when the explorer Stanley "found" David Livingstone in what was still referred to as "Darkest Africa."

In some respects, the situation was little better in the United States. Although the American Ethnological Society — the oldest anthropological society in the world — was founded in 1842, the more influential Bureau of American Ethnology did not exist until 1879. There could be no anthropology without respect for other peoples and other lifeways. Possibly the most hideous massacre of American Indians in the history of the United States took place in 1864 at a place called Sand Creek. A peaceful camp of Cheyenne and Arapaho led by a man named Black Kettle was attacked by a militia regiment known as the Third Colorado Cavalry — and this despite the fact that Black Kettle flew an American flag over his tipi, with a white flag above that. Commanded by a fanatic named John Chivington — a minister, of all things, in private life — the Third Colorado Cavalry (a force of 750 men) literally murdered the unsuspecting Indians. Of 46 Arapaho in the camp, 4 survived. There were 137 Cheyenne killed — 28 were men, and the rest were women and children. The dead were scalped and mutilated. More than 100 Indian scalps were exhibited at a theater in Denver to delight the populace. In 1868 we find General Phil Sheridan remarking that "the only good Indians I ever saw were dead." This was the basis for a common saying of the period: "The only good Indian is a dead Indian." Although Sheridan was not entirely typical of regular army commanders of that time, some of whom admired and felt deep sympathy for the Indians they had to fight, it was Sheridan again, as late as 1875, who made a speech to the Texas Legislature advocating the extermination of the buffalo to starve the Indians from the Plains. He suggested that each buffalo hunter be given a bronze medal with a dead buffalo on one side and a discouraged Indian on the other.

Examples might be multiplied, but to little purpose. The point is that the world of 1859 was (I hope) very different from the world we know today. Perhaps the best way to emphasize how new most of our knowledge about human beings really is would be to remember that in 1859 Sigmund Freud was three years old.

SOME PIONEERS OF THE NINETEENTH CENTURY

As we have seen in our preliminary discussion of Tylor, anthropology did not come into existence out of nothing; it developed at a specific time and place and within a specific intellectual background. There were a number of developments which set the stage for anthropology. It is impossible to discuss all of them, but a trio of figures must be mentioned to provide some understanding of why the early anthropologists formulated problems the way they did.

Charles Lyell (1797–1875)

One of those revered ancestral figures that grace the beginning phases of various fields of science was Charles Lyell. He was among the ''fathers'' of scientific geology. An Englishman, Lyell published his classic work *Principles of Geology* between 1830 and 1833. (The book originally came out in several volumes.)

At the time that Lyell wrote, assorted ''catastrophe'' theories of geology were much in vogue. The basic idea was that the earth was very young and that the character of the earth's surface had been shaped entirely by a series of sudden cataclysmic events: terrific floods, devastating earthquakes, vast volcanic eruptions, and the like.

As opposed to this prevailing view, Lyell advocated a position that he saddled with the somewhat cumbersome name of *uniformitarianism.* Lyell's essential argument was not complicated. He stated that the same processes that were operating in the present had also operated in the past. Thus, wind, rain, erosion, freezing, and thawing (along with known volcanic activity and the upthrust of mountain masses) could account for the nature of the earth's crust if enough time were allowed for their actions to take effect. Consider a deep canyon with a river flowing through it. In catastrophe theory, this whole structure was created explosively by a single violent event. In Lyell's view, the canyon was produced by the flowing water of the river: It was cut gradually over immense periods of time. In other words, the earth was old, not young, and conditions during much of the past were not drastically different from what they are today.

A volcanic eruption.

Of course, despite his terminology, what Lyell was really talking about was evolutionary geology: gradual change occurring over long time spans through observable processes. Lyell had a profound influence on the intellectual atmosphere of his time. For one thing, it might be said that he provided the *possibility* of the existence of early hominids. If the earth were very old, and if the earth hundreds of thousands of years ago was not totally different from the earth we know, then early mankind had a place to live. Hypothetical people would not have to charge around dodging catastrophes all the time. As a matter of fact, Lyell published in 1863 a somewhat cautious book called *The Antiquity of Man.* To mention one other point, there was a close relationship between Lyell and Charles Darwin. When Darwin sailed on the H.M.S. *Beagle* in 1831 on one of the great scientific voyages of all time, the first volume of *Principles of Geology* sailed with him.

Boucher de Perthes (1788–1868)

Not as well known to most people as he should be, a Frenchman named Boucher de Perthes was instrumental in providing some of the basic groundwork for anthropology. He was an interesting and versatile man. He made his living as a customs official in the town of Abbeville, but he was also a writer of some note, producing two books of fiction, several plays, and various other

A canyon caused by erosion.

works. However, the importance of Boucher de Perthes is due to still another facet of his life: He was one of the first prehistoric archeologists.

Beginning in 1837, Boucher de Perthes searched for and found prehistoric artifacts in the gravels of the Somme valley. Not only did he find artifacts—chipped flint handaxes and the like—but he found them in association with the bones of extinct animal species such as the mammoth, the woolly rhinoceros, and the cave lion. Furthermore, he drew the correct conclusions from his discoveries. First, he recognized the artifacts for what they were—tools made by prehistoric mankind. This may not seem particularly remarkable, but such chipped flints were often dismissed as "freaks of nature" or explained away by a variety of fantastic theories. Second, he realized that the association of the artifacts with the bones of extinct forms of animals meant that people had lived on the earth at the same time as those ancient animals. In other words, mankind was far older than the "experts" believed. Boucher de Perthes was convinced that he had found evidence of what he called "antediluvian man"—people who had lived long before the Flood. In fact, he had discovered critically important early Paleolithic artifact assemblages.

Not surprisingly, when Boucher de Perthes reported what he had found, he was generally dismissed as a madman. When he showed up at scientific meetings, the prevailing attitude was reflected in a kind of a groan: "Here comes

Boucher de Perthes with another sack of rocks." However, in time, Boucher de Perthes was vindicated. A number of scientists, including Charles Lyell, visited his sites and were convinced of the general authenticity of his work.

Obviously, the major contribution of Boucher de Perthes was his demonstration of the antiquity of the human animal. Less obvious, perhaps, is the fact that his work had strong evolutionary implications. In his history of archeology, Glyn E. Daniel puts it this way:

> The doctrine of evolution not only made people more ready to believe in the antiquity of man; it made the roughly chipped artifacts from Devon and the Somme not only credible, but essential. If man had gradually evolved from a prehuman ancestor with no culture to the cultured animal of Egypt and Greece, then there *must* be evidence of his primitive culture in the most recent geological levels. Evolutionary beliefs not only made Boucher de Perthes's handaxes easy to believe in, they made it necessary that more evidences of early human culture should be found, and that traces should also be found of other stages of culture leading from these simple tools to the complex equipment and buildings of the known early historic civilisations. (Daniel 1950: 66 – 67)

From simple to complex through time. This can serve as a crude but workable definition of evolution. Without hammering the point too powerfully, it is worth noting that technology (artifacts) is a part of culture. Therefore, the discoveries of Boucher de Perthes suggested an intriguing possibility. Not only had the earth evolved—and the plants and animals that lived upon the earth—but culture itself could be understood in evolutionary terms. We will be coming back to this idea shortly.

Charles Darwin (1809–1882)

Our trio of significant pioneers is completed by Charles Darwin, one of the intellectual titans of all time. One of the most fascinating things about the man is that his popular image is so different from the reality. People tend to think of Darwin as a militant iconoclast, but he was diffident and cautious almost to a fault. A confirmed hypochondriac, Darwin frequently took to his bed with imaginary ailments when his ideas were challenged. (It was usually Thomas Henry Huxley, known as "Darwin's bulldog," who defended Darwin's position.) For a genius, Darwin got off to a singularly unpromising start. As a young man, he was so addicted to hunting that he was the despair of his family. His father once exploded: "You care for nothing but shooting, dogs, and rat-catching, and you will be a disgrace to yourself and family" (Irvine 1955: 45).

Darwin was not the kind of genius who proceeded by lightning flashes of insight. He was a supremely patient man, and he had a passion for facts. He knew what he was doing, of course, but his triumph was due in large part to his respect for *evidence*. When Darwin said something it was not an offhand opinion: It was a carefully reasoned conclusion backed up by masses of factual data.

Charles Darwin did not invent the idea of evolution. The general notion

Charles Darwin.

was an old one, and, as a matter of fact, Darwin finally published his conclusions — after working on them for nearly 20 years — only after Alfred Russel Wallace sent him a short paper outlining a very similar approach to the problem. The importance of Darwin was that he clearly explained the major *mechanisms* of evolution — the processes by which it worked — and *documented* his arguments with a wealth of factual examples.

It is difficult to communicate the impact that *The Origin of Species* had in 1859. The first edition was sold out on the day of publication. It caused what might politely be called an intellectual uproar. Meetings were held, debates raged, and tempers flared. Quite simply, the theory of evolution dominated the intellectual atmosphere of the time. Whether you were for it or against it, there it was.

That was the legacy that the gentle naturalist left to the world. Aside from the fact that Charles Darwin was essentially correct in what he had to say, after 1859 it was impossible for thoughtful people to ignore the concept of evolution. It was an idea whose time had come, and from that time forward it had to be taken into account.

THE EARLY EVOLUTIONISTS

Against the background that we have been discussing, it is hardly surprising to discover that the early anthropologists tended to frame their theories in evolutionary terms. This was not a simple transfer of evolutionary principles from geology and biology to the realm of culture, because it is clear that the thinking of the early anthropologists had other sources as well. Among many influential sources, we might mention the Scottish historian William Robertson (1721–1793), who discussed the evolution of human society; Auguste Comte (1798–1957), who coined the word *sociology* and was one of that field's pioneering thinkers; and the English philosopher Herbert Spencer (1820–1903), who put forth evolutionary interpretations of all sorts of phenomena—inorganic, organic, and social—before Darwin published *The Origin of Species*. Nevertheless, it is beyond dispute that evolutionary ideas derived from geology and biology were very much in the air when anthropology got underway, and the early anthropologists were by no means unaware of them.

By and large, the first anthropologists believed in *cultural evolution:* They argued that the culture of mankind had developed from simple to complex through time, just as animal species or the strata in the earth itself had evolved through time. They felt that in the idea of evolution they had a kind of master key that would unlock the basic riddles of human development.

One of their most important contributions was to disengage the concept of culture from the concept of race. They ruled out the pernicious idea that "simple" cultures were the products of "inferior" races. Although these scholars were not totally free of the taint of racism in some of the language they used, the fact remains that they did not base their theories on racial factors. Indeed, as we shall see, they argued persuasively that all human beings were essentially alike in terms of their abilities and potential.

The two men who best represent this early period in the development of anthropology are Edward Burnett Tylor (1832–1917) in England and Lewis Henry Morgan (1818–1881) in the United States. Tylor and Morgan were complex men, and their views were by no means identical. They did share, however, a common faith in social and cultural evolution.

I will here attempt to sketch the main outlines of the evolutionary theory of the early anthropologists. It should be understood that this is a composite of the thinking of a number of anthropologists, not just Tylor and Morgan. After presenting the broad scheme, I will have some specific comments to make about Tylor and Morgan.

In general, these theorists thought in terms of a series of *cultural stages* through which all cultures were supposed to pass sooner or later. There was an inevitable sequence involved. The idea was that a culture would naturally unfold through preset stages, just as a flower grows from a seed. The basic stages were known as the Age of Savagery, the Age of Barbarism, and the Age of Civilization. (Sometimes the stages got more complicated; for example, Morgan subdivided his first two stages, talking about Lower, Middle, and Upper Savagery and so on.) Translating these "stages" into more modern terminology, the early evolutionists meant roughly that the "savages" were hunters and gatherers, the "barbarians" had farming and domesticated animals, and "civilization" was marked by the presence of writing.

Not only was evolutionary development inevitable, but it also indicated *progress*. In other words, culture tended to get better and better—morally as well as technologically—culminating in the glorious civilizations in which the evolutionists themselves lived. It was this notion that led the theorists into a subtle trap. It is usually implicit rather than explicit in their writings, but it is vital in understanding what they did. In its naked essence, the argument went like this: Since modern civilization, such as nineteenth-century Europe, represents one end of the evolutionary sequence, and the Age of Savagery represents the other end, the two "stages" must be opposites. Therefore, to find out what was going on in the Age of Savagery, it was only necessary to postulate the reverse of current "civilized" conditions.

Consider how this worked in practice. In the civilization the evolutionists knew, monogamous marriage between one man and one woman was the very keystone of society. What is the opposite of that? Obviously, it is a situation in which there is no marriage — everyone just mates at random with everyone else. Ergo, the Age of Savagery was characterized by something called the *primeval promiscuous horde,* a concept that had a real fascination for the Victorian mind. Well, what would the consequences of that be? Clearly, it was impossible to know who the father of a child would be in such a situation. However, since females are the ones who get pregnant, the mother of a child would be known. Therefore, descent would be reckoned *matrilineally,* that is, through the mother. This fitted the scheme well, since in "civilized" Europe the child received its name through the father's side of the family. (There are some problems here, inasmuch as the kinship systems in which Tylor and Morgan participated are not patrilineal except in some respects. This need not concern us here; the interested reader might look ahead to Chapter 14.)

To continue with our hypothetical "savages," it was argued that they were all communists. Since private property was held in such high esteem by the "civilized" societies of Europe and the United States, there would be no private property in the Age of Savagery. (It was this aspect of Morgan's work, in particular, that interested Karl Marx and Friedrich Engels, the coauthors of the *Communist Manifesto.* It seemed to indicate that communism was the original or "natural" state of mankind.)

What about religion? Obviously, the societies in which Tylor and Morgan lived believed in *monotheism* — a belief in one God. What might the opposite of that be? Here, the various evolutionists parted company. Some suggested that there was no god in the Age of Savagery, others argued that there was a belief in many gods *(polytheism)*. Tylor felt that *animism* (a belief in spirit beings) was the original religion of humanity. Something of Morgan's attitude can be gleaned from the following amazing statement:

> Religion deals so largely with the imaginative and emotional nature, and consequently with such uncertain elements of knowledge, that all primitive religions are grotesque and to some extent unintelligible. (Morgan 1877: 5)

Enough has been said to give the general flavor of the early evolutionary arguments. Two additional (and related) ideas must be mentioned before we view Tylor and Morgan from a different angle. The early evolutionists had to spend a great deal of time attempting to refute a popular idea of the period, the theory of *degeneration.* Degeneration is the view that mankind had been created in a perfect, civilized state but had in some instances degenerated (backslid) to a savage state. It is, of course, the exact opposite of evolution. Ac-

E. B. Tylor.

cording to degeneration theory, primitive peoples were the outcasts of the human race — those who had fallen from grace because of their evil ways. As such, they really weren't worth studying except as horrible examples. The evolutionists had to justify their own work by demonstrating that culture had in fact evolved from simple to complex through time, rather than going the other way, and that the people who lived in primitive societies were not fundamentally different as people from anyone else — it was their *culture* that was different. The evolutionists referred to this principle as "the psychic unity of mankind." They meant simply that human minds were much the same everywhere and that modern primitive peoples were not different in kind with regard to basic human nature.

Let us sum up the basic point of view of the evolutionists with a quotation from Tylor:

> The institutions of men are as distinctly stratified as the earth on which he lives. They succeed each other in series substantially uniform over the globe, independent of what seem the comparatively superficial differences of race and language, but shaped by similar human nature acting through successively changed conditions in savage, barbaric, and civilized life. (Tylor 1889: 269)

New World pyramid.   Old World pyramid.

Tylor and Morgan were not just evolutionists; they each made other contributions to anthropology. (This is not to suggest that their evolutionary ideas had no value. The general idea of cultural evolution, as opposed to the details of specific nineteenth-century schemes, was not without merit. It must be remembered that when we summarize a complex theory we always run the risk of caricature. Reading Tylor or Morgan in the original can still be stimulating today.) In any event, suppose we now look more closely at Tylor and Morgan as individuals rather than as representatives of the evolutionary perspective.

E. B. Tylor

E. B. Tylor was a Quaker, and his father ran a brass foundry. He had no formal university training in any subject and yet wound up as a professor at Oxford; this in itself is no mean distinction. He started to work in the family business when he was 16 years old. While still a young man, he became sickly and was advised to travel for his health. In 1856, he found himself in Cuba, and there he met a fellow Quaker named Henry Christy. Christy was an amateur archeologist with some stature in the field; he was among the scholars who had examined the discoveries of Boucher de Perthes. Christy persuaded Tylor to join him on a trip to Mexico.

Tylor spent about six months in Mexico. That was as close as he ever came to actual fieldwork, but Tylor was hooked on anthropological questions for life. He was fascinated by what he saw. What had happened to those great civilizations whose ruins lay all around him? Where had those civilizations come from? How old were many of the customs still being practiced, and how had they survived into modern times? Tylor was alive intellectually; he was curious. When he returned to England, he would test a stone scraper from Tasmania at a local butcher shop, butt into a children's street game to ask them to explain the rules, visit a school for those who could not hear or speak to understand gesture languages. Lacking field experience himself, he encouraged others to study primitive societies, and he was skilled at evaluating evidence.

As we have observed, Tylor was the first to come up with a reasonably modern and widely accepted definition of culture. ("Culture . . . is that complex whole which includes knowledge, belief, art, law, morals, custom, and any other capabilities and habits acquired by man as a member of society.") The least dogmatic of the evolutionists, Tylor was very much concerned with the problem of *diffusion* (the process by which cultural elements spread from one culture to another: if you find a Coke bottle in an igloo, this is an example of diffusion). He was struck by the similarities between the Aztec game of *potolli* and the game of *parchesi* played in India. Because they shared a whole series of distinctive features, he concluded that it was unlikely that they had been independently invented in the two regions. Therefore, he reasoned, the two games must have had a common origin. This implied that there must have been some ancient contact between the Old World and the New World — an idea that is only now beginning to be accepted by scientists.

To mention just one more point about Tylor, he was one of the first — and most successful — scholars who attempted to work out correlations between different sorts of social phenomena. In other words, he was seeking laws or principles of social connection. (If X is present, then you can expect to find Y.) He had a good word for correlations: He called them *adhesions* (things that stick together). In a classic study, working with a sample of more than 300 human societies, he found a strong correlation between a type of residence in which a husband goes to live with his wife's family and what is termed the mother-in-law tabu — a pattern of avoidance between a man and his mother-in-law.

Lewis Henry Morgan

Lewis Henry Morgan was quite different from Tylor. He was trained as a lawyer and never worked as a professional anthropologist. Although technically an amateur, it is somewhat misleading to think of him in those terms. He was president of the American Association for the Advancement of Science at one time and founded its anthropological section.

Morgan developed an interest in the American Indian, and particularly in the Iroquoian-speaking tribes, early in his career. He was a member of a literary and social club that was organized along lines suggested by the famous League of the Iroquois. He really got involved, though, in his capacity as a lawyer. In the 1840s, the Seneca tribe (an Iroquoian group) found themselves in a depressingly familiar situation: They were being swindled out of their territory by white land speculators. Morgan went to work to defend the Senecas, carrying the fight all the way to Washington. He had some success, and the Seneca tribe adopted Morgan in 1847. He was given the name of Tayadaowuhkuh ("One Lying Across"), meaning someone who bridged the gap between the whites and the

Lewis Henry Morgan.

Indians. Morgan made many visits to Iroquois reservations; he was one of the few early anthropologists who did something approximating fieldwork. In 1851 he published *The League of the Ho-de-no-sau-nee, or Iroquois.* (The league was a tribal confederation of Iroquoian-speaking peoples centered in New York and Canada and comprising the Mohawk, Seneca, Oneida, Onondaga, and Cayuga Indians. Later, the Tuscarora also joined the League. It was one of the most remarkable political systems developed by the American Indians north of Mexico.) Morgan was not a sloppy worker, and his study of the Iroquois League remains one of the classics of anthropology.

Partially as a result of his Iroquois studies, Morgan developed an intense interest in kinship phenomena. This interest was quickened in 1858 when he discovered that the Ojibwa Indians—whom he met and interviewed on a business trip to Michigan—classified relatives in a way that was very similar to the Iroquois. Much intrigued, Morgan sent out questionnaires and traveled extensively in the American West. This investigation culminated with the publication of his *Systems of Consanguinity and Affinity of the Human Family* in 1871. (The title refers to ways of reckoning kinship. *Consanguineal links* are descent links, such as that between father and daughter. *Affinal links* are marriage links, such as that between a woman and her husband's brother.) Based on data from all over the world, *Systems* is a key work in anthropology. Morgan quite literally founded the scientific study of kinship, and his work lies at the base of all subsequent analysis of the subject.

In 1877, Morgan published his most famous book: *Ancient Society.* Its subtitle tells the story: *Researches in the Lines of Human Progress from Savagery through Barbarism to Civilization.*

Having restored Tylor and Morgan to something like proper perspective, let us venture a final comment on the early evolutionists in general. Bearing in mind that Tylor and Morgan were probably the best of the lot, and recognizing the very real contributions made by the evolutionists, it might be said that this period of anthropology suffered from the defects of many pioneering investigations. It combined bold and often biased speculation with an inadequate data base. It was a time of rather too much theory and too little solid field research.

The danger, of course, was not that cultural evolutionary theory was put forth as a hypothesis to be tested. The danger was that the details of particular evolutionary schemes would be frozen as a kind of dogma, thus precluding critical investigations that were yet to be undertaken.

A FEW TOUGH QUESTIONS: FRANZ BOAS

Of all the anthropologists, I find Franz Boas (1858–1942) the most difficult one to discuss. There were so many sides to the man, and evaluations of his work differ so widely, that the problem becomes one of presenting him neither as a creator god nor as a crippling devil.

To some extent, the history of anthropology can be read as a series of reactions and counterreactions to theoretical positions. In this sense, Boas represents the reaction against the formulations of the cultural evolutionists in anthropology. But Boas was much more than that. Just as Tylor and Morgan have a way of confounding simplistic characterizations, Boas is a tough bird to cram into a neat pigeonhole.

Suppose we begin with a few facts—an approach that Boas would have found congenial. Franz Boas was the first significant professional academic anthropologist in the United States. He founded the first American department of anthropology (at Clark University in Massachusetts) in 1888. The first Ph.D. in anthropology granted by an American university (to Alexander F. Chamberlain) was given under Boas's direction. After Boas moved from Clark to Columbia University, he trained virtually an entire generation of American anthropologists. The list is truly impressive, including such people as A. L. Kroeber, Robert H. Lowie, Edward Sapir, Melville J. Herskovits, Alexander Goldenweiser, Clark Wissler, Paul Radin, Leslie Spier, Jules Henry, E. Adamson Hoebel, Ruth Bunzel, Ruth Benedict, and Margaret Mead. This is only a partial list. Not all of these names have become household words, but their significance is readily apparent to anyone familiar with American anthropology—or world an-

Franz Boas.

thropology, for that matter. They are among the most influential anthropologists of all time. When it is remembered that they in turn went on to train other anthropologists, the impact of Boas can begin to be appreciated.

In this light, it is not enough just to ask what Boas did. Indeed, a mere summary of his books and articles — Boas published more than 700 articles, incredibly enough — is not particularly revealing. We must ask, rather, who Franz Boas was and what it was that he communicated to his students.

Franz Boas was born in Germany. Unlike Tylor, who had no formal university training, and unlike Morgan, who was a lawyer, Boas was a trained scientist. Before he left Germany he had earned a Ph.D. degree. His doctorate was not in anthropology, of course. At the time Boas received his Ph.D. (1881), there was no such thing as a doctorate in anthropology. Boas got his Ph.D. in physics with a minor in geography. His doctoral dissertation dealt with the color of sea water.

Several logical questions intrude themselves at this point. How did a man trained in physics become an anthropologist, and how did Boas turn out to be the father of academic anthropology in the United States? The questions are not

The Eskimo.

easy to answer because the evidence — including statements by Boas himself — is not entirely consistent. In any event, the motivations of real human beings, unlike the phantoms that stalk the pages of textbooks, are probably never clear and simple.

We do know that in 1883 Boas went on an expedition to Baffin Island in the Canadian Arctic. Regardless of what his original intentions were, Boas came face to face with the Eskimo. The experience marked him deeply. The Eskimo people fascinated Boas, and in later years he wrote about them with an emotion that is seldom encountered in Boas's writings. In particular, one fact stood out from his Arctic experience. Boas had been taught that human beings were rather passive creatures, rigidly ruled by climate and geography. In essence, the idea was that the harsher the environment the more ''pressed down'' a people would be. The Eskimo, living in perhaps the most difficult environment the human animal has ever had to contend with on earth, were a surprise and a revelation. Boas found them lively, inventive, resourceful, and good-natured. In other words, they were directly contrary to what he had been taught they should be. It is quite possible that this experience left Boas with a lifelong distrust of fancy theoretical schemes. His crusade against the theories of the cultural evolutionists was due in large part to the simple fact that those were the theories that were in vogue at the time. It is characteristic of Boas that he was suspicious of all unproven speculations. It was the real world that interested Boas, and for him the real world was made up of facts.

Boas first came to the United States in 1884, after his return from the Arctic. For a time he divided his activities between the United States and Germany — sandwiching in another field trip to study the Bella Coola Indians in 1886 — but eventually he found the intellectual atmosphere in the United States more congenial. By 1888, as we have seen, he was teaching at Clark University.

What did he teach? In essence, Boas taught *method,* that is, technique. He was a tough-minded man, and he was after facts, not theories. He wanted *information* rather than speculation. To Boas, the first requirement of a scientific anthropology was a *solid factual foundation.* Therefore, he argued, students must do fieldwork. They must live with the people they study — learn their language and participate as much as possible in their lifeway. As far as Boas was concerned, an armchair anthropologist was no anthropologist at all.

He taught students to be scrupulously accurate reporters. The data were the important things, not what the student thought about the data. His credo boiled down to this: Get the facts before they disappear forever. The theories could wait.

Boas and his followers demolished the details of schemes of cultural evolution. Boas argued that specific outlines of cultural evolution, such as Morgan's, must be rejected as either unprovable or factually false. The Boasians were able to show that there was no "promiscuous horde" among "savages." There were no people anywhere in any society who did not have rules about who could marry or mate with whom. There was no primitive communism; there were no societies anywhere without some concepts of private property. It was not true that "savages" traced descent through the mother; in fact, most hunters and gatherers did it the other way around or else (like the Eskimo) reckoned descent through both sides of the family, as we do. Moreover, there are no preset stages through which all societies have to pass; there is too much variability at every level to permit such generalizations.

(It may be observed that the Boasians delighted in finding exceptions. In their view, it was not the exception that proves the rule but rather the exception that *disproves* the rule. This has been characterized as the "Pago Pago" approach to anthropological theory. Whenever a generalization was advanced, someone would point out that they don't do it that way in Pago Pago — or wherever — and that presumably ended the matter. The end result of this was that generalizations about human society were impossible. Let us pose a question here. If a generalization holds in 99 percent of known cases, is not the real problem to explain the exceptional 1 percent rather than to dismiss the 99 percent as false?)

Boas was more of a critic than an advocate of a theoretical system of his own. However, his rejection of cultural evolutionary ideas as frameworks for explanation left him in a difficult position. If you throw out evolution and cannot accept geographical determinism, then how *do* you account for the observable difference between cultures?

Boas coauthored a textbook on general anthropology. He gives his answer to this question in the very first lines of his Introduction. He wrote:

> The science of anthropology deals with the history of human society. It differs from history in the narrower sense of the term in that its inquiries are not confined to the periods for which written records are available and to peoples who had developed the art of writing. (Boas 1938:1)

The key word here is *history.* Every human group, he argued, had its own unique history. It was what it was because of a series of cumulative historical accidents. The business of anthropology was to unravel historical sequences.

The problem is obvious. If primitive societies have no written records, how do you find out what their histories are? Apart from archeology—and Boas understood the uses of archeology very well—his answer was a technique called *historical reconstruction.* (It is also sometimes referred to as *historical particularism.*) In trying to "reconstruct" history, Boas favored an intensive analysis of neatly delimited problems. He chopped cultures up into bits and pieces called *culture traits,* plotted the distribution of these traits, and attempted to explain each trait or cluster of traits in terms of history and diffusion. (That is, he tried to infer where particular traits had originated and how they had spread from one group to another.) The method can get quite complicated in practice; it can also get somewhat dubious. (A. R. Radcliffe-Brown, whom we will be meeting shortly, referred to the method as *hypothetical* reconstruction.) The details of the method need not detain us here. The important point to remember is that in seeking his historical goals Boas worked not with cultural wholes but with particular cultural items: folktales, needle cases, art motifs, even recipes for blueberry pie recorded in the original Kwakiutl. At its most restrictive, it represented a kind of tipi-pole-counting approach to ethnology.

Franz Boas—or someone like him—was absolutely necessary. Until anthropology acquired a solid factual foundation, it could not proceed. His skepticism was a healthy thing, and so was his determination to make anthropology as methodologically rigorous as the physics in which he was trained.

Several points need to be emphasized here. First, the Boasian era did produce extensive field investigations and a much more accurate understanding of the actual lifeways of primitive societies. Second, the writings of Boas are by no means as monolithic as I have here suggested. He did vital pioneering work in physical anthropology, ethnology, linguistics, and folklore. There is no lingering hint of racism in his approach to anthropology. Finally, the students trained by Boas did not all slavishly imitate the master. There is a considerable theoretical range between, say, Robert H. Lowie and Margaret Mead.

Still, Boas did dominate American anthropology for many years, and there is a great paradox in his career. Boas was a man trained as a scientist, and science by definition is more than fact collecting. Science is concerned with the quest for laws and principles and generalizations about phenomena. Boas ultimately retreated from science into a special kind of history, which is particularistic rather than generalizing in its approach. To say that every human society is unique and is the product of unique historical experiences may be true enough on one level of analysis, but it is also the equivalent of saying that it is what it is because it is what it is — which doesn't get us very far.

Boas felt, perhaps, that *no* theory was better than *wrong* theory. There is a persistent strain in his work that suggests that it was "premature" to attempt any sweeping generalizations. He may have been right, of course, but the impact of his caution was such that the facts piled up without very much concern about what was to be done with all this information.

It is possible to admire Franz Boas — and even to wish occasionally that he were still around to puncture hasty theories with his passion for evidence — and still to recognize that anthropology had to move beyond the Boasian stance in order to tackle the fundamental questions that lie at the heart of its scientific study of mankind.

PUTTING IT BACK TOGETHER: FUNCTIONALISM AND THE INTEGRATION OF SOCIOCULTURAL SYSTEMS

If it is true that the history of anthropology can be interpreted as a series of reactions and counterreactions, then we might expect that the next logical step would be a shift in orientation away from the standard Boasian position. To some degree, that is what happened.

Boas, with his emphasis on historical reconstruction, had advocated a *diachronic* (time-oriented) approach to the study of culture. (The evolutionists likewise had a diachronic point of view.) In addition, the emphasis in Boasian anthropology was on relatively isolated parts of cultures rather than on cultural wholes. There was a reaction against both of these orientations. The focus moved to *synchronic* studies (the examination of a culture at one point in time; a dynamic snapshot, as it were, rather than a long-running historical or evolutionary movie) and a concern — at least in ideal terms — for total sociocultural systems.

The movement away from the Boasian tradition began in England, and its two leading figures were Bronislaw Malinowski and A. R. Radcliffe-Brown.

Bronislaw Malinowski (1884–1942)

Bronislaw Malinowski was a bit like Boas in two respects: his early training and his movement away from his homeland. Malinowski was born in Poland, and while still in Poland he received his doctoral degree in mathematics and physics. Before his career in the physical sciences was well launched, Malinowski

Bronislaw Malinowski.

did a dangerous thing—he read a book. The book was an anthropological classic of an earlier generation, Sir James Frazer's *The Golden Bough.* According to Malinowski, that did it: Malinowski decided to become an anthropologist. He went to England and studied anthropology at the London School of Economics.

Malinowski did his most important fieldwork in the Trobriand Islands (not far from New Guinea), and the timing of the fieldwork was important—it roughly coincided with the duration of World War I. Malinowski was technically an Austrian citizen—Cracow, Poland, where he was born, was a part of the Austrian Empire—and he could not return to England until the war (1914–1918) was over. Malinowski stayed in the field for a very long time, his knowledge of the culture of the Trobriand Islands was deep, and his field experience strongly affected his theoretical position.

It has been said that Malinowski was the greatest of all the anthropological fieldworkers. Whether or not this is true, he did live with the people of the Trobriand Islands, he learned their language, he participated in their lifeway, and he generally got his facts straight. These were all traits that Boas—or any anthropologist—might have appreciated.

Ritual kula object.

The effect of his immersion in the culture of the Trobriand Islands can best be understood in terms of two of Malinowski's most famous books. His *Argonauts of the Western Pacific* (1922) is an analysis of a ceremonial system of exchange in the Trobriand Islands. Men on one island have trading partners with men on other islands. There is a continuous exchange of ritual objects between the trading partners: red shell necklaces travel in one direction around a circle, while white shell bracelets move in the other direction. A man receives a necklace or a bracelet, keeps it for a time, then passes it on to a trading partner on another island. The ceremonial trading network is called the *kula ring*.

Malinowski discovered that he could not discuss the kula ring separately and make sense of it; it was too closely connected with the rest of the culture of the Trobriands. Thus, a large-scale economic trade was associated with the kula exchanges; the people going on a kula expedition would load up their canoes with surplus food and artifacts and trade these for whatever their hosts had to offer. In order for the exchanges to take place at all, the people had to be able to manufacture and navigate seagoing canoes. Moreover, the whole system was "rooted in myth, backed by traditional law, and surrounded with magical rites" (Malinowski 1922:85). Already, we have moved far beyond the exchange of

Canoe building, Trobriand Islands.

ceremonial objects; we are talking about technology and magic, economics and law.

Malinowski makes his point of view quite explicit in the foreword to the book. He states:

> One of the first conditions of acceptable ethnographic work certainly is that it should deal with the totality of all social, cultural, and psychological aspects of the community, for they are so interwoven that not one can be understood without taking into consideration all the others. (Malinowski 1922:xvi)

Meanwhile, what has happened to evolutionary theory and historical reconstruction? Malinowski relegates these, quite literally, to a footnote:

> It is hardly necessary perhaps to make it quite clear that all questions of origins, of development or history of the institutions have been rigorously ruled out of this work. The mixing up of speculative or hypothetical views with an account of facts is, in my opinion, an unpardonable sin against ethnographic method. (Malinowski 1922:100)

Coral Gardens and Their Magic (1935) expresses the same set of ideas. Here, the focus was on horticulture — the gardens of the title. Again, Malinowski

The Trobriand Islands today.

found that he could not discuss his subject (farming) without reference to the rest of the cultural system. For example, no gardening activities could take place without the proper magical rites being performed. The chief could control the magic, and he got a portion of each crop for redistribution in time of need. In addition, a part of each crop had to go to the farmer's sister's family. It was all interconnected: To understand the gardening you had to understand the supernatural beliefs, the role of the chief, and the nature of kinship obligations.

To put it simply, Malinowski was not interested in isolated parts of a culture and where they came from. He was interested in the ongoing culture as a system of interrelated parts. He wanted to know how the system worked.

The most important emphasis in the theoretical position called *functionalism,* associated with Malinowski's name, is precisely this: Cultures are treated as integrated wholes, and the function of any part of a cultural system is the contribution it makes to the operation of the total culture. By way of analogy, we might say that the function of water in the radiator of an automobile engine is to cool the engine. Note that this approach is nonevolutionary and nonhistorical. It treats the culture as an operating system and examines each part of a culture within the context of the cultural whole.

It must be mentioned that Malinowski also used the term *function* in a different sense. He argued in *A Scientific Theory of Culture and Other Essays* (1944) that ultimately the function of culture was to meet or satisfy the basic needs of the human organism. Thus, a kinship system was a response to reproductive needs, techniques of food acquisition were a response to metabolic needs, and so forth. This aspect of Malinowski's work is overly simplistic, but it does have some historic importance: It was one of the few early attempts in anthropology to relate cultural categories to the biology of the human animal.

A. R. Radcliffe-Brown (1881–1955)

Radcliffe-Brown shares with Malinowski a synchronic approach and a concern with how sociocultural systems operate. A society, he said, was like an organism—it was made up of interrelated parts. The function of any part of the system was the part it played in the operation of the system. Remembering his comparison of a society to an organism, let us employ his own example:

> The processes that go on within a human body while it is living are dependent on the organic structure. It is the function of the heart to pump blood through the body. The organic structure, as a living structure, depends for its continued existence on the processes that make up the total life processes. If the heart ceases to perform its function the life process comes to an end and the structure as a living structure also comes to an end. (Radcliffe-Brown 1952:12)

Note carefully the choice of words here and what they imply. Radcliffe-Brown is talking about *society* rather than culture. He is interested in the *structure* of social systems. His conception of the *function* of parts of the social structure involves what the parts do to enable the system to go on working. If the heart stops, the organism dies. If a part of the social structure does not function, the social system ceases to operate.

Radcliffe-Brown was trained at Cambridge, and he was one of the founders of social anthropology. His thinking was strongly influenced by the great French sociologist Emile Durkheim (1858–1917). He is probably best understood as a kind of comparative sociologist who specialized in the study of primitive societies. He put it this way: "My conception of social anthropology is as the comparative theoretical study of forms of social life amongst primitive peoples" (Radcliffe-Brown 1952:4).

Like Malinowski, Radcliffe-Brown did his first important fieldwork with people who lived on islands. He published *The Andaman Islanders* in 1922, the same year that Malinowski's *Argonauts* came out. (The Andaman Islands are located in the Bay of Bengal, off the coast of India.) He was not the fieldworker that Malinowski was, but the precision of his analysis of social institutions had a lasting influence on anthropology.

Much ink has been spilled over the somewhat less than earth-shaking question of whether or not Radcliffe-Brown was a true functionalist. In my opinion, he was. Malinowski and Radcliffe-Brown were two very different personalities, and they tended to stress the differences between their respective theoretical positions. Once it is understood that Radcliffe-Brown was talking about society (rather than culture) and that he confined his explanations to the requirements of the social structure (rather than derive the social structure from human needs), Malinowski and Radcliffe-Brown stand on common ground. They shared a synchronic approach, they both emphasized the integration of sociocultural systems, and they both were concerned with how such systems worked.

SUMMARY

There were no professional (academic) anthropologists until E. B. Tylor began teaching at Oxford in 1884. However, some anthropological work was done prior to that date, and there were a number of developments that paved the way for the development of anthropology as a discipline.

The geologist Charles Lyell published *Principles of Geology* between 1830 and 1833. Although he did not phrase it in quite that way, Lyell advocated an evolutionary approach to the study of geology. Beginning in 1837, Boucher de Perthes worked on the prehistoric archeology of France. He was able to establish that mankind was much older than most people believed, dating back to a time when animals now extinct roamed the earth. Charles Darwin published his monumental *The Origin of Species* in 1859. It clearly explained the major mechanisms of evolution and presented a wealth of factual evidence. After that, no thoughtful person could ignore the concept of evolution.

The first anthropologists, men like E. B. Tylor (1832–1917) in England and Lewis Henry Morgan (1818–1881) in the United States, tended to cast their inquiries in *evolutionary* terms. They felt that there were a series of cultural stages through which all cultures were supposed to pass, such as the "Age of Savagery," the "Age of Barbarism," and the "Age of Civilization." It was a time when comparatively little was known about the actual lifeways of primitive peoples, and therefore a great deal of speculation entered into their formulations. However, Tylor and Morgan did not confine themselves to the idea of cultural evolution. Tylor, for example, is credited with one of the first acceptable definitions of culture, and Morgan did pioneering work in the analysis of kinship systems.

The early history of anthropology (and much of its later history as well) can be viewed as a series of reactions and counterreactions to various theoretical positions. The reaction against the doctrine of cultural evolution took place under the leadership of Franz Boas (1858–1942). Trained in Germany in physics and geography, Boas became the first significant academic anthropologist in the United States. He trained virtually an entire generation of American anthropologists.

Boas stressed the importance of *fieldwork* to provide a factual foundation for anthropological studies. He rejected sweeping theories of cultural evolution as either unprovable or demonstrably false in terms of specific detail. According to Boas, every human group had its own unique history, and therefore one task of anthropology was to attempt to unravel particular historical sequences. This he tried to do by a technique called *historical reconstruction,* which involved chopping cultures up into bits and pieces (traits) and plotting distributions which were supposed to reveal historical connections.

Up to this point, anthropological studies had been largely *diachronic,* or time-oriented. Then the focus moved to *synchronic* investigations—the examination of a culture at one point in time. This was largely done in the tradition called *functionalism,* a point of view articulated by two anthropologists in England, Bronislaw Malinowski and A. R. Radcliffe-Brown.

Bronislaw Malinowski (1884 – 1942) was born in Poland and took his doctoral degree in mathematics and physics. Then he went to England where he studied anthropology. A gifted fieldworker, Malinowski spent years in the Trobriand Islands. Partially as a result of that experience, Malinowski stressed the *integration* of cultural systems. His concern was in trying to understand how a culture worked: He viewed it as an interrelated whole rather than in terms of discrete traits. According to Malinowski, the function of any part of a cultural system was the contribution that it made to the operation of the total culture.

A. R. Radcliffe-Brown (1881 – 1955) was trained at Cambridge and was one of the founders of social anthropology. His approach was similar to Malinowski's, except that Radcliffe-Brown concentrated on the study of *society* (social structure) rather than on the totality of culture. He argued that a society was like an organism: It was made up of interconnected parts, and the function of any given part was what it did to enable the social system to go on working.

References

Boas, Franz (ed.). 1938. *General Anthropology.* New York: D. C. Heath.

Daniel, Glyn E. 1950. *A Hundred Years of Archaeology.* London: Duckworth and Company.

Darwin, Charles. 1967. (First edition, 1859.) *On the Origin of Species.* A facsimile of the first edition. New York: Atheneum.

Irvine, William. 1955. *Apes, Angles, and Victorians.* New York: McGraw-Hill.

Lyell, Charles. 1830 – 1833. *The Principles of Geology, Being an Attempt to Explain the Former Changes of the Earth's Surface, by Reference to Causes Now in Operation,* 1st ed. London: John Murray.

————. 1863. *The Geological Evidences of the Antiquity of Man.* Philadelphia: G. W. Childs.

Malinowski, Bronislaw. 1922. *Argonauts of the Western Pacific.* New York: Dutton.

————. 1935. *Coral Gardens and Their Magic.* London: Allen and Unwin.

————. 1944. *A Scientific Theory of Culture.* Chapel Hill: The University of North Carolina Press.

Morgan, Lewis Henry. 1851. *League of the Ho-de-no-sau-nee, or Iroquois.* Rochester, N.Y.: Sage and Broa.

————. 1871. *Systems of Consanguinity and Affinity of the Human Family.* Washington, D.C.: Smithsonian Institution.

————. 1877. *Ancient Society.* New York: World.

Radcliffe-Brown, A. R. 1922. *The Andaman Islanders.* Cambridge, England: Cambridge University Press.

————. 1952. *Structure and Function in Primitive Society.* New York: Free Press.

Tylor, E. B. 1889. "On a Method of Investigating the Development of Institutions; Applied to Laws of Marriage and Descent." *Journal of the Royal Anthropological Institute* 18:245 – 269.

Note: Since this chapter and the next are closely related in subject matter, the Suggestions for Further Reading will be found at the end of the next chapter.

12

The Later Development of Anthropology

While functionalism was being developed in England, American anthropology too began to strike off in new directions. While influenced by functionalist ideas — it was vitally concerned with the problem of how cultural systems were integrated — American anthropology brought a different slant to interpretations of culture.

MARGARET MEAD (1901–1978)

The early work of Margaret Mead provides a useful starting point. Mead was a student of Franz Boas, but she put her own individual stamp on everything that she did.

I cannot attempt here to summarize Mead's long, varied, and productive career. Instead, I want to examine briefly her very first book. It was called *Coming of Age in Samoa,* and it was published in 1928. If you glance at the book, you will find that it has a sympathetic foreward by Franz Boas. In fact, Boas encouraged Mead to do the kind of work that she did. As we have noted, Boas did not insist that his students follow slavishly in his footsteps. If you read the book, you will discover that it is a far cry from what is usually thought of as Boasian anthropology.

Mead went to Samoa to investigate the problem of adolescence. In our culture, adolescence tends to be a difficult and troubled time of life. Was this turbulence, Mead wondered, a necessary part of growing up? Or was it a cultural phenomenon, related to the way children were raised in one particular society?

Mead tells us what she did in Samoa: "I concentrated upon the girls of the community. I spent the greater part of my time with them. I studied most closely

Samoans.

the households in which adolescent girls lived. I spent more time in the games of children than in the councils of their elders'' (Mead 1928:16). She concluded that, for the most part, female adolescence was not a difficult time of life in Samoa. In general, the girls were tranquil and satisfied. She related this finding to Samoan attitudes toward personality, sex, and the social roles of females.

Without evaluating the book further, we may take note of two things about it. First, obviously, this is a new kind of American anthropology—we are a long way from counting tipi poles and plotting the distribution of folktales. Second, this was the forerunner of a whole set of theoretical interests in anthropology—

Margaret Mead.

studies that are generally referred to as the *culture and personality* school. Mead subtitled her book "A Psychological Study of Primitive Youth for Western Civilization." Of course, this indicates her early interest in communicating her findings to the widest possible audience—it is no accident that Margaret Mead was probably the most famous anthropologist in the world—but it also indicates a *psychological* orientation. Culture and personality studies ask several important questions. To what degree are our personalities shaped by cultures in which we live? Are certain types of personalities more common in some cultures than in others? How are these personalities affected by the different child-raising techniques practiced in different cultures? If the reader is intrigued by these questions, some suggestions for further reading will be found at the end of this chapter.

Top, A Kwakiutl village. *Bottom*, Kwakiutl dancers.

RUTH BENEDICT (1887–1948)

Ruth Benedict wrote one of the most widely read books ever produced by an anthropologist, *Patterns of Culture*, published in 1934. (Apart from the grace of its prose, *Patterns of Culture* was one of the first anthropological works to be published in a paperback edition, and this at a time when paperbacks were by no means as common as they are today. Until a few years ago, if a person had read only one book in anthropology it was probably *Patterns of Culture*.)

Ruth Benedict was something of a humanist in her approach, and she was interested in many things, including cultural relativism. However, *Patterns of Culture* is basically concerned with two problems: the way cultural integration is achieved and the relationship between culture and personality. Again, we may note the long arm of Franz Boas; the book begins with a perceptive introduction written by him.

Benedict argued that at least some cultures were organized (or patterned) by being built up around one dominating central idea. There was a single unifying principle, and all of the key ideas and feelings in the culture were related to that principle. To illustrate what she meant, she chose two contrasting types of cultures. One she called Apollonian and the other Dionysian. (The terms are borrowed from Nietzsche's discussion of character types in Greek tragedies.) The Apollonian cultural configuration could be described as one that aimed for balance, restraint, harmony, and unity. The motto of such a culture might be "everything in its place and all things in moderation." The Dionysian approach was the opposite. Here, the idea was to break through the mundane, to get beyond everyday experience, to seek wisdom through excess. It is the difference between calm and orderly contemplation and the kind of vision or revelation that comes from drugs or alcohol.

The Zuni Indians of the American Southwest were her example of an Apollonian culture. She calls attention to the careful, measured, repetitive character of Zuni ceremonial activities. There was no room for innovation: The idea was to repeat things precisely as they had always been done. Dreams—since they could not be controlled—were feared and avoided. Aggressive individuals were frowned upon; the ideal was to blend in with the group. The desired personality type was an easygoing, poised, predictable person who worked for group harmony.

The Kwakiutl Indians of Vancouver Island (studied by Franz Boas) were one of her examples of a Dionysian kind of culture. Here, the ceremonial life is very different. Kwakiutl dances were wild and frenzied; in some of them dancers would lunge at onlookers and bite flesh from their arms, and dance leaders were supposed to "froth at the mouth, tremble violently and abnormally, do deeds which would be terrible in a normal state. Some dancers were tethered by four ropes held by attendants, so that they might not do irreparable damage in their frenzy" (Benedict 1934:162). Dreams and visions were eagerly sought. The people were after "the power that destroys man's reason." The Kwakiutl were

Ruth Benedict.

supposed to be aggressive and hostile. There was a contant struggle for power, and the ideal personality type was a person who was suspicious, resentful, and quick to take offense. Indeed, Benedict characterizes the Kwakiutl as somewhat paranoid.

Now, Benedict clearly has something here. The Zuni lifestyle *is* different from that of the Kwakiutl, and the difference consists of more than just the sum of the parts of the two cultural systems: The difference is fundamental and it involves a difference in the *orientation* of cultural wholes, a difference in world views.

Attractive as it is, there are two major problems with Benedict's approach. On a theoretical level, it is most unlikely that any cultures are so internally consistent that they can be characterized adequately in terms of a single unifying principle. On an ethnographic level, critics have pointed out that her descriptions of the Zuni and Kwakiutl cultures are unduly simplistic. When you examine those cultures in more detail, it is apparent that not all of the values in Kwakiutl life are Dionysian, and similarly not all of the motifs in Zuni life are Apollonian.

Therefore, we must applaud Benedict's central insight, but we must also emphasize that it represents an approach that should be used only with the greatest caution. Few cultures are as strongly patterned as Benedict suggested, and they can be reduced to one key principle only by a highly selective use of evidence.

MORRIS E. OPLER (1907–   )

Morris E. Opler has proposed one way out of the Benedictian dilemma. Instead of searching for a single "master key" that supplied the framework for cultural integration, why not recognize that most cultural systems are in fact organized around a series of basic ideas or assumptions? Opler called these basic ideas or "dynamic affirmations" *themes.* (Other writers have spoken of cultural postulates or premises, which amount to the same thing.) In Opler's view, it is the interplay between the themes in a cultural system that provides cultural integration. In essence, the distinction here is that themes are multiple, while Benedict's dominant central principles are singular. Opler also notes the important point that themes tend to generate counterthemes, which have the effect of introducing variety into the cultural system.

For an example not discussed by Opler himself, consider the American (U.S.) culture pattern. It would be difficult to find a single master principle that characterizes the American culture, although some have tried to do so. On the other hand, it is possible to identify a number of basic themes. Let's look at three, bearing in mind that there are a number of other basic ones.

1. *People are rational.* This is the underlying premise of democracy—an assumption that if you give the people enough information they will make the "correct" choices. The theme has many ramifications. One obvious one is that Americans tend to pride themselves on being practical, tough-minded, and realistic. This is one reason why mysticism has had rough sledding as a dominant motif in American culture.
2. *The world (and perhaps the universe) is ours to manipulate.* The world is not a "finished product" to which we must adapt, but rather "raw materials" out of which we must build. This goes back to the heritage of a frontier society; land (and sea and air and space) is a *challenge* to Americans. Our first impulse is to change it. Cut down the trees, build the dams, tunnel the mountains! We even speak of the "conquest" of space. It is now a *fight* against air pollution, a *race* to find new energy sources, a *crusade* against social injustice. I often think of the Kamba in this regard, who tend to feel that in many situations people are powerless. Many times I heard them say: "It is a famine. We will all die." They were not complaining, but stating what was to them a fact of life.
3. *The individual is important.* This is the I'm-as-good-as-the-next-person syndrome. It is reflected in the *ideal* of equality. It too has many ramifications. Don't push me around! One person, one vote. Note our

emphasis on individual achievement—personal responsibility and competition based on self-initiative. The individual tends to become something of a social atom, which is why loneliness has been the great theme of American writers from Melville through Hemingway and Thomas Wolfe to modern authors.

It is of interest to note that many of the counterculture themes are simple reversals of these ideas; in an Oplerian sense, they too are a part of the culture— the reactions to dominant themes. Thus, we have the interest in mystical experiences, the idea that we must live in harmony with nature, and the emphasis on communal rather than individual values.

Opler's thematic approach has not been employed widely in anthropological analysis. It is, nevertheless, a useful tool and one that can be applied to any cultural system. It will not "explain" everything, of course, but it is capable of yielding meaningful insights.

THE RETURN OF EVOLUTION: LESLIE A. WHITE

If we may oversimplify a bit, it is generally accurate to state that for many years the concept of cultural evolution was pretty much a dead duck in anthropology. Boas, as we have seen, advocated a kind of historical particularism to account for cultural differences, and the functionalists and others interested in cultural integration tended to favor synchronic techniques of analysis which did not focus on the problem of cultural change through time.

However, leaving aside the details of specific evolutionary theories, the basic idea of cultural evolution has a persistent attractiveness to it. It is a demonstrated archeological fact that there is a genuine temporal sequence of ecologically based culture types: The hunters and gatherers came first, then (in the Neolithic) tribal societies based on farming and domesticated animals, and lastly the emergence of urbanism and state-organized sociocultural systems. Moreover, the ethnological data generally support the concept that these are different kinds of cultural systems: Hunting and gathering societies are fundamentally different in scale and organization from tribal societies, and state systems cannot be understood simply as overgrown tribes.

The Boasians were certainly correct in calling attention to the massive errors in the particular evolutionary schemes proposed by the early evolutionists such as Lewis Henry Morgan. But there was a growing suspicion that in rejecting the idea of cultural evolution entirely they may have thrown the baby out with the bathwater. Cultural evolution is a powerful explanatory concept. Why would it not be possible, utilizing more accurate archeological and ethnological data, to correct the errors and rescue (or resurrect) the basic idea of cultural evolution?

Leslie A. White (1900–1975) did precisely that. It was not easy. At the University of Michigan White found himself almost alone in an anthropology dominated by the Boasians and the functionalists. The battle was a bitter one—

Increasing energy yields make possible cultural complexity.

still raging when I was an undergraduate—but its details need not concern us here. It is enough to say that White was successful in making cultural evolution intellectually respectable again and that the majority of anthropologists today tend to accept White's evolutionary ideas in general if not always in detail.

There are two points that must be understood here. First, White's theoretical position involves more than the concept of cultural evolution. He viewed culture entirely as a *superorganic* phenomenon and regarded individuals (whether considered biologically or in terms of personality) as irrelevant to the culture process. People were simply the *carriers* of culture, and in White's view the science of anthropology became what he called *culturology*. In other words, culture could only be studied in terms of itself. (White was an excellent and provocative writer. Students should take a look at his essays "Ikhnaton: The Great Man vs. the Culture Process" and "Man's Control over Civilization: An Anthropocentric Illusion" to get the flavor of this aspect of his work. Both essays are included in his *Science of Culture,* published in 1949.) By no means all anthropologists would go along with White on this, and many would also dispute his extreme emphasis on technological determinism. A second point that should be remembered is that the revival of cultural evolution also involved the work of other scholars. Most notable of these was the British archeologist V. Gordon Childe (1892–1957). In such books as *Man Makes Himself* (1939) and *Social Evolution* (1951) Childe drew on his impressive knowledge of Old World prehistory to demonstrate that the cultural development of mankind through time was a fact, not merely a theory.

To return to White's evolutionary ideas, he first makes it clear that he is talking about culture as a whole. He states:

Sophisticated farming increases cultural potential.

> We may regard the human race—man—as a one. We may likewise think of all of the various cultures or cultural traditions as constituting a single entity: the culture of mankind. We may therefore address ourselves to the task of tracing the course of the development of this culture from its source to the present day. (White 1949:364)

Culture, he goes on, is an organized, integrated system. There are three basic subsystems within the cultural system: technological, sociological, and ideological. According to White, the technological system is primary and most important; that is, both sociological systems (the organization of society) and ideological systems (values and religion) are dependent on the technological system. In other words, the technological system is the determinant of the cultural system as a whole.

White uses the term *function* in a new way. The function of culture (what it does), in his view, is to harness and control *energy* for human use. This it accomplishes by means of its technology. Therefore, White arrives at his basic "law" of cultural evolution. It is: "Culture evolves as the amount of energy harnessed per capita per year is increased, or as the efficiency of the instrumental means of putting the energy to work is increased" (White 1949: 368–369).

In terms of cultural evolution, then, what do we get? As White recognizes, we wind up with something like the cultural "stages" of the early evolutionists. The first cultures were those dependent upon the energy of the human organism itself. White figures that such hunting and gathering cultures produced about one-twentieth horsepower per capita. There were severe limits to the cultural possibilities in such a culture. As he puts it, "No cultural system, activated by human energy alone, can develop very far" (White 1949: 369).

In order for culture to develop further, new sources of energy had to be tapped. This was done in the Neolithic. White states:

New energy sources have cultural consequences.

> Plants are, of course, forms and magnitudes of energy. Energy
> from the sun is captured by the process of photosynthesis and stored
> up in the form of plant tissue. All animal life is dependent, in the
> last analysis, upon this solar energy stored up in plants. All life,
> therefore, is dependent on photosynthesis. (White 1949:370–371)

By cultivating plants and by domesticating animals that lived on plants,
mankind enormously increased its available energy and thus its cultural potential. White goes on to make much the same point about such new energy
sources as coal, oil, gas, and steam and internal combustion engines. Each new
development in terms of energy yields produced a change in cultural complexity. As White says:

> The consequences of the Fuel Revolution were in general much
> like those of the Agricultural Revolution: an increase in population,
> larger political units, bigger cities, an accumulation of wealth, a rapid
> development of the arts and sciences, in short, a rapid and extensive
> advance of culture as a whole. (White 1949:373–374)

If White is correct, or even partially correct, it is interesting to speculate about
what the cultural consequences of a reduction in energy might be. What happens, so to speak, when culture runs out of gas?

Since it is concerned with the evolution of the culture of mankind as a
whole, White's position has been called *universal evolution*. The majority of
anthropologists today would accept the general idea of universal evolution, if not
all of its theoretical underpinnings and biases. (For example, are we really ad-

Eskimo seal hunter.

vanced, or are we just different?) The broad outline is clear enough. It is hardly arguable that the culture of mankind, considered as a single unit, has indeed evolved technologically through time from simple to complex.

There are two major problems connected with universal evolution. First, it is possible to grant that there has been technological evolutionary "advance" through time and to acknowledge that technology influences the rest of culture, and still to question the implied "progress" of culture as a whole. For instance, many would doubt that "civilized" values are any "better" than those of hunters and gatherers. Second, as soon as we move from grand generalizations about the culture of mankind to considerations about *specific* human cultures the concept of universal evolution does not help us very much. If we seek to understand the culture of the Kamba or the Navaho or the Jivaro, we need to employ some other technique of analysis. It won't suffice to lump them all together in one great cultural stew. It is this latter problem that points up the importance of cultural ecology.

CULTURAL ECOLOGY

In universal evolution, as we have seen, all human cultures are in effect averaged together to produce a single worldwide cultural unit. When this is done, it is apparent that there is only one meaningful environment that can be discussed, and that is the environment of the planet earth. In other words, not only are all cultures averaged together, but so are all local environmental situations.

In cultural ecology, the focus shifts to particular cultural systems and the

An early Arctic scientific base.

specific environmental contexts with which they interact. *Ecology* can be defined as the science that deals with the interrelationships between living organisms and their environment. Cultural ecology is concerned with the interrelationships between cultural systems and the environments within which they exist. The key word here is *interrelationship*. There is a dynamic interaction between the culture and its environmental setting; it is not a one-way street. If the culture is influenced by the environment, it is likewise true that the environment is influenced by the culture.

It is important to understand that cultural ecology is not the same thing as environmental determinism. In extreme form, environmental determinism asserts that the environment produces the culture: Given environment X, you can predict culture Y. This will not work, because culture itself is a part of the dynamic equation. A moment's reflection will make this clear. Taking even a simplistic view of the environment—the available flora and fauna, the soil types, the temperature ranges, the amount and distribution of rainfall, and so forth—any environment offers a variety of possibilities depending upon the cultural resources that are brought to bear upon it.

Technological systems (which are parts of cultural systems) provide the most obvious examples of this. Consider the North American Plains, for instance. The Plains offered one kind of opportunity to foot hunters with limited range and mobility. The Plains offered other possibilities to Indians mounted on horses. Still other lifeways were possible when agriculture was introduced into the river valleys. More opportunities were opened up by modern subsurface water pumping and irrigation techniques, to say nothing of industrial complexes.

Even extreme environmental situations provide more than one kind of ecological adaptation. In the Arctic, it is one thing to hunt seals with a harpoon, and something else again to introduce modern firearms — and it is quite possible to establish scientific bases supplied entirely by aircraft. Similarly, it is one thing to herd camels in the desert and quite another matter to extract oil from desert wells. This point must be grasped, but it is not complicated. *To some degree, any environmental situation will be modified by the cultural resources brought to bear upon it.* Cultural ecology is concerned with the dynamic *interrelationships* between cultural systems and their environmental contexts.

It is hardly news to point out that cultures exist in specific environments: A culture cannot exist in a vacuum or in never-never land. Moreover, there is a very long tradition in anthropology of taking some account of environmental factors. From the very beginning, all satisfactory ethnographic studies provided information on the environmental "setting," some of it quite detailed. In 1934 C. Daryll Forde wrote an influential book, *Habitat, Economy and Society.* It was subtitled *A Geographical Introduction to Ethnology,* and it by no means neglected environmental considerations. The "culture area" approach in American ethnology, developed by Clark Wissler (1917, 1926) and A. L. Kroeber (1939), also involved environmental concerns. (A culture area is simply a geographical region within which the cultures tend to resemble one another to some degree.)

Against this background, therefore, we must ask what it is about cultural ecology that makes it distinctive. What did the cultural ecologists do that was different from what anthropologists had done before? While not all cultural ecologists operate with the same basic assumptions and not all of them are interested in the same kinds of problems, it remains true that there is one characteristic of cultural ecology that usually distinguishes it from other approaches. In a nutshell, it is this: The underlying idea of cultural ecology is that ecological situations exercise a causative influence on cultural processes. In other words, particular ecological frameworks make certain cultural responses not only possible but probable. Note several points here. First, as we have indicated, this is not a return to environmental determinism: In cultural ecology, the ecological situation *includes* the interrelationships between the culture and its environment. Second, the approach does not assert that a specific cultural response is inevitable in a particular ecological context, but only that some cultural responses are more likely than others. It is not a dogmatic theory, but rather an investigative hypothesis. It is a let's-look-and-see approach. It alerts the researcher to possible interconnections between cultural characteristics and ecological bases.

It was the American anthropologist Julian H. Steward (1902–1972) who pioneered the development of cultural ecology. In 1936 Steward published a seminal article entitled "The Economic and Social Basis of Primitive Bands." (The paper was actually written several years earlier, but it was considered to be so controversial that he had difficulty getting it published.) In the article, Steward argued that hunting and gathering peoples in adverse environments could attain population densities of less than one person per square mile, a situation which resulted in social groupings ("bands") which were necessarily small (30 to 50 persons) but larger than simple (nuclear) family groups because the band was more effective than the smaller family group in providing security and food. He then went on to discuss various band subtypes and the ecological reasons for their existence, a point that need not detain us here. The critical thing about Steward's demonstration was his insistence that similar ecological situations produced similar effects among such widely separated peoples as African Pygmies and California Indians; he had identified a *type* of sociocultural organization that recurred on virtually a worldwide basis and had offered an explanation of why it took the form it did.

In "Cultural Causality and Law: A Trial Formulation of the Development of Early Civilizations" (1949) Steward, examining similar (or parallel) cultural sequences in Peru, Mexico, Mesopotamia, Egypt, and China, found strong resemblances between them, which he attributed to specific interactions between cultures and certain types of environmental situations. Note that he was not advocating a universally valid scheme of evolution; whether he was right or wrong in his conclusions, he was attempting to explain what had happened in a limited number of *particular* culture sequences. Steward referred to his approach as *multilinear evolution,* which he defined as "searching for parallels of limited occurrence instead of universals" (Steward 1953:315).

In his book *Theory of Culture Change* (1955), Steward sums up his views on cultural ecology. He states that the central problem in cultural ecology "is to ascertain whether the adjustments of human societies to their environments require particular modes of behavior or whether they permit latitude for a certain range of possible behavior patterns." He calls attention to the importance of what he terms the *cultural core* — "the constellation of features which are most closely related to subsistence activities and economic arrangements." It is his thesis that "cultural ecology pays primary attention to those features which empirical analysis shows to be most closely involved in the utilization of environment in culturally prescribed ways."

According to Steward, there are three "fundamental procedures" in cultural ecology:

1. "The interrelationship of exploitative or productive technology and environment must be analyzed."
2. "The behavior patterns involved in the exploitation of a particular area by means of a particular technology must be analyzed."
3. "The third procedure is to ascertain the extent to which the behavior patterns entailed in exploiting the environment affect other aspects of culture." Steward regards this as a "purely empirical problem." In other words, it requires "a genuinely holistic approach, for if such factors as demography, settlement pattern, kinship structures, land tenure, land use, and other key cultural features are considered separately, their interrelationships to one another and to the environment cannot be grasped." (Steward 1955:30–42)

Walter Goldschmidt.

Julian Steward is widely credited with being the founder of cultural ecology, and his reputation is richly deserved. However, Steward was not entirely alone in considering the problems of cultural adaptation during those formative years. There were other scholars who were addressing the same or similar crucial cultural questions.

Foremost among them was Walter Goldschmidt (1912–). Goldschmidt's work has been characterized by the breadth of his theoretical interests, including important work in such areas as cultural values and psychological anthropology, but his contributions to cultural ecology and his own brand of "multilinear" evolution have been substantial and of long duration.

In 1947 Goldschmidt published *As You Sow,* a book based on his study of several California farming communities. The book is not only one of the most successful anthropological attempts to deal with modern communities but also a clear reflection of his ecological orientation. Indeed, the very first sentence of the preface sets the tone of the study: "From industrialized sowing of the soil is reaped an urbanized rural society."

The next year, 1948, witnessed the publication of one of his major articles, "Social Organization in Native California and the Origin of Clans." The article is interesting for several reasons. First, it reveals in a dramatic way how unfashionable ecological and evolutionary viewpoints were in anthropology at that time. He states: "It is with a feeling of great temerity that I address myself to the problem of clan origin," and he recognizes that he has ventured "to trespass where angels do not tread" (Goldschmidt 1948:444). Second, it offers one possible explanation for the existence of clans. (For a discussion of clans, see Chapter 15.) Goldschmidt argues:

> No modern ethnologist links the clan systems of Africa, Oceania
> and the Americas. Similar social systems therefore have arisen
> repeatedly. . . . Such uniformity calls for a common causative force,
> and this force must be sought in the structural relationships of society;
> that is, it must be sociological in character. I would postulate that the
> need for clan organization and its particular value to the community
> appears when the population reaches a certain density and size. . . .
> Usually such density is the product of technological developments,
> particularly the adoption or invention of horticultural techniques. But it
> is not horticulture in itself which appears to be crucial. The California
> situation demonstrates this, for here it has been possible to assemble a
> considerable population density merely by rather advanced exploitation
> of a fairly rich environment. (Goldschmidt 1948:452)

Goldschmidt is careful to allow for alternative possibilities; he is not talking about
an inevitable sequence: "I do not want to leave the impression that I think a certain density of population will automatically bring about a clan organization of
society. Other adjustments are possible; and a people can continue, if circumstances permit, without real adjustment" (Goldschmidt 1948:453).

Goldschmidt's theoretical position is most fully presented in *Man's Way*
(1959), a tightly reasoned book that effectively unites functional social anthropology with evolutionary ecological ideas. Goldschmidt states: "Evolution is not
the unfolding of a predetermined course. Rather, it is the chance product, the
unanticipated consequences of the working out of regular forces in nature"
(Goldschmidt 1959:108).

In his view, there are five basic elements in the dynamics of cultural evolution:

> (1) The tendency for technological growth and development through
> time; (2) the social consequences of such technological development;
> (3) the process of selection of those societies and institutions that best
> cope with the exigencies which these changes bring about; (4) continuity
> through time in cultural forms (i.e., that cultural forms emerge out of pre-
> existing ones); and (5) internal congruity and functional fitness of the
> various aspects of culture. (Goldschmidt 1959:110)

Goldschmidt's ideas are both subtle and complex. Rather than attempt a
summary, let us point out just one key idea that permeates his work. Goldschmidt argues that there is a kind of natural selection that operates at the cultural level. He notes that this selection takes two forms. One is internal, involving
"the adaptive changes and adjustments taking place within a society, the shifting
of institutions that result from recognized or sensed malfunctioning." The other
is external, referring to "the processes that result from competition and warfare
with other social systems" (Goldschmidt 1959:122).

He returns to this point in *Comparative Functionalism* (1966). In discussing the ecological context within which sociocultural systems operate, he empha-

sizes that the physical environment—and the interrelationship between the physical environment and the social system—is only one factor in the ecological equation. The other factor is the *social* environment within which a particular sociocultural system exists: the presence of other competing human societies. In other words, it makes a big difference who your neighbors are. A relatively inefficient cultural system can muddle through if it is surrounded by other equally inefficient systems, but if a more powerful group develops or moves into an area the situation is radically changed. To take a classic example, consider the plight of a hunting and gathering society forced to compete with a farming or herding society with greater population resources and more complex organizational techniques. The hunting and gathering society has only three options: It can adapt by changing its economic base, it can move away into an area where there are no powerful societies, or it can become extinct. As Goldschmidt notes:

> This factor, once mentioned, is so self-evidently important that it is a wonder that so little recognition has been taken of it in sociological investigation. In truth, except for a few isolated communities, such as those of the Eskimo, it is a factor of first importance in all societies. (Goldschmidt 1966:51)

As the reader has perhaps fathomed by now, there is no lack of theories in cultural anthropology. At the same time, there has been relatively little systematic *testing* of theoretical principles. This was what Goldschmidt and his associates sought to do in the Culture and Ecology in East Africa Project. The rationale behind the research is set forth in Goldschmidt's "Theory and Strategy in the Study of Cultural Adaptability" (1965).

Goldschmidt explains:

> Our investigation is a study in cultural adaptation, in ecological analysis, in the character of economic influence on culture and behavior or in social micro-evolution—depending upon which of the currently fashionable terminologies one prefers. It is—or endeavors to be—all of these for the simple reason that they are different perspectives on the same thing. Let us use the framework of ecological adaptation. (Goldschmidt 1965:402)

The project was ambitious, utilizing the services of four ethnographers, a geographer, and an anthropologist-psychologist. Four East African tribes were chosen for field investigation: the Sebei, the Pokot, the Kamba, and the Hehe. They were picked because each tribe contained groups that were primarily herders and groups that were primarily farmers. Essentially, one ethnographer studied two groups in the tribe for which he was responsible (herders and farmers), while the geographer moved from group to group analyzing and mapping the physical environment and the anthropologist-psychologist did likewise administering a battery of psychological tests.

A characteristic scene at the Kamba herding site.

The idea, of course, was to find out if similar ecological situations did indeed tend to produce similar cultural characteristics. As Goldschmidt expressed it:

> Functional theory assumes that the institutions of a society are integrated wholes, that changes in one sector require adjustments in other sectors of the social system. This was the set of ideas which we are endeavoring to test. Let us put it this way: we treat environment as the independent variable; then, assuming a repertoire of techniques available, the pattern of economic exploitation becomes the intermediate variable, while the institutions of society, cultural attitudes and behavior patterns, become the dependent variables. (Goldschmidt 1965:403)

Although the full results of this study have not yet been published, it is possible to say that in general terms the test was a successful one. That is, despite many difficulties the research team was able to demonstrate a number of predicted sociocultural similarities between the pastoral (herding) segments of the four tribes and between the farming segments of the four tribes. I do not mean to suggest that the herders were identical to one another, or that all the farmers were the same. Nor do I wish to suggest that there was a perfect fit between theoretical expectations and what was actually found. Nevertheless, consistent tendencies did appear—and they turned up in widely separated tribes (in Kenya, Uganda, and Tanzania) speaking different languages and with different cultural traditions. While this is certainly not the final word on the subject, the study does strongly support many of the basic assumptions of cultural ecology. (For details

The Kamba farming site. Note cattle surrounded by cultivated fields.

on some of the results of the Culture and Ecology Project, see Edgerton 1971 and Goldschmidt 1976.)

A great deal of recent anthropological research has been phrased in the idiom of cultural ecology. It is impossible to list all of the significant research in a book such as this. However, mention must be made of Roy Rappaport's elegant and influential *Pigs for the Ancestors: Ritual in the Ecology of a New Guinea People* (1968). In this stimulating book, Rappaport presents an analysis of how the ritual killing of pigs among the Maring affects such matters as maintaining an effective ecological balance in the pig population (that is, reducing their numbers when the "cost" of maintaining large numbers of pigs exceeds their social value), providing needed animal protein at crucial times to combat stress, and regulating warfare over a large area (because truces require a very long ceremony called a *kaiko*, hostilities cannot resume until the ceremony is completed, and the ceremony involves a large-scale pig slaughter that cannot take place without a substantial increase in the pig population).

The study makes use of a number of innovations, the most notable of which involves treating ritual as a regulating mechanism in a complex system. As Rappaport states:

> Maring ritual, in short, operates not only as a homeostat — maintaining a number of variables that comprise the total system within ranges of viability — but also as a transducer — "translating" changes in the state of one subsystem into information and energy that can produce changes in the second subsystem. (Rappaport 1968:229)

He also notes:

> Like thermostats, rituals have a binary aspect. As the thermostat switches on and off, affecting the amount of heat produced by the furnace and the temperature of the medium, so the rituals . . . are initiated and completed, affecting the size of the pig population, the amount of land under cultivation, the amount of labor expended, the frequency of warfare, and other components of the system. (Rappaport 1968:234)

Several other points should be noted. First, Rappaport is meticulous on matters of detail, providing quantified data wherever possible. To anyone who has struggled with these problems in the field, his work commands admiration. Second, Rappaport is one of the few anthropologists to make consistent use of ethological concepts in his work. The book must be read to appreciate this fully, but he is quite explicit about his point of view:

> My belief that it is not only possible but preferable to examine man's ecological relations in terms that also apply to noncultural species has been reflected throughout this study. Anthropology has been mainly concerned with phenomena unique in man, but it seems to me that if we are to understand what is uniquely human we must also consider those aspects of existence which man shares with other creatures. (Rappaport 1968:241–242)

To put the matter simply, one of the exciting possibilities inherent in cultural ecology is that it may ultimately provide a crucial bridge between traditional anthropological interests and the larger world of animal behavior.

"AND THEN THERE'S LÉVI-STRAUSS."

One of my colleagues (Robert A. Fernea, who has himself done important work in cultural ecology) was talking about textbooks not long ago. He made the point that most of them cover the traditional anthropologists, such as Boas and Malinowski, in some detail, but that often when they get to Lévi-Strauss they tend to be somewhat perfunctory: "And then there's Lévi-Strauss." I have taken the liberty of borrowing his phrase.

It is probably impossible to view more or less current developments in anthropological theory with the same degree of perspective that one can bring to the accomplishments of an earlier generation. Nevertheless, it is possible to single out one person who has generated sharp debate within anthropology and who has at the same time become something of a popular "cult" figure. That person is certainly Claude Lévi-Strauss (1908–).

Lévi-Strauss is a philosophically trained French anthropologist who has done fieldwork in Brazil and who advocates a theoretical approach called *structural anthropology*. Beyond that simple statement — and it is about as bald and neutral as a statement can be — it is difficult to say anything about Lévi-Strauss that is noncontroversial. He has both fervent disciples and ardent debunkers, which I suppose is something of a testimonial to the originality of his thinking. Moreover, his work is sufficiently complex that it defies easy summation.

I do not pretend to know why Lévi-Strauss has the popular reputation that he does; it is definitely not due to any attempt on his part to "write down" to the public. Quite frankly, reading Lévi-Strauss tends to be rather heavy going. I suspect that one appealing element in his work is his insistence on the idea that there is discoverable meaning underlying apparent and superficial chaos; this is an attractive notion in the often confusing world in which we live. In any event, the problem is not to "explain" his popular influence but rather to understand the nature of his contributions to anthropological thought.

Perhaps the best approach is to attempt to set forth what it is that Lévi-Strauss is trying to do in structural anthropology instead of presenting the detailed results of his investigations. For the latter, the only sensible advice to the student is to go and read Lévi-Strauss. For the former, I will try to let Lévi-Strauss speak for himself as much as possible. For ease of reference, I will confine myself to a single pivotal book, *Structural Anthropology*, published in 1963. The page references are to the Anchor Books edition, published in 1967. Other works by Lévi-Strauss will be mentioned in the Suggestions for Further Reading at the end of this chapter.

Lévi-Strauss states that he begins his analysis of cultural phenomena with detailed ethnography. He stresses this point repeatedly in his work. The following passage is characteristic:

> On the observational level, the main — one could almost say the only —
> rule is that all the facts should be carefully observed and described,
> without allowing any theoretical preconception to decide whether some
> are more important than others. . . . There is a direct relationship
> between the detail and concreteness of ethnographical description and
> the validity and generality of the model which is constructed after
> it. . . . Therefore, the first task is to ascertain what those facts are.
> (Lévi-Strauss 1967:272–273)

So far, so good. We begin on an empirical level: Get the facts. This almost sounds like Boas, and indeed Boas (for this and other reasons) is frequently invoked with admiration by Lévi-Strauss. But even in this introductory passage we have learned something else about Lévi-Strauss; he is concerned with models. The ethnographic facts simply serve as a takeoff point for the construction of abstract models, and it is the models that interest Lévi-Strauss. Models are nothing new in anthropology, of course, but the models of Lévi-Strauss are distinctive, to say the least.

He is concerned not with the facts themselves, no matter how they are classified and compared, but with what the facts *mean*. He refers to "the unconscious nature of collective phenomena" and emphasizes that the people themselves do not understand why they do things:

> We know that among most primitive peoples it is very difficult to obtain a moral justification or a rational explanation for any custom or institution. When he is questioned, the native merely answers that things have always been this way, that such was the command of the gods or the teaching of the ancestors. Even when interpretations are offered, they always have the character of rationalizations or secondary elaborations. There is rarely any doubt that the unconscious reasons for practicing a custom or sharing a belief are remote from the reasons given to justify them. (Lévi-Strauss 1967:19)

In other words, the models of Lévi-Strauss are attempts to represent the *unconscious structures* (his term) of sociocultural systems.

It might be said that Lévi-Strauss is seeking to dig down below surface phenomena in order to get at the underlying structure that is not apparent on a conscious level. If we might attempt a clumsy analogy, he is not so much interested in wooden chairs and iron pipes and glass dishes as he is in the hidden atomic structure of wood, iron, and glass. (He speaks, as a matter of fact, of "atoms of kinship.") The "unconscious structures" of Lévi-Strauss are models of the *relationships* between highly abstract principles. As he puts it, "As soon as the various aspects of social life . . . are expressed as relationships, anthropology will become a general theory of relationships. Then it will be possible to analyze societies in terms of the differential features characteristic of the systems of relationships which define them" (Lévi-Strauss 1967:95).

Nor is this all. Lévi-Strauss asks the question: "Can we conclude that all forms of social life are substantially of the same nature—that is, do they consist of systems of behavior that represent the projection, on the level of conscious and socialized thought, of universal laws which regulate the unconscious activities of the mind?" (Lévi-Strauss 1967:57–58). And he answers the questions in the affirmative:

> We shall be in a position to understand basic similarities between forms of social life, such as language, art, law, and religion, that on the surface seem to differ greatly. At the same time, we shall have the hope of overcoming the opposition between the collective nature of culture and its manifestations in the individual, since the so-called "collective consciousness" would, in the final analysis, be no more than the expression, on the level of individual thought and behavior, of certain time and space modalities of the universal laws which make up the unconscious activity of the mind. (Lévi-Strauss 1967:64)

Thus, we have moved—somehow—from the facts of ethnographic description to the inner structure of the human mind. This "inner structure" of the mind tends to boil down to an assertion that the mind operates in terms of binary oppositions: distinctions between light and dark, sacred and profane, male and female, life and death, and so on. Since this is difficult if not impossible to demonstrate without recourse to intuition or revelation, one might say that we have also moved from the world of empirical reality to the world of something closely approximating metaphysics.

Be that as it may, let us stick to our original purpose, which was to attempt to explain what Lévi-Strauss is trying to do. The best analogy we have lies in the field of linguistics. Lévi-Strauss himself has repeatedly acknowledged his debt to structural linguistics, and it is from this angle that his work can be most readily comprehended. In the study of language, too, we must begin with a tangible reality: human speech. But as we have seen (Chapter 7), we cannot stop on that level. For languages have structure — phonemes, morphemes, syntax — and this structure (which can be thought of as a system of relationships or arrangements) is not apparent to the speakers of the language. We cannot articulate the rules by which we speak, but nonetheless the rules are there. The structure is unconscious. It cannot be discovered by asking a speaker, "Why do you use phonemes?" Moreover, according to Chomsky and others, the basic principles of language may be innate, which is another way of saying that they are built into the structure of the human mind. Looked at in this light, and leaving aside some of the complexities of the problem, it seems fair to say that Lévi-Strauss is attempting to apply the techniques of linguistic analysis to the analysis of social structure.

If we grant that this is his purpose, how successful has he been? It is a matter of opinion, and opinions differ. On one level, it is easy to dismiss Lévi-Strauss as inconsequential. His little diagrams of structural "realities," which tend to be somewhat fanciful combinations of lines surrounded by clusters of plus and minus signs, and his sometimes obscure pronouncements, lend themselves to ready parody. On another level, he has made significant contributions to at least two important anthropological topics: kinship and myth. Indeed, no future studies of these subjects will be able to ignore the ideas of Lévi-Strauss.

In the field of kinship, Lévi-Strauss begins with "the universal presence of an incest taboo," which he says is a prohibition against marriage between close kin. (As a number of critics have pointed out, he really has the wrong term here. Technically, incest tabus are prohibitions against mating. Marriage is another matter, and he is actually referring to rules of exogamy: the requirement that a person must "marry out" of his or her family group.) Whatever name you assign to it, this custom is a two-sided coin: The negative aspect is that a person cannot marry within that person's own family, and the positive aspect is that a person must marry someone from another family. Lévi-Strauss (1967:44) proceeds from the vantage point of the male: "A man must obtain a woman from another man who gives him a daughter or a sister." This sets up a reciprocal pattern of exchange: The family that gave up a woman eventually gets another woman back. In other words, kinship systems resolve themselves into assorted systems of exchange, and what is being exchanged are women. As Lévi-Strauss (1967:

45) says, "In human society, it is the men who exchange the women, and not vice versa."

The techniques by which Lévi-Strauss analyzes myths are too involved to discuss here, but his central insight may be simply stated: Mythical thought begins with an awareness of oppositions (or contradictions) and attempts to resolve them by means of a logical model. The story (myth), as it were, serves as a bridge between perceived contradictions (such as mortality versus immortality) and a picture of the world that symbolically reconciles or deals with the oppositions. As Lévi-Strauss might have phrased it, a myth is a mediating metaphor; it transposes a problem to a symbolic frame of reference in which the problem can be handled.

He concludes:

> Prevalent attempts to explain alleged differences between the so-called primitive mind and scientific thought have resorted to qualitative differences between the working processes of the mind in both cases, while assuming that the entities which they were studying remained very much the same. If our interpretation is correct, we are led toward a completely different view — namely, that the kind of logic in mythical thought is as rigorous as that of modern science, and that the difference lies, not in the quality of the intellectual process, but in the nature of the things to which it is applied. (*Ibid.*, Lévi-Strauss 1967:227)

If this sounds somewhat less than crystal clear, I can only repeat my original injunction: Go and read Lévi-Strauss. You may not agree with him, but I think that no objective reader can fail to be impressed by the seriousness of his purpose and the industry of his analysis. I suspect that the works of Lévi-Strauss are more the records of a lonely vision quest than an indication of where anthropology as a field of inquiry is going. Still, he has made provocative contributions to the study of the human animal, and perhaps that is enough to ask of any scholar.

THE CLOUDY CRYSTAL BALL: PARTISANS AND ECLECTICS

At times, looking at modern cultural anthropology, one is almost irresistibly reminded of the proverbial gentleman who climbed on his horse and galloped off in all directions. Aside from the trends already discussed, we have the debate between those favoring an *emic* approach (studying culture from the inside out, as it were, attempting to phrase the analysis in terms relevant to the participants in a cultural system) and those favoring the more traditional *etic* approach (utilizing, one hopes, objective categories which can be applied cross-culturally). We have various *cognitive* approaches; cognition refers to thinking, of course, and cognitive anthropology asks the question: How do people know what they know? We have *systems* theory, which deals with formal models based on cybernetic regulation and the like. We have a *symbolist* school, represented by anthropologists such as Clifford Geertz, which seeks to explain cultural dynamics in terms of a culture's symbolic definition of reality.

In anthropology as elsewhere, it is easy to miss the forest for the trees. While approaches that are novel or extreme tend to generate the most heated discussions, it is probably true that the majority of anthropologists today would at least tacitly favor an *eclectic* theoretical stance. That is, they would recognize that no single "school" of anthropology has all the answers, and they would attempt to utilize whatever theoretical approach seemed promising in terms of the problem they were trying to solve.

This open-mindedness is not without value; indeed, it is one of the more attractive aspects of anthropology. At the same time, it is an admission that we do not yet have a unified body of theory that will adequately explain what there is to explain about the human animal. At present, there is no theory of anthropology—there are only anthropological theories. The careful reader will have realized that none of the theoretical positions we have outlined are totally without merit. The cautious reader will have concluded that the grand synthesis that will put it all together has not yet been achieved.

We must ask the hard question: What is it that is lacking? If we grant that cultural anthropology has already made significant contributions to human knowledge and understanding, what more might it do? Do we simply require more information, or do we need to examine the human animal from additional perspectives?

It is striking, I think, how complete the separation has been between physical (or biological) anthropology and sociocultural theory. With the exception of Malinowski's unsatisfactory "needs" and some aspects of cultural ecology, it is as though the two sciences existed in completely distinct universes. It is also striking how little impact the amazing discoveries concerning the nonhuman primates has so far had on sociocultural theory.

If we are animals, no science that purports to deal with mankind can divorce itself from the principles of animal behavior. If we are primates, we must look at ourselves against the background of other primates. If we are culture-bearing animals, we must understand what culture is and how it works.

Like all great problems, this one is easily stated. Moreover, the solution seems obvious. We must know more, of course. But what we do know must not be sealed off in isolated compartments complete with "no trespassing" signs. Somehow, we must put it all together. When this is done, we can begin to speak of a theory of anthropology.

SUMMARY

The early work of Margaret Mead (1901–1978) shows a new direction in American anthropology. Her first book, *Coming of Age in Samoa* (1928), was basically a study of female adolescence. A forerunner of the "culture and personality" school of anthropology, the book concluded that the relatively happy adolescence of Samoan girls was related to specific aspects of the Samoan cultural system.

Ruth Benedict (1887–1948), like Mead, had been a student of Franz Boas but developed her own characteristic way of trying to understand the integration of cultural systems. In *Patterns of Culture* (1934) she argued that at least some cultures were organized around a single dominant idea that permeated the culture and affected the personalities of the participants in the culture. She suggested that some cultures, such as that of the Zuni Indians, were built around an *Apollonian* motif: everything in its place and all things in moderation. Other cultures, such as that of the Kwakiutl, were structured around a *Dionysian* principle: the idea being to break through the mundane and get beyond everyday experience.

Morris Opler (1907–) modified Benedict's approach by interpreting cultural integration as being the product of a *series* of interacting basic ideas or premises, which he referred to as *themes*.

With the advent of Leslie A. White (1900–1975), the concept of cultural evolution staged a comeback in anthropology. Viewing human culture as a whole—the culture of humankind—White argued that the "function" of culture was to harness and control *energy* for human use. With each major technological advance, such as farming in the Neolithic or the later industrial revolution, a new type of culture came into being. Essentially, White took the evolutionary ideas of Tylor and Morgan, brought them up to date, corrected their errors, and provided cultural evolution with a new theoretical base. This kind of cultural evolution is sometimes called *universal evolution,* since it refers to a rather large abstraction, the total culture of humanity.

In *cultural ecology* the focus shifts to particular cultural systems and the specific environmental contexts with which they interact. The emphasis is on *interrelationships:* a dynamic interaction between the culture and its environmental setting. In seeking to understand how particular cultures have adapted the way they have, cultural ecology tries to identify cultural tendencies rather than universal laws of cultural evolution. This approach was pioneered by Julian H. Steward (1902–1972). Steward referred to his approach as *multilinear evolution,* "searching for parallels of limited occurrence instead of universals."

The study of cultural adaptation has also characterized much of the work of Walter Goldschmidt (1912–). His theoretical position is most fully set forth in *Man's Way* (1959), a book that effectively unites functional social anthropology with evolutionary-ecological ideas. Goldschmidt and his associates sought to test the theory of cultural adaptation in the Culture and Ecology in East Africa Project, which investigated the contrasting sociocultural systems of farming and pastoral peoples.

Claude Lévi-Strauss (1908–) is a philosophically trained French anthropologist who advocates a theoretical approach called *structural anthropology.* Fundamental to this approach is the idea that there is discoverable meaning that underlies the seeming confusion of "surface" phenomena; his quest is to expose the hidden "unconscious structure" of sociocultural systems.

Most anthropologists today would agree that no single "school" of anthropology—whether those mentioned here or others—has all the answers. At the present time, there really is no wholly unified "theory of anthropology." There are only a variety of anthropological approaches, each of which contributes something to our understanding of the human animal.

References

Benedict, Ruth. 1934. *Patterns of Culture*. New York: Houghton Mifflin.

Boas, Franz (ed.). 1938. *General Anthropology*. New York: Heath.

Childe, V. Gordon. 1939. *Man Makes Himself*. New York: Oxford University Press.

———. 1951. *Social Evolution*. New York: H. Schuman.

Daniel, Glyn E. 1950. *A Hundred Years of Archaeology*. London: Duckworth and Company.

Darwin, Charles. 1967. (First edition, 1859.) *On the Origin of Species*. A facsimile of the first edition. New York: Atheneum.

Edgerton, Robert B. 1971. *The Individual in Cultural Adaptation: A Study of Four East African Peoples*. Berkeley and Los Angeles: University of California Press.

Forde, C. Daryll. 1934. *Habitat, Economy and Society: A Geographical Introduction to Ethnology*. London: Methuen.

Goldschmidt, Walter. 1947. *As You Sow*. New York: Harcourt Brace Jovanovich.

———. 1948. "Social Organization in Native California and the Origin of Clans." *American Anthropologist* 50(3, part 1): 444–456.

———. 1959. *Man's Way*. New York: Holt, Rinehart and Winston.

———. 1965. "Theory and Strategy in the Study of Cultural Adaptability." *American Anthropologist* 67 (2): 402–408.

———. 1966. *Comparative Functionalism: An Essay in Anthropological Theory*. Berkeley and Los Angeles: University of California Press.

———. 1976. *Culture and Behavior of the Sebei*. Berkeley and Los Angeles: University of California Press.

Irvine, William. 1955. *Apes, Angels, and Victorians*. New York: McGraw-Hill.

Kroeber, A. L. 1939. *Cultural and Natural Areas of Native North America*. Berkeley: University of California Press.

Lévi-Strauss, Claude, 1967. *Structural Anthropology,* trans. by C. Jacobson and B. G. Schoepf. Garden City, N.Y.: Doubleday (Anchor Books).

Lyell, Charles. 1830–1833. *The Principles of Geology, Being an Attempt to Explain the Former Changes of the Earth's Surface, by Reference to Causes Now in Operation,* 1st ed. London: John Murray.

———. 1863. *The Geological Evidences of the Antiquity of Man*. Philadelphia: G. W. Childs.

Malinowski, Bronislaw. 1922. *Argonauts of the Western Pacific*. New York: Dutton.

———. 1935. *Coral Gardens and Their Magic*. London: Allen and Unwin.

———. 1944. *A Scientific Theory of Culture*. Chapel Hill: The University of North Carolina Press.

Mead, Margaret. 1928. *Coming of Age in Samoa*. New York: Morrow.

Morgan, Lewis Henry. 1871. *Systems of Consanguinity and Affinity of the Human Family*. Washington, D.C.: Smithsonian Institution.

———. 1877. *Ancient Society*. New York: World.

Radcliffe-Brown, A. R. 1922. *The Andaman Islanders*. Cambridge, England: Cambridge University Press.

———. 1952. *Structure and Function in Primitive Society*. Glencoe, Ill.: Free Press.

Rappaport, Roy A. 1968. *Pigs for the Ancestors: Ritual in the Ecology of a New Guinea People*. New Haven, Conn.: Yale University Press.

Steward, Julian H. 1936. "The Economic and Social Basis of Primitive Bands," in Robert Lowie (ed.), *Essays in Anthropology Presented to A. L. Kroeber*. Berkeley: University of California Press.

————. 1949. "Cultural Causality and Law: A Trial Formulation of the Development of Early Civilization." *American Anthropologist* 51:1–27.

————. 1953. "Evolution and Process," in A. L. Kroeber (ed.), *Anthropology Today.* University of Chicago Press.

————. 1955. *Theory of Culture Change.* Urbana: University of Illinois Press.

Tylor, E. B. 1889. "On a Method of Investigating the Development of Institutions; Applied to Laws of Marriage and Descent." *Journal of the Royal Anthropological Institute* 18:245–269.

White, Leslie A. 1949. *The Science of Culture.* New York: Farrar, Straus & Giroux.

Wissler, Clark. 1917. *The American Indian.* New York: D. C. McMurtrie.

————. 1926. *The Relation of Nature to Man in Aboriginal America.* New York: Oxford University Press.

Suggestions for Further Reading

Barash, David P. 1977. *Sociobiology and Behavior.* New York: Elsevier. An honest book, and therefore a cautious one. Makes no wild claims, but does offer some suggestions—some plausible, some not—for collaborations between sociobiology and the social sciences. Consistently interesting.

Barnouw, Victor. 1973. *Culture and Personality,* rev. ed. Homewood, Ill.: Dorsey Press. An excellent introduction to the field. Contains a good discussion of Ruth Benedict's work.

Berreman, Gerald D. 1966. "Anemic and Emetic Analyses in Social Anthropology." *American Anthropologist* 68(2, part 1):346–354. Penetrating and amusing comments on some recent trends in anthropology.

Chagnon, Napoleon A. 1977. *Yanomamo: The Fierce People,* 2d ed. New York: Holt, Rinehart and Winston. A really remarkable ethnography of Indians living in Venezuela and Brazil. Can be read as a study of culture and personality or simply as a graphic account of a highly aggressive society. Should not be missed. Includes fine photographs.

Darnell, Regna. 1974. *Readings in the History of Anthropology.* New York: Harper & Row. A valuable and stimulating collection.

Eggan, Fred. 1954. "Social Anthropology and the Method of Controlled Comparison." *American Anthropologist* 56:743–763. A sound and sensible article.

Eiseley, Loren. 1958. *Darwin's Century: Evolution and the Men Who Discovered It.* Garden City, N.Y.: Doubleday. Well written and packed with interesting information.

Firth, Raymond. 1957. *Man and Culture: An Evaluation of the Work of Bronislaw Malinowski.* London: Routledge & Kegan Paul. A distinguished anthropologist who was a student of Malinowski's has here assembled a detailed collection of papers dealing with various aspects of his work. Firth's Introduction provides considerable insight into Malinowski's career and personality.

Garbarino, Merwyn S. 1977. *Sociocultural Theory in Anthropology: A Short History.* New York: Holt, Rinehart and Winston. A compact and reasonably objective survey of the subject.

Goldschmidt, Walter (ed.). 1959. *The Anthropology of Franz Boas.* Memoir No. 89 of the American Anthropological Association. A collection of papers about Boas; essential for the serious student.

Harris, Marvin. 1968. *The Rise of Anthropological Theory.* New York: Crowell. A very long and opinionated book. There is much of value here but the book must be read with a grain of salt.

Hays, H. R. 1958. *From Ape to Angel.* New York: Knopf. Not very sophisticated theoretically, but contains interesting information about a number of anthropologists. Entertaining reading.

Herskovits, Melville J. 1953. *Franz Boas: The Science of Man in the Making.* New York: Scribner. Almost totally uncritical, this is an evaluation of Boas by one of his disciples. Interesting nonetheless and valuable in presenting Boas as he appeared to some of his students.

Kardiner, Abram, and Edward Preble. 1961. *They Studied Man.* New York: Harcourt Brace Jovanovich. Verbal portraits of scientists ranging from Darwin to Freud. Some of this — for example, the sections on Tylor, Boas, and Malinowski — is fascinating.

Leach, Edmund. 1961. "Lévi-Strauss in the Garden of Eden." *Transactions of the New York Academy of Sciences,* ser. 2, 23:386–396. Leach has become one of the foremost interpreters of Lévi-Strauss to the English-speaking world. This elegant article is an introduction to the way Lévi-Strauss approaches the analysis of myth.

Lévi-Strauss, Claude. 1964. *Tristes Tropiques,* trans. by John Russell. New York: Atheneum. First published in 1955, this is the most accessible (readable) of his works. A difficult book to describe — part autobiography, part Brazilian exploration, part theory — but a work of great originality and perhaps even genius.

————. 1966. *The Savage Mind.* University of Chicago Press. Despite its title, this deals with nothing less than the structure of human thought.

————. 1969. *The Elementary Structures of Kinship.* Boston: Beacon Press. First published in 1949, this is an introduction to the Lévi-Strauss version of kinship theory. It is not light reading.

Linton, Ralph. 1945. *The Cultural Background of Personality.* Englewood Cliffs, N.J.: Prentice-Hall. This little book is somewhat dated, but as is true of many of Linton's works it retains its interest. A good introduction to what some of the early workers in the culture and personality field were trying to do.

Lowie, Robert H. 1937. *The History of Ethnological Theory.* New York: Holt, Rinehart and Winston. For many years, this was the standard introduction to the subject. Written with a Boasian bias, this is a work of considerable scholarship and is worth looking into.

Oliver, Symmes C. 1980. *The Kamba of Kenya: Ecological Variation in Two East African Communities.* Palo Alto, Ca.: Mayfield. In addition to providing information on the Kamba, who are mentioned frequently in this textbook, this work discusses cultural ecology in general and the Culture and Ecology in East Africa Project in particular.

Sahlins, Marshall, and Elman Service (eds.). 1960. *Evolution and Culture.* Ann Arbor: University of Michigan Press. A useful and generally sound attempt to reconcile different points of view on cultural evolution.

Stocking, George W., Jr. 1968. *Race, Culture, and Evolution: Essays in the History of Anthropology.* New York: Free Press. Original articles based on first-hand historical research. Must reading for anyone interested in the development of anthropology.

Tyler, Stephen A. (ed.). 1969. *Cognitive Anthropology.* New York: Holt, Rinehart and Winston. On the technical side, but a good collection of readings dealing with some modern trends in anthropology.

Wallace, Anthony F. C. 1961. *Culture and Personality.* New York: Random House. A good and perceptive short book on the subject.

Wax, Murray. 1956. "The Limitations of Boas' Anthropology." *American Anthropologist* 58:63–74. A very critical analysis of Boas. This is a healthy antidote to the Herskovits book cited above.

White, Leslie A. 1959. *The Evolution of Culture.* New York: McGraw-Hill. Although not up to the standard of the author's *The Science of Culture,* this is still required reading for those seeking to understand White's theoretical position.

13

Living Together: Introducing Social Organization

One of the most significant facts about the human animal is very simple: We are intensely social animals and we live in groups. We are born into groups, ranging from families to tribes and nations; we live our lives in the context of various groups that we join or to which we are assigned; and when we die we are ushered from the ranks of the living in group ceremonials. This is such an obvious point that it must be underscored; the danger is that what is truly basic is so taken for granted that we seldom think about it. The genuinely isolated human individual—the hermit totally without friends or associates or kin—is such a rarity that for all practical purposes he or she does not exist. It is not an accident that solitary confinement is widely regarded as the worst of all punishments, and it is not an accident that in many primitive societies expulsion from the social group is worse than a death sentence; it not only makes survival a very dubious proposition, but it effectively converts a person to a nonperson because much of our identity comes ultimately from our group affiliations.

To be sure, it is possible to withdraw from the company of others on a temporary basis. History records many examples of mystics and intellectuals who have done precisely that. However, such people are isolated only in a partial physical sense. There are social reasons for their retreats; they are often wrestling with social (or cultural) problems; and when they return they tend to try to "convert" existing social groups to their beliefs or to create new social groups. In any case, it is idle to focus on the few partial exceptions to the rule. We are not solitary animals; we will fight to maintain social networks even under very adverse circumstances, and the true recluse is at the very least a most unusual human being.

We do not know precisely what is responsible for the human propensity to organize in groups, although this tendency may be a very old one among the primates. (You will recall that under natural conditions an isolated chimpanzee is as unlikely as an isolated human being.) However, it is worth pointing out that a culture-bearing animal must function in a group context: The essence of culture is a shared system of ideas, and it can be neither maintained nor transmitted without enduring contact with others. Beyond this, Walter Goldschmidt has postulated a *need for positive affect* as characteristic of the human species. In his view, "this need is not a product of cultural conditioning but underlies it" (Goldschmidt 1959: 27).

A need for positive affect simply means that a person seeks and requires some measure of group support. A human being totally deprived of positive affect is psychologically crippled, often to the point of being unable to function at all. The syndrome is familiar to any clinical psychologist. Examine the records of disturbed individuals and the phrases virtually leap out at you: "I was an unwanted child. . . . Nobody loved me. . . . When I went to school the other kids all laughed at me. . . . I don't have any friends. . . . ." This is no trivial matter, anywhere, anytime.

Of course, it is not necessary to be liked (or accepted or admired) by everybody. Indeed, this is probably impossible in any society, and certainly impossible in large, complex, and diverse social groupings. (This is probably one reason for the variety of *symbolic* signs of acceptance in large groups in which people cannot all know one another personally: stripes on the sleeve, feathers in the hair, name tags, shirts with slogans, bumper stickers, scarification marks on the face, objects suspended from necklaces, and so forth.) Rather, the idea is that we do seem to require support and recognition from at least some of the people with whom we associate. Every parent knows that a child needs more than just food and shelter; a child craves love and reassurance. It is not otherwise with adults, although they may mask their disappointments better.

The need for positive affect has not been demonstrated to exist by solid experimental evidence, but without it—or something like it—a great deal of human behavior makes no sense at all. One can draw neat little diagrams of social systems until seminar tables collapse and still not come to grips with the basic questions: What makes the systems work? What is it that motivates the participants? Yes, we must obtain food and shelter and protect ourselves and seek sexual partners, but there is no society anywhere in which that is *all* that people do. Universally, human beings act in ways that are designed to win the approval of others in the group. Again, this does not necessarily mean the approval of the total society. The group in question may be very small: a family, a high school clique, an occult club, a revolutionary cadre, a bunch of tennis enthusiasts. Whatever the group, we seldom if ever "go it alone." If we did, human societies would be far different from what they are.

In previous chapters, the concept of culture was discussed at some length. Also, from time to time, I have smuggled in the word *society* but have refrained from defining it. Among human beings, there can be no culture without a society and no society without a culture; the two are linked. (That is why anthropolo-

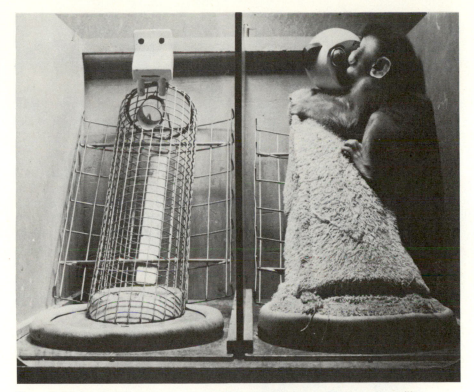

Harry F. Harlow's experiments with mother substitutes suggest that a "need" for some sort of emotional response is not limited to human beings. Monkey infants consistently sought reassurance from the more lifelike cloth-wrapped figure even when "nursed" by the wire figure.

gists often refer to *sociocultural systems* when they do not wish to distinguish between social and cultural components). Although the two are always found together among human beings, it is both possible and useful to separate them in conceptual terms.

Societies are organized groups. Human societies are organized groups of persons. (Other animals can and do live in organized groups and therefore have societies even though they lack cultural traditions. The social insects, such as ants, bees, and termites, are obvious examples.) When we speak of a particular total human society—Kamba society, say, or Hopi society—we are referring to the largest group within a given cultural domain, the group that contains or includes all of the other groups. A culture, as we have seen, is a design for living— a set of interrelated ideas that forms a lifeway. The organized groups of people that participate in a cultural system constitute the society.

Every society is built out of a series of interlocking groups. In this sense, groups are the bricks of the social structure—they are what the social system is made out of. These social groups are crucial, because it is within the context of groups that the activities of a society are carried out. Whether the activity in-

It is a rare individual who does not respond to the approval of others in the group.

volves hunting elephants, raising children, deciding legal cases, or putting on a religious ceremony, these things cannot be done without group organization.

All human societies have certain basic tasks that must be performed. Whatever else they do, societies must obtain and distribute food, train and care for children, provide shelter, work out methods for handling internal disputes, and devise some means of protection. The alternative is extinction. A social system provides the organization necessary to the accomplishment of these tasks. (Again, that is not all that a social system does, but it must at least do these things.)

One can imagine a system (or, more properly, a nonsystem) that is totally unorganized. Every person — man, woman, or child — simply goes her or his own way with the vague hope that somehow things will work out. The idea is not unattractive in an age in which fashionable rhetoric speaks of the individual versus society as though the two were in constant opposition to each other. The trouble is that such a nonsystem will not work. If it has ever really been tried, it did not survive long enough to be discovered by anthropologists. The fact of the matter is that human beings live in organized societies and cannot live in any

Human beings will go to extreme lengths to gain social acceptance. These are Cheyenne Sun Dance volunteers.

other way. It is possible to change a society, but it is not possible simply to dispense with it.

Let us return to this matter of groups. It is essential to grasp not only the fact that they exist but also how crucial they are. Earlier (Chapter 9) I discussed the crash of a plane in the Andes. The plane was flying from Uruguay to Chile transporting a rugby team. It carried 45 people, including the plane crew. Some were killed in the crash and others perished later from avalanches of snow, injuries, and malnutrition. But there were 16 survivors who were eventually rescued ten weeks later. They survived in part because they ate the flesh of their dead companions. However, a careful reading of the harrowing account of their experiences (Read 1974) reveals a critical point: They survived because they organized themselves into working groups.

Top, group structure may be informal, as in this Nuer fishing party. *Bottom,*
true groups always have an organizational structure.

Here is a kind of miniature society in desperate circumstances. It was not a
complete society, of course, for there were no children. Still, there were tasks
that had to be performed. A group of four young men was selected to try to walk
out for help. They were called the expeditionaries. Since everything depended
on their ultimate success, they were given special privileges. They could eat as
much meat as they wished. They could sleep in the most sheltered places. They
were excused from other work. Another group was formed to carry out the grim
job of digging corpses out of the snow, thawing them, and cutting off large
chunks. Still another group divided the chunks into smaller portions with razor

Top, random aggregations of individuals are not groups, because they lack structure. *Bottom,* the group structure may be formal, as in this military unit.

blades. Other "teams" were responsible for melting snow and cleaning out the cabin of the crashed plane. A trio of leaders emerged to ration the meat and make the hard decisions and settle arguments. (The three leaders were cousins, by the way. Much of their power was derived from their unity; they always stood together.)

It worked. There *were* survivors. Some of the expeditionaries did manage to bring help. It is not too much to say that without their group organization they would probably all have died in the Andes. The lesson is this: Groups form to do the jobs that a society needs or wants to have done. Some of the "jobs" are not essential: A group can form simply to have fun. But some of the tasks *are* essential. If you remove the mosaic of interlocking groups from a society, you no longer have a functioning society.

It is obvious that a group must contain more than a single person. It is somewhat less obvious that a group involves more than just multiple individuals. It is possible to assemble many people together in one place and still not have a group in the technical sense of the term. A crowd on the street or passengers on a bus are not groups; they are ephemeral aggregations of individuals who happen to be thrown together on a temporary and largely accidental basis. Such aggregations can become true groups under certain circumstances, but in order to understand what those circumstances are we must look into the nature of groups.

A group always has structure — organization. The structure may be formal, as in a military unit, or informal, as in a poker-playing club, but the structure is always there. One of the most universal characteristics of human beings is some sort of a distinction between *us* (insiders) and *them* (outsiders). In a true group, people always know who is in the group and who is not. There is yet another characteristic of groups: They always have a shared purpose or interest. This commonality of interest can range from exercising political control over a tribe or nation to a fascination with model airplanes; the principle is the same. Groups seek to maintain themselves whether they are families or secret societies or rock bands: The glue of common interests holds them together, and the members put out effort to further those group interests. When this fails to happen — when nobody cares enough to bother — groups disintegrate whether they are political parties or baseball teams.

Now think back to our crowd on the street and our busload of passengers. Such aggregations can turn into short-lived groups in a number of situations. Suppose that a sudden fire breaks out and people need help. If leaders come forward in the crowd and the crowd organizes to render aid, you have a group. When such events occur, the people in a crowd begin to think of themselves as belonging together; they form a unit. Similarly, imagine that the driver of the bus pulls over to the curb, stops, switches off the engine, and begins to read *Moby Dick*. It is safe to assume that the passengers will form a protest group in a hurry.

GROUPS

Before getting into the problem of different types of groups, it is useful to ask a couple of basic questions. First, what determines group membership? How does a person get into a group in the first place? Second, what is it exactly that groups do?

Group membership is determined in two main ways. There are groups that you are *born* into and there are groups that you *join,* voluntarily or otherwise. A group that you are born into is termed an *ascribed* group. The most obvious example is the family in its various permutations, although the family is not the only ascribed group. There is no fully satisfactory term to describe groups that are joined. They have been called *achieved* groups and *volitional* groups, among other things. The trouble is that a person can join a group where there is not much of an achievement involved, and groups can also be joined on an involuntary basis, as when a person is drafted into the army. However, it is probably true to say that most nonascribed groups are joined on a more or less voluntary basis. As a general rule, although the distinction is not absolute, primitive societies tend to have a higher proportion of ascribed groups.

I have already tried to explain the fundamental sociological purpose of groups: They form to carry out the tasks that the society needs or wants to have done. Without the structure of interlocking groups, it is impossible to organize social action. This is true whether the "task" involves hunting bison, harvesting a field of maize, raising children, defending a village, making sacrifices to ancestors, or getting together on Saturday afternoon to play soccer in the park.

Another way of saying the same thing is to point out that groups have not only an organization (structure) but also a function (a sociological job to do). In understanding the function of a particular group, it is often necessary to go beyond the obvious level of explanation. The sociologist Robert K. Merton has stressed the important distinction between *manifest* and *latent* functions (Merton 1949:21–81). To reduce a complex argument to the simplest possible terms, a manifest function is overt and proclaimed: It is the stated purpose of the group. A latent function is whatever else the group does, whether this is apparent to the participants or not.

Consider an advertisement for a dancing class. The ad offers you one free lesson and a chance to sign up for umpteen more at a stated price per whirl. "Learn to do such exotic dances as the fox-trot, the boogie, and the hound dog country fling!" Here we have a clear manifest function: Join the group and it will teach you how to dance. Now read the advertisement more carefully, and read between the lines as it were. Note the photograph of the dancing couple transported to surprising realms of ecstasy. Note the claim that dancing will "enhance your popularity." Note the discreet mention of frequent dancing parties for those enrolled in the dancing class. We are now dealing with a latent function: You can meet people, be popular, and have fun. The not-so-hidden message of the ad is: "Are you lonely? Tired of sitting home with a six-pack and the TV? Get out of your rut! Join our dancing class and be a happy person with unlimited prospects before you!"

Of course, latent functions are often much more subtle. In addition to the psychological support that almost all groups provide, the groups may have key parts to play in the operation of a society which are different from their stated purposes. For example, a clan (which is a kind of superfamily constructed according to different principles from those that operate in our own society; see Chapter 15) may have as its stated objective the honoring of the clan ancestors and the perpetuation of the clan name or line. It does indeed do this, but it also does other things: It may be the major group in the society that deals with legal cases, it may allocate farmland, it may determine who marries whom, and so on. Similarly, a literal witch hunt has an obvious manifest function: Find the supposed evil doer and eliminate the witch. However, even a witch hunt may have important latent functions. It may operate as a kind of psychological safety valve for the society: When social pressures build to the point where people are suspicious of their neighbors and the group seems to be falling apart, it is a way of blowing off social steam and reducing tension. It isn't worth it from the viewpoint of the ostensible witch, of course, but it is a technique that makes the survivors feel that they have dealt with their problems. It goes without saying that the real problems—epidemics, malnutrition, feuds, or just plain bad luck—have nothing to do with witches. The point is that the people *believe* that a witch is responsible, and in any case they may not have the means—such as adequate medical knowledge—to cope with the situation in which they find themselves.

When one first becomes aware of groups, their seeming diversity appears to defy analysis. There are so many of them, and they do so many different things, that it is difficult to make sense out of what is going on. This should not surprise us: Virtually everything that happens in a society occurs within the context of groups, and therefore a total inventory of groups for all practical purposes involves a consideration of nearly all the activities in which people engage.

Take a moment (or a week or so) and jot down the names of all the groups to which you belong. Some of them will not have names, to be sure, but no matter, make up a name. (Informal groups, like a group of close friends or a group that gets together for lunch, often lack names.) Start with the family and work up through school groups, clubs, and work groups. Go all the way up the most inclusive group you can put yourself into—American citizen, or whatever. Then list all the groups in this society that you have ever heard of: everything from the Admirers of Aristotle to the Rotary Club to the New York Yankees to the American Medical Association to the Daughters of the Alamo to the Tenth Street Tigers. Then remember that the groups you have listed—only a fraction of all those that *exist*—are only the groups in a single human society. Suppose you tried to list all of the groups in all of the societies of the world . . . ?

To put it mildly, there are a lot of groups. Whatever our other failings may be, human beings do not lack a propensity for forming groups. Fortunately, there is a way to make sense out of the seemingly vast variety of groups. When you examine them closely, you will find that almost all groups can be assigned to one of three major *types* of groups. *In any human society, there are only three major kinds of groups.*

Kin Groups

As the name suggests, *kin groups* are groups that are based primarily on kinship. That is, the group is formed on the basis of how people are related to one another, whether by descent or by marriage. The example that springs most readily to mind in terms of the experiences of most Americans is the unit we call the family. It should be noted, though, that when we use the term *family* we can be referring to several groups. It may mean a small group—a married man and woman and their children—or it may mean a larger group, including grandparents, uncles, aunts, cousins, and whatnot. Nevertheless, those persons included are all kin in some way. Similarly, in other societies, what is meant by *family* may vary a good deal, but family members are always reckoned as kin in some sense. As a rule, in primitive societies—and some not so primitive—kin groups tend to be more important than they are in American society. Kinship may be reckoned in different ways, more sorts of groups may be based on kin ties, and the groups may have many functions which we assign to other kinds of groups. In particular, the kin groups known as lineages and clans are often critical in other societies (see Chapter 15).

Territorial Groups

Territorial Groups are sometimes referred to as *spatial* groups or *coresidence* groups; the choice of terms is largely a matter of taste. A territorial group is a group composed of people who live together in a particular locality. Some of the people involved may in fact be kin, but the criterion for group membership is where you live rather than what kin connections you may have. In American society, some familiar kinds of territorial groups are cities, neighborhoods, and small towns. (There are others, of course: counties, states, and so forth.) In other societies, common examples of territorial groups include villages, bands, tribes, and the wandering "local groups" of hunters and gatherers (see Chapters 17 and 18).

Associations

It would be only moderately facetious to define an *association* as a group that forms on some basis other than kinship or territoriality. Robert H. Lowie referred to such groups as *sodalities,* remarking that such a classification was "merely a convenient lumber room for a great variety of associations" (Lowie 1948:294).

However, it is useful to think of associations as either *special interest* groups or as groups based on persons with *special characteristics*. Examples of the former would include labor unions, social clubs, a group of bass fishermen, or a secret society. Examples of the latter would include a group made up of all young men between 16 and 25 or a group like Mensa, supposedly composed of people who are unusually intelligent.

All human societies have kin groups and territorial groups. Most human societies contain associations as well, but not all of them do; there are human societies which manage to get things done without associations. The American society is particularly rich in associations, possibly as a result of our restricted emphasis on kin ties and the sheer sprawl of some of our territorial groupings. Indeed, if you will think back to your personal list of groups, you will find that most of them are associations of one kind or another. The Girl Scouts, a fraternity, church groups, civil rights groups, a football team, or the students who get together regularly to drink beer at the Purple Armadillo—all are associations.

In some primitive societies, important types of associations include secret societies of various kinds, warrior clubs, craft guilds, age grades, and age sets. Age grades and age sets will be discussed in Chapter 18; at this point, we can simply indicate that they are groupings of people on the rough basis of relative age: "elders" and the like.

STATUS

As we noted earlier, all groups have structure: They are not just random collections of individuals. A useful tool for uncovering the structure of groups is the concept of status and role. It will not explain everything about how groups are organized, but it will provide a convenient starting point.

Within each group of which he or she is a member—whether it be a family, a village, or a club of some sort—a person occupies a particular *status*. Stated simply, a status is a social position. Technically, the position (the status) exists independently of the person who occupies it. Indeed, a status may in some instances be "vacant" in the sense that there is a position but nobody in it at the moment. Military ranks are a good example of this; so, for that matter, are the "slots" in an anthropology department. (If an assistant professor leaves and the department retains the position, the position is "open" until a new professor is hired.) However, let us take a more familiar example. A football team is a group. Within that group, there are a series of positions to be filled—tackle, guard, quarterback, and so on. Usually, of course, someone occupies each position. But it is possible to think of the position whether anyone occupies it or not; the position still exists. If Joe Blow is the center and Joe Blow breaks his leg, you still require a center if the group is going to continue to function as a football team.

Every group is made up of a series of statuses, whether the positions are formally named or not. The statuses may be vertical—ranked—or merely different. A major is higher than a private, and a university president outranks a mere professor. But which is higher, a tackle or a guard? Which is more important, a trumpet player or a trombone player? In a group of writers, does the poet outrank the novelist, or is it the other way around?

It can be argued that there are generalized statuses that are not directly linked to specific groups. For example, a poet is a poet whether or not the poet interacts with other poets, and a teenager is a teenager. However, it seems to me that when society itself is regarded as a group this distinction disappears. After all, the status of poet differs from one society to another, and so does the status of teenagers; as a matter of fact, the status of teenager does not exist as such in most societies.

With the possible exception of infants, all people have more than one status. This is because all persons occupy positions in more than a single group. A woman may (or may not) be a wife and mother, but she may also be a magazine editor, a newspaper reporter, a tennis star, an actress, or the mayor of a city. A person's "total status" in a society is a function of all the statuses that person occupies.

To some extent, status is like group membership generally: It may be either ascribed or earned (or sometimes conferred). Essentially, an ascribed status is one that a person is born into. Clan membership is such a status; clan affiliation is determined by descent, and a person has no control over it. The caste system in India works the same way; a caste is a fixed social class that a person is born into and cannot move out of, at least in one lifetime. Age and sex are ascribed status criteria in all known human societies. This does not mean that the statuses linked to age and sex are the same in all societies. It only means that it makes a difference in all societies whether you are male or female, old or young. There are no societies in which the facts of sex and age are simply irrelevant. Barring a sex change operation or an accident of birth, one is biologically either a female or a male, and we all get older with time whether we like it or not. It must be stressed again that the statuses linked to age and sex differ from one society to another. To a Kamba in East Africa, it is a good thing to be old: Elder males pretty much run the show politically, and older females can turn much hard work over to younger females. Elderhood confers status. In the United States, nobody wants to be old. Our elders are not venerated, although we pay lip service to the notion. Often they are forced to retire and packed off to what we euphemistically refer to as "rest homes" for "senior citizens." Our cultural injunction is: Think young! (If possible, *be* young. If you can't be young, then at least *look* young!)

Other statuses are earned or achieved. Election to a political office is an obvious example, and so is a promotion in a business firm. Wealth is frequently a component of status; if you earned it yourself it represents an achieved status, and if you inherited it the status was conferred. By and large, earned statuses involve skills of one sort or another. It is hardly news that good connections — especially kinship connections — do no harm in any society, but, nevertheless, demonstrated ability is very much a part of the picture. The skills that confer status are legion, and they too vary from society to society. Here the ability to go into a trance and contact the ancestors, there skill as a hunter, elsewhere eloquence or athletic ability or a talent for music or skill in farming or a capacity to lead or a knack for settling disputes — the list is endless.

Although all societies have both ascribed and earned statuses, they differ greatly with regard to the emphasis they place on one or the other. The Arunta of Australia, one of the first hunting and gathering societies to be systematically studied by anthropologists, stressed ascribed statuses. There were few significant positions in Arunta society that were not determined by age, sex, or one's place in the kinship network. By contrast, American society stresses earned status as a cultural ideal. In fact, there is a definite feeling on the part of Americans that ascribed status is somehow wrong. Our ideal model is one of social mobility, which runs counter to the idea of ascribed status. Ideally, Americans earn their place in society by work and ability; our children are taught in school that anyone can be president. Of course, we all know that we fall short of our own ideals; no woman has ever been elected president, no black, no Chicano, no American Indian. Nevertheless, the ideal remains, and we tend to be uncomfortable with ascribed status positions. Perhaps that is the firmest index we have with regard to the direction this society will take in the future.

It is worth noting that each system has both advantages and disadvantages. An ascribed system has a certain stability to it; by placing persons in largely predetermined slots it reduces the necessity for making hard choices. The drawback is that it blocks talented people from positions in which they might perform with distinction. The advantages of an earned status system may seem overwhelming to us, but such a system is seldom a comfortable one: It requires constant competition and a high level of stress anxiety. After all, in any contest there are both winners and losers, and in an earned status system the losers often feel that they are personal failures.

Status alone is not enough. The sociological function of group organization is to get things done; to make the society work. Clearly, this involves something more than just sorting people into positions — the occupants of those positions must *perform*. A social role is often referred to as the dynamic aspect of status: The role linked to a status position is the appropriate action that should be taken by the person occupying the status. A necessary component of role behavior is that it involves people doing what they are expected to do when placed in a particular status.

In any society, people have to have a reasonable idea of what to expect from their neighbors and those with whom they associate. If every social encounter were totally unpredictable, that would be the very opposite of social organization — it would be social chaos. When you go to the grocery store and wheel your cart up to the check-out stand, you must have a reasonable expectation that what you have selected will in fact be checked and put in a bag. When you go to class, you have a right to expect that the instructor will instruct and not just sail paper airplanes out the window. If you are on a baseball team and a ground ball is hit to the shortstop, you expect the shortstop to field the ball and throw it to the appropriate base rather than sticking the ball in his pocket and reciting a poem by Robert Frost.

As Walter Goldschmidt has put it:

> Thus it is that in each social status there are blueprints which set forth customary behavior. It follows that role is not merely a matter of action, but specifically a set of expectations for action. Whenever we enter a normal social situation, we anticipate the behavior that others will exhibit. (Goldschmidt 1959:83)

In short, a social role is the part a person is supposed to play when occupying a particular status. The roles linked to particular statuses may differ from one society to another. Thus, within the family, our role of "father" includes the duty of the father to discipline a child in certain situations. In the Trobriand Islands, that is not part of the father's role; that unpleasant task is allocated to the mother's brother.

It is also the case that we all have more than one role to play. A child acts one way with his playmates, another way with his family, and still another way at school. I have one role as a professor, another as a writer of science fiction, an-

For every status there is an appropriate role. We expect a doctor or a priest to
act differently from a circus clown.

other with friends on a trout stream, another with my family, and so on. The
problem of role conflict, it seems to me, is sometimes overstressed. The fact of
the matter is that we seem to move rather easily from one role to another depending on the situation. We are intensely social animals, and role playing is a
crucial part of social behavior among humans.

There is one aspect of role behavior that is particularly difficult to discuss at
the present time, and this is the connection between sex and "appropriate" social roles. The simple fact that the subject is a touchy one should tell us something: The social situation is in flux, we are in a time of transition from one
system to another, and the cultural problem involved has not been wholly
resolved.

We have already noted that sex is one basis for status in all societies: It
makes a difference whether one is male or female. We have also noted that
there are roles linked to statuses; there are patterns of expectations associated

with the parts we are supposed to play in society. In terms of modern American society, then, two basic questions suggest themselves.

1.* Are there any fundamental differences between males and females?
2. If such differences exist, how relevant are they to the statuses we occupy and the roles we enact?

Rhetoric aside, it is nonsense to argue that there are no differences between women and men. Moreover, it is dangerous nonsense because the proposition is so palpably false that it obscures the real issue. The evidence for psychological differences between males and females, if any, is too shaky to evaluate. However, the evidence for biological differences is about as solid as evidence can be.

To state the obvious, only a female can get pregnant and bear a child. We are mammals, after all, and only a female can nurse an infant with milk from her breasts. The other major differences are succinctly stated by Bernard G. Campbell.

> Differing roles suggest evolutionary shaping to fit those roles. For example, men are usually bigger and stronger than women now, and they surely have been for millions of years. These attributes are predictable for protectors and hunters; the relationship between role and physique is simple and direct. But men can also run faster than women, and here the reason is neither simple nor direct. If speed on foot were merely a matter of size and strength, then the largest and strongest man would be the faster runner. Since this is demonstrably not the case, there must be another reason why a lithe woman should not be so swift as a bulkier man: she cannot be if she is going to be the mother of larger-brained children. The best-designed pelvis for bearing such children is not the best-designed for running, or even for the most efficient walking. (Campbell 1976: 181)

This means exactly what it says, no more and no less: On the average, males are bigger, stronger, and faster. Of course, there are some females who are superior to some males in all these categories; the differences apply to populations but not necessarily to all individuals. The real question is, so what? The answer is: It all depends. Specifically, it depends on the sociocultural context within which females and males are operating.

Both sexes lived in hunting and gathering societies for millions of years before any other kind of human society existed. As Jane B. Lancaster has pointed out, in discussing the key change that made the human adaptive pattern possible and distinguished it from that of the nonhuman primates, ''More than anything else the new pattern must have rested on a unique way of exploiting food resources: gathering and hunting based on a division of labor between adult males and adult females with offspring'' (Lancaster 1975: 78). It will be recalled that in the great majority of nonhuman primate societies each animal forages as

Traditional American sex roles: *Top left*, the female as homemaker; *bottom left*, the male as businessman. American society is changing: *Top right*, a male in a nontraditional role; *bottom right*, Chris Evert in a nontraditional role.

an individual. Among the primates, a division of labor by sex and a resultant sharing of foods of different kinds is a human (or hominid) specialization. (It will also be recalled that the chimpanzees foreshadow this characteristic: The males do some hunting and share the kill with both sexes. However, the females do not gather wild plant foods for the males.)

In all human hunting and gathering societies, the division of labor by sex is the same: The men are responsible for the hunting, and the women are responsible for collecting wild plant foods. (In societies in which there are few wild plant foods to gather, such as that of many Eskimo groups, the males still do the hunting.) If any hunting and gathering society tried some other arrangement, it vanished without a trace. Moreover, the role separation tends to be sharp: Hunting is "man's work" and females are excluded except under special circumstances. Janet Siskind is one of the relatively few female anthropologists who has worked with a hunting people, the Sharanahua Indians of Peru. In her fine book, *To Hunt in the Morning,* she candidly reports:

> I have never gone hunting since no man at Marcos would tolerate a woman's presence in this context. Ndaishiwaka agreed several times to let me accompany him, but somehow he always left earlier than he had indicated or changed his mind at the last minute. What I know of hunting, therefore, is known only through my informants. (Siskind 1973: 89)

There is really nothing very mysterious about this division of labor. Suppose that you were going to design a hunting and gathering society. You have just two sexes available, obviously. One sex gets pregnant and can nurse children. The other sex is bigger, stronger, and faster. The tasks assigned to each sex are critical: Survival depends on successful performance. How would you arrange it? Remember that you can gather plant foods perfectly well when pregnant or with an infant in tow, but you cannot hunt effectively under those conditions. Remember too that a woman will begin to bear children while she is quite young, and during her fertile years she is apt to be either pregnant or responsible for young children, or both. Neither an old woman nor an old man can contribute much to sustained hunting in a primitive society. It is also true that there is an element of danger involved in hunting. Especially in a society with a small population, the group can afford the loss of males more readily than it can tolerate the loss of females; the future of the society depends upon the capacity of the females to bear children.

The point of all this is simple. There are societies in which the biological differences between men and women are useful in allocating separate social roles for the two sexes; it makes sound survival sense. However, this does not mean that it makes equally good sense in all human societies. In modern American society—and in many other societies as well—there is no clear connection between sexual differences and most of the social roles we play. We do not live in a hunting and gathering society. We need skilled workers, lawyers, doctors, politicians, pilots, and possibly even anthropology professors. In those jobs, it is irrelevant that males are bigger, stronger, and faster. There is no biological reason why a woman cannot fly a plane or run a business as well as a man. The problem here is one of social learning (role models) and the patterns of expectation taught to the sexes, and there is plenty of room for flexibility.

Women must still bear the children, of course. However, not all women must have children; our problem is too many people rather than too few. For those women who do choose to have children, there are still options open. There are day care centers, fathers who don't mind staying home, and available years before and after the children arrive.

Given our professed system of values, we seem to be moving toward a situation marked by two characteristics:

1. Sex will probably remain one criterion for status in the sense that it will continue to make a difference whether one is male or female. We are not a "unisex" species regardless of our philosophical inclinations. However, the status differences will not be ranked: One is as "good" or as "high" as the other.
2. Most specific social roles will increasingly be freed from sex linkage as such. In large part, social roles will be earned rather than ascribed. The "appropriate" social role will be defined in terms of interests, personality, and ability rather than gender.

An optimistic projection? Perhaps. However, it is difficult to examine the changes that have taken place in American society over the past half-century and come to any other conclusion. The only way in which rigidly "traditional" sex roles can be maintained is to blast us quite literally back to the Stone Age.

SUMMARY

Human beings are intensely social animals who live in groups. Since cultures are shared systems of ideas, it is necessary for people to lead a group existence. In addition, Walter Goldschmidt has suggested that a *need for positive affect* is a characteristic of the human species: We require some measure of group support in order to survive.

There can be no culture without a society and no human society without a culture. Since the two are linked, the term *sociocultural system* is used to refer to both components together. However, culture and society are not the same. Human societies are organized groups of persons. A particular total human society—all of the Kamba, for example—is the largest group within a given cultural domain, the group that contains or includes all of the other groups. A culture is a design for living. The organized groups of people who participate in a specific design for living constitute the society.

Every society is built out of a series of interlocking groups. The groups are critical because it is within the context of social groups that the activities of the society are carried out. A group is more than simply an ephemeral aggregation of individuals. Groups always have structure, whether the organization is formal or informal. In a true group, people always know who is in the group and who is not, and groups always have a shared purpose or interest.

Group membership is determined in two main ways. There are groups that you are born into, which are called *ascribed groups*; and there are groups that you join, which are referred to as *achieved* or *volitional groups*. Groups have functions—sociological work to do. Robert K. Merton has divided these functions into two kinds: *manifest functions*, which are overt and proclaimed, and *latent functions*, which are more subtle and may not be explicitly stated.

Despite their seeming diversity, in any human society there are really only three major types of groups. All human groups are either *kin groups* (such as families or clans), *territorial groups* (such as villages or tribes), or *associations,* which are either special interest groups or groups based on persons who have special characteristics. Examples would include social clubs or age grades.

Within each group of which he or she is a member, a person occupies a particular *status.* A status is simply a social position — a slot in the group structure. The statuses may be ranked, as they are in a military organization, or merely different. Like group membership itself, statuses may be *ascribed* or *earned.* Age and sex are ascribed status criteria in all human societies. This does not mean that the statuses are the same everywhere, but only that it makes a difference in all human societies whether one is young or old, female or male. The American ideal model places a strong emphasis on earned status.

A *role* is the dynamic aspect of status — the part a person is expected to play while occupying a particular status. The roles linked to specific statuses may differ from one society to another. Beyond this, the roles associated with particular statuses can change within a society through time. In the American society at present, significant changes are taking place in both male and female sex roles.

References

Campbell, Bernard G. 1976. *Humankind Emerging.* Boston: Little, Brown.

Goldschmidt, Walter. 1959. *Man's Way.* New York: Holt, Rinehart and Winston.

Lancaster, Jane B. 1975. *Primate Behavior and the Emergence of Human Culture.* New York: Holt, Rinehart and Winston.

Lowie, Robert H. 1948. *Social Organization.* New York: Holt, Rinehart and Winston.

Merton, Robert K. 1949. *Social Theory and Social Structure.* Glencoe, Ill.: Free Press.

Read, Piers Paul. 1974. *Alive: The Story of the Andes Survivors.* Philadelphia: Lippincott.

Siskind, Janet. 1973. *To Hunt in the Morning.* London: Oxford University Press.

Suggestions for Further Reading

Divale, William Tulio, and Marvin Harris. 1976. "Population, Warfare, and the Male Supremacist Complex." *American Anthropologist* 78 (3): 521–538. Although not easy reading, this tightly reasoned article should be consulted by anyone seeking solid data on status differences between males and females.

Friedl, Ernestine. 1975. *Women and Men.* New York: Holt, Rinehart and Winston. An anthropological study of sex roles written from a feminist point of view.

Goldschmidt, Walter. 1977. *Exploring the Ways of Mankind,* 3d ed. New York: Holt, Rinehart and Winston. Goldschmidt's introduction to chapter 6 is an excellent brief statement dealing with groups, statuses, and roles.

Linton, Ralph. 1936. *The Study of Man.* Englewood Cliffs, N.J.: Prentice-Hall. Sometimes old books are the best books. Many of Linton's observations on social organization are pertinent today. A model of clarity.

Selby, Henry A. 1975. *Social Organization: Symbol, Structure, and Setting.* Dubuque, Iowa: Brown. An elegantly written little book. Presents a different perspective on social organization in a thoughtful and persuasive manner.

Service, Elman R. 1962. *Primitive Social Organization: An Evolutionary Perspective.* New York: Random House. A good introduction to the subject.

14

Who Goes Where: Principles of Marriage, Descent, and Residence

The purpose of this chapter is to introduce some necessary terminology. It is unfortunate but true that not all anthropologists use the same words to mean the same things. Sometimes there are valid reasons for this: Different terms convey different shades of meaning and different ways of viewing the same phenomena. Sometimes the reasons are trivial: A certain prestige adheres to a specialized vocabulary, and jargon has the dubious advantage of concealing whatever it is that a person is talking about. In any event, I have tried to use the simplest and clearest terms that will get the job done.

In the previous chapter, I stressed the importance of groups in human social systems. There is no more basic type of group in human society than the kin group. Kinship counts for something in all human societies, and in many primitive societies kinship is supremely important: It is a major organizational technique. Despite our tendency to assume that kinship is pretty much the same everywhere, this is not the case. It is true that all cultures have kinship systems, but it is not true that all cultures have the same kinship system.

Different cultures categorize kin in different ways. It is perfectly possible that persons considered to be kin in one system will be regarded as nonkin in another. The range of variation is certainly not infinite, but it is considerable. In addition, marriage customs and ideals vary from culture to culture. Beyond this, residence "rules" are not the same everywhere; where you will live and with whom depends in large part on the cultural matrix. All of this means that the kinship *groups* that form in different societies are the products of various combinations of how descent is reckoned, how marriage is viewed, and where people are supposed to live.

Without terms by which we can refer to these variables we can only resort to lengthy descriptions to make our meaning clear. This is also the basic reason for the use of kinship diagrams. With a few key symbols, it is possible to represent clearly any type of kin relationship. This is far less cumbersome and less confusing than referring to "the mother's brother's daughter's son's wife" and the like.

So let us begin with the elementary symbols of a kinship diagram. They are not complicated at all, but it is important to get them straight right from the beginning. A triangle represents a male. A circle stands for a female. Therefore:

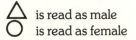

△   is read as male
○   is read as female

Anticipating current thinking on the subject, an equals sign (=) means "married to." Therefore, the series

△ = ○   is read as "this man is married to this woman."

In other words, the two are spouses.

A vertical line is a descent line. Consider this diagram:

△ = ○
  |
  △

This simply means that the male at the bottom of the vertical line is the child of the married couple at the top of the diagram.

Now we need just one more kind of line, and that is a horizontal line. A horizontal line is a sibling line. This means that the persons connected by a horizontal line are the children of the same parents. Obviously, such persons may be brothers, sisters, or brothers and sisters.

Examine this diagram:

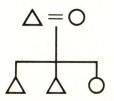

In this example we are indicating that the married couple has three children, two boys and a girl.

The following diagram also involves a sibling line:

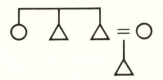

Here we are showing that the child's father has a brother and a sister.

That is all that *we* need. Additional devices can be employed to convey more information, such as drawing a slanted line through a symbol to indicate that the person is deceased or using dotted lines to indicate adopted children, but these devices are not necessary to grasp the basic principles.

Bearing in mind that we cannot simply transfer our own kinship terminology to the kinship system of a different society, it remains the case that there must be some point of reference on a kinship diagram. Nobody is a *father* or an *uncle* or a *cousin* except with reference to someone else. In reading a kinship diagram, there must be a starting place. This point of reference—the *slot* in the diagram from which all relationships are read—is designated *Ego*. It is quite arbitrary *who* is selected as Ego; it is strictly a matter of convenience. Ego may be either a male or a female.

Take a look at the following diagram:

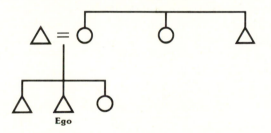

Ego

Here, we have designated a male as Ego. In the first ascending generation (the set of persons above Ego) the symbols may be read (left to right) as *father, mother, mother's sister,* and *mother's brother.* In Ego's own generation, the symbols may be read as *brother, Ego (male),* and *sister.*

In order to make a critical point about kinship, let us briefly examine the problem of *incest* and *incest tabus.* In all human societies, there are rules that regulate who may mate with whom and which persons are acceptable marriage partners. There are no human societies in which either mating or marriage occurs in a completely random fashion. Incest refers to sexual relations between persons who are considered to be close kin. An incest tabu is a prohibition against such a relationship. The prohibition is not a mild one on the order of, "You really shouldn't do that, you know." Tabus are strong; they refer to forbidden acts, and they frequently involve the idea of supernatural punishment for offenders.

All human societies have incest tabus. There is what might be termed a core of forbidden relationships in almost every human society, and that core shows practically no variation. Regardless of the particular structure of the family, it is tabu for a mother to mate with her son, a father to mate with his daughter, and a brother to mate with his sister.

We do not actually know the origin of these prohibitions. There are a plethora of theories but none of them are entirely satisfactory. Judging by their virtual universality, it is probable that they are very old. Some of them may have their roots in our primate heritage, while others (notably involving the sociological role of the father) may be as ancient as the first hominids. While we cannot yet speak with confidence about origins, it is possible to suggest two probable functions of these core prohibitions. First, by reducing or eliminating sexual rivalry between close kin, they contribute to the stability of the family unit. Second, by forcing offspring to seek mates outside their own family unit they contribute to ties or alliances between different families. Marriage is not the same thing as mating, but it is nevertheless true that marriage usually involves mating. As we shall see, it is possible to devise a system in which spouses do not have sexual relations with each other; however, such instances are so rare as to be statistically insignificant.

There are some infrequent and partial exceptions to the universality of incest tabus between core relatives. The best-known examples involve brother-sister marriages among the royal families of ancient Peru, Hawaii, and Egypt. Here, the individuals had such a high status — that of virtual gods and goddesses on earth — that there was nobody else they could marry; it was a way of preserving the "purity" of the ruling line. It must be emphasized that these exceptions did not apply to the bulk of the population, but only to the royal families.

Be that as it may, once you get beyond what I am here calling the core relatives, you still find incest tabus. The reason that they are important in terms of theory is that the tabus in this area clearly demonstrate that what is involved goes far beyond biology. The way people reckon kinship and the manner in which they determine who is kin and who is not cannot be reduced to simple biological principles. Although it may take off from biologically based relationships, such as that between a mother and her child, kinship is a *cultural* phenomenon. It is a fundamental part of the way people view their social universe.

You will recall that incest refers to sexual relations between persons who are *considered* to be close kin. With that in mind, examine the following diagram until the biological relationships are clear:

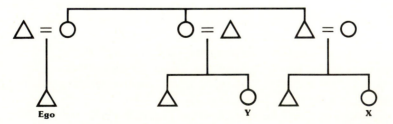

In biological terms, the females I have here designated as X and Y are related to Ego in exactly the same way; that is, they are equally "close" to Ego in terms of genetics. In our own kinship terminology, both girls are Ego's first cousins.

However, in other societies, we frequently find a situation in which Ego is forbidden to mate with or marry Y — it would be regarded as incest — but at the same time Ego is encouraged to marry X, and sexual play between them is pretty much taken for granted. To put it differently, other things being equal, X is the female that Ego is supposed to marry.

Obviously, in some societies a distinction is made between these two females that we do not make. In discussing other social systems, anthropologists have found it convenient to make the same distinction. We sometimes refer to Y as Ego's *parallel cousin.* This is because she is the child of Ego's mother's sister. The sex line in the parental generation is not crossed: Ego's mother and his mother's sister are the same sex. (On the other side, not shown in the diagram, a child of Ego's father's brother would also be a parallel cousin for the same reason.) We sometimes refer to X as Ego's *cross cousin.* This is because she is the child of Ego's mother's brother — the sex line is crossed in the parental generation. (A child of Ego's father's sister would likewise be a cross cousin for the same reason.)

By giving these cousins different names we have not actually explained anything, of course. The significance of the distinction will be discussed shortly when we talk about the effect of different descent systems. At this point, the idea I am trying to communicate is simply this: Here we have two females who are equally closely related to Ego in biological terms, but a sexual relationship with one would be incestuous while a sexual relationship or marriage with the other would be ideal. Whatever is going on here, it cannot be accounted for solely within the framework of biology. Beyond this, as we shall see in the next chapter, incest tabus can also be extended to some persons to whom Ego is not related at all in a genetic sense. In dealing with kinship, the cultural factors involved must always be carefully considered.

SPOUSES

It is clear by now that incest regulations will affect the composition of kin groups (and indeed the recognition of kin), since they partially determine who can marry whom. In addition to this, societies also differ with regard to the number of spouses a person may have at the same time. I do not want to get into the thorny problem of what constitutes marriage at this time — that, too, will be taken up in the next chapter — but it is necessary to emphasize that when we discuss spouses we are talking about persons who are *married* to each other. Spouses may indeed be lovers, but lovers are not always spouses — at least not to each other.

In our culture, of course, the approved (or ideal) form of marriage is *mo-*

nogamy: each person may have just one spouse at any given time. (Legally, if you want more than one spouse you must wait until your spouse dies or get a divorce.) Although the ideal of monogamous marriage is by no means confined to our own society, it is definitely not the most common type of approved marriage. In most cultures, the ideal is to have plural spouses; that is, a person is encouraged to have more than one spouse at a time. A system of marriage involving plural spouses is called *polygamy.* On the basis of conservative estimates, polygamy is the preferred form of marriage in about four times as many societies as those favoring monogamy. In other words, statistically speaking, it is monogamy that is somewhat unusual, not polygamy.

Polygamy is a general term; it does not specify which sex is permitted to have plural spouses. To gain a better understanding of what polygamy actually involves, it is necessary to divide the category into two basic types. *Polygyny* is the variety of polygamy by which a male is allowed or encouraged to have more than one wife at a time. *Polyandry* is the kind of polygamy by which a female is allowed or encouraged to have more than one husband at a time. The essential point here is a simple one: Polygyny is very common and polyandry is very rare. *Almost all polygamous marriages are in reality polygynous marriages.* To put this in more specific terms, less than 1 percent of polygamous marriages involve polyandry.

It must be understood that we are here discussing ideal or preferred marriage patterns. In stating that a given society is polygynous, we do not mean that all marriages in that society take that form. We just mean that the polygynous marriage is permitted and viewed as desirable. Not every person can attain that goal; the poor man tends to be a monogamist in all societies.

Nevertheless, several obvious questions occur concerning polygyny. First, how does it work in structural terms? Second, why does it occur so frequently? What makes it attractive as a marriage arrangement? Given roughly equal numbers of males and females in a society, it would seem that if some men have more than one wife some other men are not going to have *any* wife. It does not work that way. The reason usually is that males and females marry for the first time at different ages. A male may be relatively old when he first marries; he may be 30 or so before he is in an economic position to take a wife. Females tend to be much younger when they first marry; it is not unusual for a girl to be married when she is 14 or 15 years old. It follows, for this and other reasons, that the husband will probably die first. In effect, this makes the wife available again to marry another man. It is a truism to point out that when males or females marry for a second or third time they are older than they were the first time around.

Housing arrangements vary from society to society. It is quite common in Africa for the husband to have a cluster of houses with one wife in each. Sometimes he visits one, sometimes another. In other areas, all of the wives are housed in the same structure, but each wife has her own part of the household. In either case, mothers are usually found with their own children; all the wives and children are not just jumbled up together, although it may appear that way to a casual observer.

Why does polygyny occur so often? There is no single answer that will satisfactorily explain all known cases, but a start can be made by bearing in mind that a polygynous society does not have the same set of values that a monogamous society has; the ideal family form is different. A woman does not regard a second or third wife as an insult; on the contrary, they are marks of distinction inasmuch as they show the world that her husband is a successful man. (I do not mean to suggest that sexual jealousy between cowives never occurs; it sometimes does. I mean only that it is not supposed to occur, and when a man takes an additional wife this is not viewed as a criticism of the first wife.)

Sex is only one of the usual attributes of marriage, and by no means the most important one. (Sexual activities, after all, do not require marriage; it is not at all uncommon for males and females to have lovers both before and after polygynous marriages. The same is true for monogamous marriages, of course.) Families have work to do, and in many primitive societies the division of labor is such that the women must work harder than the men. In addition to caring for children, they must often gather firewood, cultivate crops, milk the cows, walk miles for water, cook the meals, and make the clothing. This is both difficult and time consuming. An additional wife may be pleasant for the male, but it is a blessing for the first wife. Simply put, she has less work to do; the jobs can be divided up. Moreover, her status is enhanced both because she is a participant in an "important" household and because she becomes the senior wife — she can delegate some of the tougher tasks. Frequently, it is not the male who is so eager to have another wife. Rather, it is the first wife or wives who encourage him to marry another woman. The new wife, too, has certain advantages. By moving into a household where there are already adult females, she does not have as tough a time as she would if she had to do everything by herself.

Polyandry is another matter. There are less than ten known polyandrous societies; the best known are the Todas of India and the Marquesans of Polynesia. Polyandry is so rare that special circumstances are probably required to produce it. It appears to be associated with a shortage of females; there simply are not enough women to go around. (A shortage of females can be produced by the practice of female infanticide — the killing of unwanted female children — or by neglect of female children, which lessens their chances for survival.) There are other possible reasons for polyandry, but it must be noted that polyandry is always a poor reproductive strategy. A single male can produce pregnancy in a large number of females, but a single female can have only a limited number of children no matter how many husbands she has.

There is also the phenomenon sometimes referred to as *group marriage*. It is a complex system in which several men, two brothers for example, are simultaneously married to several women. About all that can be usefully said about it is that it is a possible arrangement. It is best documented for the Kaingang of Brazil. It is quite rare, and there are no societies in which it is the cultural norm. Group marriages, when they do occur, are never free and easy instances of collective promiscuity. They are always sharply limited and involve complicated and well-defined marriage rules.

PRINCIPLES OF DESCENT

Just as the rules regarding incest or marriage may differ from society to society, the principles of *descent* may also vary. Descent relationships refer to kin links that are established between parents (or ancestors) and children. Thus, the link between me and my father is a descent link; so is the relationship between me and my grandmothers.

Although there is often some connection between the two, descent principles do not necessarily follow genetic relationships. Difficult as the idea may be to get used to, it is best to view descent ties as culturally recognized kinship relationships. To take a simple example, if I had an adopted child, that child would be my daughter or son and I would be the sociological father of the child. Since I would not be the biological father of the son or daughter, there is no genetic relationship between us.

In our society, we have what is called a *bilateral descent system.* It seems entirely "natural" to us for the elementary reason that this is the way in which we have been conditioned to look at descent; in any culture, people feel that what *they* do is obvious and natural, while what *other* cultures do is perhaps a bit weird. In a bilateral system, a child is regarded as equally kin to both the child's father (and father's relatives) and the child's mother (and mother's relatives). That is what "bilateral" means—two sides. Ideally, the child has the "same" kinds of kin on both sides of the family: a grandfather and a grandmother on the mother's side, a grandfather and a grandmother on the father's side, and so on. (You will find a bilateral system outlined in Chapter 16.) The system is not unique; indeed, it is often referred to as an "Eskimo system" because the Eskimo descent system has the same basic design.

The joker in the ethnological deck, from our point of view, is that the majority of cultures on this planet do not reckon descent the way we do. Their ideas about what is "natural" differ from ours. The plain fact is that most human societies do not have bilateral descent systems. Instead, their systems are based on the principle of *unilineal descent.* "Unilineal" means one line. A unilineal descent system counts descent just through *one* side of the family. In other words, sociologically speaking, a child is viewed as being kin *either* to the child's father (and father's relatives) *or* to the child's mother (and mother's relatives)—not to both. Remember our earlier caution here—this does not involve genetics (or biology) as such, but rather the cultural definition of who is regarded as being kin to whom. Another way of looking at it is to regard it as a method of determining which of two kin groups you will belong to, your mother's or your father's. The key factor is not the recognition by the child of its father and mother. Rather, it involves the roles played by the father and mother and the degree to which they provide links to larger groups of kin.

Essentially, there are two main types of unilineal descent systems. If the descent links are through males, the system is called *patrilineal.* If the descent links are through females, the system is called *matrilineal.* Although the matrilineal form might seem at first glance to be the better choice — recalling the deeply rooted primate ties between mothers and their children — most unilineal systems are in fact patrilineal. Patrilineal systems outnumber matrilineal systems by a ratio of about three to one.

In passing, it may be noted that there is also a type of system referred to as a *double descent* system. This utilizes both patrilineal and matrilineal descent principles in the same society. In effect, a person is affiliated with two different descent groups. The person is linked with the father's kin group through patrilineal ties and with the mother's kin group through matrilineal ties. Frequently, the two kinds of descent groups will have different functions. For example, among the Toda of India, property is inherited through the patrilineal kin group, while ritual obligations are assigned on the basis of membership in the matrilineal kin group. What is going on here is that two unilineal systems are operating at the same time. A double descent system is fundamentally different from a bilateral system. Ideally, in a bilateral system, a person acquires membership through descent in just one kin group composed of both the father's and the mother's relatives.

What is important to understand here is that these different ways of reckoning descent have critical social consequences. They affect what is going on in a society — and with whom. We will be seeing more of this in the next two chapters, but to illustrate what can be involved let us go back to our diagram dealing with cross and parallel cousins (p. 246). This time, using the same basic diagram, let us assume that a matrilineal descent system is in operation. If this is so, the members of the matrilineal kin group are indicated by solid triangles and circles:

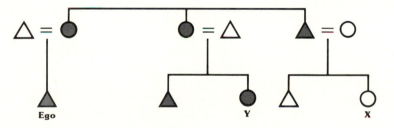

Let us spell out the key relationships here to avoid the possibility of misunderstanding. It may help to give the matrilineal kin group a name; suppose we call the members Grasshoppers. Ego is a Grasshopper because his mother is a Grasshopper. Ego's mother's sister and mother's brother are Grasshoppers because Ego's mother, mother's sister, and mother's brother are siblings; they are all the children of the same female Grasshopper, who would be in the next generation up. The children of Ego's mother's sister are Grasshoppers because their mother is a Grasshopper.

Note also who is *not* a Grasshopper. Ego's father cannot be a Grasshopper because Ego's mother *is;* if two Grasshoppers married, that would be incest. Similarly, the wife of Ego's mother's brother cannot be a Grasshopper for the same reason. In turn, this means that the children of Ego's mother's brother cannot be Grasshoppers either; they will take their kin affiliation from their mother (Ego's mother's brother's wife), and whatever she is she cannot be a Grasshopper.

The distinction between cross and parallel cousins now should make more sense. Note that Ego's parallel cousin (Y) is in Ego's kin group; she is a Grasshopper. Ego might very well address her by the same term he would apply to his sister; she is in the same generation as Ego and in the same kin group. If you think of Ego and Y as the equivalents of brother and sister, it is clear that they are not suitable marriage partners for each other.

Moreover, Ego's cross cousin (X) is *not* in Ego's kin group. Beyond that, she cannot be a relative as long as a matrilineal descent system is in operation. Therefore, she is a potential marriage partner for Ego. There is another factor that is important here. The father of X (Ego's mother's brother) *is* a Grasshopper. There is already a key social relationship between Ego and his mother's brother; since Ego's mother's brother is a Grasshopper and in the generation above Ego, he may be "like a father" to Ego. Indeed, he has certain advantages over Ego's biological father, since the biological father is not a member of Ego's kin group. This is why X is not only a *possible* marriage partner for Ego but also a *preferred* marriage partner.

To repeat, it is essential to realize that varying descent principles have important social consequences. Until the descent system is understood, it is nearly impossible to figure out what is going on in any human society.

RULES OF RESIDENCE

Whenever two people marry, somebody has to move. It is difficult if not impossible for a marriage to work if both the man and the woman remain in their original households. Therefore, when a marriage occurs this involves a certain amount of personnel reshuffling.

All human societies have *rules of residence* which state where people are supposed to live when they get married. Such rules are perhaps better thought of as general principles which serve as guidelines with regard to residential locations after a marriage has taken place; the rules are seldom so inflexible that no exceptions are permitted. They are really statements about what is supposed to happen, other things being equal.

In our society, we have *neolocal* residence. The word means "new place." The suggestion is that a newly married couple should set up housekeeping in a place separate from the original households of both the bride and the groom. The couple establishes a place of its own—an apartment, a trailer, a house, or whatever. Neolocal residence patterns occur in a fair number of societies and tend to be associated with a high degree of social mobility; it is a system that does not tie a person to a particular locality, and it does not require that a person must remain locked into a large functioning kinship network.

The majority of human societies have *patrilocal* residence. This means that after a marriage occurs the wife moves in with the household of the groom; that is, she joins the household of the groom's father. Speaking from the viewpoint of a male in such a society, when I married I would bring my bride home to live with my parents — either in the same house or in effect right next door. Patrilocal systems tend to be associated with patrilineal descent. The Kamba of Kenya have such a system, and they have a saying that expresses the basic idea very well. "A son," they say, "is like the center post of the house — he stays put. A daughter is like a bird — she flies away."

The converse of patrilocal residence, of course, is *matrilocal* residence. This means that after marriage the groom goes to live in the household of the bride's mother. The bride stays put this time, and the groom moves. Matrilocal systems are often associated with matrilineal descent.

This does not exhaust either the possibilities or the ethnographic realities of residence patterns. There are societies in which a choice can be made between patrilocal or matrilocal customs; there are societies in which the couple lives for a time in a matrilocal arrangement and then switches to a patrilocal one; there are societies in which the couple lives with or near a maternal uncle of the groom, and so on. (To get an inkling of why this last pattern occurs, refer back to the diagram on p. 251.) However, nearly all human societies fall into the first three categories: They are either neolocal, patrilocal, or matrilocal.

We have already discussed the fundamental fact that in all human societies there are some people a person can marry and other people that a person cannot marry. It is useful to extend this concept beyond the individual level and return once more to the characteristics of groups.

There are groups — and they are very numerous — that require a person to go outside the group when seeking a marriage partner. Such groups are called *exogamous* groups. By definition, a member of an exogamous group cannot marry another member of the same group. There is nothing complicated about this; it simply means that if you are a Grasshopper (to utilize our earlier example) you cannot marry a Grasshopper — you must marry a member of some other group. In our society, the immediate family is an exogamous group. Since you cannot marry your brother or sister or father or mother, you must look outside of your family in order to find a suitable person to marry. We will encounter some other kinds of exogamous groups in the next chapter.

The principle of exogamy is probably a very ancient one among the hominids. While its origins remain somewhat obscure, the results of exogamy are not difficult to see. Whether or not the custom establishes a reciprocal pattern of exchange between families, as Lévi-Strauss suggested (see p. 216), it is clear that exogamy greatly enlarges social networks based on kinship. Instead of one closed group, exogamy produces a series of kin-linked groups. This enhances the possibility of peaceful cooperation between the component groups of a society. It may not solve all social problems to have relatives in different groups, but it helps.

The opposite of an exogamous group is an *endogamous* group. This is a group that a person must remain within when seeking a marriage partner. The most familiar examples are the castes of India. A caste is a fixed social class, and marriages can occur only within castes — not between them. In a formal sense, endogamy is much less common than exogamy. However, in terms of what actually occurs as opposed to stated rules, endogamy is not really rare. Most total (the sum of all internal subdivisions) human societies — the Masai, say, or the Hopi or the Kwakiutl — are in fact largely endogamous. That is, a Masai usually marries a Masai even though there may be no rule to this effect. Similarly, villages are often endogamous, and it is by no means unusual for religious groups to bring pressure to bear to encourage a person to marry someone of the same religious faith. If exogamy functions to extend the social network, endogamy operates to preserve and intensify the solidarity of particular social groups.

As most of us discover sooner or later, a marriage is far more than a tie (or a contract) between individuals. A marriage creates a reciprocal relationship between groups — at a minimum, a relationship between two families. This factor is partially responsible for the widespread customs known as the *levirate* and the *sororate*.

Both institutions are ways of coping with a recurrent social problem — what to do with a family if one spouse dies. In the levirate, a man is supposed to marry his brother's widow. In other words, if the levirate were in operation in this country, if I died my wife would marry my brother. In the sororate, a woman is supposed to marry her sister's widower. In the above example, if my wife died she would be replaced by her sister.

Two points merit emphasis in connection with these phenomena. First, in either the levirate or the sororate, the deceased spouse is replaced by his or her social equivalent — the tie between groups is maintained. Second, there is obviously a kind of social insurance at work here. If the father or the mother of a family dies, a "substitute" moves in, and the family can continue as a functioning unit. Moreover, the replacement is no stranger either to the children or to the larger kinship network.

Certain questions invariably arise when the levirate and the sororate are mentioned. The problems are more apparent than real, but suppose we take a look at them. The common questions are:

1. What if the husband does not have a brother, or the wife does not have a sister?
2. What if the brother or the sister are already married to somebody else?
3. What if the people involved cannot stand one another?

Specifically, the answers are as follows. If the husband does not have a biological brother, or the wife does not have a biological sister, there will usually be an *equivalent* person available in the community. As we have noted, kinship is a cultural phenomenon. This means, as we shall see in the next two chapters, that a person may have many "brothers" or "sisters" apart from those acquired through genetic relationships. Marriages that occur through the operation of the levirate or sororate are almost always secondary marriages; that is, they involve one spouse taking an additional marriage partner. Obviously, such a situation will occur normally in a polygamous society. As a rule, the levirate and sororate deal with *categories* of kin rather than with specific persons. If the most logical choice is not acceptable for one reason or another, some alternative arrangement can usually be worked out. It is true that many marriages are arranged with little or no regard to the feelings of the potential partners, but in the majority of cases this occurs in primary (first) marriages rather than secondary ones.

In more general terms, the key to the whole situation is to remember that customs like the levirate or sororate tend to be ideal solutions to social problems: They are a kind of shorthand statement about what is supposed to happen under normal circumstances. People everywhere recognize that things do not always work out as they theoretically should; that is why there are divorces as well as marriages. Under unusual conditions, there are ways to tinker with the levirate or sororate. Indeed, they can be avoided altogether by the surviving spouse marrying someone other than the "ideal" social choice.

It is a mistake to imagine that people in other societies have no room to maneuver. They know the ropes of their cultures as well as we know the ropes of ours, and there are always social games that can be played. I knew a Kamba man who had been avoiding the levirate for 20 years. His brother had died, and the man was supposed to marry his brother's wife. He recognized the obligation, but he had his reasons for not wanting an additional wife. Moreover, the brother's wife was quite content as she was. They worked out an arrangement that was satisfactory to both parties. The man visited the household of his brother's wife from time to time and made decisions when they had to be made. (The woman had a grown son, but as the Kamba say, "A son cannot be the head of his mother's household.") He was available in emergencies. It was all quite amiable, but the two never married. I asked the man about it and his answer was a good one. He said, "Nobody follows all the rules. Sometimes, there are better ways." It is a principle that has wide application in human societies.

SUMMARY

The kinship groups that form in different societies are the products of various combinations of how descent is reckoned, how marriage is viewed, and where people are supposed to live. Incest regulations also affect the composition of kin groups, since they partially determine who can marry whom. Although it may take off from biologically based relationships, such as that between a mother and her child, kinship is essentially a cultural phenomenon. Once you get beyond a core of forbidden sexual relationships — mother-son, father-daughter, brother-sister — the definition of incest cannot be reduced to simple biological principles.

Monogamy is a form of marriage in which each person can have only one spouse at a time. In most cultures, the ideal is to have plural spouses. A system of marriage involving plural spouses is called *polygamy.* There are two basic kinds of polygamous marriage: When a male is allowed or encouraged to have more than one wife at a time this is termed *polygyny,* and when a female is allowed or encouraged to have more than one husband at a time this is called *polyandry.* In point of fact, almost all polygamous marriages are in reality polygynous marriages.

Just as the rules regarding incest or marriage may differ from society to society, the principles of descent may also vary. Descent relationships refer to kin links that are established between parents (or ancestors) and children. A *bilateral* descent system is one in which a child is regarded as being equally kin to both the child's father (and father's relatives) and the child's mother (and mother's relatives). Ideally, the child has the same kinds of kin on both sides of the family. This seems quite natural to us simply because this is the type of kinship system that exists in American culture. However, most cultures do not reckon descent in this fashion. Instead, in the majority of human cultures, descent is figured on *unilineal* principles. Such a system counts descent through just one side of the family. A child is viewed as being kin either to the father's side of the family or to the mother's side, but not to both. The key factor here is not the recognition by the child of its father and mother, but rather the roles played by the father and mother and the degree to which they provide links to larger groups of kin. There are two main types of unilineal systems. If the descent links are through males, it is a *patrilineal* system. If the descent links are through females, it is a *matrilineal* system.

All human societies have *rules of residence*, which state where people are supposed to live when they get married. A *neolocal* system is one in which the newly married couple establish a new residence separate from the original households of either the bride or the groom. The majority of human societies have *patrilocal* residence, which means that the wife is supposed to move into the household of the groom. The converse of this is *matrilocal* residence, in which the groom moves into the household of the wife.

Some human groups are *exogamous,* which means that a person must go outside the group in seeking a marriage partner. Other groups are *endogamous,* which means that a person must remain within the group when seeking a marriage partner.

When the *levirate* is in operation, a man is supposed to marry his brother's widow. When the *sororate* is in operation, a woman is supposed to marry her sister's widower. Both institutions are designed to cope with a recurring social problem: what to do with a family if one spouse dies.

Suggestions for Further Reading

Bohannan, Paul. 1963. *Social Anthropology.* New York: Holt, Rinehart and Winston. Part 2 of this book, which is divided into six chapters, presents a clearly written discussion of kinship and marriage in less than 100 pages.

Buchler, I. R., and H. A. Selby. 1968. *Kinship and Social Organization.* New York: Macmillan. Heavily theoretical, this will prove rewarding to the careful reader.

Fox, Robin. 1967. *Kinship and Marriage.* Baltimore: Penguin Books. This little paperback — a volume in the Pelican Anthropology Library — may well be the best single book in the field. It is beautifully done and continuously interesting. Not the sort of thing to polish off before breakfast, but you will be glad you read it.

Murdock, George Peter. 1949. *Social Structure.* New York: Macmillan. A classic example of cross-cultural analysis. Provides both statistical data (how many societies do what) and theoretical interpretations.

————. 1957. "World Ethnographic Sample." *American Anthropologist* 59: 664–687. For the serious student. Presents information on a number of variables, including kinship terminology, based on a sample of 565 cultures.

Schneider, David M. 1968. *American Kinship: A Cultural Account.* Englewood Cliffs, N.J.: Prentice-Hall. A thoughtful examination of kinship in America.

Schusky, Ernest L. 1972. *Manual for Kinship Analysis,* 2d ed. New York: Holt, Rinehart and Winston. If kinship phenomena intrigue you, you will have some fun with this one.

15

Kin Groups: The Family, the Lineage, and the Clan

In one form or another, the family is virtually a cultural universal. In fact, there are no human societies that totally lack family systems. However, taking into account an abundance of ethnographic evidence, it is difficult to make unqualified assertions about "the" family. Families are not always simple, and they are not everywhere the same.

By the same token, however, there is more than one way to read the ethnographic evidence. We can either seek out the rare and the unusual or we can focus on the vast majority of cases, that is, talk about what holds true for almost all human societies. It seems to me to be a mistake to concentrate on the exceptional cases insofar as families are concerned. It is misleading because it leaves the impression that this is what most families are like, and the impression is false. The exceptional cases reveal the range of the possible, but they should not obscure the central issue, which is to find out what families usually are and how they operate.

The simplest type of family consists of a married man and woman together with their dependent children. This elementary family unit is called a *nuclear family.*

THE NUCLEAR FAMILY

Technically, it is possible to have a married pair but not a family. In most societies, the idea is that the family does not really exist until at least one child has been born. In some societies, such as our own, a married couple tends to be regarded as a family unit whether or not there are children. However, most mar-

The nuclear family is the simplest type of family system.

riages do produce (or adopt) children, and there are sound reasons for including dependent children in the definition of a nuclear family. In a very real sense, many of the functions of a nuclear family cannot operate without the existence of children.

More critical, perhaps, is the problem of marriage. All human societies distinguish between those persons who are married and those who are not. All human societies recognize a difference between marriage relationships and other types of sexual arrangements. A marriage involves something more than an agreement to meet occasionally in the forest, and something more than just living together. There is no need to inject "morality" into the picture. The point is simply that marriages are different.

What is a marriage? Any marriage has at least two components to it, and I am not referring to the participants themselves. A marriage has both a symbolic (or ceremonial) aspect and a functional aspect. The two should not be confused. The symbolic element is a *signal* to the participants and to the rest of the community. It announces in no uncertain terms: "We are married." The functional element is something else again. It concerns what the marriage *does*. That is, it deals with the social effects of the marriage relationship.

You have to "get married" in any culture. You must *do* something — perform some act or series of acts — to formalize the marriage and show that it has taken place. What you do depends on your culture. It can be a church wedding, a signing of documents in the presence of witnesses, a public embrace, an acted-out abduction, or a ceremonial meal of whale blubber. Quite frequently, it in-

Although the form of ceremonies may vary a great deal from one culture to another, you have to *get* married to *be* married.

volves a transfer of property from the family of the groom to the family of the bride. These property transfers are called *bridewealth payments;* they are often complex and extend over many years, but as a rule there is a key payment in the series that finalizes the marriage. The specific method of "getting married" is not the crucial thing; what counts is that the society has some recognized procedure to indicate that a marriage has occurred.

The functional aspect of marriage involves what it means to be married—

the social consequences of the existence of a marriage. Rather than talking about theories, let us return to the nuclear family. This is what the nuclear family unit usually does:

1. It establishes legal or socially sanctioned parentage. That is, it places the children of a married couple in a recognized kinship network. Among other things, by clearly defining descent links, it greatly simplifies both social and material inheritance.
2. It has the primary responsibility for the enculturation of children. By providing a reasonably stable unit to care for the slow-maturing young primate, it makes it possible for the child to learn its culture. This is why the family is sometimes called "the transfer point of culture." Certainly, not all of any culture is learned within the family. Nevertheless, enculturation begins at home.
3. It establishes a recognized economic unit. A division of labor by sex is a human characteristic, and that is what happens in a nuclear family: The participants divide up the work and share the results. Whether the man hunts and the woman digs roots, or the woman farms and the man forges iron tools, or they both work in a factory and bring home paychecks, the result is the same: The family is a working group that benefits from the labor of all of its members. (It may be noted that taking care of the kids is a form of work, no matter who does it. The division of labor here is that one member of the family can do whatever else must be done. The very essence of the division of labor is that it is virtually impossible for one person to look after the children, prepare meals, make clothing, gather firewood, conduct ceremonies, fight enemies, and hunt elephants—all at the same time.)
4. It sets up a relationship between several families. That is, at a minimum, it establishes firm social links between the husband's original family and the wife's original family. This can be clearly seen in bridewealth payments—they are exchanges between families, not a purchase of a bride by a husband. In our own society, it is interesting to observe how the two families become intertwined, even if they have never met before the marriage of their children. These interconnections can have important economic and social implications. To mention just one obvious example, with our kinship system a newborn child acquires two sets of grandparents. Conversely, both sets of grandparents have a new grandchild. Hence, the eternal question: Which house do you visit at Christmas? Or whom do you invite to your house?
5. It establishes a socially approved pattern of sexual rights between the spouses.

Not all nuclear families are identical, although they tend to be similar wherever they are found, and not all marriages result in nuclear families. Therefore, the social consequences of marriage are not everywhere the same. It is possible for a marriage to occur that does not produce a family unit that carries out all of the above functions. However, the plain fact is that the overwhelming majority of marriages do either create or add to family units, and families generally perform all or most of those functions. In this sense, the functions will serve to indicate what it usually means to be married.

Anthropologists are divided on the question of whether or not nuclear families occur in all human societies. George Peter Murdock, on the basis of a sample of 250 cultures, argued that they do: "The nuclear family is a universal human social grouping. Either as the sole prevailing form of the family or as the basic unit from which more complex familial forms are compounded, it exists as a distinct and strongly functional group in every known society" (Murdock 1949: 2).

The question is not simple. On a kind of common sense level, it would seem that there is no more basic primate characteristic than the ties that exist between a mother and her offspring. If you bring a specific husband-father into the picture, which is probably a very old hominid pattern, you have, in effect, a nuclear family. Beyond this, it is usually possible in any human society to identify a social unit composed of a married couple together with their children — which is what a nuclear family is. The danger is that we may be viewing other family systems through our own cultural lenses and thus failing to see how other cultures perceive their families.

Specifically, there are two questions that must be asked. First, if something like a nuclear family exists primarily as a subunit of a larger family structure, should that be counted as a nuclear family? Second, if there is some clear alternative to the nuclear family, is this arrangement characteristic of the society in question or is it exceptional? In other words, does the alternative apply only to specialized segments of the society or to the society as a whole?

There is no doubt that the nuclear family as a functioning unit usually does not occur in isolation. The degree to which the nuclear family operates by itself in our society is not unique, but it is definitely unusual. Like neolocal residence, it tends to be associated with a high degree of social mobility. The more or less isolated nuclear family makes sense in a hunting and gathering culture like that of the Eskimo, where people must sometimes move around in very small groups to find food, and in industrial cultures like our own, where people must go to where the jobs are. However, not all hunting and gathering cultures are organized around a core of nuclear families, and even in our own society the nuclear family is not totally isolated. When Uncle Joe and Aunt Ruth come to call, they are "family." The problem — or the blessing, depending on your point of view — is that they can't come to call very often because they live someplace else. Indeed, it could be argued from a worldwide perspective that the nuclear family only operates as an independent unit when there is no other workable option. In most cultures, people live their lives surrounded by kinfolk. When anthropologists describe our nuclear family system to tribal peoples with whom they work, the reaction is often one of pity or amazement.

And that is precisely the point. Although something like nuclear family units can be identified in almost all cultures, they are usually embedded in larger kinship groupings. If I may paraphrase a useful observation of Murdock's, the nuclear family does not as a rule exist as a kind of social atom but rather is found in molecular combinations. To extend the analogy a bit, we all know that water is composed of hydrogen and oxygen. Therefore, when we go jump in the lake, we can say, "That's water!" Alternatively, we can holler, "That's hydrogen and oxygen!" Both statements are correct, of course. Leaving aside some special situations that we will get to shortly, the problem of the universality of the nuclear family is similar. If the nuclear family unit is there — if you can spot a group made up of mother, father, and the kids — but it is just one part of a larger family grouping, do you call it a nuclear family or do you call it something else? Do you recognize that hydrogen (the nuclear family) is present, or do you talk about water (the larger family) instead?

If you accept the presence of nuclear families whenever they can be detected, regardless of the context of larger family groups, then the nuclear family is reasonably close to a cultural universal. If you count only fairly isolated nuclear families — those that are not plugged into larger functional family groups — then the nuclear family is clearly not a cultural universal. It is not a matter of who is right and who is wrong. As is so often the case, it is a question of which definition you use. To repeat the essential point, in most human societies the family consists of something more than the nuclear family alone. It is a larger group. Since this is true, we must examine the nature of these larger family groups.

LARGER FAMILY GROUPS

They can take several forms. As we saw in the previous chapter, most human societies have polygamy as the preferred form of marriage, and most polygamous marriages are in fact polygynous. In plain English, this means that the most common type of ideal family in terms of spouses consists of one male and two or more females, together with their children. This is a *polygamous family*. Obviously, such an arrangement can be interpreted in nuclear family terms. Suppose that a man has two wives who live in separate dwellings in a compound. Each woman's children reside with her. When the male visits one wife, that is one nuclear family. When he visits the other, that is another nuclear family. In other words, there are two nuclear families that share a single husband-father. However, the nuclear family interpretation is strained to say the least. Polygamous families do not really work that way. Although there may be recognized divisions within the family, from the viewpoint of the participants it is still *one* family. It performs all of the functions of the family (see p. 262) and it *thinks* of itself as a family. Therefore, it *is* a family.

To clarify the distinction here, think of a situation that pops up from time to time in our society. A man has a job that requires travel. He marries one woman in Dallas and another in Los Angeles and has children by both. This is illegal, of course, but more to the point, it is not socially sanctioned: This is not an accepted form of marriage in our society. Neither family knows that the other exists. In fact, the arrangement depends on total secrecy. The children are emphatically not enculturated in a total group situation, and social descent links are not clear—think of the inheritance problems, for instance. The wives do not interact with one another, and there is no large group structure. There is not one economic unit, but two. Whatever name you give to it, this is not a single family by any stretch of the imagination.

Apart from the question of spouses, the type of family encountered in most cultures is an *extended family*. Definitions can do more harm than good here, and for this reason it is probably best to set forth a series of principles that will apply to extended families of various kinds. The problem here is one of recognition: How do you know one when you see one?

1. An extended family is always larger than a nuclear family.
2. The enlargement involves more than just polygamous households. (This does not mean that polygamous families cannot also be extended families. It just means that a polygamous household *by itself* is not usually considered to be an extended family.)
3. An extended family is best thought of as a kind of residence group. This does not mean that all family members must live in the same dwelling, although sometimes they do, but only that they must live close enough to one another to form a functioning interacting group. Think of a brush fence forming an enclosure with a series of houses inside or a row of dwellings in a village.
4. The members of an extended family will be tied together by kinship links. In other words, it is not just a group composed of friends and neighbors. The kinship links may be lineal (as from mother to son or daughter) or collateral (as between siblings), or both.

Let us diagram the simplest kind of extended family:

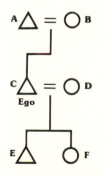

Here we have in essence two nuclear families with one member (Ego) in common. One nuclear family is composed of A, B, and C. (From the viewpoint of Ego, this is the *family of orientation*. It is the family within which Ego grew up.) The other nuclear family is composed of C, D, E, and F. (From the same viewpoint, this is the *family of procreation*. It is the family Ego establishes when

This is an extended family. A person is surrounded by relatives.

he marries and has children.) If all of these people live together, they form an extended family. This particular type of extended family is a *joint extended family*.

I have deliberately drawn this diagram as a kind of extended family skeleton, employing the bare minimum of symbols. A full-fleshed extended family will normally involve more people, but the principle is the same. For example, A may have more than one wife and more than one set of children, A and B may have several married sons in addition to Ego, and so on. Beyond this, extended families may be either patrilineal or matrilineal, which further complicates the picture. The diagram presented is most easily interpreted as a simple patrilineal extended family.

So far, we have been talking about a type of extended family that is formed on the basis of lineal (descent) links. A very simple type of extended family that is formed from collateral (sibling) links looks like this:

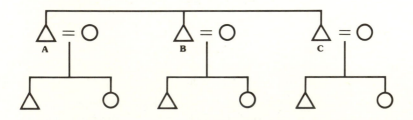

All that is going on here is that several brothers (A, B, and C) have formed a residence group; they share a dwelling or a compound. Each is married, and

This is a nuclear family group among the San. A few key relatives must do it all.

each has children. The group is a *fraternal extended family;* if the siblings were sisters, it would be a *sororal extended family.*

Again, this can get more complex. One of the brothers (or all of them) may have more than one wife. The parents of the brothers may live with them. Nevertheless, the point remains—an extended family is a larger group than a nuclear family, and the kinship linkages may be either linear or collateral, or both.

Some understanding of the structure of extended families is necessary, although at first it may seem somewhat confusing. More important, though, is an understanding of what it means to live in an extended family. People do not live in a social world of triangles and circles. In family terms, they live in a world of relatives. The key thing about an extended family is that there are lots of relatives around. It isn't just that you have relatives; everybody has relatives. It is that the kinfolk are *right there with you.* You are surrounded by kin, enmeshed by kin, supported by kin, working with kin, relaxing with kin. Privacy you do not have. What you do have is a measure of warmth and security that a nuclear family has difficulty in supplying; from the critical viewpoint of a child, you live in a social universe conveniently supplied not only with fathers and mothers but also grand-parents and aunts and uncles and other children who are related to you. If it were not satisfying and effective, it would not be the most prevalent type of fami-ly system on this planet.

We often view families from the perspective of a child, just as I did in the preceding paragraph. Sometimes, we tend to forget the other members of a family. I am not thinking here of relatively young spouses but rather of the el-derly. Older people are members of families too. One great advantage of ex-tended family systems is that they take care of the elderly. An old person is not alone or shunted off to a "rest home" to wait for death. The older people can still contribute; they are secure in a meaningful social network. This is no small matter, for the role of the aged is one that most of us have to play sooner or later.

Earlier I suggested that there are two basic questions that must be asked concerning the universality (or nonuniversality) of the nuclear family. We have examined some data bearing on the first question, and we have indicated that there are good reasons for classifying polygamous and extended families as something more than clusters of nuclear families. We must now take a look at the second question. If family systems exist that do not involve nuclear families at all, singly or in combination, how typical are they of the societies in which they occur?

Anthropologists have discovered a number of unusual types of families. They have received a great deal of attention, and many textbooks discuss them in detail. This should not obscure the central fact about them, which I have al-ready indicated: They are unusual. Two examples will serve to illustrate the na-ture of the problem.

The Cheyenne Case

The historic Cheyenne were Plains Indians. Like many other Plains peo-ples, collectively called the Grasslands tribes, their lifeway was based on the mounted hunting of bison (buffalo) and raiding for horses. (There were other Plains groups, the Riverine tribes, who lived in stable villages and practiced agri-culture, but they need not concern us here.) Cheyenne males were warriors: A man had to prove himself as a warrior before he could be anything else. As George Bird Grinnell, one of the outstanding authorities on the Cheyenne, put it: "The Cheyenne men were all warriors. War was regarded as the noblest of pursuits, the only one for a man to follow" (Grinnell 1923:5). E. Adamson Hoe-bel, in his classic work on the Cheyenne, states: "Public glory is the ever-present reward of the man who fights bravely and well. The fighting patterns of the Cheyennes are embellished with virtuosities that go far beyond the needs of victory. Display in bravery tends to become an end in itself" (Hoebel 1960:70).

The Cheyenne were not unusual in this respect; it was a pattern that showed itself among all of the Plains Indians of the Grasslands type. For example, the Blackfoot started their males on the psychological warpath at a rather tender age: "When a boy was born it was customary for his father to hold him up toward the sun, and pray, 'Oh Sun! Make this boy strong and brave. May he die in battle!' " (Ewers 1955:214).

The male role was difficult and demanding. To play the role successfully a man had to have or affect a particular kind of personality. Most Cheyenne males managed to cope with the role; many obviously enjoyed it. However, it was not an attractive role for *all* Cheyenne men. There were some Cheyenne males who could not (or would not) dedicate a large part of their lives to being warriors. For such men there was essentially one alternative open. Unable or unwilling to function as males, they became sociologically females. Known as *berdaches,* they were transvestites who wore women's clothing and enacted female roles.

Such men, who may or may not have been homosexual, could marry other men. On the face of it, we would seem to have here a clear example of a marital arrangement very different from a nuclear family grouping. Two biological males cannot produce children, and the married pair therefore cannot perform many of the functions of a nuclear family as the term is ordinarily understood.

On a superficial basis, then, one might list the Cheyenne as an example of a society in which the nuclear family did not exist either as an isolated grouping or as a component of a large family system. It should already be obvious that such a listing would be nonsense. In fact, almost all Cheyennes live in quite familiar family groupings: Males married females and they lived in their own tipis (tents) with their unmarried children. Beyond this, they formed matrilocal extended families that camped together in tipi clusters. (That is, the married daughters stayed in the vicinity with their husbands and children. When sons married, they camped elsewhere with their wives and children.)

However, polygyny was permitted in Cheyenne society and this is where the transvestites enter the picture. As a rule, a married couple consisting solely of a transvestite and a warrior (or two transvestites) simply did not occur. When a transvestite married, he joined a household as an additional wife. Hoebel is quite specific on this point: "The transvestites are male homosexuals who wear women's clothes and often serve as second wives in a married man's household" (Hoebel 1960:77). Moreover, there were very few transvestites among the Cheyenne: Hoebel states that there were only five in the entire tribe.

The Cheyenne transvestites were not social outcasts. They often became doctors, and the Cheyenne generally liked them. They had an accepted place in Cheyenne society. The point is not that they are somehow peculiar, but only that they constituted the exception rather than the rule among the Cheyenne.

The Nayar Case

As far as the family is concerned, the Nayar of India have become perhaps the most famous people known to anthropology. They have achieved this distinction because they had the most unusual family system so far discovered by ethnologists.

The Nayar were a subcaste of warriors who lived in Malabar. The structure of the Nayar family system has been described with clarity and precision by Kathleen Gough (Gough 1959). She had to reconstruct the details of the former Nayar lifeway, but this is standard operating procedure, and there is no reason to question her accuracy.

The core of the Nayar social structure was composed of matrilineal descent groups. Such a group was a *taravad*. When she was still very young—before puberty—a Nayar girl was married in a specific ceremony to a man from another taravad. (In other words, the taravad was exogamous.) Up to this point, we are on familiar ground; there are many societies that arrange marriages when the females involved are quite young.

After the marriage ceremony, things begin to get complicated. The Nayar husband did not go to live with his bride, nor did she go to live with him. The newly married couple might have sexual relations on their wedding night, or they might not. In effect, the Nayar husband participated in the wedding ritual and then had little or nothing to do with his wife. He went on being a warrior, and warriors were away a lot. He could take other lovers, and lower caste men did the necessary farm chores.

The peculiarity here is that the Nayar marriage does not really create an economic unit, the spouses are not sexual partners to any meaningful extent, and the husband does not become the sociological (or biological) father of his wife's children. This does not mean that the marriage ceremony was insignificant. Without it, a Nayar girl could not (in Nayar terms) become a Nayar woman: She could not have sexual relations, and she could not become a mother.

As you have probably suspected by now, the plot thickens. Once she was properly married, the Nayar girl was free to take other lovers. There were restrictions on this. It was by no means total promiscuity; only certain classes of males were acceptable, and there could be no sexual relations with men of the woman's own taravad. Still, within limits the woman could participate in a number of sexual relationships of either long or short duration. It was customary for a warrior-lover to leave his spear outside the door of her dwelling to indicate what was going on.

When the woman became pregnant, there was another ceremonial act. One or more of the males having sexual relations with the woman publicly acknowledged that they were the father of the child. This was done by paying the fee of the midwife. The ritual payment was necessary both for the child to be "legitimate" and for the mother to be regarded as "proper." However, the father continued to be referred to as such only as long as he maintained a sexual relationship with the mother, and he had no social responsibility for the child and no authority over it. Sociologically speaking, as Gough indicates, "No Nayar knows his father" (Gough 1962:364).

It must be understood that Nayar children are not simply left to fend for themselves in an anonymous social universe. The mother is a constant. She is there. It is the husbands and the fathers who come and go. The place of the child in the kinship network is supplied by the matrilineal taravad groups, which also provide much of the child's psychological security and enculturation.

The Nayar system should not be dismissed as being bizarre. For one thing, it is an example—albeit an extreme one—of a rather widespread tendency in some family systems. What is going on with the Nayar is that the kinship link that counts is the *descent* link in the female line rather than the tie between spouses. For another thing, it worked.

Certainly, the Nayar must give pause to anyone who wishes to make unqualified assertions about the universality of the nuclear family. Still, there are some additional points that should be recognized. As Walter Goldschmidt has noted, "the Nayars are a part-culture in a plural society" (Goldschmidt 1966: 101). The Nayar system operated in a small segment of a larger caste-divided culture. The males had specialized roles as soldiers in the larger society of which the Nayar were a part, and they were excused from economic (agricultural) work by the operation of the caste system. This makes the detached-male family system possible. What makes the system sensible in functional terms, as Goldschmidt has pointed out, is that it is designed to make ideal soldiers of the Nayar males: They are freed from economic and household responsibilities, they are provided with sexual partners, and they can give their full loyalty and attention to the military organization (Goldschmidt 1966:103).

Perhaps the major ethnographic lesson that anthropology can offer about "the" family is indicated by the word in quotation marks; beware of unsupported generalizations concerning "the" family. Whatever definition one chooses, it is abundantly clear that all families are not identical.

On the other hand, I think it is a mistake to leave the impression that family systems vary wildly without rhyme or reason. Families are not whimsical play combinations of men, women, and children: Families are serious sociological business. The other lesson that ethnography teaches is that the overwhelming majority of families represent variations on a common theme. You can have one spouse or several; you can live one place or another; you can reckon descent through one side or the other, or both; you can isolate the conjugal unit or surround it with kin—but still men must marry women, or vice versa, children must be produced and cared for and placed in a recognized social network, and families must perform the tasks that will enable the society to continue. I am confident that you could visit almost any culture anywhere and spot a family without much trouble: The details might be different from what you are used to, but you would know one when you saw one.

The nuclear family, about which so much has been written, is interesting because it is the simplest possible type of family structure. It is a bare-bones family. (This does not mean that it is necessarily either the best or the worst kind of family. It only means what it says: It is the simplest kind of family.) As I have already indicated, whether or not the nuclear family is a cultural universal is a matter of both opinion and definition. If we are speaking of total societies and isolated nuclear families, then the nuclear family is not universal—indeed, it is on the uncommon side. If the reference is to total societies with larger family groupings of which nuclear families are one discernible component, the question can be argued either way. My own view is that polygamous and extended families are significantly different from nuclear families: The whole is greater than the sum of its parts.

The exceptional and unusual types of families, such as those encountered among the Cheyenne or the Nayar or other peoples who might be mentioned, are not characteristic of total societies. They are produced by special circumstances, and they are found in parts of larger sociocultural systems. They illustrate the range of forms that a family can take, but it is a distortion of reality to employ them as examples of family norms in any total human society.

THE KINDRED

When we think of a family, regardless of what particular type of family it is, we normally think of a residence group. The members of a family—nuclear, polygamous, or extended—either live together or live in close proximity to one another. But kinship ties can extend far beyond residence groups, and in all human societies there is always some recognition of a larger group of kin. This larger kin group does not have to live together—although sometimes it does—and it may meet as a group only infrequently. Indeed, it may never come together as a total group. Despite this, it exists, it has social weight, and in some instances it is even more important that the family hearth group.

To establish the principle, let us begin at home. In our society, the largest meaningful kin group is that composed of the people who are considered to be "close" or "near" relatives. There was a time in the United States when this group was functionally highly significant. These days, with some notable exceptions involving kin enclaves in small towns or city neighborhoods, it seldom counts for much. Nevertheless, we all know what it is.

Who is in this group? The best way to answer this question is to picture a situation. You are with your family, and it is Christmas or Thanksgiving. The turkey is about to be served when there is a knock on the door. You open the door. Forget about manners now; that is not the issue. The person standing there walks into your home, plunks himself or herself down at the table, and says, "I'd like some white meat, please." If that person had a recognized social right to behave in that manner, then that person is a near relative. It might be a grandparent, an uncle, an aunt, or whatever. If the person was clearly out of line—simply an intruder with a distant kin link—then the person is not a near relative. If you are not sure—if the situation is socially ambivalent—then the person is probably a cousin.

In effect, we establish cutoff points on both sides of our kinship networks (that is, on the father's side and on the mother's side). Those relatives within the cutoff brackets are regarded as near relatives. Those people outside the brackets are excluded—they are kin, but not close kin.

This type of kin group is called a *kindred*. It is best defined as the group of culturally determined near relatives in a society with a bilateral descent system. Since kindreds are more or less familiar to us, they need not be discussed further at this point.

LINEAGES

As we have seen, most human societies do not have bilateral descent systems. They reckon descent on unilineal principles; descent is counted either through males or females, but not both. In societies of this type, we often find the large kin groups known as *lineages* or *clans.* When they occur—and they usually do—they tend to be critically important. Lineages and clans are not the same, although the two types of groups are similar in some respects. Since the lineage is the simpler of the two, we will consider it first.

It will be useful to begin with a definition: *A lineage is a named, exogamous, unilineal descent group the members of which can actually trace their ancestry back to a real person.* Before getting into a specific example, there are two points that need to be understood. First, you are born into a lineage: It is not a group that you join. At birth you become a member of either your father's lineage or your mother's lineage, depending on whether the descent system is patrilineal or matrilineal. Second, you can never change your lineage affiliation. You are stuck with it for life. It is not affected by where you live or who you marry. If Male Fox marries Female Rabbit, he's still Fox and she's still Rabbit.

To illustrate what the definition means, let us turn to the Kamba of Kenya. The word for lineage in the Kamba language is *mbaa.* I worked with the Kamba, and what follows is a fictional discussion that paraphrases a great many actual conversations I had with these people. The material included in the brackets represents a commentary on the discussion.

Picture a mature Kamba man whom we will call Kithome wa Nzwili. (The name means that Kithome is the son of a man named Nzwili.) Anthropologists in the field spend much of their time asking questions. I start with this one:

Q. Kithome, what is your mbaa?

A. I am mbaa-Kioko. [The answer comes readily and with a touch of pride. This is not sensitive material, and people like to talk about it. The answer always comes in this form, rather like a bound morpheme: first the name for lineage and then the name of a person.]

Q. How did you get to be a member of mbaa-Kioko?

A. My father, Nzwili, was mbaa-Kioko. His father was mbaa-Kioko. Therefore, I am mbaa-Kioko. [Kithome is a patient man, and a polite one. To him, the question is the question of an ignoramus. Any child would know the answer. But what he is telling me is that he was born into the lineage and that the descent system is patrilineal. The lineage links are through males only. This means that the Kamba mbaa is a *patrilineage.* If the descent links were through females, it would be a *matrilineage*—which is what the Nayar taravad was.]

Q. Could you marry a woman who was also mbaa-Kioko?

A. Never! It is forbidden! It would be crazy! [Again, Kithome is being polite. The question is an insulting one, similar to asking him if he would marry his sister. It must be asked, however, because the answer reveals an essential fact: The lineage is exogamous.]

Q. Kithome, you tell me that you belong to mbaa-Kioko. Who or what was Kioko?

A. Ah, Kioko! You do not know who Kioko was? That is amazing! Kioko was the father of my father's father's father's father! Oh, he was a very important man. Look, do you see that hill over there? That was where Kioko lived. I will take you there and show you the place. He had four wives and many cattle. He had a scar on his left arm from a Masai spear. Let me tell you about Kioko! He was born early in the morning. . . . [This answer is much condensed. Kithome can tell me plenty about Kioko. The basic point, however, is simple. Kioko, the founder of the lineage, was a real and well-remembered human being. He was not a legendary or supernatural figure of some sort. His name, as a matter of fact, is a common Kamba name; the literal meaning of *kioko* is "morning," and it is a name frequently given to children born at that time of day.]

If you will think about it a bit, you can learn several other things about lineages from the above example. For one thing, lineages are often relatively shallow: They go back a number of generations, but hardly into the dawn of time. For another thing, the members of a lineage are actually genetically or biologically related to one another; they can trace out the descent links. There are exceptions to this in the case of adopted children or fictive kin, but it is still useful to think of lineages in this way. (Fictive kin links are inserted after the fact; they are "made-up" links sometimes supplied to make everything "come out right.") Finally, it is entirely possible and even necessary for new lineages to start up from time to time. If they didn't, lineages would get so cumbersome that—as the Kamba say—it would be almost impossible to keep track of who was "really related" to whom.

Bearing this last point in mind, examine this fragment of a lineage spanning three generations. The lineage is patrilineal, and all those persons represented by solid triangles and circles are members of the lineage:

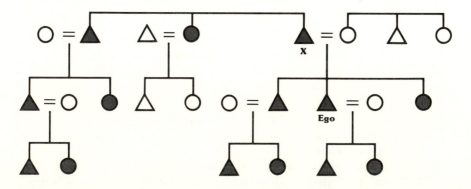

Unless Ego's father (X) is the founder of the lineage — which he isn't, because his brother and sister are in the same lineage — there will be other branches of the lineage which are not shown on the diagram. By way of example, just suppose that the father of X had two brothers.

In other words, when you deal with lineages you are talking about a fair number of people. All of the lineage members regard one another as kin and will address each other by kinship terms. That is why, in such a system, a person is apt to have a large number of people who are sociologically equivalent to "brothers," "sisters," and so on.

Although all the members of a lineage do not have to live together, lineage systems are most effective in situations of residential stability (such as farming villages) or in situations in which well-defined lineage segments can unite if necessary to take common action (as in herding societies). A lineage, after all, is a group. If the group is going to function, there must be some contact between its members.

What lineages actually do varies a good deal from society to society. In effect, once you have a lineage group there are a number of functions that can be assigned to it. These can range from the simple regulation of marriage, in which lineage members get together to decide upon suitable spouses for the younger generation, to major political or ceremonial activities, in which a particular lineage is charged with supplying village leaders or has the responsibility for conducting religious rites. As a general rule, lineages tend to be involved in the regulation of property division and in the control of some aspects of family life. Lineages are often land (or stock) holding units, and they have a collective voice in the sale, trade, or inheritance of fields or livestock. Any lineage has a vested interest in the orderly continuity of generations; that is the very core of the lineage. Therefore, when spouses or children get out of line, the lineage frequently meets to decide upon an appropriate course of action.

CLANS

Clans are rather like superlineages, and in truth the distinction between the two is not always as sharp as ethnologists would like. However, there are differences, and it might be useful to spell some of them out.

1. If both clans and lineages exist in the same society, the clan is the larger group. This means that lineages can be subdivisions of clans but not the other way around.
2. All of the members of a given clan cannot actually trace out the descent links between themselves. They regard one another as kin, but they cannot as a rule demonstrate their kinship with real family histories. In our society, if we had unilineal descent, a similar situation would prevail if everyone with the same last name — Jones, for example — simply assumed that they were related.

3. Clans are not only larger than lineages but they also tend to take on broader social functions. A clan composed of many thousands of persons is a powerful group. Although it may intercede in family matters, its concerns are typically wider than that. Indeed, many clan-organized societies are just exactly that: The clan is the most crucial element in the entire society; it provides the framework for getting things done.

The definition of a clan begins like the definition of a lineage. It goes like this: *A clan is a named, exogamous, unilineal descent group whose members cannot actually trace their ancestry back to a real person. The clan is frequently but not always involved with totemism.*

Let us return to our hypothetical Kamba, Kithome wa Nzwili. The Kamba have clans as well as lineages; each clan is made up of a series of lineages. The Kamba word for clan is *mbai*. Some of the questions that follow are ones that I routinely asked of many Kamba; the answers given here are representative of many actual answers.

Q. Kithome, what is your mbai?
A. I am Atangwa!
   [We can skip some questions here because you should already know the answers. Kithome is Atangwa because that is what his father was, and his father before him; the clans are patrilineal. Kithome could not marry a woman of the Atangwa clan; the clans are exogamous.]
Q. What is Atangwa? What does the word mean?
A. Atangwa are hawks. That is what it is. That is what we are. (The word is in the plural form, which is how the Kamba refer to their clans. The singular of Atangwa is Mutangwa.)
Q. How did your clan begin?
A. Oh, that is a very long story!
Q. Would you tell it to me?
A. It is just what some people say.
Q. What do some people say? [This give-and-take goes on for quite some time, but eventually Kithome tells his story. It is a story he only half believes; the Kamba do not worry much about clan origins. The clans simply *are.*]
A. It is said that long, long ago the first Kamba woman was walking up a hill very far from here. She saw a hawk circling in the sky. That hawk landed on the hill. He mated with that woman. Her children were the first Atangwa! That is what some people say. [The story is actually much longer than this; I have only given the essence here.]
Q. Would you ever kill a hawk?
A. Never! The hawk is my brother.
Q. Would you eat a hawk?
A. Never! I would get very sick. It is very impossible! [Kithome was somewhat defensive in telling his story. Now, he is quite positive—

he would no more eat a hawk than I would swallow poison.]

Q. You said that the hawk was your brother. Has a hawk ever really done anything for you?

A. Oh, yes. Once there was a fire in my shamba [cultivated field]. I did not see it. A hawk saw it! He circled the field in the sky until I came to see what was the matter. He saved my crop!

[At this point, let us pause to see what we have learned. When Kithome is pressed about the founding of the clan, he does not tell a story about a real person. Instead, he gives an origin myth—a story that he recognizes as belonging to the world of the supernatural. The special relationship that exists between a social group and some aspect of the natural world, such as a plant or an animal, is *totemism*. In this case, the relationship is between the clan and the hawk. Not all clans are totemistic, but many of them are. Commonly, when a totemistic relationship exists, a person is forbidden to kill or eat the totem animal.]

Q. Of all the groups you belong to—family, tribe, village, and so on— which one is the most important?

A. Oh, it is the clan! The clan is so important that it cannot even be compared with anything else.

Q. Why is the clan so important to you?

A. Because if I get into trouble—real trouble, like killing someone—the clan will help me out. The clan must help! It is a post you can lean on. It is always there. Without it, a man is alone. You cannot live without the clan!

Q. Are some clans better than other clans?

A. Yes, definitely. A big clan like Atangwa is the best.

Q. Why is that?

A. Because a big clan can help you more when you get into trouble. No matter what you need, the clan can give it. It can make the blood payment in a single day! [We will return to the matter of the "blood payment" shortly.]

Q. Can you tell me about an actual case where your clan helped somebody?

A. Many cases, many cases. You know Kisilu? He is Atangwa. Just two years ago, he burned a man's house down. It was an accident, but Kisilu was in real trouble. The clan replaced that house within one week!

The Kamba clans are neither more nor less "clanlike" than other clans in other societies. Without meaning to imply that all clans operate in that manner, the above example will serve to illustrate some common characteristics of clans. Obviously, they can be extremely important. As far as the Kamba are concerned, the clan is in a class by itself. In Kithome's terms, a person cannot live— that is, function in the society—without the support of the clan. Among other things, the clan is a kind of mutual aid society; its existence serves as a kind of social insurance. Beyond this, the clan is a critical legal group: It handles certain types of major legal disputes.

In traditional Kamba law, the killing of one Kamba by another was a matter that was settled by the involved clans; the homicide was not a tribal or village problem but a clan problem. (We will discuss this further in Chapter 18.) Whether the killing was intentional or not, a payment had to be made to the clan that had lost a member. This is the "blood payment" to which Kithome referred. It consisted of 11 cows and 1 bull—a small fortune for most Kamba. The man who had done the killing did not supply the livestock himself. As a matter of fact, he was not allowed to make the payment even if he could afford it. His clan provided the animals, appropriating one here and another there on a rotating basis so that no clan member became impoverished. (It was a central feature of Kamba law that the basic idea was to make restitution rather than to seek vengeance.)

As I indicated earlier, clans can get quite large. There are roughly one million Kamba and only about 40 Kamba clans. Although clan traditions often tell of a time when clans were localized—and sometimes they still are—it is commonplace to find clan members scattered throughout a society. This is an important integrating mechanism, because a person can travel into a distant area and find fellow clan members there; it makes no difference whether they have ever met before or not, or even whether they know of one another's existence. It takes only a few moments to determine clan affiliations, and if two strangers find they belong to the same clan they treat each other as kin. When clans are scattered in this way, the clan segments in particular areas tend to form the effective groups. They meet and make decisions and speak of themselves as "the whole clan" even though they know perfectly well that most of the clan is not present.

Families, kindreds, lineages, clans—all of them are kinship groupings, and all of them provide vital organizational features to human societies. The ramifications and elaborations of kinship ties are not mere doodlings on the surfaces of cultural systems; they are part and parcel of what it means to be human. No human society has ever survived without a kinship system, and the phenomenon of kinship is one of the key universal attributes of the human animal.

SUMMARY

The family is virtually a cultural universal. The simplest type of family consists of a married man and woman together with their dependent children. This elementary family unit is a *nuclear family.*

Families perform various functions. At a minimum, they (1) establish legal or socially sanctioned parentage; (2) provide an enculturation unit for the children; (3) establish an economic unit; (4) set up a relationship between several families; and (5) establish a socially approved pattern of sexual rights between the spouses.

Although something like nuclear family units can be identified in almost all cultures, they are usually embedded in larger kinship groupings. The most common type of ideal family in terms of spouses is a *polygamous* family. Apart from the question of spouses, the type of family encountered in most cultures is an *extended* family. An extended family is always larger than a nuclear family, and it is best thought of as a kind of residence group.

Beyond the immediate family, there is always recognition of larger kinship groupings. In societies with a bilateral descent system, the largest meaningful kin group is that composed of the "close" relatives on both sides of the family. This group is called a *kindred*.

In societies with unilineal descent systems, the most common large kin groups are the lineage and the clan. A *lineage* is a named, exogamous, unilineal descent group in which the members can actually trace their ancestry back to a real person. *Clans* are rather like superlineages. The definition is the same except that the members of a clan cannot actually trace their ancestry back to a real person. Rather, clan origins go back to a world of myth. This is why clans are frequently involved with *totemism,* a special or ritual relationship between the social group and some aspect of the natural world such as a plant or animal.

References

Ewers, John C. 1955. *The Horse in Blackfoot Indian Culture.* Bureau of American Ethnology, Bulletin 159. Washington, D.C.: U.S. Government Printing Office.

Goldschmidt, Walter. 1966. *Comparative Functionalism.* Berkeley and Los Angeles: University of California Press.

Gough, E. Kathleen. 1959. "The Nayars and the Definition of Marriage." *Journal of the Royal Anthropological Institute* 89:23–34.

———. 1962. "Nayar: Central Kerala," in David M. Schneider and E. Kathleen Gough (eds.), *Matrilineal Kinship.* Berkeley and Los Angeles: University of California Press.

Grinnell, George Bird. 1923. *The Cheyenne Indians,* vol. 2. New Haven, Conn.: Yale University Press.

Hoebel, E. Adamson. 1960. *The Cheyennes.* New York: Holt, Rinehart and Winston.

Murdock, George Peter. 1949. *Social Structure.* New York: Macmillan.

Suggestions for Further Reading

Goldschmidt, Walter. 1959. *Man's Way.* New York: Holt, Rinehart and Winston. Along with many other good things, this excellent book contains useful discussions of families, lineages, and clans.

Lowie, Robert H. 1948. *Social Organization.* New York: Holt, Rinehart and Winston. Allowing for a certain Boasian bias, this remains a clear and coherent account.

Oliver, Symmes C. 1980. *The Kamba of Kenya: Ecological Variation in Two East African Communities.* Palo Alto, Ca.: Mayfield. If you would like more information about Kamba clans and lineages, this is the place to look.

Radcliffe-Brown, A. R., and C. D. Forde (eds.). 1950. *African Systems of Kinship and Marriage.* London: Oxford University Press. On the technical side, this is a classic in the field.

Sahlins, Marshall. 1961. "The Segmentary Lineage: An Organization of Predatory Expansion." *American Anthropologist* 63:322–343. Stimulating reading, this article explores some of the functions that certain types of lineage systems can sometimes perform.

Stephens, William N. 1963. *The Family in Cross-Cultural Perspective.* New York: Holt, Rinehart and Winston. The title tells the story. A good place to look for specific information.

Note: The reader should consult the Suggestions at the end of the previous chapter, since most of the titles are relevant here also.

16

A World of Relatives: The Difference Kinship Makes

Consider, for a moment, the noble trout. When a female trout spawns, she fans out a depression in the stream gravel with her tail. This is a redd. Into this rather flimsy nest she deposits her eggs. A mature female trout will carry roughly 1000 eggs per pound of body weight; therefore, a large trout will deposit 3000–4000 eggs in a single spawning. The male follows the female and fertilizes the eggs. When this is done, the adult trout separate and abandon the redd. The eggs are on their own.

It is a costly way to reproduce. Many of the eggs never hatch at all; trout eggs are eaten by other fish and a variety of organisms. If they do hatch, the fry (baby trout) are very vulnerable. Even when they reach the fingerling stage, they have about the same chance as a minnow in a pool of hungry bass. Of the thousands of eggs that are deposited, perhaps 2 percent of the trout live as long as a year. (A wild trout has to survive about three years before it is capable of spawning.)

Obviously, there would be no wild trout except for the tremendous numbers of eggs that are deposited. Out of 100 eggs, it is likely that *no* trout will live to reproduce. The trout need to produce thousands of eggs to have any real chance at all. Equally obviously, there is no social kinship between trout. A trout emerging from the egg into a hostile world knows neither its mother nor its father. It recognizes no brothers or sisters—they are all just trout or even just fish, although presumably a trout can tell a trout from a catfish. Despite Disney interpretations of fish, a trout has no grandparents, no uncles and aunts, no cousins. The kinship system is simple; there isn't any at all.

I have chosen this extreme example to drive home a basic point: When we talk about kinship, we have to talk about something more than simple biological

Chimpanzee mother and child.

relationships. As animals become more complex, there is a clear tendency for them to produce fewer offspring and to provide the young with some protection. Among mammals, the females must nurse the young if the young are going to survive. Moreover, there is a clear recognition factor between mothers and their children—a mare knows her foal and vice versa, and the same is true for fawns, puppies, and kittens. As we saw in Chapter 5, the maternal links are quite strong and long enduring among nonhuman primates. Although there are exceptions, it tends to be the male role that is sociologically shaky: The males in the group relate with the immature animals in general rather than with specific infants.

There is nothing more characteristic of human beings than the incorporation of the males into recognized family groupings and the extension of kinship ties beyond the immediate reproductive unit. Although examples such as that of the Nayar (discussed in the previous chapter) remind us that it is possible to devise a system in which the males are only loosely attached to the conjugal unit, this is still quite different from the situation that prevails among most nonhuman primates. The Nayar males are firmly linked to their matrilineages; moreover, the females do "get married" and there is a sociological acceptance of paternity by a male.

To help us understand the difference that kinship makes, let us examine a couple of simple examples. When I was a child, my parents frequently had guests in the house. Very few of these people—the close friends of my father and mother—were relatives. It is typical of our culture that we interact socially more with nonkin than with kin; the larger kin group, if it meets at all, tends to

Among humans, the males are usually integral parts of
the family groups.

get together only on special occasions. Invariably, the close friends of my parents
were presented to me as *if* they were kin. They were Uncle Les and Uncle Elmer
and Aunt Patsy and Aunt Mary. My parents were not anthropologists, but what
they were doing would have made good sense to any anthropologist. By presenting these people as kin, they placed them at once in a behavioral network
that was understood by all parties concerned. A man named Lester became
Uncle Les; I treated him as an uncle and he treated me as a nephew. (He expected a hug when he came to the house, and I expected a small gift now and
then.) This is what a kinship network does: it sets up a reciprocal pattern of statuses and roles, establishing expected or customary ways of behaving for the
participants in the system. In short, what you call a person determines how you
are supposed to act toward that person and vice versa. This is why members of
many social societies or ethnic groups address one another as "brother" or "sister"; it defines the role relationship that is supposed to exist between them.

There was a time when large groups of relatives, such as kindreds, were far
more important in our society than they now are. Suppose we go back in time a
century or so and imagine a big, isolated house in a rural area. Think of one of
those rambling structures with an upstairs and a downstairs, plenty of rooms,
and about 20 miles of nothing between it and the nearest neighbors.

Who might we find living in such a house? Our old friend Ego lives there,
and we will make him a young male for purposes of illustration. With Ego will be
his father and mother, thus providing the kernel of a nuclear family. Already we

have three people, all of whom are kin to one another either by marriage or descent. These people operate in a predetermined social universe; each person has a status and a role with respect to the others. These statuses and roles are not something you must figure out as you go along; they are supplied by the system. Ideally, it makes no difference what individual personalities are involved. Father is supposed to behave one way, Mother another, and Ego has his own particular role. In those bygone days, the father was responsible for "making the living." He worked the fields and tended the stock. He was the authority figure in the home, and he made the basic decisions. He was not a "buddy" to his son, and certainly not a playmate. He was Father rather than Dad, and if Ego had to go to the woodshed for a thrashing it was his father who took him there. The mother was responsible for the home. She provided the meals, made the clothing, cleaned the house, and took care of the younger children. Mother, too, was the comforter: If Ego got hurt, he could go to his mother for some soup and soft words. Ego, too, had a job to do. He was supposed to "do the chores" — gather firewood, perhaps, or milk the cows. In effect, each person knew what to expect from the others, and all of this was supplied by the kinship roles. (One of our problems today is not so much that kin roles are changing but that they have become ambiguous. Another problem is that the minimal nuclear family is often all there is, and even it may be incomplete. A very small family must somehow try to do what a very large family once did.)

Since Ego seems lonesome, let us supply him with two brothers and two sisters. Once again there will be preset social relationships. How Ego will behave toward them will depend on their age and their sex — you do not treat an older brother the same way you treat a kid brother, and you do not treat a brother like a sister. However, for all of the brothers, the major requirement is to stick together. A brother is a ready-made ally. Again, personalities do not matter. Ego may detest his kid brother as a person, but he is still his brother. Picture a situation in which the three brothers go into town. The youngest brother gets into a fight with five village boys who are taking turns pounding Younger Brother's head with a rock. What is the reaction of Ego and his older brother? They do not say, "Why, look there! Our kid brother is being beaten to a pulp. I never liked him anyway." No, the *role* is supportive: If you do not go to your brother's aid, you are not much of a brother.

Toward his sisters, Ego's role is likewise set. He has a teasing relationship with his younger sister. His older sister is different: She is "female" and therefore somewhat mysterious. Although she is tabu to Ego, she can initiate him into some of the puzzles of sex roles. Suppose that Ego has to go to a dance. He doesn't know how to dance, and he is petrified at the prospect of actually *talking* to a girl. (Remember, this was a long time ago.) His older sister can show him how to dance and can even suggest some conversational gems. Beyond all this, the role of all the brothers toward their sisters is essentially protective, particularly in sexual matters. ("Let me tell you something, mister. You can't talk that way about *my* sister!")

There would be other people in our old farmhouse. It would not be unusual to find one set of grandparents living upstairs. Once again, Grandpa and

Grandma are securely placed in the reciprocal role system. I will not spell this out in detail because the role relationships have not changed a great deal through time. Their major components are love and permissiveness. Ideally, grandparents and granchildren are very close: The warmth is there without (except in extreme cases) the disciplinary structure. If Ego wants something, say a quarter to go to the country fair, if he has any sense at all he will pursue the following route: Go first to Mother, then to Father, then to Grandma, and finally to Grandpa. Grandpa will wrap it up: "Run along now, Ego. I'll take care of your father."

This relationship between grandparents and grandchildren is not at all unusual, by the way. Radcliffe-Brown pointed out what he called "the combination of alternate generations" (Radcliffe-Brown 1952:69). He meant that there is a kind of tension between adjacent generations (parents and children), but a commonality of interests between alternate generations (grandparents and grandchildren). Consider what happens in an American home when the grandparents come to visit. A child picks up a bowl of oatmeal and dumps it on the floor. Grandpa or Grandma says, "Isn't that cute!" Meanwhile, the parents of the child are thinking something like: "Just wait until I get that kid alone!"

We could put some additional residents in this hypothetical farmhouse of ours — an aunt and an uncle, for instance. However, the basic point should be clear by now. A kinship system provides a kind of built-in social organization, and all of the participants in the system know what is expected of them and how they are supposed to behave. In very small human societies, where nearly everyone is kin to everyone else, the kinship system can supply the major component of the social structure. Although there are no human societies organized exclusively in terms of kinship, in theoretical terms kinship principles are almost all that you really *need* to get the necessary jobs done. In larger and more complex human societies, the social situation is not that simple but it is nevertheless true that kinship systems are *always* one key to understanding how human societies organize for social action.

The literature dealing with kinship systems is both rich and technical; the study of kinship has been one of the primary focuses of anthropology for as long as there have been anthropologists.

Kinship systems are beautiful examples of the fact that the universe is not the same to all observers. Participants in different cultures "see" the world in somewhat different ways.

When you get right down to it, all kinship systems do the same basic job: They classify and sort out kinds of relatives. The pioneering figure in the study of kinship, Lewis Henry Morgan (whom we met in Chapter 11), suggested that there were two fundamental varieties of kinship terms. He referred to them as *descriptive* terms and *classificatory* terms (Morgan 1871). At least by implication, in a descriptive kinship system all primary relatives are called by separate terms. That is, to take an easy example, only one person within a family would be called *mother* or the equivalent, only one person called *father,* and so on. In a classificatory system, some of the primary relatives would be lumped together under a single term or category. Thus, for example, the father and the father's brother might be called by the same tag.

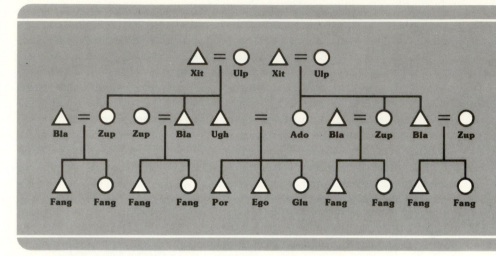

Figure 16.1 One type of kinship system.

This is a useful distinction, but it obscures a key point that must be appreciated. In actual fact, there is no such thing as a purely descriptive kinship system. All kinship systems classify relatives into categories — that is one of their basic functions. To put it another way, you never find an arrangement in which there is a completely separate term for every person included in the kinship system. There are always more persons than there are terms. Therefore, some persons must always be grouped with other persons under a common label, and what you call a person influences how you regard that person and how you are supposed to act.

Look at Figure 16.1, for example, which illustrates a portion of a truly bizarre kinship system. Recognize it? This is, of course, our own kinship system. You should have no trouble understanding it once you realize what you are looking at. Here is a translation of the invented terms:

Xit = grandfather
Ulp = grandmother
Ugh = father
Ado = mother
Bla = uncle
Zup = aunt
Por = brother
Glu = sister
Fang = cousin

Although our kinship system is technically a descriptive one, for reasons that will be explained shortly, our term *uncle* will serve to make a point concerning classificatory kinship terminology. Note that here we have one term that is applied to several different kinds of relatives. Specifically, it can refer to the father's brother, the father's sister's husband, the mother's brother, and the mother's sister's husband. This does *not* mean that we cannot tell the difference between them. We know perfectly well that the father's brother and the mother's brother are not the same. It merely means that the distinctions between one kind of uncle and another are not crucial to us: It is convenient to lump them all together because we expect all of our uncles to play essentially the same social role.

I want to emphasize this idea because — to anticipate a bit — if you encounter a system in which the father and the father's brother are called by the same term, this does not imply that a person does not know who the "real" father (the biological father or the person married to the mother) is. It only means that the two relatives are in the same social category and that in many respects similar behavior is expected from each. Looking at our own kinship system, we might point out a few features:

1. Once you get beyond the nuclear family group, within which descriptive terms are employed, one side of the system is a mirror image of the other side. In other words, it is a simple bilateral system — no terminological distinction is made between the father's relatives and the mother's relatives.
2. Somewhat confusingly, it is also a simple lineal system. Don't confuse this with *uni*lineal descent. It simply means that lineal and collateral kin are separated. (Lineal kin are linked by descent. Collateral kin are siblings.) The easiest way to see this is to examine the first ascending generation from Ego. There you see that Ego's lineal kin (his father and mother) are distinguished terminologically from his collateral kin (his father's brother and sister and his mother's brother and sister). However, the collateral kin are not separated from each other except by sex. (That is, the father's brother and the mother's brother are called by the same term; another term applies to both the father's sister and the mother's sister.)
3. In Ego's own generation, all cousin terms are merged (the same) and the cousin terms are distinguished from sibling terms (brother and sister).

All of this may seem like much ado about nothing, but that is not the case. Every single one of these principles may vary from one kinship system to another, and understanding who is grouped with whom — and which relatives are separated — provides an important insight into how people view the social universe in different cultures.

Rather than deal with the more complex systems — and some of them can get complicated indeed — two simplified examples of different ways of doing the job will serve to indicate something of the range of variation.

To avoid confusion and because they are not required in understanding the way the systems operate, I am omitting the terms for spouses except for Ego's mother and father.

Take a look at Figure 16.2. The first clue that you are dealing with a true

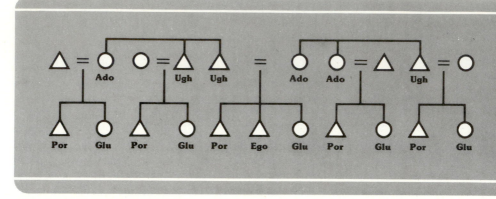

Figure 16.2 A simple classificatory kinship system.

classificatory system is this: At least some of Ego's lineal kin will be called by the same terms as some of Ego's collateral kin. Therefore, the diagram represents a classificatory system. (Compare the terms applied to Ego's father and mother — lineal kin — with the terms applied to Ego's father's brother and Ego's mother's sister, who are collateral kin.)

In addition, we might call attention to the following points:

1. Once again, we see a bilateral kinship system. One side of the system is a mirror image of the other side, and this time that basic principle extends to the nuclear family itself.
2. Conceptually — that is, with reference to the number of terms employed — this is about as simple as a kinship system can get. The only distinctions that are employed are those of generation and sex. Notice that all relatives of the same sex and the same generation are lumped together. Here, there are no "cousins" — only brothers and sisters. Here, there are no "aunts" and "uncles" — only mothers and fathers.
3. This is not an imaginary system. It is known as a *generational* or *Hawaiian system,* and it is widespread among Malayo-Polynesian speakers and elsewhere.

Figure 16.3 is one more example of a kinship system, of a rather different sort. An inspection of this chart shows the following points:

1. This system is obviously not a bilateral one. When you compare one side of the chart with the other, you find markedly different terminologies.
2. There is some merging of lineal and collateral kin. (For instance, Ego's father and father's brother are called by the same term.) However, the *mother's* brother is called by a separate term. This means that a distinction has been introduced that we have not encountered before: Name-

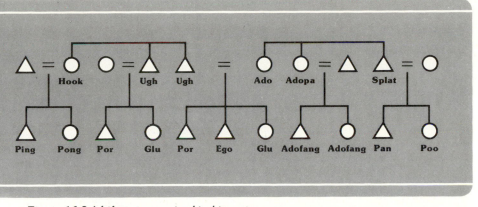

Figure 16.3 A bifurcate merging kinship system.

ly, the sex of the relative standing between Ego and the person named. In other words, it makes a difference whether the relative is linked to Ego through his father or through his mother.

3. On both sides, in Ego's own generation, cross cousins are distinguished from parallel cousins (see pp. 244–245). Moreover, on one side (the father's) parallel cousins are merged with siblings.

4. This is basically a patrilineal system. What is really going on here is that the unity of the patrilineal group supersedes other distinctions. Thus, the father and the father's brother "go together" because they are both males of the same generation in the same unilineal kin group—a clan, for example. Similarly, the children of Ego's father's brother will be in the same group as Ego and his siblings; therefore, these children are "like" Ego's brother and sister.

5. Although I have simplifed it somewhat, this is essentially what is known as a *bifurcate merging system.* To bifurcate is to split or divide; it just means that a distinction is made between one side of the family and the other. To merge means just what it says: Some of the terms are going to be combined. In this case, the father's brother and the mother's brother are divided. However, the father and the father's brother are combined—thus, bifurcate merging.

In the system we have just discussed, you may have noticed that I named Ego's mother's sister with a term similar to that given for Ego's mother. (I called the mother *Ado* and the mother's sister *Adopa.*) In reality, these two females are often called by the same term. One reason for this is that the mother's sister is a potential replacement for Ego's mother. If the sororate were in operation here (see p. 254) and Ego's mother died, his mother's sister would become his sociological mother.

With regard to the father, the father's brother, and the mother's brother, we have so far seen three common arrangements:

1. In the lineal system (our own, which is also called an *Eskimo system*) there are two terms, *father* and *uncle.* The collaterals are merged, with a separate term for the lineal relative.
2. In the generational system, there is just one term. All three kinsmen are merged terminologically.
3. In the bifurcate merging system, we again have two terms, but they are sorted out differently from a lineal system. One collateral term is merged with the lineal term (*father* and *father's brother*), but the other collateral term (*mother's brother*) is separated.

The other logical possibility, obviously, is to employ *three* separate terms, one for each of these key relatives. This does occur, and such an arrangement is called a *bifurcate collateral system.* In effect, the collaterals are separated (*father's brother* and *mother's brother*) and neither is merged with the lineal term (*father*).

Since the time of Morgan, anthropologists have produced a tremendous number of books and articles dealing with kinship terminology and kinship systems. Indeed, anthropologists have probably written more about kinship than any other single topic.

Without in the least meaning to downgrade the important contributions that have been made to kinship theory in recent years, it is fair to say that the essential features by which kinship terms were distinguished from one another were clearly set forth long ago by two scholars associated with Franz Boas.

In 1909, A. L. Kroeber pointed out that there were eight basic criteria by which kin could be sorted into different categories (Kroeber 1909). Most of his distinctions have been utilized in this chapter, but not all of them. For instance, Kroeber noted that the sex of the speaker could make a difference in the terminology employed. That is, a male might call his father by one term, but a female might call her father by another term. He also made the interesting observation that terminology could change depending on whether a connecting relative were dead or alive. For example, Ego might call a father's brother by one term if Ego's father were living but switch to another term if the father died.

In a series of contributions highlighted by a classic article called simply ''Relationship Terms,'' included in the fourteenth edition of the Encyclopedia Britannica, Robert H. Lowie did a great deal to clarify the study of kinship (Lowie 1920, 1929, 1932, 1948). It is impossible to discuss all of Lowie's ideas in a short space, but mention can be made of one feature to which Lowie called attention. He noted that there was a principle of *reciprocity* involved in the terminology employed in some kinship systems. One example of this is found between lineal kin of the same sex but of alternate generations. For instance, grandfathers may call grandsons by the same term that grandsons apply to grandfathers. This is not at all uncommon, but it can be disconcerting—keeping in mind the obvious translation problems—when you hear an elderly gentleman referring to a child as his grandfather.

In thinking about kinship, it is all too easy to get lost in a welter of sometimes confusing terms and fancy names. Be of good cheer: You may never have

Kinship roles are important elements in the organization of social action.

heard of a *bifurcate merging kinship system* before, but then neither have the people who *live* in societies with bifurcate merging kinship systems. As with language itself, you do not have to be able to articulate the rules of a kinship system in order to use the system. You may never have thought about the distinction between lineal and collateral kin, but you never made the mistake of calling your father's brother your father — you called him your uncle.

The analysis of the structures of different kinship systems is not — or should not be — a sterile exercise in term juggling. Kinship is an essential organizational technique in the ordering of human societies, and an understanding of the different ways in which the job can be done is necessary to appreciate how people view the social universes in which they live. It would matter very little whether cousin terms were merged or separated or whether or not one side of a family is addressed the same as the other side unless these distinctions provided vital clues about which social relationships were important in a given society and how people were supposed to treat one another. In fact, they do.

Remember our hypothetical farmhouse? The people in that farmhouse were all linked in a social network of kinship: They all knew what was expected of them and how they were supposed to behave toward one another. In a very real sense, all kinship systems are like that. The principles involved are not obscure; they are simply variations on a handful of basic themes. Different kinship systems represent different ways of doing the same job, and that job is to set up a kin-based pattern of statuses and roles that makes sense with regard to specific cultural contexts.

While there are no human societies organized exclusively in terms of kinship roles, it is also true that there are no human societies without kinship systems. The cultural ramifications of kinship contribute a great deal of what it means to be human, and all people everywhere recognize the invisible links that assist them in forming the groups and performing the organized actions that enable human societies to continue.

SUMMARY

In thinking about kinship, it is crucial to remember that much more is involved than simple biological relationships. As animals become more complex, there is a clear tendency for them to produce fewer offspring and to provide the young with some protection. There is nothing more characteristic of human beings than the incorporation of the males into recognized family groupings and the extension of kinship ties beyond the reproductive unit.

In human societies, what you call a person determines how you are supposed to act toward that person and how that person is supposed to act toward you. There was a time in our society when large groups of relatives — kindreds — were far more important than they now are. Quite sizeable groups of people could be organized primarily in terms of kinship. Although there are no human societies organized exclusively along kinship lines, kinship principles are capable of providing nearly all the structure you really need in order to get necessary tasks performed.

The variety of human kinship systems drives home a crucial anthropological lesson: The universe is not the same to all observers, and people in different cultures tend to "see" the world of kinship in somewhat different terms.

All kinship systems classify and sort out kinds of relatives. Lewis Henry Morgan suggested that there were two basic varieties of kinship terms; he called them *descriptive* and *classificatory*. In actual fact, there is no such thing as a purely descriptive kinship system. All kinship systems classify relatives into categories, and you never find a situation in which there is a completely separate term for every person included in the kinship system, However, some systems "lump" more relatives together than others, and which kin are "merged" differs from one culture to another.

In simple classificatory systems, the only distinctions that are employed are those of generation and sex. In other systems, additional distinctions may be used, such as separating one side of the family from the other or distinguishing between siblings and cousins.

There are no human societies without kinship systems. Kinship is an important part of what it means to be human, and it is an essential organizational technique in the ordering of human societies.

References
Kroeber, A. L. 1909. "Classificatory Systems of Relationship." *Journal of the Royal Anthropological Institute* 39:77–84. (This article is reprinted in Kroeber's book, *The Nature of Culture*. 1952. The University of Chicago Press.)

Lowie, Robert H. 1920. *Primitive Society*. New York: Liveright.

———. 1929. "Relationship Terms," the 14th ed., *Encyclopedia Britannica,* 19.

———. 1932. "Kinship," in *Encyclopedia of the Social Sciences,* 8.

———. 1948. *Social Organization*. New York: Holt, Rinehart and Winston.

Morgan, Lewis H. 1871. *Systems of Consanguinity and Affinity in the Human Family*. Washington, D.C.: Smithsonian Contributions to Knowledge, 17.

Radcliffe-Brown, A. R. 1952. *Structure and Function in Primitive Society*. Glencoe, Ill.: Free Press.

Suggestions for Further Reading

Service, Elman R. 1978. *Profiles in Ethnology,* 3d ed. New York: Harper & Row. Just this once, we will abandon the sacred rule of alphabetical order. I have listed this book first because it is a logical starting point. It contains brief descriptions of 22 different human societies. Although the primary focus is not on kinship, kinship is presented as an integral part of each sociocultural system. The references are excellent, permitting the reader to consult, for example, such primary sources as Evans-Pritchard's works on the Nuer.

Beattie, John. 1960. *Bunyoro: An African Kindom*. New York: Holt, Rinehart and Winston. Offers a clear account of how kinship operates in one state system.

Chagnon, Napoleon A. 1977. *Yanamamo: The Fierce People*. 2nd ed. New York: Holt, Rinehart and Winston. This remarkable book is must reading for many reasons. Dealing with a society in Venezuela and Brazil, it is a lively and honest account of a people far removed from some of the stereotypes of anthropology, and it is also a penetrating analysis of kinship.

Goldschmidt, Walter, 1976. *The Culture and Behavior of the Sebei*. Berkeley and Los Angeles: University of California Press. Of considerable theoretical interest, this book about a society in Uganda is also a solid ethnography. Chapter 4 offers a sensitive interpretation of Sebei kinship from the perspective of role behavior.

Hart, C. W. M., and Arnold Pilling. 1960. *The Tiwi of North Australia*. New York: Holt, Rinehart and Winston. The hunting and gathering cultures of Australia have long been famous for their intricate kinship systems. This is a vivid picture of one Australian lifeway, particularly interesting as an example of how people sometimes tinker with a kinship system "to make things come out right."

Turnbull, Colin M. 1972. *The Mountain People*. New York: Simon & Schuster. A portrait of the Ik of Uganda, a people living under horrifying conditions of cultural disintegration. It shows in memorable fashion what happens when vital organizational systems — such as kinship — fail to function as they should.

Note: The reader should also consult the Suggestions at the end of Chapter 14.

17

Hunting for the Food Collectors: Introducing Political Organization

When we speak of a people—the Hopi or the Kamba or the Andamanese or the Aztecs—we are essentially talking about territorial groupings. The reference is to a sociocultural arrangement of persons in a delimited space. When we ask how these people organize their lives—how they maintain order, how they make crucial decisions, how they resolve internal and external conflicts—we are dealing with political questions.

No matter how tightly it is defined, political organization tends to be a somewhat slippery subject. It is difficult and perhaps even impossible to draw a neat little box and stuff something called *political behavior* into it. Of course, this is simply another way of saying that political organization does not exist by itself. It is part and parcel of a larger sociocultural system and cannot be entirely divorced from it. However, the creation and enactment of public policy in any human society necessarily involves decision making, and it is in this area that political organization comes most sharply into focus.

In the broadest possible terms, political organization concerns the types of leadership and the kinds of authority systems that are associated with various territorial groupings. It is a fact of life that there are times when important decisions must be made that affect the cohesion and indeed the existence of large groups of people, and it is another fact of life that someone must make these decisions. There must be a recognized decision-making process, and the key word here is certainly *recognized*. As we all know, it is one thing to make a decision, and it is quite another thing to have that decision accepted by a group. In matters of public policy, whenever more than a single kinship unit is involved decisions cannot be handled in the context of kinship roles alone. At the very least, there must be some mechanism that articulates one kin group with another.

In dealing with political organization, it is particularly important to avoid the trap of imagining that all primitive societies are essentially the same. We all slip up now and then and use sweeping phrases like "the primitive world." This will get us exactly nowhere in understanding how political activities are organized. The very first necessary step is to get rid of an ancient stereotype. The stereotype is that primitive societies are all composed of two types of people. On the one hand you have the "chiefs," and on the other hand you have everybody else. According to this simplistic view, the system works in an engagingly straightforward manner: The "chiefs" just tell all the other people what to do.

In fact, different kinds of human societies have different techniques for handling "political" problems. It follows from this fact that the most sensible way to come to grips with actual political processes is to examine them *in context*. This means we have to look at how political questions are resolved in *specific types* of human sociocultural systems.

Of course, it is a truism that every human society is unique to some degree. Ideally, an examination of political processes in context would involve an analysis of individual societies. The construction of sociocultural types or categories necessarily sacrifices sharpness and clarity of detail. Still, a taxonomy of some sort is required in any orderly scientific procedure. Beyond that, it is manifestly impossible to discuss *all* human societies one by one; and if a selection is made for purposes of illustration, this too becomes a kind of typology. It just approaches the problem through the back door, as it were.

Whatever classification is employed in looking at these systems, the categories must be thought of as models built on general tendencies. No claim is made that all actual human societies placed in a given category are identical. It is not asserted that the generalizations made have no exceptions. Rather, we must acknowledge the limitations of the approach and spell out exactly what it is that we are doing. In sorting out societies into "types," we are making statements about how things *usually* work in certain *kinds* of sociocultural systems. We are talking about tendencies — expectations, if you will — and not absolutes. The tendencies are not spun out of the air; they are based on known ethnographic facts. By the same token, the world of ethnography is a world of the particular and the highly specific. Any model involving general tendencies does some violence to the world of concrete detail.

It seems to me that the approach that does the least violence to the facts of human existence is rooted in cultural ecology. By establishing categories that are ecologically based, it is possible to define the categories in plain language and with some precision.

The ecological situation (see Chapter 12) involves a dynamic interrelationship between a cultural system and the total environment within which it exists. One vital component of a cultural system is its technology. It makes a difference what you do for a living, and this difference is nowhere more apparent than in the realm of political organization. Even a casual examination of the facts will reveal that the ecological situation clearly *influences* the nature of political institutions. This does not mean that ecological involvements determine the precise forms that political arrangements will take; there are always alternatives and variations possible in any conceivable ecological context. In other words, politically speaking, there is more than one way of getting the job done. However, some organizational techniques are much more probable than others in specific ecological situations, and there is a good reason for this: They are more effective and more attainable in terms of the cultural resources available.

In a sense, we all began in the same kind of ecological situation. There was a time—and it was not really so long ago—when all peoples on this earth were hunters of wild animals and collectors of wild plant foods (see Chapter 10). Although such societies are rapidly disappearing from this planet, they are of immense importance because they provided the frameworks within which the human animal was formed. We were hunters and gatherers for millions of years before we were anything else, and therefore the surviving societies of this type can tell us a great deal about what we were like during most of our existence as hominids. Let us look, then, at the hunters and gatherers and see how they dealt with basic organizational problems.

HUNTERS AND GATHERERS

There are two questions which must be posed. First, what is the most appropriate term to use in referring to this kind of society? Second, exactly what type of society are we talking about? Traditionally in anthropology such peoples were called hunters and gatherers for rather obvious reasons. They hunted for meat and collected (gathered) wild plant foods. Sometimes, using a sort of shorthand, we simply called them *hunters.*

There is nothing particularly wrong with this; surely, it is idle to pretend that such peoples do not hunt. The difficulty is that the picture tells only part of the story—namely, what the men are doing. The implication, whether it is intended or not, is that the women are not doing anything worth mentioning. This is a distortion of reality. Studies of surviving "hunters" show that at least in some cases *most* of the food consumed consists of wild plants brought in by the females. However, even in the best-documented examples of this sort of situation, it seems clear that the less productive hunting activities are more highly regarded by the people themselves. As Richard B. Lee notes with reference to the Bushmen of the Kalahari Desert,

> The essence of their successful strategy seems to be that while they depend primarily on the more stable and abundant food sources (vegetables in their case), they are nevertheless willing to devote considerable energy to the less reliable and more highly valued food sources such as medium and large mammals. The steady but modest input of work by the women provides the former, and the more intensive labors of the men provide the latter. It would be theoretically possible for the Bushmen to survive entirely on vegetable foods, but life would be boring indeed without the excitement of meat feasts. (Lee 1968:41)

San (Bushman) hunters bring down an antelope.

It must also be remembered that surviving groups of hunters and gatherers — and after all they were the only ones who were around long enough to be studied by anthropologists — tend to be located in difficult environmental situations. In effect, they have often retreated into land that nobody else wants, such as the Arctic, remote islands, and semidesert areas. It may well be that when societies of this kind were operating in game-rich territories the yield from hunting was far greater than it now is.

Still, the evidence cannot be ignored, and its message is plain: Hunters don't just hunt. (The only exception to this statement would be groups like some of the Eskimo, who have virtually no plant foods available to them. And the Eskimo do not just hunt sea mammals; they also fish.) Because of the importance of wild plant foods — and I would argue that the importance is there whether the relative contribution to the diet is 15 or 75 percent — some anthropologists believe that these societies should be called food collectors, or foragers, or even gatherer-hunters. It is a moot point. My own opinion, based on the central importance given to hunting in the value systems of the people who live in such societies, is that we might as well continue to refer to them as hunters *and* gatherers, with the stress on the conjunction. Most societies of this type do engage in *both* activities.

Top, A San group on the move. The male hunters are in the rear. *Bottom*, San females gathering wild plant foods.

At the very least, we should avoid misrepresentation in the illustrations we use. At a bare minimum, we need two (see page 299).

It is a general characteristic of human societies that men and women *share* the food that is obtained, regardless of who provides what.

In setting up an ecologically based type of sociocultural system, definitions can be somewhat tricky. In regard to hunting and gathering societies, it is essential to specify what kind of a society we are talking about. I define it this way: "We mean a society that practices no farming, lives by hunting wild animals and collecting wild plant foods, lacks domesticated animals other than the dog, and does not have access to concentrated fish resources" (Oliver 1976:37).

Some of this—the absence of farming and the emphasis on hunting and collecting—requires no comment. The other two points need a brief explanation. It is not just the lack of farming that produces a typical hunting and gathering society. Viewed ecologically, it is the amount and distribution of the available foods, the low population densities that result, and the need for frequent movements within a territory. When nonfarming peoples can remain in fixed villages and build up relatively dense populations, they are no longer organized in the manner of hunters and gatherers. This is what happens when abundant fish are present in the environment. The classic example involves the peoples of the northwest coast of North America. They were able to "harvest" immense quantities of spawning salmon from the fish-choked rivers and store them. This made possible an essentially sedentary lifeway that was drastically different from that of true hunters and gatherers.

Similarly, the introduction of domesticated horses into a game-rich area profoundly alters the ecological situation. Game becomes much easier to locate, kill, and transport. The yields are very different from those produced by uncertain foot hunting; indeed, in terms of both quantity and reliability, the yields are similar to those usually obtained through primitive methods of agriculture. Here, the historic Plains Indians, who relied upon the mounted hunting of the bison, are the best-known examples. As John C. Ewers notes, "Two Blackfoot hunters on horseback could kill enough buffalo to provide over a ton of meat in a matter of minutes on a single chase" (Ewers 1955:169). Although the historic Plains Indians are often referred to in anthropology as typical hunters and gatherers, they were in reality nothing of the sort. True hunters and gatherers do not possess herds of horses.

Now that we have named them and defined them, let us do what we set out to do: Examine the political lifeways of the hunters and gatherers.

POLITICAL ORGANIZATION OF HUNTERS AND GATHERERS

Hunters and gatherers must move around, and they must have a lot of room to do it in. There is no way that they can stay put in one place for long periods of time, because the game and wild plant food resources in a small area are quickly exhausted. Since it is difficult and time consuming to cover long distances on foot, it is easier to move the base camp than to go on extensive foraging expeditions. The seasonal availability of water can also be a factor in determining the location of a camp, but the essence of the situation is that it requires mobility. This does not mean that a hunting and gathering population must be constantly on the move, but it does mean that such a group must shift locations with some frequency within an annual cycle.

Since it takes a lot of room in order for hunters and gatherers to operate effectively, this is another way of saying that population densities are going to be low. It has been observed that for hunters and gatherers it is more meaningful to speak of square miles to the person than the more customary image of persons per square mile; very few surviving groups of hunters and gatherers attain a density of even one person per square mile (Lee and DeVore 1968:11). It must be remembered that the number of persons a given territory can support will be determined by the *least* productive segment of the annual cycle. In the absence of storage techniques, it doesn't matter if there is plenty of food for six months out of the year if people are going to starve during the other six months.

Not only are population densities low, but group sizes must be small. It is suicidal to mass large concentrations of people in one area, because there is no way to feed them. The largest effective social groups among hunters and gatherers rarely contain more than 50 persons. Such a group is sometimes referred to as a *band,* but the more neutral term *local group* is probably preferable.

A local group is simply a small group of people that moves around in a large territory searching for wild animals to kill and wild plant foods to collect. As a rule, these local groups tend to be somewhat fluid and unstable. This is true in several senses. Small as it is, the local group may not be able to function as a unit all year round; when food resources are particularly scarce and scattered, the local group must divide into still smaller units — sometimes down to the nuclear family level.

Membership in a local group is usually not fixed and immutable. Even though the core of a group may persist for long periods of time, it is possible for people to leave one local group and join another. Hunters and gatherers have the option of voting with their feet: If they don't like the way things are going where they are, they can pick up their digging sticks and bows and arrows and go elsewhere. There is very little to hold them, really.

A person living in a society in which movement is essential and limited to what can be transported on foot cannot accumulate significant amounts of property. Land is not owned; it is an arena within which a person is free to hunt or gather. Boundaries are not sharply defined in most cases — one territory more or less fades into another. The wild animals are not owned; they are available to any hunter in the group. When they are killed, they may "belong" to the hunter who first got an arrow or a spear into the animal, but all this means is that the hunter can direct the division of the meat; the kill is always shared. With rare exceptions, wild plant foods — roots, berries, melons — are not owned either. They don't "belong" to anyone until they are collected and brought into camp. The effect of all this is that the people are not tied to the land by property rights. It is relatively easy to move and to shift from one local group to another.

Within a given cultural domain, then, the people live in small and widely

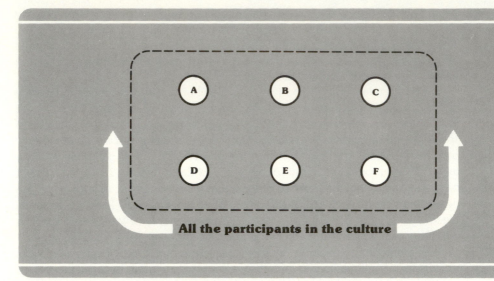

All the participants in the culture

Figure 17.1 Schematic diagram of a hunting and gathering society.

separated local groups. In a very simplified fashion, imagine a hunting and gathering population divided into just six local groups. The people all share a common language and culture. We might diagram this as in Figure 17.1. Here, the dotted line indicates the people within a given cultural domain—all the Bushmen, say, or all the Eskimo. The lettered circles represent local groups.

Normally, each local group is separate. However, there will be occasions when two or even three local groups might get together on a temporary basis. During a bountiful part of the year—plenty of water, plenty of game—groups A and D might camp together briefly, or groups B and C and F might get together. This is a time of celebration and ceremonial activity, a chance to visit with old friends or relatives, and an opportunity for men to find wives and women to find husbands. Still, it is a temporary phenomenon: After a week or two, the groups must go their separate ways again.

This leads to the central point in understanding the political organizations of hunters and gatherers. *At no point do all of the local groups within a cultural domain unite to take common political action.* They do not get together physically and they do not get together through some system of delegates. The participants in the culture do not act as a unit. In effect, each local group is autonomous: It makes its own decisions. Beyond the local group, there is only a consciousness of kind—an awareness of cultural identity. The larger group—all the Bushmen, all the Eskimo—has cultural but not political significance. There is no Bushman "tribe." There is no Eskimo tribe.

Politically speaking, the local group is all there is. The local group is the largest effective social unit, and whatever political action there is must be taken in the context of the local group. Therefore, in discussing political organization—or the lack of it—among hunters and gatherers the focus must be on the local group. How does it make decisions, and what kinds of decisions have to be made?

A local group is an intimate, face-to-face group. Everyone knows everyone else, and social interactions are intensely personal. Think of what it means to live a large part of your life in a group of 50 persons or less. If you split it evenly, you have 25 males and 25 females. Some will be old, some will be young, and some will be infants. How many friends could you have the same sex and approximately the same age? How well could you know them?

It has been said that hunting and gathering societies are profoundly egalitarian. This is true in the sense that nobody can accumulate significantly more property than anyone else. There are no social classes, and there are no marked wealth differences. There is a sexual division of labor: The women gather and the men hunt. There are meaningful age differences: A child does not have the same responsibilities as an elder. But that is about as far as it goes.

The societies are egalitarian in quite another sense as well: There are very few specialized social roles. By and large, within the confines set by age and sex, everybody does pretty much the same thing. There are only two partial exceptions to this statement, and they are embodied in the persons known as the *headman* and the *shaman*. The shaman is a part-time supernatural practitioner, and in the local groups of hunters and gatherers the shaman is a kind of all-purpose dealer in supernatural concerns; since the shaman is all there is, the shaman must do whatever needs doing in the supernatural area. However, the major task of the shaman is to serve the people as a healer. (Shamans are discussed in detail in Chapter 20.)

The role of the headman is pivotal in understanding what can and cannot be done in hunting and gathering societies. Each local group has a headman, and he tends to be the focus of whatever political activity there is. I am designating this individual as a male because to the best of my knowledge headmen are always male; in this case, some sort of euphemism like "headperson" only confuses the issue.

The headman is not a chief. In fact, although this distorts the people's own perception of what a headman is and what he does, it is necessary to specify the negative attributes of headmanship. We have to know what a headman is *not* before we can appreciate what a headman *is*.

The headman is not formally selected to hold down the job. When asked how a person became a headman, the usual explanation is some variant of the classic description, "He just got to be that way." The authority that he has derives mainly from his own personality; it is a case of the man making the office rather than the other way around. However, the headman *cannot* give orders: He cannot force anyone to do anything. He is usually not an adjudicative official, which means that it is not his job to hear legal cases and render decisions.

What, then, does the headman do? Basically, he makes suggestions and offers advice. He discusses matters with the other senior males in the local group and decides when the camp should be moved and where it should go. If the other people follow his advice, he continues as headman. If he is ignored, he is by definition no longer headman.

It is true that his role may be somewhat larger than this. He can give "permission" to others who wish to hunt or gather in the territory that his group occupies. He can make suggestions about any problem that arises. He may have some degree of authority because of his place in the kinship structure; indeed, the position of headman is spoken of as being inherited in some groups. However, a person who is incompetent—or merely unlucky—does not remain as headman for very long. He has no group to lead—everybody leaves.

The headman is a classic example of a charismatic leader. It is the force of his own personality rather than the authority inherent in the office that gets things done. He may be a mighty hunter or a skilled craftsman, but what he really needs is sound judgment coupled with eloquence. The power that he has is the power to persuade, and headmen are notoriously good talkers.

If you look at a local group there is no way to tell who the headman is on the basis of his appearance. He dresses like everybody else; he has no insignia or badge of office. He participates in the daily round of activities like anyone else. Being a headman is not a full-time specialized job that sets a person apart from others; it is something done in addition to the usual role of adult male.

There are no human societies in which conflicts do not occur. Somehow, these conflicts must be resolved; they cannot be left like festering sores that will in time cause the group to disintegrate. Similarly, in all human societies there are basic policy decisions that have to be made. The alternative is to drift without a compass, and that is a fatal course to follow.

From what we have discussed it should be obvious that whatever "political" or "legal" decisions are made in hunting and gathering societies, they must be made within the context of the local group. There is no larger social grouping that has political significance. It should be equally obvious that problems are not going to be settled and crucial decisions made simply by appealing to the headman. He does not have that kind of authority.

In Walter Goldschmidt's terms, such societies exhibit *governance* but they lack formal *government* (Goldschmidt 1977:304–309). This means that there is no agency that has a monopoly on the legitimate use of force but that the functions of social control and conflict resolution are effected by other techniques.

What are they? Essentially, there are four. First, there can be *consensus*. In small societies, there is usually general agreement as to what is right and proper and what is not. The steady pressure of public opinion can be a powerful thing. When the effective social groups are small, it is by no means impossible to determine a course of action by mutual agreement. If all the members of a group view a situation in the same way, there is no need for coercion.

Second, there can be *disengagement*. If a serious dispute occurs within the group, one of the disputants (or one of the factions) can simply move away. Third, there can be *self-help*. A person who has been wronged can take direct individual action against the offender. This often takes the form of a duel, and kinship alliances can play a prominent role in providing support. When a crime such as murder occurs, it is not uncommon for a relative of the murdered person to exact blood vengeance, that is, to kill the murderer.

Fourth, there is *feud*. Sometimes, problems are not satisfactorily resolved and bitter feelings result. For example, suppose a relative of a murdered person kills the murderer, and then the relatives of the murderer decide to execute the executioner. You get a kind of Ping-Pong effect; there is no end to it. The violation of the social code does not have to be murder, of course. Any serious dispute can result in an uneasy settlement. A feud situation cannot be tolerated for long in a group of 50 people; the group would cease to exist. However, feuds can occur between local groups, and there can be chronic hostility for long periods of time. (Remember that a party to a dispute may move away, but not to the ends of the earth. There is still sporadic contact.)

Hunters and gatherers — at least the ones who have survived — are not warlike in any meaningful sense. There are no pitched battles between large forces; they have neither the population resources nor the organizational techniques for such fights. Even raiding is uncommon for the excellent reason that there is nothing to raid *for* — your neighbors have nothing you want. There are no herds of cattle or horses to serve as tempting targets. There are no cultivated fields to harvest. Territorial expansion is not a sensible goal as long as there is plenty of room for everybody and a group is already controlling as big an area as it can handle.

There is a tendency to think of hunters and gatherers as being engaged in a constant struggle for survival. It used to be argued that they were so busy just getting enough to eat that there was no time available for anything else. This is an area in which modern research has come up with a bit of a surprise. Elman R. Service has characterized the Arunta of Australia as "literally one of the most leisured peoples in the world" (Service 1978:19). Richard B. Lee estimated that the people in one Bushman group "worked" only about two and one half days a week and that the working day was only around six hours long (Lee 1968: 37). Marshall D. Sahlins has gone so far as to describe hunters and gatherers as "the original affluent society" (Sahlins 1968:85).

While it is clear that some hunting and gathering groups live a much more difficult existence than others, it does seem to be a fact that in many hunting and gathering societies there is a lot of time in which there is literally nothing to do. Since they cannot store food, it is pointless to bring in more than can be eaten. Since they cannot accumulate property, there is obviously no incentive to do so. When times are good, the food quest is relatively easy; and when times are tough there is not much a person can do about it except to wait for better days. If there is nothing to hunt it is senseless to exhaust yourself in hunting. Hunters and gatherers have a remarkable ability to adapt themselves to what is available. When food is plentiful, they gorge themselves. When food is scarce, they can get by on very little.

There is another sense, though, in which the struggle for survival is very real. The most serious problem that confronts hunters and gatherers today is not internal but external. It is not necessary to idealize the hunting and gathering lifeway to appreciate that there are rewards in such existence: Not only does it work but it has worked for millions of years longer than any other hominid lifestyle. The tragic catch is that hunters and gatherers cannot compete with other types of human societies. They are few in numbers and loosely organized. When confronted with more efficient cultural systems — farmers, herders, state-organized societies — they have only three options. They can change and adopt the new lifeway, in which case they are no longer hunters and gatherers. They can become extinct, and many of them did. Or they can retreat into land that nobody else wants, and that is where the survivors are.

Even this last option is now being taken from them. Like the chimpanzee, their peril comes not from a war of extermination but from loss of habitat. Soon there will be no place left on earth that can sustain a hunting and gathering lifeway. By the end of this century, there will probably be no hunting and gathering societies remaining on this planet.

They deserve to be remembered, and more than that. These were the "savages" of the old schemes of cultural evolution. These were also the cultural ancestors of all of us, the people who enabled the human species to endure.

Savages? From them we inherited an intact and living earth. Will we be remembered with the same distinction when our time too has passed?

SUMMARY

In the broadest possible terms, *political organization* concerns the types of leadership and the kinds of authority systems that are associated with various territorial groupings. The creation and enactment of public policy in any human society necessarily involves decision making, and it is in this area that political organization comes most sharply into focus.

Different kinds of human societies have different techniques for handling "political" problems. Therefore, the best way to come to grips with actual political processes is to examine them *in context*. For this reason, we must examine *specific types* of human sociocultural systems.

There was a time when all peoples on this earth were hunters of wild animals and collectors of wild plant foods. Although such societies are now rapidly disappearing, they are of immense importance because they provided the frameworks within which the human animal was formed. Thus the first type of society we need to look at is that of the *hunters and gatherers*.

A true hunting and gathering society is one that practices no farming, lives by hunting wild animals and collecting wild plant foods, lacks domesticated animals other than the dog, and does not have access to concentrated fish resources. In ecological terms, the possession of herds of domesticated animals or the availability of concentrated fish resources — such as annual salmon runs — permits the development of a kind of sociocultural system that is outside the normal range of variation for hunting and gathering peoples.

True hunters and gatherers must *move around* a good deal, and *population densities* are low: Few surviving groups of hunters and gatherers attain a population density as high as one person per square mile. The largest effective social group among hunters and gatherers seldom contains more than 50 people. These somewhat fluid and unstable groups are sometimes called *bands,* but the more neutral term *local group* is probably preferable.

Land is not owned—it is an arena within which a person is free to hunt or gather. In most cases, boundaries between local groups are not sharply defined. Although several local groups may get together on a temporary basis, all of the local groups within a given cultural domain never unite to take common political action. In effect, each local group is autonomous; it makes its own decisions. Beyond the local group, there is only an awareness of cultural identity. Functionally speaking, there is no "tribe."

A local group is an intimate face-to-face group. Everyone knows everyone else, and social interactions are intensely personal. There are no social classes and no marked wealth differences. There is a sexual division of labor: The women gather (and often produce the bulk of the food) and the men hunt. There are meaningful age differences: A child does not have the same responsibilities as an elder.

The only semispecialized social roles within the local group are those of the *shaman* and the *headman.* The role of the headman is pivotal in understanding how political action works in a hunting and gathering society. The headman is not a chief, is not formally selected, cannot force anyone to do anything, and is not an adjudicative official. The headman is an informal charismatic leader. The headman makes suggestions and offers advice. It is not the authority inherent in the office that gets things done, but rather the influence of the headman's personality. When decisions must be made in a local group, they are not made just by the headman. Decisions are reached and problems resolved on the basis of *consensus, disengagement, self-help,* or *feud.*

Although hunters and gatherers are often pictured as being engaged in a constant struggle for survival, there is actually a good deal of leisure time in such societies. The real problem that they face is external rather than internal: They cannot compete effectively with other types of human societies.

References

Ewers, John C. 1955. *The Horse in Blackfoot Indian Culture.* Bureau of American Ethnology, Bulletin 159. Washington, D.C.: U.S. Government Printing Office.

Goldschmidt, Walter. 1977. *Exploring the Ways of Mankind,* 3d ed. New York: Holt, Rinehart and Winston.

Lee, Richard B. 1968. "What Hunters Do for a Living, or, How to Make Out on Scarce Resources," in Richard B. Lee and Irven DeVore (eds.), *Man the Hunter.* Chicago: Aldine, pp. 30–48.

Lee, Richard B., and Irven DeVore. 1968. "Problems in the Study of Hunters and Gatherers," in Richard B. Lee and Irven DeVore (eds.), *Man the Hunter.* Chicago: Aldine, pp. 3–12.

Oliver, Symmes C. 1976. "The Plains Indians as Herders," in James P. Loucky and Jeffrey R. Jones (eds.), *Paths to the Symbolic Self: Essays in Honor of Walter Goldschmidt. Anthropology UCLA* 8:35–43. Los Angeles: University of California.

Sahlins, Marshall D. 1968. "Notes on the Original Affluent Society," in Richard B. Lee and Irven DeVore (eds.), *Man the Hunter.* Chicago: Aldine, pp. 85–89.

Service, Elman R. 1978. *Profiles in Ethnology,* 3d ed. New York: Harper & Row.

Suggestions for Further Reading

Coon, Carleton S. 1971. *The Hunting Peoples.* Boston: Little, Brown. In a word, fascinating. One of anthropology's most vigorous writers and wide-ranging intellects surveys the world of the hunters and gatherers.

Drucker, Philip. 1963. *Indians of the Northwest Coast.* American Museum Science Books. Garden City, N.Y.: Natural History Press. A reliable guide to the Indians of the region: people who neither farm nor possess domesticated animals but who are very different from hunters and gatherers because of their utilization of extensive fish and sea mammal resources.

Freuchen, Peter. 1961. *Book of the Eskimos.* New York: Harcourt Brace Jovanovich. A vivid personal account by a Danish explorer who spent many years with the Eskimo.

Marshall, Lorna. 1965. "The !Kung Bushmen of the Kalahari Desert," in James L. Gibbs, Jr. (ed.), *Peoples of Africa.* New York: Holt, Rinehart and Winston, pp. 241–278. A very good, short account of the Bushman lifeway by a noted authority. (The mark ! in the title indicates a "click" phoneme in the Bushman language.)

Oliver, Symmes C. 1962. *Ecology and Cultural Continuity as Contributing Factors in the Social Organization of the Plains Indians.* University of California Publications in American Archeology and Ethnology 48(1). Berkeley and Los Angeles: University of California Press. A comparative study of the historic Indians of the Plains, this shows how misleading it is to consider these peoples as traditional hunters and gatherers.

Service, Elman R. 1966. *The Hunters.* Englewood Cliffs, N. J.: Prentice-Hall. A good little book that offers a useful overview of the subject.

Steward, Julian H. 1938. *Basin-Plateau Aboriginal Sociopolitical Groups.* Bureau of American Ethnology, Bulletin 120. Washington, D.C.: U.S. Government Printing Office. Despite its somewhat forbidding title, this is a fascinating and insightful account of the hunters and gatherers who lived in the Great Basin region of the United States.

Thomas, Elizabeth Marshall. 1965. *The Harmless People.* New York: Vintage Books. A beautifully written and personal account of the Bushmen, this is probably the best single book on a hunting and gathering society. Must reading.

Turnbull, Colin M. 1962. *The Forest People.* Garden City, N.Y.: Doubleday (Anchor Books). This one deals with the Pygmies of Central Africa. Like the Thomas book mentioned above, it is reliable, well written, and deeply felt.

18

Let's Get Organized: Middle-Range Societies and States

The hunting and gathering societies we discussed in the previous chapter can be characterized as *small-scale societies*. They tend to be small in total population, low in population density, and small in terms of the number of important groups and roles that exist in the society. The next basic type of sociocultural organization is that represented by *middle-range societies*. These are the peoples who live in what are usually called *tribes*.

For many years in anthropology, the word *tribe* really had no very precise referent. One person's tribe was the other person's band and vice versa. That situation is changing now, but there still is not total agreement on exactly what a tribe is. My own view is that it is useful to begin with the economic base. From this angle, tribal societies are generally based on simple farming or herding, or on some combination of the two. By "simple" I merely mean to exclude large-scale, more-or-less industrialized farming and sophisticated ranching operations that produce livestock for profit.

It is true that not all tribal societies rest on that economic foundation. There are exceptions, and I indicated some of them in the last chapter. However, the vast majority of tribes are farmers or herders or both, and that is the least confusing way of thinking about them.

Therefore, the word *tribe* can be taken to mean: the largest group of people (society) that shares a common culture and language, occupies a common territory, and thinks of itself as a unit—with specific reference to a sociocultural system based on simple farming or herding or on some combination of the two. In other words, the tribe is the largest meaningful sociocultural group found in a middle-range society. By a middle-range society I mean one that is between a small-scale society of hunters and gatherers, on the one hand, and a state-or-

Masai tribesmen with cattle.

ganized system on the other. If the group in question is not composed of hunters and gatherers and it is not a state or a portion of a state, then it is a tribe. Certainly, it does make sense to speak of a Hopi tribe or a Kamba tribe or a Jivaro tribe or a Masai tribe — just as it does *not* make sense to speak of a Bushman tribe or an Eskimo tribe.

Regardless of how they are defined, tribes are notably diverse. There are many kinds of tribes, and they cannot be described as neatly as hunters and gatherers. This is not an accident. Hunters and gatherers are the way they are because there are few sociocultural alternatives open to them; indeed, this is one of the characteristics that marks the hunting and gathering lifeway. The introduction of farming or herding alters the ecological situation profoundly, and many more alternatives open up. Whenever you have viable alternatives, you are also going to have diversity.

Nevertheless, some generalizations are possible. Perhaps the most obvious one involves population. To put it plainly, in middle-range societies you tend to find *more people* than can exist in hunting and gathering societies. Farming is not surefire — crops can fail — and herding is not without its perils, but crops in the soil and domesticated animals under control offer a more bountiful and stable food supply than that available to hunters and gatherers. Tribal societies contain populations ranging from a few thousand to hundreds of thousands of people. Population densities will vary — farmers are always thicker on the land than are herders — but the densities will be higher than those found among hunters and gatherers. Around 50 persons per square mile is not unusual, and population densities of several hundred persons per square mile are sometimes encountered.

It is not just the size of the population that makes the critical difference, although that is a factor. It is the kind of settlement unit that exists. The living groups in tribal societies, whether they are relatively fixed villages or portable herding encampments, are always more stable than the somewhat fluid local groups of hunters and gatherers. It is certainly possible to leave one group and join another, but this is not as simple as switching local groups among hunters and gatherers. In villages, the people are tied to their farmland, which they often obtain by inheritance. In herding groups, the people are directly linked to their stock, and their movements are conditioned by the seasonal requirements of the animals; the people move through the annual cycle together, and they cannot abandon the herds to try their luck somewhere else. In effect, the result is a fairly permanent cluster of people who spend their lives together.

The settlement groups — they can be thought of as villages, although there are many different kinds of villages — tend to be larger than the local groups of hunters and gatherers. It is possible to keep more people together in one place. A typical village will contain hundreds of people, and it may contain thousands. It must be emphasized that *stability* is a village characteristic — even if a village moves, the whole village goes together. It is not at all unusual for a person to spend a lifetime in a particular village, just as the parents did in the preceding generation and the children will do in the next generation.

TRIBAL LINEAGES AND CLANS

It is partly because of this stability that large kinship units such as lineages and clans are characteristic of tribal societies. When kin groups ramify beyond a family level they work most effectively as organizational techniques in a fixed and stable population. A group like a clan is not very efficient when its members are scattered all over the map. In a settled village context with a large population, however, it is another story. Clans or subdivisions of clans — which is what lineages often are — can be localized and politically potent. They sometimes control the farmland, allocating the fields to clan kin on a use basis. They can be crucial in replenishing herds or dictating the conditions for stock trades.

Not all tribes have lineages and clans, but when they occur they tend to *divide the tribe into a series of socially equivalent units.* That is, the tribal structure consists of a number of large groupings based on kinship, and each of these groupings may operate to some extent as an equal and independent unit within the larger society. Frequently, when clans exist they are the largest effective social groupings. In crucial situations, it may be the clan that takes action rather than the village or the tribe.

For example, let us return to the problem of homicide. In a clan-based society, it is usually the clan that deals with the situation. If a person belonging to one clan kills a person belonging to another clan, then the two clans involved get together to work out a solution. This may entail a payment of wealth from one clan to the other, or it may require the sacrifice of a clan member to pay the debt. (This does not always mean the execution of the actual murderer; the idea is to restore the balance between the two clans, and the clan may select some other

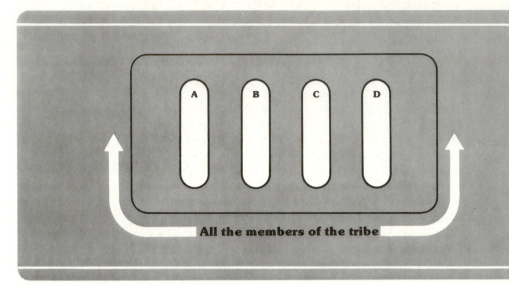

Figure 18.1 Schematic diagram of a tribal society with clans.

person as being more nearly equivalent to the person who was killed.) Obvious-ly, you are not going to kill someone with the idea that one of your clan kin will pay for your deed; this would be like knowingly committing a crime that would send your brother to the gallows. Murder is wrong by definition, but murder *within* the clan is particularly bad for the same reason—you are killing a relative. Nevertheless, it happens, and when it does the problem is handled within the confines of a single clan. The Kamba of Kenya require a payment for any killing, whether the killing was intentional or not, and the payment consists of 11 cows and 1 bull. If the killing occurs within the clan, the payment is made from one clan segment—such as a lineage—to another. Even if the killing involves just a single family, the payment is made within the family.

Homicide is just a particularly dramatic illustration of the much larger ques-tion of resolving disputes. The point is that when major disputes occur in clan-based societies it tends to be the clans that deal with the situation. As the Kamba put it, "The clan will decide and take action. The others just argue."

A society of this kind can be visualized as in Figure 18.1. Here the solid enclosing line represents the tribal domain and within it there are four large clans designated with letters. As a rule, there would be more than just four clans, but that does not alter the principle involved. When problems arise or decisions have to be made, it is not the tribe that constitutes the arena for political action. Rath-er, it is the clan or clans. If the difficulty is limited to Clan A, then Clan A deals with it. If both Clan A and Clan D are involved, then those two clans work the problem out; Clan B and Clan C stay on the sidelines.

I do not mean to suggest that all tribes are organized in this fashion. I also do not mean to suggest that the tribe as a whole is insignificant. There is more going on here than the vague consciousness of kind found among hunters and gatherers. We shall return to these points shortly.

In the final analysis, perhaps, clans and lineages tend to occur in tribal societies because they are useful there; they are effective devices for getting things done. However, there are other ways of organizing stable populations for social action. The most common alternative organizational techniques involve age grades or age sets.

AGE GRADES AND AGE SETS

Both age grades and age sets are ways of grouping people on the basis of relative age. In an *age grade* system, the society is divided into a series of ranks or categories. For instance, insofar as males are concerned, there might be three basic groups or grades. The young unmarried men belong to the warrior age grade, the middle-aged married men belong to a second grade, and the older men form an elder age grade. Each grade or group is responsible for specific tasks; the warriors, as the name suggests, were traditionally the soldiers, the elders decided the legal cases, and so on. The essence of an age grade system is that a person enters or leaves a particular grade as an individual, and actual chronological age may not be the primary determining factor. It may depend on a man's wealth or the wealth of his father — since a payment is often required to move from one age grade to another — or it may depend upon his capacity for judgment, his skill with weapons, or whether or not he has children. Regardless of exactly what is required, as he goes through life he participates as an individual first in one age grade and then in another.

An *age set* system is similar, but it has one basic difference: You do not go through the ranks as an individual but rather as a member of a fixed group. That is, you are initiated into the first "rank" with others of about your own age and after a predetermined interval — say ten years or so — the whole group or set passes on into the next rank. In effect, you spend your life in the company of a stable group of age mates, and the "set" passes together from one rank to the next. Age sets work particularly well as systems of military organization, and they are quite common in herding societies that tend to be involved in cycles of raids and counterraids. When age sets are strong, they may have the primary responsibility for social control: Each set has its leaders, and each set keeps its own people in line.

It is perfectly possible to combine an age set or an age grade system with a clan system, but to some extent they are alternative structuring devices; they represent different ways of organizing tribes for social action. As a rough general rule, if the clans are very strong the age sets or age grades will be relatively weak, and vice versa.

Since clans are vertically organized and age sets or age grades are horizontal in structure, we might diagram a tribal society with both kinds of groups, as in Figure 18.2. Here, as before, units A, B, C, and D indicate clans, while units E, F, and G represent age sets or age grades.

ACEPHALOUS TRIBES

Contrary to popular belief, many tribal societies have no real tribal leader. That is, there is no head or "chief" of the whole tribe. Such tribes are referred to as *acephalous societies* — literally, "without a head." The basic reason for this kind of organization has been implied in the preceding discussion: The critical units, the ones that count in getting things done, are the lineages or the clans or the age sets or the age grades, or sometimes the villages or the secret societies. The tribe is subdivided into a series of more or less equivalent units, and it is there — in the subtribal groupings — that the real organization exists.

Acephalous tribes can be thought as *felt tribes*. That is, the people involved — all of the Kamba, for example — recognize their tribal identity, they have a name for themselves, they know that they are distinct from other tribes, and they feel that they belong together. There is a strong sense of "tribalness," but there is no overall inclusive tribal government. In point of fact, there is no person or group of persons who have the authority to speak for the tribe as a whole.

In my view, this does not mean that there is no government. Important decisions and conflict resolutions are not just left to consensus or individual initiative. Rather, the question that must be asked is: What kind of government is it, and over whom does the government have jurisdiction? The answer is that regardless of the particular form the government takes (which may range from powerful techniques of persuasion through supernatural sanctions to the direct use of force) it exists only on the local or subtribal level. The village will generally have a council of leaders of some sort, the age groups have their officers, and the clans too have their councils and leaders. Decisions can indeed be made, and they are stronger than mere expressions of opinion. However, the decisions that are made apply only to the group in question — the village, the age set, the clan, or whatever — and not to the entire tribe. Thus, one clan can elect to fight another clan, or one village can choose to plant millet instead of maize, and the tribe itself — as a tribe — has no effective say in the matter.

TRIBAL LEADERSHIP

All tribes are not acephalous, of course. There are tribal societies that have some integrating mechanism that makes it possible for the tribe to act as a unit with a cohesive overall policy. There are many ways in which this situation can come about. Perhaps the two most common techniques involve *ranked clans* and *a response to an outside threat*. In a clan-based tribe, it is often the case that one clan is larger and more powerful than the others. The hereditary chief of that clan sometimes becomes the paramount chief of the tribe, with the leaders of the other clans serving as a kind of advisory council. When a tribe is under severe outside pressure, it must respond as a tribe to counter the threat. It isn't enough for clans or villages to operate as independent units; the situation requires a tribal military organization. In such instances, a strong military leader — a war chief —

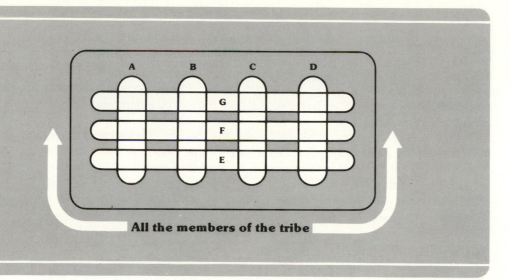

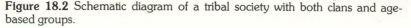

Figure 18.2 Schematic diagram of a tribal society with both clans and age-based groups.

can assume overall tribal leadership. As a rule, a chief of this sort remains as paramount chief only as long as the threat persists; when the pressure lessens, the tendency is for the subtribal leaders to assert themselves once again.

In truth, there is a considerable range of variation in nonacephalous tribal societies. They run the gamut from tribes with rather nebulous leaders to tribes with a strong and well-defined system of tribal leadership. It is this latter type of society that Elman Service calls a *chiefdom*.

The great advantage of the presence of a real chief, in Service's terms, is that it provides a society with a "central nervous system" (Service 1978:6). That is, it gives the tribe a mechanism by means of which it can integrate social action. A system of centralized leadership offers a sense of direction that makes possible a cohesive tribal-wide policy. To be truly effective, such leadership must be of long duration; it can't amount to much if it lacks continuity. That is why the leadership in chiefdoms usually has a hereditary basis.

As Service points out, the existence of a "controlling center" in a chiefdom enables it to function as an agency of economic redistribution. That is, it can pool tribal products and parcel them out to those who need them. We have already encountered a system of this kind in Malinowski's analysis of the sociocultural organization of the Trobriand Islands (see Chapter 11). The Trobriand Islanders constituted a chiefdom. A portion of every crop grown was allocated to the chief, who had the responsibility of dividing up the food and distributing it in an equitable manner.

What exactly is a chief? One way of looking at it is that a chief is more than a headman and less than a ruler. Chiefs are found in middle-range (tribal) societies, and logically enough they are middle-range sorts of leaders. They are like headmen in some ways and like true rulers in others, and yet they have certain attributes that make them distinctive.

A chief has a definite title of some kind and is usually formally selected for office either through descent or by some other process of recognition. A chief does not just "get to be that way." Rather, a chief is chosen and assumes the office in a public ceremony. Unlike a headman, a chief does not look just like anyone else in the society. A chief is marked off from the rest by a particular style of dress or some badge of office.

A chief may have considerable authority; the role of a chief involves more than just making suggestions. Consider a chief of the Trobriand Islanders. By controlling the allocation of food resources, he can bring considerable pressure to bear. Beyond this, being in charge of magical practices gives him substantial social leverage. A chief by definition has superior social status. Rather than being "just one of the boys," he holds the highest rank in a nonegalitarian social structure. A chief is treated with respect and deference, and his opinion carries weight.

Chiefs can and do make decisions on a wide range of problems. They can give judgments in legal disputes and determine strategies in conflicts with other tribes. However, being a chief is not easy. Much depends on the personality and shrewdness of the chief. Although a chief has high status and can manipulate things to some extent, the actual power of the office is limited. There can be weak chiefs and strong chiefs; it all depends on how effectively the person holding the office operates. A chief does not have absolute power. This means that a chief can strongly influence the course of events but lacks a monopoly on the use of legal force. The coercion employed by a chief is a subtle kind of thing. A chief cannot just issue orders and then call out the troops to ensure that the orders are obeyed. In the true sense of the term, a chief must be a politician. That is, a chief must read the situation carefully and bring pressure to bear that stops short of the use of physical force.

OTHER CHARACTERISTICS OF TRIBAL SOCIETIES

Tribal societies do not usually have strong class divisions, although these can occur in chiefdoms. However, marked individual wealth distinctions are characteristic of tribal groupings. Unlike hunting and gathering societies, where in effect there is little or nothing to own, tribal societies tend to be very involved with property. Cultivated fields or herds of domesticated livestock can obviously be owned, and the successful farmer or herder can accumulate significant amounts of wealth. To put the matter briefly, both individuals and families tend to sort themselves out along a continuum that ranges from the relatively prosperous to the relatively poor. For this reason, tribal societies are not egalitarian to the same degree that is characteristic of hunters and gatherers.

While it cannot be maintained that all tribes are "warlike," it is true that organized conflict between different political groupings is far more common on the tribal level than among hunters and gatherers. Although the motivations for tribal warfare are not well understood, it can be pointed out that in tribal societies there is something to fight *about*. Herds of livestock make tempting targets, and pastoral (herding) societies frequently find themselves involved in long-term cycles of raids and counterraids. Indeed, such societies tend to be quite militaristic, and the role of the warrior often enjoys very high prestige. Farmers as a rule are more defensively oriented, but — as the old saying goes — sometimes the best defense is a good offense. Farming peoples must be concerned with the territories they occupy, and they must protect their crops or risk starvation. It is difficult to generalize here; some farming tribes fight only when they must and others live in a chronic state of semiritualized warfare with their neighbors. Massed troops and pitched battles to the death are not really characteristic of tribal societies, but raiding hit-and-run attacks and quasi-ceremonial combats between warriors are too much a feature of tribal life to be ignored.

The supernatural systems of tribal societies are so diverse that facile generalizations about them should be avoided. However, it is noteworthy that the shamans who are all-purpose supernatural practitioners in hunting and gathering societies tend to be joined in tribal societies by another kind of specialist (or semispecialist) in dealing with supernatural affairs. The shaman is still there, but the role of the shaman is reduced in scope. In tribal societies, major ceremonial activities — such as planting and harvesting rituals — are often the responsibility of persons best referred to as *priests*. The distinction between shamans and priests will be explored in Chapter 20.

STATES

When the explorer John Hanning Speke, who was searching for the source of the Nile River, found the Kingdom of Buganda on the shores of Lake Victoria (in modern Uganda) in 1862, he encountered a ruler who was about as far removed from a local group headman or a tribal chief as a man could be. He was called the *Kabaka*, and he was the very embodiment of power, pomp, and authority. The Kabaka never walked outside his own residence; he was carried on the shoulders of human bearers. When people approached the Kabaka, they crawled on the ground, thumping the earth with their hands, feet, and heads. If someone sneezed in his presence, that person was executed. If he disliked a meal, he called in the cook and had the man speared on the spot.

When Hernan Cortes and his Spanish conquistadors invaded Mexico (1519–1521), they found the fabulous city of Tenochtitlan (on the site of modern Mexico City) at the heart of the Aztec Empire (see photograph on p. 12). There they encountered a ruler, Montezuma, who had been virtually a god on earth. Surrounded by pyramids and temples that were festooned with the bones of human sacrifices, Montezuma lived in an impressive palace that was nothing if not well equipped — there was a zoo, a swimming pool, rooms stacked with gold and jade and magnificent feather mantles, apartments for wives and mistresses, and kitchens that regularly served hundreds of guests at each meal in addition to roughly 1000 guards and attendants. When Montezuma waged war, which he did frequently to exact tribute from his neighbors, he summoned his war leaders to his throne. Before they could approach him, the war leaders had to divest themselves of all signs of rank and present themselves to the god-king "bare-headed and barefooted, with downcast eyes" (Vaillant 1962:189).

Shaka, the king of the South African Zulus, was a military genius who ruled with an iron hand. He had a superbly disciplined army, and he kept it that way by executing any of his troops who retreated in battle. When his mother died, Shaka showed his grief by having some 7000 people killed. Deciding that the mourning had not been intense enough to suit him, he ordered a general massacre of all citizens who did not seem properly distraught. As a final gesture, he ordered all citizens to refrain from sexual intercourse for one year (Gluckman 1960:165).

Even if we knew nothing else about the sociopolitical systems involved, the presence of such all-powerful figures should alert us to the fact that we are now dealing with something that is quite different from a tribally organized society. Specifically, we have encountered the primitive (or nonindustrialized) *state*.

It is not that the heads of states must behave in such regal and arbitrary ways — some do and some don't — but that they have the power to do so if they wish. Structurally, a state is built like a pyramid. There is a single powerful figure at the apex of the pyramid, and it is instructive to think of all authrority as flowing from the top down. (This is not always literally true, of course. In democratic states, the ultimate authority in theory rests in the hands of the citizens. In effect, they select a representative or group of representatives; this person or group then exercises the authority. However, there is always a strongly centralized power structure in state systems.) In most primitive states, the head of the state can *delegate* authority to others. Indeed, it is necessary to do so if there is going to be effective government. Nevertheless, the key point is that the authority is there to delegate.

The very essence of a state system is that a state has a monopoly on the legal use of force. The head of a state — either in person or through appointed councils and officials — can not only make decisions and issue orders but can back up these edicts with the threat of coercion.

A number of logical consequences follow from the few features we have mentioned. (Remember that god-kings and centralized power structures cannot exist in isolation; they are parts of systems.) As a matter of fact, state systems tend to resemble one another rather strongly. They are not all identical, but they are not as diverse as tribal societies. Apparently, just as there are only so many ways to organize a hunting and gathering society, there are likewise relatively few variations that will work in state-organized societies.

States require specialists in the art of government. States have populations ranging from thousands of people to millions of people, and the ruler cannot cope alone. There must be ministers, officers, and local officials to carry on the everyday tasks of administration. Bureaucrats may be a modern disease, but

Left, A Nigerian head of state; *Right,* The Queen of England.

their counterparts are found in primitive states as well. This means that an essential characteristic of a state system is that a portion of the population must be freed from food production. The food producers—usually farmers, but sometimes herders as well—must not only feed themselves but also provide enough food to support the specialists. There is a basic division of labor in state systems between the food producers and those providing administrative or other state services.

Food producers, obviously, must live in "rural" areas. Equally obviously, a centralized power structure must be centered somewhere. The focal point of a state system must be a place where there are lots of people; it must house the ruler and key officials, the treasury, the ceremonial plazas, the markets, the military organization, and the people who surround the seats of power. In other words, a state must have a capital. Technically, this does not have to be a true city, but urbanism is highly correlated with state organizations. You do not find cities in tribal societies, and you certainly do not find them among hunters and gatherers. (The old term *city-state* is a very revealing one. There you had a kind of state in miniature—an urban center controlling the adjacent food-producing areas.) Sometimes the connection is quite clear. The Aztec Tenochtitlan was a city by any standards. In other instances, the state has a capital—an administrative center—but not necessarily a city. The Zulus, for example, had no urban areas. Still, the royal residence was located in a thickly bunched circle of dwellings that were built around a central cattle enclosure that was 2 miles across—big enough to hold some 80,000 warriors.

The threat of coercion implies the existence of a police force of some kind. Professional soldiers tend to be a prominent feature of state societies. They are employed by the state and they perform a double function. They can act as police, enforcing the laws of the state. Beyond this, they can serve as a professional officer core in a militia army in times of war.

When states form, one of the first things that they do is to establish a centrally controlled legal system. Major crimes and disputes are no longer handled by individual clans or local independent villages. The state steps in to prohibit feuds and the private pursuit of justice. This means that the state must set up a system of local courts with state-appointed (or state-approved) judges. This is where the legal cases are thrashed out—whether they involve theft or witchcraft or murder—and where decisions are reached. Frequently, there are appeal courts as well, and in theory a case can be appealed all the way to the head of the state. (This takes some financial muscle, of course; appeals are not automatic.) It is characteristic of state systems that the head of the state can reverse any lower court decision. In thinking of courts, one need not imagine a series of pseudo-Greek buildings scattered through the territory of a state; a court can be a simple clearing in the bush. What counts is that it is a recognized place for the disposition of legal cases and that it is equipped with officials who have the authority to reach decisions in the name of the state.

As a rule, the populations of states are quite diverse socially. This involves a good deal more than just wealth differences. The people who inhabit state systems are emphatically not all alike in terms of social status. There are profound differences between rural food producers and state officials, between members of the royal family and artisans, between nobles (who receive grants of land from the state) and slaves. In fact, strong class divisions tend to be characteristic of state systems. If we return to our analogy of a pyramid, there is a vast social distance from the top to the bottom—and there is a good deal of jockeying for position in the middle.

The authority structure of a state does not rest solely on secular power. It takes more than squads of police to make a state system work. The citizens must believe in the rightness of the state organization. For this reason, there is usually a very close link between the state and what might be termed a supernatural charter. There is a kind of official state religion that generally provides a supernatural basis for the structure of the state. For example, states are usually equipped with elaborate origin myths—sacred stories—that tell how the state came into being and why it is organized the way it is. The head of the state is frequently regarded as a divine being, a god on earth. As such, the ruler is the ultimate head of the state religion. Here again, the authority can be delegated, and head priests tend to be influential figures in state systems. Operating under the direction of the head priest, other priestly officials conduct the annual rounds of public ceremonies that serve to dramatize the sacred character of the state. There may still be shamanlike figures — curers — but they are less directly tied into the official state structure.

Communication is the lifeblood of a state. It does no good to issue proclamations and perform ceremonies if nobody knows about them. In small states this may not be a major problem, but states have a way of expanding. When they grow large, they need roads and messengers. The roads are also useful in military operations, making it possible to shift soldiers around in a hurry. Messengers mean messages and, as we all know, the least effective form of a message is oral; things get garbled. Writing is a tremendous asset to a state, not only for sending information but for keeping records. There were plenty of states that made do without writing, but on the other hand it is no accident that systems of writing first appeared in conjunction with state organizations.

In any state there must be a regular flow of commerce. Sometimes this is critical. There are states that owe their very existence to occupying strategic positions on important trade routes. They require controlled markets, and states have an unpleasant habit of collecting taxes to replenish the treasury. Goods must be exchanged between the food producers and the rest of the people. Craft specialists must have markets for their wares. It is not that markets and commerce and even taxes are found *only* in state systems. However, they are more developed there and probably more essential to the successful operation of the system.

Finally, as we have noted, states have armies. They have the manpower, the discipline, and sometimes the economic incentive to wage true warfare with competing states. It is here that we finally encounter pitched battles, heavy casualties, and wars of territorial expansion. Peaceful states do exist, but the histories of most states are stained with the chronicles of war. Succession to power is a tricky business in nondemocratic states; there are no elections. The position of head of the state is usually defined in hereditary terms, but there are often rival claimants to the throne. When the dust settles after the death of a monarch, the new ruler often fights a war or two to show his prowess. Of course, there are more compelling reasons for fighting wars, including the very survival of the state itself, but the fact remains that when true wars are fought it is states that fight them.

It is all too easy to focus on the highly visible features of state systems — the imperial potentates and the mighty armies — and it is tempting to conclude that the game is hardly worth the candle. There is a tendency to contrast the repressive characteristics of state societies with the more easygoing nature of hunting and gathering groups, and to view the transformation to state systems as a loss rather than a gain. Philosophically, there is something to be said for this position. However, there is another side to the coin. Perhaps it is true that all sociopolitical systems have both advantages and disadvantages. The emergence of states marks the transition from informal sanctions to the rule of law. It is not really quite that simple — there are tribal societies with fairly sophisticated legal systems — but codified laws and state organizations go hand in hand. Beyond this, the structure of the state often makes possible the specializations that mark the positive accomplishments of civilization. Modern medicine, literature, technology that can send a primate to the moon, and science itself — all are products of the developing state.

Anthropologists understandably have stressed the values and the rewards of nonstate societies. This has been both a useful and a necessary enterprise. But one of the primary lessons of anthropology is the necessity of perspective. Viewed from that angle, we might remember with a dash of humility that there would be no such thing as anthropology without the state.

In cultural evolution as in life, you can't go home again. It is desperately important to know where you came from and who you are, but life must be faced as it is. We are no longer hunters and gatherers culturally, and tribal societies too are rapidly disappearing from this earth. Most of us now live in states whether we like it or not.

Therefore, the choices we have are simple. We must make them work, perish, or go on to something else.

SUMMARY

Hunters and gatherers can be characterized as living in small-scale societies. It is in *middle-range societies* that *tribes* are found. The great majority of tribes are based on simple farming or herding or some combination of the two. A tribe is the largest meaningful sociocultural group found in a middle-range society. Tribes are more diverse than are hunters and gatherers. However, in tribal societies you will find *larger* social groups, more *stable* social groups, and higher population densities of 50 persons per square mile or more.

Large kinship units such as *lineages* or *clans* are characteristic of tribal societies. When they occur, lineages or clans tend to divide the tribe into a *series of socially equivalent units*. Often, when clans are present, they are the largest effective social groupings in the society. That is, in crucial situations it may be the clan that acts rather than the village or the tribe as a whole. Alternative organizational devices include *age grades* or *age sets*.

Many tribal societies have no real tribal leader. Often, there is no head or "chief" for the whole tribe. Such tribes are called *acephalous* or "felt" tribes. There is a strong sense of tribal identity but no overall inclusive tribal government. This means that governmental functions operate on a *subtribal* level. The villages have their leaders, the age groups have their officers, and the clans have their councils and leaders. Decisions can be made, but they apply only to the group in question.

All tribes are not acephalous. When tribes have a strong and well-defined system of tribal leadership, they are referred to as *chiefdoms*. A chief is more than a headman and less than a ruler. Chiefs are formally selected, but the actual power of the office is limited.

There are marked individual wealth differences in tribal societies. They are often militaristic in a fashion unknown in hunting and gathering societies. Both shamans and priests are found in tribal cultures.

A *state* is marked by a distinctive form of political organization. Structurally, a state is built like a pyramid. There is a single powerful figure at the apex of the social pyramid, and in theory all authority flows from the top down. The head of a state can *delegate* authority to others, but the key point is that the authority is there to delegate.

The essence of a state system is that a state has a monopoly on the legal use of force. The head of a state can not only make decisions and issue orders but can back up those edicts with the threat of *coercion*.

States frequently have large populations, and they require *specialists* in the art of government. Therefore, a portion of the population must be freed from food production. The food producers must not only feed themselves but also provide enough food to feed the specialists. This results in a division of the population into *rural* and *urban* (or quasi-urban) segments.

Professional soldiers tend to be a prominent feature of state societies, as is a centrally controlled legal system; there are local courts with state-appointed or state-approved judges, and the ultimate appeal court is the head of the state. Strong class systems are also characteristic of states, and there is usually a very close connection between the state and some form of state religion that provides a supernatural sanction for the structure of the state. States have armies, and they have the manpower, the discipline, and sometimes the economic incentive to engage in *true warfare*.

References

Gluckman, Max. 1960. "The Rise of a Zulu Empire." *Scientific American* 202(No. 4): 157–168.

Service, Elman R. 1978. *Profiles in Ethnology,* 3d ed. New York: Harper & Row.

Vaillant, George C. 1962. *Aztecs of Mexico.* Garden City, N.Y.: Doubleday.

Suggestions for Further Reading

Beattie, John. 1960. *Bunyoro: An African Kingdom.* New York: Holt, Rinehart and Winston. A good, short account of an African state, particularly interesting in showing the interconnections between the supernatural system and the state structure.

Cohen, Yehudi A. (ed.). 1974. *Man in Adaptation: The Cultural Present,* 2d ed. Chicago: Aldine. A well-organized collection of readings that covers the spectrum from hunting and gathering groups to state societies. Especially useful in conveying something of the diversity in tribal systems, with an emphasis on the ecologically based differences between farmers and pastoralists.

Fortes, Meyer, and E. E. Evans-Pritchard (eds.). 1940. *African Political Systems.* London: Oxford University Press. A classic (if somewhat dated) survey that deals with two types of political systems: those with centralized authority and those without.

Goldschmidt, Walter. 1959. *Man's Way.* New York: Holt, Rinehart and Winston. Although this penetrating book is recommended in its entirety, the reader will find the section titled "The Evolution of Society" particularly useful in setting forth the major distinctions between tribal and state societies.

Hoebel, E. Adamson. 1954. *The Law of Primitive Man.* Cambridge, Mass.: Harvard University Press. There are a good many more recent treatments of the subject, but this is still a good place to begin. The book is clearly written, and the middle — which presents detailed materials on societies ranging from the Eskimo through the Plains Indians to the Ashanti state — is a gold mine of information, regardless of the theoretical stance one takes toward legal analysis.

Meggitt, Mervyn. 1977. *Blood Is Their Argument.* Palo Alto, Ca.: Mayfield. For those who still believe that tribal societies always exist in a milieu of peace and harmony, this book is a useful corrective. Dealing with the Mae Enga of New Guinea, this is both a masterful study of tribal warfare and an excellent ethnography.

Middleton, John, and David Tait. 1958. *Tribes Without Rulers.* London: Routledge and Kegan Paul. Somewhat specialized and with an exclusive focus on Africa, this is the classic study of acephalous societies.

Roscoe, J. 1911. *The Baganda.* London: Macmillan. Allowing for a certain bias — the author was a missionary — this work remains a singularly vivid and carefully observed portrait of the Kingdom of Buganda.

Sahlins, Marshall D. 1968. *Tribesmen.* Englewood Cliffs, N.J.: Prentice-Hall. A brief and useful overview of life in tribal societies.

Service, Elman R. 1962. *Primitive Social Organization.* New York: Random House. A generally sound and engaging study of the subject. The premises are evolutionary and the focus is on bands (hunters and gatherers), tribes, and chiefdoms.

————. 1975. *Origins of the State and Civilization.* New York: Norton. Not always totally convincing, this work nevertheless provides a good introduction to modern thinking on the subject and discusses competing theories.

Speke, J. H. 1863. *Journal of the Discovery of the Source of the Nile.* London: Blackwood and Sons. Speke was the first European explorer to visit the Kingdom of Buganda. This is a fascinating story, and despite a fair amount of observer bias it is illuminating.

Wolf, Eric R. 1966. *Peasants.* Englewood Cliffs, N.J.: Prentice-Hall. A noted authority on the subject explains just what peasants are and what their importance is in the world of today. A lucid and valuable little book.

19

The Supernatural

Superstition is the religion of the people who live on the other side of the river.

— attributed to Ambrose Bierce

Most people are intrigued by the supernatural, and there is probably a good reason for this. I suspect that it interests us for the same reason that we like to talk, speculate about kin, and fiddle with tools. There is no need to get fancy about it. Supernatural involvements are a part of being human.

Supernatural beliefs and practices are a cultural universal. Nobody has ever found a human society that was completely devoid of supernatural concerns. Even in some modern states in which religious beliefs are officially discouraged or forbidden, they keep popping up with a sublime disregard for any party line. This tells us something important about the supernatural. It is not a kind of superficial frosting on the cultural cake. It is part of the cake itself.

This does not mean that all individuals participate with fervor and deep conviction in supernatural systems. Indeed, we are now beginning to appreciate that there is considerable individual variation that applies to *any* aspect of cultural sharing. It simply is not true that human beings are a series of identical cultural sponges, each one soaking up exactly the same version of whatever culture it is exposed to. Cultures are not that uniform, and neither are human beings. There are probably both skeptics and true believers in any sociocultural system, or at least those who are strongly attracted to supernatural beliefs and practices and those who are not.

This should not obscure the fundamental point. If something is a cultural universal, it is reasonable to assume that it is contributing in a useful manner to the ways in which cultures work. However, if supernatural systems have, so to speak, sociocultural work to do, what functions do they perform?

It is worthwhile to begin with the understanding that supernatural involvements affect both the individual and the society. There is no hard and fast dividing line here — the individual is a member of a group and social concerns have an effect on the individual — but it is still possible to recognize supernatural activities that are *primarily* aimed at one or the other.

Let us examine two examples, both dealing with the historic Plains Indians.

The Vision Quest: An Individual Rite

Among most of the American Plains Indian tribes, ranging from the Sarsi in the north to the Comanche in the south, visions were a necessary factor in the coming of age of a male. Visions were deliberately sought, and they were crucial. Without them, a young man could not acquire the guardian spirit that would protect him in the course of his life. He could not know the "medicines" — charms — to place in his bundle. He would be without the designs to be painted on his shield or his tipi. He might even be without a true — that is, adult — name. All of these things were revealed in visions. Without his vision, a man was defenseless — indeed, he was not a man at all but only a kind of half-man who could not marry or participate in the adult activities of males.

As a rule, a young man went out alone to seek his vision. He went to some sacred place — a hill or a valley that had been "lucky" for others. He ate nothing and drank as little as possible. He prayed and offered smoke to the spirits. And he waited — sometimes for many days. The vision might come to him in a dream, or he might be given a sign while he was awake — a bolt of lightning, a strange animal, a voice on the wind. Psychologically, he was ready — he expected to see a vision. Culturally, he was prepared — he knew the forms the visions took. If all went well, the vision came. He acquired his spirit — a buffalo, a bird, a horse. He was given instructions, some of which were very detailed: how to wear his hair, what kind of stone might be lucky for him, how and when to plan a raid.

But sometimes the vision did not come. In such a case, the only thing to do was to try again. The experience could not be faked — after all, *you* knew whether you had a guardian spirit or not. If a young man had repeated failures, he had to resort to extreme measures. He might go without water until he fainted, cut off a finger, lacerate his flesh. Sooner or later, the vision usually came. (Drugs were not traditionally used on Plains vision quests; peyote, in particular, arrived very late in the Plains area.)

There are several points of theoretical interest here. For one thing, the vision quest raises an old problem that plagues students of the supernatural. Those that argue that the role of the supernatural is supportive can point to the obvious sense of well-being and confidence that a successful vision quest produces in an individual. Those who argue otherwise can point out that if there were no cultural belief in the necessity for a vision quest, then failure wouldn't matter. We have already suggested that individuals differ in their receptiveness to supernatural ideas. The Plains Indians knew that. They recognized that it was impossible for some men to see visions, no matter how hard they tried. Some tribes even provided a loophole. If all else failed, a man could purchase the contents of vision from someone who had, in effect, more than he needed. It was expensive — it might cost a string of prized horses — but it could be done.

The Sun Dance: A Group Ceremony

Many of the Plains Indians—those tribes that did not practice farming in the river valleys and who depended on the mounted hunting of the bison (buffalo) for survival—followed an annual life cycle that precisely mirrored the life cycle of the bison. During the winter months, the bison were widely scattered in small groups (herdlets) throughout the plains. In order to hunt them effectively—and also because of the difficulty in finding pasturage for large horse herds in winter—the Plains Indians likewise were dispersed at that time of the year. A tribe could not stay together as a tribe, and therefore it divided into scattered bands. (The Cheyenne once tried to keep the whole tribe together in the Plains country during the winter. They very nearly starved to death, and never tried it again.)

Beginning in the late spring, with the return of good grass, the bison began to congregate in larger groups. By late summer, the mating season, the bison formed enormous herds. (This was when, in the classic phrase, they "blackened the earth as far as the eye could see.") This meant two things. First, the concentration of the bison—the drawing in to common centers—effectively removed the animals from some parts of the range. In other words, a hunting strategy based on widely distributed bands was not a wise policy. Second, the concentrated herds were a magnificent hunting opportunity if you could hit the herds with every available hunter.

Therefore, the tribes too reformed. The scattered bands of Plains Indians came together in *tribal* groups. This was when the great tribal camp circles occurred. All the Cheyenne (or all of the Kiowa, or all of the Blackfeet) camped together as a tribe. Tribal members who might not have seen one another all winter were suddenly face to face again. This was when the Sun Dance took place.

The Sun Dance was a complex ceremony that lasted for many days. It required the construction of a special Sun Dance lodge that was built around a strong central pole. The lodge contained an altar the basic feature of which was a sacred buffalo skull.

The details of the ceremony varied somewhat from tribe to tribe, but common features included performances by the warriors that dramatized military exploits, ritual intercourse involving the tribal priests, dancing around the center pole, blowing on bone whistles, and self-torture. (This was the ceremony in which some men were hung from the center pole. This was a voluntary action on their part. Ropes were skewered in their chests, with the other ends of the ropes fastened to the top of the pole. Those making the sacrifice danced all night, trying to tear the ropes out of their flesh.)

The Sun Dance was a dramatic affair, and what it symbolized ultimately was tribal unity. Because it was dramatic, it provided a focus for the tribe—something to look forward to all year long. It required extensive tribal organization; this was no slapdash performance that could be thrown together by a few people. It got everybody involved for a week or more, and it pulled the tribe back together after the fragmentation of the winter months.

The Sun Dance illustrates how misleading it can be to isolate a supernatural observance from its context. It cannot be understood as a thing apart; it was tightly integrated with the cultures of the Plains peoples. (Consider the symbolism of the buffalo skull, the emphasis on bravery, the performances of the military clubs, the role of the priests, and so on.) Beyond this, it was intimately bound up with the ecological situation within which the Plains tribes existed: The uniting of the tribe was made possible by the habits of the bison. There was also a clear economic aspect to the Sun Dance. It took some doing to get all the equipment together, and the whole ceremony was a prelude to a mass tribal bison hunt.

These two examples, of course, do not begin to exhaust the full range of functions of supernatural observances. They can only suggest two common involvements. The reader who might like to explore this problem a bit more deeply is referred back to Chapter 12, in which Roy Rappaport's *Pigs for the Ancestors* is discussed in some detail.

In part, supernatural systems are belief systems. The essence of a belief system is that some people believe in it. Therefore, the supernatural cannot be a neutral topic. There is a quite human tendency to feel that whatever *we* (whoever "we" happen to be) believe is entirely right and proper. There is nothing inherently wrong in this. The mischief comes from the other side of that coin. This is the feeling that what *other* people believe is somehow "wrong." This can only lead to dismissing the supernatural ideas of other peoples and other societies as so much superstition and mumbo-jumbo. Such an attitude is unacceptable from a humanistic or anthropological perspective.

We must make an active effort to *understand* what other people believe and do. As individuals we will likely have our own opinions on such matters as human sacrifice, witchcraft, the Inquisition, or going to church on Sunday. As students of anthropology, we must learn to suspend those judgments at least for the duration of the investigation. We can no more divide supernatural systems as "good" and "bad" than we can divide languages into "true" and "false."

We began this chapter with a little aphorism about superstition being the religion of the people who live on the other side of the river. The point is that what is regarded as being right and correct depends on where you live, that is, on which sociocultural system you participate in. One person's nonsense is another person's deeply held conviction. There is no place for concepts like "superstition" in anthropology.

ORIGINS OF THE SUPERNATURAL

We know virtually nothing about the origins of supernatural ideas. They may very well be as old as the human animal itself. We do know that evidence for the existence of supernatural beliefs takes us quite a distance back in time.

The Neanderthals of the Middle Paleolithic—some of them living as much as 100,000 years ago—practiced intentional burial of the dead. The Neanderthal graves, frequently near the mouths of caves, are significant in themselves; they show some concern for the bodies of the deceased. But what is much more impressive is the nature of the burials. Placed with the bodies in the graves were food offerings and kits of flint tools. In one case (from Iraq) a man was buried on a bed of flowers and the body was then covered with more flowers. Wherever this practice is encountered — whether in the elaborate tomb of a pharaoh of ancient Egypt with its extensive furnishings or in the humble grave of some anonymous tribal warrior equipped with a bow and some arrows — the significance is the same. It indicates some sort of a belief in an afterlife. You don't bury perfectly good tools or weapons or food unless you feel that they will be used by the occupant of the grave. Beyond this, there are shrines of cave bear skulls deep within some of the Neanderthal caves; they were almost certainly used in ceremonial activities of some kind.

Of course, this tells us nothing about the beginnings of supernatural belief systems. Ideas do not always leave a record in the earth. It does indicate how far back such evidence as we have goes. After the Neanderthals, as is well known, the cave paintings of Upper Paleolithic peoples (going back some 40,000 years) are replete with supernatural symbolisms. Indeed, much of this dramatic art may have been motivated in part by supernatural concerns: The many paintings of animals, including pregnant animals and wounded animals and animals with spears flying toward them, may represent what has been termed "art for meat's sake" — that is, a kind of hunting magic.

It can be argued that the human animal lives not in one world, but in two. As cultural animals, with our heads crammed full of symbols and ideas and speculations, we move rather easily from the everyday practical world where we think we know what is going on to another kind of world, a world of the strange, unseen, and unpredictable. It is this second world that we call the supernatural. That is the literal meaning of the word — something that is beyond natural comprehension.

There are scholars who are distinctly uncomfortable drawing a line between the natural and the supernatural, or even using the words at all. Their argument is essentially twofold. In the first place, it is not always possible to distinguish clearly between the two concepts: The "natural" and the "supernatural" may flow together and merge, and what might seem to be "supernatural" to us might seem quite "natural" to others, as well as vice versa. In the second place, the two categories are deeply rooted in our own thinking and speaking. In other words, the distinction is culture bound. In some cultures, it is maintained, people do not distinguish between the "natural" and the "supernatural" at all. For these reasons, among others, some anthropologists — notably those of what has been termed the *symbolist* persuasion — avoid the words in their interpretations. By way of example, the astute Clifford Geertz states that a religion is:

(1) a system of symbols which acts to (2) establish powerful, pervasive and long-lasting moods and motivations in men by (3) formulating conceptions of a general order of existence and (4) clothing

Detail from Upper Paoeolithic cave painting, Dordogne, France.

> these conceptions with such an aura of factuality that (5) the moods
> and motivations seem uniquely realistic. (Geertz 1965:4)

It is certainly possible to view religion as simply a symbolic interpretation of
the sociocultural universe. That is one way to do it. The difficulty with such an
approach, in my opinion, is that it is so all-inclusive that it virtually precludes any
focus on what may be unique (or at least different) about what William James
once called the "varieties of religious experience."

I would argue that most peoples do make some sort of a distinction between the natural and the supernatural, even though they may not conceptual-
ize it in quite that way. In most societies, people are perfectly well aware that
constructing a house and feeding a baby are fundamentally different activities
from praying to the moon or divining the future from the entrails of a cow. As
the old saying goes, nobody ever tries to build a tipi with a spell.

The distinction between a secular realm and a nonsecular (or
supernatural) orientation has a long history in anthropology and elsewhere. We
have already encountered it in Chapter 10 in connection with Robert Redfield's
contrast between the sacred values of folk-primitive societies and the secular
values of urban life (see pp. 159–160). Long ago, the pioneering French sociologist Emile Durkheim carefully distinguished between what he called the "sacred" and the "profane" — meaning the supernatural and the ordinary or natural
(Durkheim 1915). More recently, in a penetrating analysis of religion, Edward
Norbeck suggested:

> The least constricting terms our vocabulary provides to enable us to set
> off the realm of religion from the rest of culture are the natural and
> the supernatural. Most if not all peoples make some sort of distinction
> between the objects, beliefs, and events of the everyday, workaday,
> ordinary world and those which transcend the ordinary world. Using this
> distinction, as others have done, we shall define religion as ideas,
> attitudes, creeds, and acts of supernaturalism. (Norbeck 1961:11)

One of the most distinguished modern scholars of the subject has been Anthony F. C. Wallace. Wallace (1966:52) argues:

> It is the premise of every religion — and this premise is religion's defining characteristic — that souls, supernatural beings, and supernatural forces exist. Furthermore, there are certain minimal categories of behavior which, in the context of the *supernatural premise*, are always found in association with one another and which are the substance of religion itself.

THE PRACTICE OF THE SUPERNATURAL

Having presented a bit of background on the subject, let us return to the main thread of the argument. If we assume that the concepts of the natural and the supernatural constitute one useful way of approaching the problem, then what is the connection between the two? Under what circumstances do people turn to the supernatural, and what techniques do they use?

The basic situation, I think, is much the same for all peoples. It is a product of the kind of creatures that we are: big-brained primates who have the capacity both to think and to imagine.

As we live our lives, there are some things that are known and understood and can be handled without recourse to the supernatural. If you want to build a fire or make a spear or dial a number on a telephone, there are practical ways of going about it. All it takes is the know-how. But there are other things that are unknown, mysterious, and potentially dangerous. The most obvious example is death itself: We know that it is coming but dealing with it is another matter. The problem need not be that extreme. Take the question of "luck." What makes one person lucky and another unlucky? Or consider the strange situations that people face from time to time: the hunter when the game animals suddenly disappear, the farmer whose crops fail for no apparent reason, the dreams that disturb our sleep, the child that goes into a coma, the life-giving rains that will not come. There are no well-understood natural solutions to mysterious problems. That is why they are mysterious. And that is where the supernatural comes in.

It is a great fallacy to believe that the people who live in "primitive" societies are so enmeshed in supernatural involvements that they cannot operate in a practical (or secular) way. What they know for sure, they do. As Malinowski pointed out about the Trobriand Islanders who employ magical practices to *assist* in crop production, "If you were to suggest to a native that he should make his garden mainly by magic and scamp his work, he would simply smile on your simplicity." (Malinowski 1948:11). Malinowski provides another interesting example. He notes that when the Trobriand Islanders fish in the safe lagoons where everything is under control, they use no magic. However, when they take their canoes out into the open seas where they face "danger and uncertainty, there is extensive magical ritual to secure safety and good results" (Malinowski 1948:14).

In the same seminal book, *Magic, Science, and Religion,* Malinowski suggests that all cultures have a body of "empirical and rational knowledge" akin to the knowledge produced by science—just as all cultures have a belief in "supernatural forces." The real distinction between primitive cultures and those that have developed strong scientific traditions is that in primitive cultures fewer things are "known." That is, the sphere of the supernatural spreads to cover a wider area. For instance, in a society that lacks much of the knowledge of scientific medicine, almost any illness can be attributed to supernatural causation. Similarly, if there is little or no understanding of scientific geology, phenomena such as volcanic eruptions are likely to be explained in supernatural terms. Nevertheless, there is no such thing as a society completely lacking in practical techniques for dealing with the secular world. To quote Malinowski once more:

> A moment's reflection is sufficient to show that no art or craft however primitive could have been invented or maintained, no organized form of hunting, fishing, tilling, or search for food could be carried out without the careful observation of natural process and a firm belief in its regularity, without the power of reasoning and without confidence in the power of reason; that is, without the rudiments of science. (Malinowski 1948:1)

It must be realized that we are all much the same in this respect. There are no cultures in which scientific knowledge can explain everything, and there are no cultures in which secular techniques are always sufficient.

Suppose that you have an automobile and that you are equipped with the usual hazy idea of how an internal combustion engine works. Suppose that you get into the car one morning and it won't start. What do you do? In part, that depends on how much technical knowledge you have. You do the obvious things: kick the tires, lift the hood and peer inside, check the battery cables, look at the gas gauge. The car still won't start. Then what do you do? It is the situation that now becomes critical. How serious is it? Perhaps it is not all that important whether the car starts or not—you were just going to an anthropology class. But perhaps it *is* serious. Suppose you are a man whose wife is more than nine months pregnant and the labor pains are coming *every few seconds.* You have done everything you know how to do. The car *must* start. What do you do? Cross your fingers before you hit the starter again? Touch a lucky charm? Pray?

Take the problem of health. When you feel good, fine. If you get sick and go to the doctor and the doctor can fix you up, fine. You take the pills. But suppose that the doctor cannot help you. Suppose you discover that you have an incurable disease and will be dead in six months. Then what? Well, try another doctor, of course. But suppose that the diagnosis is the same: There is no "scientific" technique that can save you. Right about there, we all turn to the super-natural. There is nowhere else to go. We try "cures" that have been rejected by scientific medicine. We consult "faith healers" and join cults that promise deliverance. We pray to whatever gods we know.

From this perspective, it is worth remembering that in a "primitive" society almost any disease is potentially fatal. It is a grim situation where any cough, any fever, any feeling of discomfort can be a warning of death. The link between illness and supernatural beliefs is immensely strong. Every field anthropologist has had the experience of being besieged by desperate would-be patients. The people are grateful for anything, even an aspirin. Of course, the medicines are more or less supernatural to them — they don't know how they work, but they believe in their power. (This is a tough ethical problem for an anthropologist. Most of us are not medical doctors. We are not qualified to offer reliable medical advice. And yet we must do what we can. My own solution was to transport seriously ill people to a hospital clinic in a Land Rover.)

In one sense, we are profoundly unusual animals. All peoples ask the great unanswerable questions. Where did we come from? What is the purpose of life? What happens to us after we die? People not only ask these questions, they then proceed to answer the questions: The reason that you are here is that long ago a Great Turtle fished your island up from the bottom of the sea and carried the first woman and the first man to the island on its back; the purpose of life is to increase the solidarity of your clan; when you die, you become an ancestral spirit and live in the trees.

The supernatural supplies solutions to many problems, great and small. If you love her and she does not love you — or the other way around — there is always a spell you can use. (In our culture, we call this kind of magic *toothpaste* and *deodorant soap* and *hair styling*.) If the crops are failing and you must have rain, there is a rain-making ceremony available. If the animals you hunt are getting scarce, you can perform a fertility ritual to increase the herd. If you think your wigwam is haunted, there is a technique that will get rid of the ghost. If you are afraid of the darkness that lies beyond the fire, you don't have to worry: There are gods who look after such things, and they are on your side; or at least you *hope* they are on your side.

There, perhaps, is the key problem. Once you postulate the existence of the supernatural, how do you make sure that it is working *for* you rather than *against* you? In short, how do you deal with the supernatural?

Although supernatural phenomena are extremely diverse and complex, it is still useful to sort out two polar types. You can attempt to *coerce* the supernatural — force it to do your bidding. Technically, this is *magic*. You do the proper thing — say the secret word, burn the special plant, jump over a rabbit by the light of the full moon — and the supernatural *must* respond. It has no choice. It is very much like a scientific formula based on nonscientific principles. Just as you can put two chemicals in a test tube and apply heat and predict the results (the chemicals themselves have no say in the matter), you can get a sliver of your enemy's toenail, mix it with a mushroom, smash it with a rock, and wait for your rival to go lame. (It helps if your opponent knows that you have done all this, of course, and believes that it will have an effect. But that is another story, the story of how magic works.) The essence of magic is that it is a technique designed to make the supernatural do what you want it to do. Rub the bottle and out pops the spirit. Say the right words and the spirit must obey your commands. Conceptually, the spirit cannot say no.

The alternative is to *plead* with the supernatural. You ask the supernatural for help and do things that are designed to make the supernatural look favorably upon your request. In other words, you pray and offer sacrifices and perform ceremonies. Technically, this is *religion* rather than magic. Here, the supernatural is conceived of as having the power of choice, or the right of decision. You cannot force it—you can only *petition* it. Fundamentally, you are trying to stay on the good side of the gods.

William Howells, a distinguished physical anthropologist, wrote a delightful book called *The Heathens* (Howells 1948). The title, it must be noted, was chosen with tongue in cheek. The book has influenced my thinking on the subject for many years, and I have probably stolen from it shamelessly. Howells is responsible for the following example. In using magic, he says, you do the equivalent of going up to a supernatural slot machine, such as a machine that dispenses soft drinks or sandwiches. You drop your supernatural coin (the spell or whatnot) in one slot and out comes the supernatural sandwich (the favor) from the delivery mechanism. You can't *see* inside the machine, but you are satisfied that there are gears and levers and wheels in there and that the machine will always work the same way: Drop in the spell and out comes the supernatural gift. (If nothing comes out, you must adjust your spell or tinker with the machine.) In using the art of worship or religion, the procedure is different. You fill out an application in a standardized way (pray) and send it off to the proper authorities. Then you wait. The answer may be yes, no, or maybe, depending on how the gods feel about you at the time.

The polar concepts of magic and religion are only first approximations of the ways in which people try to cope with the supernatural. Clearly, there are magical ideas in religions and religious ideas in magical systems. Moreover, there are supernatural entities that can be neither manipulated nor petitioned. Nevertheless, the two concepts are often helpful in trying to understand why people sometimes proceed as they do.

RITES OF PASSAGE

In a very real sense, all human beings walk the same path. We are not so very different from one another after all. We are born, we grow up, we get married, we have children, we grow old, and we die. That may not be a particularly ecstatic way of viewing human existence, but it is undeniably a true one. Minor alterations are possible, of course. We don't *have* to get married and we don't *have* to produce children. But the vast majority of human beings do.

Everywhere in the world, people feel that these significant events — birth, adolescence, marriage, death — mark crisis points in the individual life cycle. In effect, they are transition points, times when a person stops being one thing and begins to be something else. They signal a change in status: from unborn to born, from youth to maturity, from unmarried to married, from living to nonliving. Transition points can be dangerous for the individual — you might get stuck between one status and another — and they also require some social advertising. The other people in the society must be made *aware* that a change in status has taken place. Therefore, a little supernatural oil is useful in easing the transition. It is a good time for some ritual and ceremony.

Rituals of this kind are a cultural universal. A culture may omit some of them — choose to emphasize one transition point rather than another — but no cultures ignore them all. Children are almost never just born, like a cow dropping a calf. There is generally a ceremony of some kind, either at the actual birth or shortly afterward when the child is named. There are almost always rituals at or around puberty. Girls are commonly isolated for a few days or even weeks at the time of their first menstruation. Often they go to live in a special house, eat only special foods, scratch themselves with sacred sticks, and so on. At the end of this time of isolation, there is a literal coming-out party. The girl takes a ceremonial bath, dresses in adult clothing, and is presented to the males as a woman eligible for marriage. When boys come of age, there are frequently elaborate initiations with all sorts of supernatural overtones. They may be circumcised or have teeth knocked out or have their bodies scarred with ritual markings, all the while being instructed in the lore of their culture. Marriages tend to be big social events everywhere, with all sorts of supernatural involvements. The transition to elderhood is very important in many societies, and accounts of supernatural rituals connected with death — when a person moves from this world to another, or becomes one with the ancestors — would fill a book much longer than this one.

These ceremonies which punctuate the significant transition points in the life cycles of individuals are called *rites of passage.* The term was coined by Arnold Van Gennep (1908), who pointed out that such rites always involve three stages: separation from the old group or relationship, transition, and incorporation into a new group or relationship. It should again be mentioned that the occasion for a rite of passage is determined by progress through the individual life cycle, but the social functions of the rites involve both the individual and the group within which the person lives.

RITES OF INTENSIFICATION

There is another sense in which it may be said that all human beings walk the same path. As we have discussed at length, all of us live in groups — we are members of groups ranging from families and associations to large communities.

A rite of passage involving the initiation of younger boys by older boys.

Just as there are crisis points or significant occasions in the life cycles of individuals, there are likewise recurrent transition points in the cycle of groups. They are times of change, frequently seasonally based, or periods of importance for the solidarity of the community. These occasions too tend to be marked by ceremonial observances. Earlier in this chapter, we discussed a ceremony of this kind—the Sun Dance. It was observed by the Plains Indians when the tribe reunited after the dispersal of the winter months. Chapple and Coon refer to such observances as *rites of intensification* (Chapple and Coon 1942:398–400). The term was chosen because it is characteristic of such ceremonies that interaction rates go up sharply. The people intensify their relationships with one another, thereby dramatizing the unity of the group.

   Rites of intensification can occur in any type of society. Among hunters and gatherers, they often take place when animals migrate or wild foods ripen. In tribal societies, planting and harvesting rituals are virtually universal. In state systems, rites of intensification frequently are tied in with the operations of the state's political structure—for example, an annual confirmation of the authority of the head of the state. Among the Aztecs of Mexico, because of the cycles imposed by their calendrical system, a new sacred fire was kindled in the chest of a sacrificial victim every 52 years. This was a time of great rejoicing—for everybody except the victim—because it symbolized a new lease on life, a sign that the world would continue through another cycle.

   I have sought to stress the idea that all peoples are much alike when it comes to the supernatural. We may believe in different things and express our beliefs in different ways, but the occasions and types of supernatural observances do not vary greatly between one society and another. Certainly, we will never get anywhere in understanding the phenomenon by assuming that "we" have been blessed with the power of clear thinking while "they" are hopelessly confused and don't know what they are doing.

It follows from this that our society too has its rites of passage. Just as the Plains Indians had their vision quests, we have our "coming of age" ceremonies. We too have our rituals at birth and marriage and death. Similarly, we also have our rites of intensification. Christmas is an obvious example, and so are Thanksgiving and New Year's Day. It is instructive to think of our ceremonies in this light. The supernatural aspects are too clear to require comment, and so are the ritual proclamations by government officials. But think how these observances do "draw us together," from the family level all the way up through the highest echelons of the state. How often we hear some variant of the idea, "If only this spirit of good will and togetherness could last all year long." Well, that's what it is all about. And it is interesting to note that interaction rates *do* go up—even symbolic interactions such as the exchanging of Christmas cards.

SUMMARY

Supernatural beliefs and practices are a cultural universal. There are no human societies that lack some kind of involvement with the supernatural. Supernatural concerns affect both the individual and the society. Among the Plains Indians, the vision quest by which a young man sought a guardian spirit is an example of a rite that primarily involved the individual. The ceremony of the Sun Dance—which also occurred among some of the Plains Indians—is an example of a group-oriented supernatural observance. After being divided into bands during the winter months, the tribes reunited and put on an elaborate ceremony that dramatized the values of the total society.

The anthropological approach to the supernatural demands that we make an active effort to understand the beliefs of others. Anthropologists make no attempt to divide supernatural systems into "good" ones or "bad" ones; nor do they take a position as anthropologists on the "truth" or "falsity" of any group's supernatural convictions.

Supernatural ideas may be as old as the human animal itself, but we have no real evidence on this point. The earliest evidence that we have for the existence of supernatural beliefs dates back to the Neanderthals of the Middle Paleolithic, some of whom lived as much as 100,000 years ago.

Human beings live not in one world, but in two. One is the world of the mundane and the practical in which we think we know what is going on and why. The other is the world of the strange, the unseen, and the unpredictable. It is this second world that we call the *supernatural*. Some scholars avoid making distinctions between the natural and the supernatural, arguing that the two tend to flow together and that the opposition between them is rooted in our own ways of thinking and speaking. Clifford Geertz represents this point of view, presenting "religion" as essentially just a symbolic interpretation of the sociocultural universe. However, the distinction between a secular realm and a nonsecular (or supernatural) orientation has a long history in anthropology. Among others, Robert Redfield, Emile Durkheim, Edward Norbeck, and Anthony F. C. Wallace have maintained that the concepts of natural and supernatural are both meaningful and useful.

As we live our lives there are some things that are known and understood and therefore can be handled without recourse to the supernatural. Other areas of living are mysterious; they have no obvious natural solutions, and that is where the supernatural comes in. Bronislaw Malinowski has argued that all cultures have a body of "empirical and rational knowledge," just as all cultures have a belief in "supernatural forces." Which system we use depends on the situation we find ourselves in. No society attempts to cope with life exclusively through supernatural techniques, and no society has been able to solve all problems through secular means.

Once you postulate the existence of the supernatural, the problem is making sure that it is working *for* you rather than *against* you. How do you get the supernatural on your side? Essentially, there are two main ways. You can attempt to coerce the supernatural, force it to do your bidding. Technically, this is *magic.* Alternatively, you can plead with the supernatural—ask it for assistance and do things that are designed to make the supernatural look favorably upon your request. Technically, this is *religion.*

In a very real sense, all human beings walk the same path. We are born, we grow up, we get married, we have children, we grow old, and we die. Everywhere in the world, people feel that these significant events—birth, adolescence, marriage, death—mark crisis points in the individual life cycle. Rituals that are designed to ease the individual across these areas of transition are called *rites of passage,* a term first used by Arnold Van Gennep.

Just as there are crisis points or significant occasions in the life cycles of individuals, there are also recurrent transition points in the cycles of groups. Planting and harvesting occasions are obvious examples. Ceremonies that occur at such times are called *rites of intensification,* a term coined by Chapple and Coon. The name refers to the fact that people intensify their relationships with one another during such ceremonial observances, thereby dramatizing the unity of the group.

References

Chapple, Eliot D., and Carleton S. Coon. 1942. *Principles of Anthropology.* New York: Holt, Rinehart and Winston.

Durkheim, Emile. 1915. *The Elementary Forms of the Religious Life,* trans. from the French by Joseph Ward Swain. London: Allen & Unwin.

Geertz, Clifford. 1965. "Religion as a Cultural System," in Michael Banton (ed.), *Anthropological Approaches to the Study of Religion.* London: Tavistock.

Howells, William. 1948. *The Heathens.* Garden City, N.Y.: Doubleday.

Malinowski, Bronislaw. 1948. *Magic, Science and Religion.* Glencoe, Ill.: Free Press.

Norbeck, Edward. 1961. *Religion in Primitive Society.* New York: Harper & Row.

Van Gennep, Arnold. 1908. *The Rites of Passage.* Chicago: University of Chicago Press, 1960. (The first date indicates the date of first publication.)

Wallace, Anthony F. C. 1966. *Religion: An Anthropological View.* New York: Random House.

Suggestions for Further Reading

Evans-Pritchard, E. E. 1956. *Nuer Religion.* Oxford: Clarendon Press. A classic study, based on years of experience, of the religion of an African people.

Firth, Raymond. 1940. *The Work of the Gods in Tikopia,* two vols. London: The London School of Economics and Political Science. A very detailed, eye-witness account of the ritual cycle of a people on a small island in the Pacific.

Geertz, Clifford. 1960. *The Religion of Java.* Glencoe, Ill.: Free Press. A rich study by an innovative scholar in the field of religion.

Lessa, William A., and Evon Z. Vogt (eds.). 1972. *Reader in Comparative Religion,* 3d ed. New York: Harper & Row. If you only read one book on the subject, this should be the one. Sharp and lively, it contains authoritative articles on the whole spectrum of supernatural activities.

Lowie, Robert H. 1954. *Indians of the Plains.* New York: McGraw-Hill. Contains good, brief accounts of both the vision quest and the Sun Dance.

Oliver, Symmes C. 1962. *Ecology and Cultural Continuity as Contributing Factors in the Social Organization of the Plains Indians.* University of California Publications in American Archeology and Ethnology 48(No. 1). Berkeley and Los Angeles: University of California Press. Discusses the relationship between the annual cycle of the bison and the patterns of concentration and dispersal of the Plains tribes; treats the Sun Dance as a rite of intensification.

Radcliffe-Brown, A. R. 1922. *The Andaman Islanders.* Cambridge, England: Cambridge University Press. Although by no means confined to a study of the supernatural, this is a classic social anthropological analysis of the relationship between ceremonial activities and the social structure.

Radin, Paul. 1937. *Primitive Religion.* New York: Dover. Not much read today, and that's a pity. Radin was an engaging writer, and this is often an insightful book. Particularly recommended for Radin's perceptive comments on how individuals differ in their receptiveness to supernatural ideas.

20

How to Do It: Supernatural Practitioners and Supernatural Concepts

All cultures, as we have seen, include a body of beliefs relating to the supernatural. This is another way of saying that all cultures postulate the existence of the supernatural, and therefore the participants in a culture act on the assumption that the supernatural exists. Whether or not the supernatural—or a supernatural since the idea takes a variety of forms—exists in actuality may be an important question, but for anthropological purposes it is not vital. If people believe that it exists and act as though it exists, that is enough. In any case, there is no method by which anthropology can establish the "truth" or objective reality of any particular supernatural system.

Similarly, it is not absolutely necessary to ask the perplexing question of *why* people feel the urgency of postulating the existence of a supernatural. One reason seems to be that it introduces an element of security in an uncertain world—it gives people at least an illusion that they have some say in matters that are beyond their secular knowledge and control. There are, however, other ways of looking at it. Be that as it may, once you assume the existence of a world of the supernatural, you have to come to terms with it in some manner. That is, you have to deal with it. In the preceding chapter, I discussed several common techniques for doing precisely that. However, techniques alone will not get the job done. Someone has to *use* the techniques.

In all societies, there are some supernatural tasks or observances that anyone can attend to, and there are other occasions that require the services of a supernatural specialist. If you wish to say a blessing before a meal or insert a good luck charm in your baseball glove, you do it yourself. If a Kamba wants to make an offering of food or beer to the family ancestors, that is what the man or woman does. On the other hand, some situations are more serious or need specialized skills. If a Kamba wishes to protect the beehives that are scattered over wide areas, particular spells are required. (You can't keep all your beehives under personal observation; the hives are placed in trees and the spells are supposed to "freeze" a would-be honey thief to the tree.) There are also supernatural devices — strings of sinew that are suspended on poles and placed at the entrances to cattle corrals — that are designed to protect the herds from disease or theft. This important business is not an occasion for a "do it yourselfer." You need the services of an expert, and you pay for the services rendered.

Everywhere there are persons who are thought to be more skilled than others in dealing with the supernatural. Whether by personality or training or both, some people have the knack or the authority to handle supernatural problems. If you are confronted with a situation that requires supernatural ability, you seek out the skilled practitioner — someone who has a good track record in that area. Fundamentally, it is no different than consulting any other kind of expert. If you want a canoe that will float, you go to a talented canoe maker. If your problem involves the supernatural, you go to someone who has specialized knowledge or ability.

There are a host of supernatural practitioners in human societies. Indeed, their number and variety are a sure index of how involved with supernatural considerations we are. There are fortune tellers and astrologers, diviners and weather magicians, ghost chasers and custodians of sacred tribal lore, gurus from Atlantis and paraders of reincarnation, sacrificial authorities and dispensers of love potions. Some of them are full-time specialists — they make their living at it — and some of them dip into supernatural waters as a sideline. But all of them have (or claim to have) special credentials for dealing with supernatural problems.

While their numbers may be legion, it is still possible to identify and isolate two major kinds of supernatural practitioners. Not *all* supernatural operatives will fit neatly into one or the other of these two categories, but the concepts they represent are virtually worldwide in their distribution, and in the great majority of human societies the categories are useful in understanding what supernatural experts do and how they do it.

The two major types of supernatural practitioners are the *shaman* and the *priest*. Note that these terms refer to categories of persons, not just to those individuals who happen to be so named in a particular culture. The word *shaman* is a Tungus word; the Tungus are reindeer herders in Siberia. Shamans were first identified among some of the Siberian peoples and across the Bering Strait among the Eskimos of the New World. Over the years, however, the term has been applied in a much broader sense. It includes both the shaman "proper" — the original shaman — and any other practitioner with similar characteristics. The same is true of the word *priest*. It has come to refer to a type of supernatural practitioner. Let us take a closer look at these two major categories.

THE SHAMAN

The shaman, as William Howells aptly put it, is a kind of lone wolf of the supernatural (Howells 1948:142). As people, shamans tend to be fascinating individuals, highly intelligent and articulate and often with a dash of razzle-dazzle about them. As supernatural practitioners, shamans usually have a set of distinguishing characteristics:

1. The shaman generally is a part-time operator. The shaman is a specialist, true enough, but the shaman does not as a rule work full time at being a shaman. Shamans go into action when they are called upon, and they are paid for their services; but the rest of the time they hunt or farm or work like anyone else in their society. (Shamans may be either male or female.)
2. The shaman almost always works alone. That is, there is no organized group of shamans. Each shaman operates as an individual, sometimes with an apprentice in tow. Other people may watch a shaman's performance, but the shaman is performing as an individual.
3. The shaman gets his or her power from a personal source. In other words, the basic reason why the shaman is thought to be effective in dealing with the supernatural is because of the personal qualities of the individual shaman. The shaman is felt to have a special ability, a gift. Shamans may be unstable psychologically and subject to "fits" or trances. They may have been marked from birth by some curious happening: a bump on the forehead, a strange sign in the sky, the call of a forest animal. (The Kamba say that a shaman is born with beans clutched in the hand.) Often, too, a shaman is a person who has "died" and come back to life. That is, we assume, the person has gone into a deep coma and recovered. It is believed that the person has visited the land of the dead and come back to tell the tale.

If these are the identifying characteristics of a shaman, what do shamans do? First and foremost, the shaman is a healer—a doctor. The shaman is the person who is referred to in popular parlance as a "medicine man" or a "witch doctor." In this connection, it must be noted at once that the shaman is *not* a witch. Rather, the shaman is the individual who *combats* the actions of witches. Shamans and witches are on opposite sides of the fence. As we have indicated, sickness in primitive societies (and in some not so primitive) usually involves the supernatural in some way. It may be believed that the supernatural is a direct causative factor: You become ill because the ancestors are angry or you have violated a tabu or a witch is after you. It may be believed that the supernatural is just a contributing factor: The disease may be "natural" enough, but the reason it happens to you instead of someone else is due to supernatural reasons. In either case, the reasoning is that if the illness has a supernatural dimension, then the treatment of the illness must also involve the supernatural.

That is what the shaman does. The shaman diagnoses the illness (figures out exactly what the supernatural involvement is) and then intercedes with the supernatural on the behalf of the patient. The shaman may use other remedies as well—splints for broken bones, concoctions of herbs—but the primary technique is a supernatural one. An important part of the shaman's job is simply to

A female Kamba shaman. She holds a special bow used to contact ancestral spirits.

convince the patient that something is being done for the sick person. There is a critical psychological aspect to almost all healing; you must believe in the power of the doctor.

When a shaman goes into action, the performance tends to be very dramatic. There are reasons for this. In the first place, it impresses the patient with the effort that is being made to effect a cure. In the second place, it can influence the fee that is charged. A tough case ought to be worth more than an easy one. The shaman is expected to put on a lively show—a fight with the unpleasant aspects of the supernatural—and people come to watch the performance much as we might attend a play.

There are tricks to the shaman's trade. They may employ ventriloquism, sleight of hand, or "speaking in tongues." A common gadget is a sucking tube, like an overgrown straw. A cut is made in the patient's flesh, the tube is inserted, and after considerable heaving and thrashing around the shaman "extracts" some substance from the body which is then shown to the patient. Very often, the shaman goes into a trance, contacts the supernatural, and then announces the "revealed" treatment to the patient. The essence of the thing is that the shaman must convince the patient (and the audience, if there is one) that it isn't just the shaman as a person that is offering a cure. The shaman is using his or her power to get the supernatural to intercede on the side of the patient. That in itself is potent medicine.

Even though the shaman may employ a variety of tricks to enhance the treatment—convince the patient that the cure will work—the shaman must believe in what he or she is doing. It is a great mistake to dismiss the shaman as a fraud and a fake. Shamans do achieve cures. They are not always successful, of course, but neither is any other kind of doctor. A shaman who consistently loses

A Bushman (San) shaman and his patient.

patients will not be a shaman for very long. The ultimate test of their faith, perhaps, is that when one shaman becomes ill the sick shaman will go to another shaman for treatment.

   To repeat, the shaman is primarily a doctor. What else the shaman does depends in large part on the sociocultural system involved. In hunting and gathering societies, the shaman is usually the only kind of supernatural practitioner there is. Therefore, the shaman may be called upon in a wide variety of situations. The shaman performs hunting magic, seeks to control the weather, divines the future, deals with ghosts, and does whatever else needs to be done in the supernatural realm. In tribes and states, where there are usually other types of persons engaged in supernatural activities, the role of the shaman tends to be both more restricted and more specialized. In such societies, the shaman is normally a doctor and nothing else, but the shamans often specialize in the sense that there will be particular shamans who are considered to be expert in dealing with specific kinds of disease.

THE PRIEST

The priest, unlike the shaman, usually does not work alone. The priest acts as one member of a group of priests, rather than as an individual. The priest is a specialist in the art of worship, and the source of the priest's power is not personal. The priest gains the ability to deal with the supernatural—and the authority to do so—from an association with an organized religious group. Once the priest is initiated into the group, or confirmed as a member of the group, the priest is by definition qualified to handle supernatural problems. The priest may, of course, have personal talents in this area, but the right to act as a priest does not derive from this personal ability. The right and the power come from the fact that the priest is a recognized member of an organized group. Priests may or may not be full-time specialists. In state-organized societies like the Aztecs of Mexico, they usually are. In tribal societies, such as that of the Zuni Indians of the Southwest, they often are part-time practitioners.

The existence of priests, with their sometimes extensive training and their affiliation with an organized group, implies several things. For one, it makes possible a more codified supernatural belief system than would otherwise be the case. If we define a myth as a sacred story, the myth—accounting for the origin of the state or the nature of the gods—becomes standardized and formalized. (For another view of myth, refer back to the discussion of Lévi-Strauss in Chapter 12.) With full-time specialists—or even part-time experts who share their knowledge with a group—the supernatural can get very complicated and detailed. In such a system there is a tendency toward dogma: a fixed belief system interpreted by experts rather than countless individual variations on some hazy basic themes. For another, it supplies the necessary personnel to conduct the annual round of public ceremonies and rituals for the community. Ceremonies of this kind can be elaborate and time consuming. With organized priests on the job, the people can be assured that the right rituals will be performed at the proper time.

As with magic and religion, it is not always possible to distinguish sharply between shamans and priests. The polar examples are clear enough, but there is some blurring in the middle ground. However, as a general rule a priest is not

A male Mundu Mue or shaman.

primarily a doctor. The roles of the shaman and the priest tend to be distinct. Often, the same person cannot hold both positions. The priest is a specialist in staying on the good side of the gods, in prayer and sacrifice and complex ceremonial activities. The shaman is essentially a healer.

Let us return to the Kamba of Kenya to illustrate the basic distinction. Among the Kamba, nearly every *utui* (''community'') has at least one *mundu mue*. The term literally means ''wise person,'' but the mundu mue is clearly a shaman. I have already referred to the Kamba belief that shamans are singled out at birth by being born with beans clutched in their hands. There are other ways to become a mundu mue; a person with inclinations in that direction can apprentice himself or herself to a practicing shaman to learn the required lore and techniques. Nevertheless, you either have the ability or you don't. The power is personal, and no amount of training can compensate you for an individual lack of talent.

The mundu mue can readily be recognized. They have special bows strung with wire and equipped with a gourd resonator. Males usually carry their special bows with them, even on a bus or a bicycle. Females as a rule keep their bows in their houses. Most of the time, the mundu mue works at an everyday job — farming or herding or making baskets or whatever. But when someone gets sick the mundu mue goes into action.

The Kamba believe that most medical problems have their roots in the supernatural; the primary cause of disease is witchcraft. The mundu mue takes a special stick and taps it against the wire string of the bow. This summons the

Kamba priests making offering at sacred tree.

ancestral spirits, who are then "questioned" by the mundu mue. Usually, the basic questions involve who is doing the "witching", and why and what particular methods are being employed. Armed with this information, the mundu mue — using other techniques, such as casting objects on an animal skin and "reading" the pattern — determines a course of treatment. This may involve a counterattack against the witch, a defensive spell against witchcraft, offerings to the ancestors, or special foods that are felt to be effective in such cases.

The shamans are sometimes quite specialized. One man I knew dealt only with respiratory problems. Another was particularly skilled in working with people who had difficulty in walking. A female mundu mue that I interviewed many times was an expert in treating women who were unable to get pregnant or who had problems with giving birth. The mundu mue herself was childless.

The Kamba have an age-graded society (see Chapter 18, pp. 313 – 314). A man advances into the senior age grade, that of the *utumia* ("elders"), by making a series of payments to the existing elders in his community. These payments consist of goats and cattle and beer, which are used to provide "a feast for the elders." Once a man becomes an elder, he has a very high status. He is entitled to carry a special staff and can sit in judgment on legal cases. That is as far as most men go. However, it is possible to make still more payments and move up to the highest notch of all. These additional payments of livestock and beer — which must be accepted by the group in question — confirm a man as not just an elder but a particular kind of elder. The man becomes *utumia wa ithembo* (an elder of the place of sacrifice). After a period of instruction, the man is in effect a priest. Each community has a place of sacrifice, usually a Sacred Tree. Once or twice a year, a ceremony is held at the Sacred Tree. A goat is strangled in a ritual way, the blood is collected in a special gourd and mixed with other substances, and the concoction is poured over the roots of the tree. At that time, prayers are offered for the well-being of the community. That is basically what the utumia wa ithembo do: They are the priests responsible for making the offerings at the Sacred Tree. The mundu mue (shaman) has nothing to do with this. Indeed, the mundu mue does not even attend the ceremony. Similarly, the priests have nothing to do with treating illness.

SOME ASPECTS OF THE SUPERNATURAL

Evolutionary theories of the development of supernatural systems have had a long history in anthropology and elsewhere. By and large, the various theories have in common the fact that they are not very convincing. At first glance, it is an attractive approach. If the idea of cultural evolution has merit—and if supernatural belief systems are a part of culture—then it should logically follow that supernatural systems have evolved with the rest of culture. Unfortunately, perhaps, the data have resisted the theories.

There are a few ideas along this line, however, that are worth considering. There does appear to be a trend away from all-purpose, part-time supernatural practitioners, such as shamans, and toward specialized, full-time practitioners, such as priests. (That is, to take the two ends of the cultural spectrum, you tend to find the shamans emphasized in hunting and gathering societies and priests the main focus of attention in state-organized societies.) With the development of priesthoods, there is a tendency toward more standardized and codified belief systems.

It may be that our conceptual tools are not adequate to do the job. More likely, supernatural beliefs are in the same kind of category as languages. We cannot arrange languages on a scale from "simple" to "complex" because no such distinctions exist or because the evidence bearing on the question has long since disappeared. All languages spoken today are complex. Similarly, all supernatural systems that we know about are complex. Certainly, it is far easier to demonstrate evolutionary change in technology—where we have the archeological evidence—and in those areas directly affected by technology, such as population densities and stability of residence. I would not dismiss all evolutionary approaches to the supernatural out of hand. Some of them, such as the system proposed by Robert N. Bellah (1964), merit further investigation. However, it is better, I think, to put the evolutionary schemes on the back burner in discussing the supernatural. There are many ideas that are frequently encountered in supernatural systems, and it is possible to identify some of the commoner ones without implying some sort of evolutionary sequence. Although we cannot discuss all of them, we can note a few concepts that have a wide distribution.

Witchcraft

Witches provide an intriguing test case of the "reality" of supernatural beliefs. Clearly, there are people who think they are witches and act as though they are witches. There are many documented cases in which witchcraft has had an effect on people. There are also many instances in which people who did not profess to be witches were accused of witchcraft. In a large number of diverse societies, people have been killed or otherwise punished for that reason. One of the commonest questions put to anthropologists is, "Do witches really exist?" There is no easy answer, particularly if you happen to have known a witch or two. Perhaps the best way to put it is to say that there are people who believe themselves to be witches and do things that supposedly produce supernatural effects. The real question is whether or not anything supernatural is actually involved. It can all be "explained" in psychological terms. If you believe in witchcraft and think a witch is after you, you are in trouble. There is nothing mysterious about that.

What is a witch? Anthropologically speaking, a witch is someone who is believed to have the supernatural power to do evil. Despite *The Wizard of Oz,* there are no "good" witches.

Witches can do harm either inadvertently or by intent. If you are a witch, you may injure people just by looking at them—the so-called evil eye. Or you may aim your witchcraft at a selected target. People tell stories about witches: They eat corpses, hold secret meetings by the light of a full moon, collect scraps of clothing or parings from fingernails or locks of hair, and direct their baleful supernatural influence toward their enemies. This is why the link between witchcraft and illness is so strong. If you become ill, it is always possible that a witch is responsible. Therefore, the shaman must combat the witch. (Sometimes, people get a bit cynical about the whole thing. One Kamba informant told me, "It takes two—a witch to make you sick and a doctor to cure you. They work together. It is a kind of business.")

What has survived of our own witchcraft beliefs tells us a good deal about witches. Our stock Halloween witch is an old woman who flies on a broomstick and has a cat as her "familiar." Although witches may be either male or female, they are commonly believed to have the power to fly—or at any rate to move from place to place at supernatural speeds. Kluckhohn describes Navaho witches as follows: "Witches are active primarily at night, roaming about at great speed in skins of wolf, coyote, and other animals" (Kluckhohn 1944:15). This suggests the other ingredient in standard witchcraft beliefs. Witches are closely identified with animals. It is believed that either they use animals (such as the cat) in their nefarious doings or they have the power to transform themselves into animals. This idea, of course, lies at the root of the vampire and werewolf stories that have such an enduring popular appeal.

It is easy enough to describe witches. It is much less easy to account for the very widespread existence of witchcraft beliefs. If they are found in so many cultures, they must have a cultural function that goes beyond simply providing materials for ghastly tales that are whispered around campfires. In short, what good is a witch? Why postulate their existence in the first place?

Evans-Pritchard, in a classic study of witchcraft among the Azande of Africa, has suggested that witchcraft is a way of explaining unfortunate events

(Evans-Pritchard 1937). When something goes wrong and there is no natural explanation, witchcraft enters the picture. It not only clarifies the inexplicable, but it also provides a way out of the difficulty: Get the witch. Many studies have shown that witchcraft accusations are correlated with social structure; in other words, who accuses whom of witchcraft depends on where the points of tension are in the social system (see Nadel 1952). It can be argued persuasively that witchcraft beliefs are most intense in situations in which people are crowded and cannot get away from one another.

Still, this does not entirely explain witchcraft. Perhaps its major function is to provide scapegoats for all the ills of a society. It enables people to fire off pent-up hostilities and discharge aggressions; it lets off "cultural steam." As Howells puts it,

> Under it as a heading, a tribe can gather and impute to witches
> a number of recognized evil desires and emotions, and so make the
> witches serve as a horrible example; witches are easy to believe
> in, and witchcraft can be hated communally, so that it makes a bond;
> and for these reasons and because it is beyond the pale it makes a
> safe shooting gallery in which to expend the floating hatred present in a
> group, which cannot be shot off in the group's own circle. (Howells
> 1948:127)

Of course, it is tough on the supposed witches: They are tormented and frequently killed. Sometimes the witchcraft accusations hit pretty close to home: Cowives in polygynous societies often hurl charges of witchcraft at one another. But if the social benefits of witchcraft keep a society from tearing itself to pieces, the cultural gains outweigh the cultural costs. That is at least a partial explanation of the function of witchcraft beliefs. Why the beliefs take the particular forms they do is a riddle that remains locked in the human mind.

Animism

Animism is simply a belief in supernatural spirits: the idea that some sort of supernatural essences live all around you, inhabiting springs or trees or animals. Basically, it is the notion that other things besides human beings have "souls" or supernatural counterparts. The first professional academic anthropologist, E. B. Tylor (see Chapter 11), argued that animism was the origin or first stage of religion. This is an idea that has long since been discarded, but even today we read occasional popular accounts that report blithely that the religion of some "primitive" society is animism. This is nonsense. Many peoples have animistic beliefs, but such beliefs are only part of their supernatural systems. Another anthropologist, R. R. Marrett, noted that there was a related concept that he termed *animatism*. This is the idea that inanimate objects — trees or rocks, for instance — are themselves capable of sentient feelings or emotions. If you believe that the spring near your camp is in a sense alive and that it will be made happy or unhappy by what you do to it, this is animatism.

A Kamba Kithitu keeper at work.

The distinction need not detain us long. If you figure that there is an evil spirit living in your bathtub, that is animism. If you believe that the bathtub *itself* is out to get you, that is animatism.

Tabus

A *tabu* is a supernatural prohibition. It tells you what *not* to do if you wish to avoid supernatural punishment. In Polynesia, where the idea of tabu was developed to an extraordinary degree, the concept was quite complex. However, the basic nature of a tabu is not difficult to grasp. A tabu is a way of forbidding things that are culturally unacceptable. It fences in certain aspects of behavior with a symbolic warning sign: If you do what you are not supposed to do, you will be punished by the supernatural. Although tabus may have many functions, the most obvious thing that they do is to maintain the existing social order. By underscoring what is forbidden, tabus direct people along the paths that are deemed right and proper.

Oaths and Ordeals

Oaths are a very common feature of supernatural systems. Oaths involve swearing—indeed, in English, we still call swear words *oaths*—but in a different sense from run-of-the-mill profanity. An oath is fundamentally an if-then statement with a supernatural clause. A standard oath takes the form: "If I am not telling the truth, then may the gods strike me dead!"

Oaths can get complicated and they sometimes involve special objects or apparatus. Earlier (see p. 17), I mentioned the Kamba use of the *kithitu*. The kithitu is a wrapped bundle or container (such as two shells fastened together) that contains secret ingredients. The kithitus are owned by selected individuals who are summoned by the elders in important legal cases. One of the disputants swears on the kithitu that his version of the case is correct. (Kamba women cannot swear on the kithitu.) The Kamba believe that if the man is telling the truth nothing will happen. If he is not, the power of the kithitu begins to kill. It does not affect the swearer himself but acts on his relatives — all the way out to clan kin. Swearing on the kithitu is not something that one does lightly. Moreover, if you are not telling the truth — and people usually know who is in the wrong in such cases — powerful social pressures are brought to bear to see that justice is done. All the miscreant has to do is admit the facts and make restitution. Then the kithitu keeper is authorized by the elders to perform a cleansing ceremony and the killing stops.

Ordeals are just what they sound like. They are tests or contests in which the outcome is believed to be determined by supernatural factors. In its simplest form, an ordeal is a literal contest between two rivals. It there is a dispute and it is not clear who is in the right, there is a ritual combat between the disputants. The idea is that the virtuous person will prevail with supernatural assistance. If you win, you are right. If you lose, you are wrong.

There can be tests administered to a single person. You can be ordered to walk through a fire or swim a difficult stretch of water. If the gods are with you, you will emerge not only unharmed but cleared of any charge that has been brought against you. If you are badly burned or if you sink like a stone, that is taken to be evidence that the supernatural has ruled against you. Obviously, faith plays a strong part in all this. If you believe in the correctness of your position, the odds are pretty good. If you are nervous and afraid because you know that you are in the wrong, you are nearly beaten before you start.

Sometimes, the ordeals are more involved. The Azande of Africa constitute a classic example (Evans-Pritchard 1937). They have a poison called *benge,* which is fed to chickens. The poison is unusual in that it kills some chickens and has no effect on others. When there is a serious question — is a particular person a witch or not — the problem is in effect "put to the chicken." A specialist gives benge to a chicken and then the supernatural is implored to kill the bird if the person is a witch or spare the bird if the person is innocent.

Other Supernatural Beings

Gods. These supernatural beings tend to be remote in several senses. They are remote in that they usually live fairly far away — up in the sky, on Mount Olympus, across the river in the Great Forest. They are also remote in that they keep their distance socially. Gods are usually named, and they are frequently rather specialized.

Howells suggests that gods can be divided into three major categories: creator gods, culture bringers, and departmental deities (Howells 1948:215). It is true that these categories will not cover them all, but the three basic types are encountered so frequently that they merit particular mention. A creator god is one who is believed to have created the world and everything in it. Oddly enough, perhaps, many peoples have a belief in a creator god but not much involvement with that god; the idea is that the creator god did the initial creating and then pretty much left things alone. A culture bringer (sometimes referred to as a culture hero) is a being with supernatural attributes who is felt to be responsible for introducing crucial elements of culture — a god who first brought fire or the idea of the state or the concept of agriculture. A departmental deity is a god who is in charge of a specific area of activity, such as the weather. A belief in a single god is *monotheism.* A belief in a variety of gods is *polytheism.*

Spirits. These beings are less remote than gods and a good deal more approachable. Spirits have limited powers; their authority is not as all-inclusive as that of the gods. Often, they are not named individually. In the previous chapter, we met the guardian spirit of the Plains Indians. Another familiar example would be the amiable spirit of the hearth. In actuality, spirits are almost infinitely diverse, and about the only generalization that can be made about them is that they are plentiful.

Souls and ghosts. A belief in souls is virtually a cultural universal. A soul is an invisible counterpart or essence or double of the body we see. (Many peoples believe that a person has more than one soul.) The most common belief is that the soul (or a soul) leaves the body when the body is asleep; dreams are said to represent the adventures of the wandering soul. In other words, the soul can have a kind of quasi-independent existence. The soul is also believed to leave the body at death. When the soul remains after the body has died, it is technically a ghost.

Ancestral spirits. These spirits were once people. They are like ghosts in that they do not go away after death. However, they are not really ghosts conceptually, the distinction being that ancestral spirits are *supposed* to remain in contact with the living and take an interest in their welfare. Ghosts tend to be troublesome and people wish that they would go away. Ancestral spirits are generally protective and people gain confidence from their presence; indeed, people try to entice them to remain in the vicinity (by offerings of food and by speaking their names) so that the ancestors can help them out. It gives a feeling of continuity to life to believe that your ancestors are still with you and looking after your interests.

REVITALIZATION MOVEMENTS

There is always a danger in dividing up supernatural practitioners and supernatural concepts into a series of more or less neat little categories. The danger is that we tend to lose sight of the rich tapestry of complete supernatural systems and tend to forget that such systems play vital roles not only in what people believe but in what they do. Supernatural systems are not inert, like so many lead weights. They are active ingredients in the culture process.

One of the best-documented examples of how supernatural systems operate in the area of culture change concerns *revitalization movements.* The term was first proposed by Anthony F. C. Wallace (1956). Revitalization movements typically appear in periods of cultural stress. A supernatural leader such as a prophet or a messiah comes forth and proclaims a novel version of a traditional religion — usually one that contains elements of both the "old" supernatural system and the "new" ideas that may be borrowed in contact situations or may come from within the "revitalized" culture itself. Wallace has suggested that the basic aim of revitalization movements is "to construct a more satisfying culture" (Wallace 1966:30). In other words, people who find themselves in a difficult and frustrating situation — such as cultural disintegration produced by the imposition of a dominant outside group; the colonial experience is a classic case in point — seek to restore meaning to their lives by creating an intense new supernatural structure. The revitalization movement is perceived as a way out of deep cultural trouble.

Revitalization movements have been most commonly reported from North America, Melanesia, and Africa, although they are by no means unknown in other areas. To illustrate a basic point, mention must be made of the Melanesian examples, which were generally referred to as "cargo cults" (Worsley 1957). The so-called cargo cults occurred after the island peoples had been oppressed and humiliated at the hands of the Europeans. The island peoples, understandably, were impressed by the power and the wealth of the Europeans, and they sought to adjust their cultures to get in on the winning side. In a typical cargo cult, a supernatural leader would go into a trance and announce some revelations. A great steamer (boat) was coming, and aboard it was a miraculous cargo. The ship was carrying the spirits of the dead ancestors, wonderful food, and rifles. (Note the characteristic combination of old and new features: ancestral spirits and rifles.) In order to obtain the cargo, the people were supposed to abandon many of their rituals and ceremonies; they were told to collect their ritual masks and other gear into piles and set them afire. At the same time, they were instructed to engage in new rituals: everything from mortuary feasts for the departed ancestors (an old element in their supernatural systems) to setting up flagpoles and sitting at European-style tables and making marks on paper — in effect, "signing for" the expected cargo. There is a terrible pathos about these events, for the basic point is all too obvious: In a literal sense, the cargo never comes. However, this does not mean that the revitalization effort was entirely futile. We will return to this idea after a more extended discussion of one of the most famous revitalization movements of them all.

As is often the case with such phenomena, it is difficult, if not impossible, to assign a precise date to the beginning of the movement known as the Ghost Dance. Nevertheless, since we must begin somewhere, let us start with a vision that was seen by a man named Wovoka on the first day of January in the year of 1889. Wovoka was a Paiute Indian in Nevada; he was also known as "Jack Wilson." (The latter name had been given to him by one David Wilson, a rancher for whom Wovoka worked. This point is significant because the Wilson family had given Wovoka some exposure to Christian theology.) The vision was a dramatic one. There was an eclipse of the sun, and "when the sun died," Wovoka, who had a fever at the time, became unconscious and had his vision. The vision was quite similar to an earlier one seen by a Paiute in 1870.

The Paiutes, like so many other American Indians at the time, were faced with the loss of their traditional lifeway. Wovoka's vision promised to save it —

and even improve it. In the vision, he was taken up into heaven and "saw God." He also saw all of the people who had died long ago engaged in their old-time activities in a pleasant land full of game. Wovoka was told to go back and tell his people to be good and love one another, work hard, tell the truth, and put away all practices having to do with traditional warfare. He was shown a dance and told to instruct the people in the new dance. This dance, it was said, would reunite the dead and the living. All would be happy and there would be no more sickness and trouble. The original vision was a nonviolent one. The idea was that "when the earth shakes at the coming of the new world" the Indians would not be harmed and the white Americans would simply disappear. To put it another way, the "good old days" would return, better than before.

The doctrine spread very rapidly, aided by Indians riding on trains. Wovoka became known as the "Indian Messiah." Many Indian tribes sent delegations to talk to Wovoka. As news of the vision spread, each tribe adapted the basic vision to its own needs and interests. When the movement reached the Teton Dakota (popularly known as "the Sioux") it took on threatening overtones. The Dakota version involved a return to the old ways and a return to traditional dress. The dancers wore buckskins when they could get them and otherwise donned so-called ghost shirts, which were made of cloth but cut and decorated in Indian style. The ghost shirts were believed to be bullet proof. The idea was that the dead warriors would come back to life again, and then anything might happen.

The Indians did not attack anyone. They just danced. However, the Indian agent at Pine Ridge (South Dakota) went into a panic and insisted that the army be called out. The War Department was reluctant, but eventually 3000 soldiers were sent to put down the "uprising." As luck would have it, eight troops—some 470 men—were from the Seventh Cavalry. That, of course, was Custer's old outfit, and it had been mainly the Teton Dakota along with the Cheyenne who had destroyed Custer and five troops of the Seventh Cavalry at the Little Big Horn in 1876.

The Indians, understandably, were nervous. Many of them, after the death of Sitting Bull at Standing Rock (who was shot by Indian police sent to arrest him), fled from the reservations. A group of Teton Dakota—about 340 people, including women and children—were rounded up at Wounded Knee Creek, some 20 miles from the Pine Ridge Agency. The Seventh Cavalry was responsible for "guarding" the camp, which flew a white flag.

As might have been predicted, there was trouble. The Indians had guns and felt that they were protected by their ghost shirts. The soldiers had long memories and itchy trigger fingers. A fight broke out, and the soldiers opened up with Hotchkiss guns which fired 50 shots a minute. Within minutes, over 200 Indian men, women, and children had been cut down. About 60 soldiers were killed or wounded.

Then the massacre began. With more than half their number dead or dying, the Indians tried to run away. The battle, if that is the right name for it, was over; but the killing continued. The fleeing Indians, most of whom were women and children, were pursued and butchered. Women with nursing infants were shot down as much as 2 miles from the scene of the battle.

The dead and wounded Indians were left where they fell. There was a heavy snowstorm. On New Year's Day, 1891, a detachment was sent out to bury them. There was no burial service. All the bodies were thrown into a long trench. Before earth was pitched into the trench, the corpses were stripped by whites seeking souvenirs. The most prized souvenirs, of course, were the ghost shirts.

In one sense, as we noted, the stories of many revitalization movements make for mournful reading: The cargo never comes, the warriors of a vanished past do not rejoin the living, and the ghost shirts prove to be all too vulnerable to bullets. However, there is often a happier perspective from which to view revitalization movements.

The slaughter at Wounded Knee Creek was by no means the end of the matter. Wounded Knee has become a powerful symbol for modern American Indians and has served as a rallying point in the drive to obtain basic political rights for the Indian peoples. It has been a crucial factor in uniting the American Indians against oppression.

In *New Lives for Old,* one of Margaret Mead's most insightful books, she describes what happened to the Manus of the Admiralty Islands (Mead 1956). There was a rather typical cargo cult movement (called "The Noise") in the region, and as usual the cargo did not come. But that was not the end of the story. The excitement and the organization of the cargo cult pulled a fragmented people together, and out of the ashes of the old movement a new vision appeared. A man named Paliau became disenchanted with cargo cults and organized a predominantly secular political plan among the Manus. Building on the existing organization and utilizing European and American models for political action, Paliau was largely responsible for the modern transformation of Manus society.

It should not be concluded, however, that supernatural systems are only effective when they can be translated into secular movements. Rather, it should be remembered that supernatural beliefs and practices do not exist in isolation; they are deeply embedded in the cultures of which they are one part. People everywhere are involved in the supernatural, trying to come to terms with a world that lies beyond the everyday and the commonplace. The supernatural provides one variety of answers to the problems and questions that confront all of us sooner or later. Opinions may differ about the quality of those answers, but the human animal has come a long way with the supernatural as one cultural dimension.

SUMMARY

In all societies, there are supernatural tasks or observances that anyone can attend to and others than require the services of a supernatural specialist. The two major kinds of supernatural practitioners are the shaman and the priest.

The *shaman* has three distinguishing characteristics: (1) he or she is usually a part-time operator, (2) who almost always works alone, and (3) whose power comes from a personal source. Primarily, the shaman is a healer or doctor. What else the shaman does depends on the type of society involved. In hunting and gathering societies, the shaman is apt to be the only supernatural practitioner and for this reason may be called upon to provide a variety of supernatural services. In tribes and states, the role of the shaman tends to be more restricted: the shaman is a doctor and nothing else.

The *priest* gains the ability to deal with the supernatural through an association with an organized religious group. The priest usually does not work alone. An expert in the art of worship, the priest may or may not be a full-time specialist. As a rule, the priest is not a doctor but is instead involved in prayer, sacrifice, and complex ceremonial activities.

Some supernatural concepts have a very wide distribution. *Witchcraft* is the belief that certain persons are endowed with the supernatural power to do evil. Frequently, illness is attributed to witchcraft. That is why shamans are sometimes referred to as "witch doctors" — it is the shaman's job to combat the witch and thus cure the disease. *Animism* is the belief that there are supernatural spirits living around you, in springs or trees or animals. It is the notion that other things besides human beings have "souls" or supernatural counterparts. *Animatism* is a related idea; its essence is that inanimate objects such as trees or rocks are themselves capable of sentient feelings and emotions. *Tabus* are supernatural prohibitions. They tell you what not to do if you wish to avoid supernatural punishment. *Oaths* involve swearing; they are "if-then" statements with a supernatural clause. *Ordeals* are tests or contests in which the outcome is believed to be determined by supernatural factors.

There are a host of supernatural beings. *Gods* are rather remote supernatural beings, remote in that they are believed to live in some distant place and tend to keep their distance socially. There are three major types of gods: creator gods, culture bringers, and departmental deities. A belief in a single god is *monotheism*. A belief in a variety of gods is *polytheism*.

Spirits are less remote than gods and more approachable. Their authority is more limited than that of gods. *Souls* and *ghosts* are very widespread concepts. A soul is an invisible counterpart or essence or double of the body we see. When the soul remains after the body has died, it is a ghost. *Ancestral spirits* are like ghosts in some ways, but they are supposed to remain in contact with the living and take an interest in their welfare.

One of the best examples of how supernatural systems operate in the area of culture change concerns *revitalization movements*. Such movements typically appear in periods of cultural stress. A supernatural leader comes forth and proclaims a novel version of a traditional religion. It is an attempt by troubled people to restore meaning to their lives by creating an intense new supernatural structure built out of both "old" and "new" elements. The *cargo cults* of Melanesia and the *Ghost Dance* of the American Indians were revitalization movements. Although such movements tend to fail in literal terms — the cargo never comes, the dead do not live again in a restored cultural world — they often provide the foundations that enable people to adapt to changing circumstances.

References

Bellah, Robert N. 1964. "Religious Evolution." *American Sociological Review* 29: 358–374.

Evans-Pritchard, E. E. 1937. *Witchcraft, Oracles and Magic among the Azande.* London: Oxford University Press.

Howells, William. 1948. *The Heathens.* Garden City, N. Y.: Doubleday.

Kluckhohn, Clyde. 1944. *Navaho Witchcraft.* Papers of the Peabody Museum of American Archeology and Ethnology, Harvard University 22(2). Cambridge, Mass.

Mead, Margaret. 1956. *New Lives for Old.* New York: Morrow.

Nadel, S. F. 1952. "Witchcraft in Four African Societies: An Essay in Comparison." *American Anthropologist* 54:18–29.

Wallace, Anthony F. C. 1956. "Revitalization Movements." *American Anthropologist* 58: 264–281.

———. 1966. *Religion: An Anthropological View.* New York: Random House.

Worsley, Peter. 1957. *The Trumpet Shall Sound: A Study of "Cargo" Cults in Melanesia.* London: Macgibbon and Kee.

Suggestions for Further Reading

Note: The reader is urged to refer to the works cited and recommended at the end of the previous chapter. In addition, the following two books should be of interest.

Frazer, Sir James G. 1958. *The Golden Bough,* abridged 1 vol. ed. New York: Macmillan. First published in 12 volumes between 1911 and 1915, this is a classic collection of supernatural phenomena. Old fashioned as it may be, it is an eminently readable book and a veritable goldmine of information.

Mooney, James. 1896. *The Ghost-Dance Religion and the Sioux Outbreak of 1890.* Fourteenth Annual Report of the Bureau of American Ethnology, part 2. See also the revised edition by Anthony F. C. Wallace, which contains some new material. The title is the same. 1965. University of Chicago Press. This is another classic, and the best single source on the Ghost Dance. Mooney interviewed the surviving participants in the Ghost Dance, including Wovoka himself, and he danced in ghost dances. In short, he knew what he was talking about. His few errors are corrected in the Wallace edition.

21

Culture Change

     In a sense, it is a truism to say that culture changes. Yet it is surprising how deeply most of us resist the reality of culture change. Within our own culture—the culture that we know best, whoever "we" are and whatever "our" culture happens to be—we experience frustration, anxiety, and disappointment when the familiar social universe that produced us becomes transformed before our very eyes. It is rather like playing in a game when the rules keep changing in the midst of the action.

     When we think about other cultures, particularly so-called primitive ones, there is a tendency to regard them as being somehow fixed, static, and inert. The image that comes to mind is that they are living fossils, existing in pristine isolation in some distant never-never land. The proverbial "outside observer" arrives on the scene, describes a "traditional" lifeway that supposedly has endured since the beginning of time, and preserves it for posterity like a stuffed bird. Thus, we speak glibly of fierce Comanches raiding into Mexico, remote Eskimos chewing blubber and harpooning seals, and the Kamba as an isolated tribe somewhere in Africa. We do this when we know perfectly well—as anthropologists, or simply as people who have some knowledge of the modern world—that the Comanches have not raided anyone for a century and are among the best educated of all American Indians, that the Eskimos have rifles and snowmobiles and are more affected by the Alaskan pipeline and radar stations than they are by sea mammals, and that the Kamba are actively engaged in the politics of the nation of Kenya.

     The myth of the totally changeless and completely isolated primitive culture is precisely that—a myth. All cultures undergo some modifications through time; the only culture that is fixed forever in a frozen pattern is a dead one. All

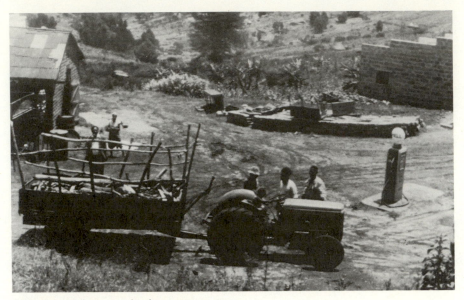

A Kamba child tries out his first tractor.

human societies have contact — peaceful or otherwise — with other human societies. It is true that circumstances can bring about temporary periods of relative isolation; there was one group of polar Eskimos who reportedly believed themselves to be the only people in the world, and the Andamanese were separated from other groups long enough so that they had no knowledge of how to make fires — they had to carry the embers with them when they moved. But these were exceptional situations. Long-distance travel was not easy in the Arctic, and the Andamanese, as we have seen, lived on rather remote islands in the Bay of Bengal. For most human societies most of the time, interaction with other groups is the name of the game. And all peoples have had at least some contact with others. After all, the Eskimos did not originate in the Arctic, and the Andamanese did not appear on their islands by a process of spontaneous combustion.

There is another point here that is frequently overlooked. With the exception of cultures reconstructed by archeologists, all of the documented societies on this earth are societies that flourished after the major cultural transformations of the Neolithic. There were no anthropologists in the Paleolithic, and no written records. It is a sobering thought to realize that we have not a single eye-witness account of any true Paleolithic lifeway — and those lifeways were the ones that nourished us for the vast majority of the time we have been on this planet. The ethnographic record that we have is of what happened after one of the most dramatic cultural changes of all time. To be sure, hunting and gathering cultures are not yet quite extinct, but the surviving ones have been profoundly affected by the development of new kinds of cultures. Hunters and gatherers were forced into marginal areas that nobody else wanted; people who once dominated the earth were converted into refugees. The other characters who crowd the rich chronicle of human existence — the horticultural tribes and pastoral nomads, the

Eskimos turn out for the whale hunt in snowmobiles.

city-dwellers and the rural peasants, the states and kingdoms and empires—are all recent arrivals on the cultural scene.

At the beginning of this chapter, I mentioned the frustration many people feel when their culture changes its shape within the span of a single lifetime. We can see the evidences of this all around us—in the so-called generation gap, in the nostalgia for the "good old days," in the confusion of coping with different standards of morality and competing "life-styles." The frustration is understandable. It is a difficult thing to learn one set of cultural rules and expectations only to discover that they are no longer applicable. Indeed, since the specific content of any cultural system is always learned, it is even possible that a culture will not work if it changes too fast. There must be someone to learn *from,* and much of the orientation of any culture is inculcated in childhood.

Of course, a culture does not change totally overnight, unless it is destroyed, and there is continuity as well as change in the culture process. It is doubtless true that we tend to exaggerate the degree to which "our" culture has changed, and the reason for this is not hard to see. Relatively minor changes can hit us deeply on an emotional level simply because they are happening to *us* as opposed to being charted by some neutral observer.

Nevertheless, the feeling that "everything is moving too fast" is not just an illusion, and it is not merely an aberration of one particular culture. Whether or not "things" are really moving too fast may be a matter of opinion, but it is a fact that the *rate* of culture change is increasing with every passing year. Cultures have always changed, but they have not always changed as rapidly as they are now doing. As far as one can judge from the archeological record, there were spans of time that could be measured in terms of tens of thousands of years when the changes between one human generation and another were very slight.

Even within the brief period covered by written records and anthropological field investigations, there were many societies in which the future was believed to be essentially an extension of past experience: People expected that their lives would be basically similar to those of their parents or even of their distant ancestors.

That cultural world is gone, or nearly so. We may lament its passing or we may welcome the new challenges we face. In either case, that cultural condition is unlikely to return. In some respects, the situation in which we find ourselves is unique in human experience. Cultural processes that seemed at least moderately intelligible even 50 years ago have become bewildering in their speed and complexity. The study of culture change is no longer a minor academic specialization—it is an urgent worldwide problem.

It would be idle to pretend that we have solutions to all of the questions posed by the explosive increases in the rates of culture change. It is not only that there are no easy answers, but also that in some areas we as yet have no answers at all.

Still, there are three major questions that can be explored in the search toward understanding the problems we face. First, what are the known basic mechanisms or processes of culture change? What ideas or explanatory frameworks can we use in clarifying the dynamics of cultural development? Second, how adequate are these principles when we attempt to apply them to the modern world? Third, what are the implications of modern cultural transformations for anthropology itself? Can a field of study that was shaped by one set of historical circumstances continue to make meaningful contributions in a drastically different situation?

Before proceeding directly to these questions, a brief detour will be useful. Let us look at a specific research project to provide a background for many of the problems we will be discussing.

THE KALAHARI RESEARCH GROUP

In 1963, Richard B. Lee and Irven DeVore went to Africa to begin a field investigation of the Bushman people who are now known as the San. (*San* simply means "aborigines," but many scholars feel that it is a more respectful term of reference than *Bushmen.*) The San are the true old settlers of Southern Africa; they have been there much longer than either their Bantu-speaking African neighbors or the white populations of South Africa. Traditionally, the San were a hunting and gathering people, and as of 1976 a significant fraction of them—about 5 percent—were still following that ancient lifeway (Lee 1976:8). They are primarily located in the Kalahari Desert region of Botswana and Namibia. The Republic of South Africa is situated immediately to the south of this area.

The Bushmen had been studied before (most notably by Laurence and Lorna Marshall, who began their work in 1951), but the increasing recognition of the vital importance of hunting and gathering societies in the evolution of mankind stimulated the further research of DeVore and Lee. Although their research

San hunters stalking giraffe.

strategies were quite sophisticated, it seems fair to say that at first their intentions were relatively uncomplicated: They wanted to try to find out as much as they could about how hunters and gatherers actually lived. The work was eminently successful, providing new insights on the hunting and gathering way of life. It led to a symposium in 1966 that brought together specialists on hunting and gathering societies from all over the world; this in turn resulted in a landmark book, *Man the Hunter,* which had a profound impact on anthropological thinking (Lee and DeVore 1968).

If they had stopped at that point, Lee and DeVore would have contributed a solid enough piece of anthropological research: They would have substantially enriched our knowledge of surviving hunting and gathering societies. They had not found an intact and unchanged Paleolithic lifeway, of course; the San were smoking tobacco (a plant of New World origin), trading with their neighbors for metal knives and arrow points, and even sometimes working for wages for nearby cattle keepers. However, they had been able to study a kind of society that resembled ancient human lifeways in many respects. They had learned a great deal about the intricate adjustment that the San had made to a near-desert environment: their careful utilization of water resources, their seasonal gathering of nutritious wild roots and melons and nuts, their effective arrow poisons that enhanced the chances for a kill, their detailed understanding of the behavior of animals and birds, their sharing ethic which ensured that there would be enough food for their small populations, their camp movements that enabled them to exploit the possibilities of very limited environmental opportunities.

Sharing the meat from the kill.

But like most really good studies, this one raised as many new questions as it answered old ones. Some of the questions were aimed at a more complete understanding of the San way of life. What child-rearing practices did the people follow? How many children did women have? What was the average life expectancy? How healthy were the people? How adequate was their diet? What was their folklore like? What were the genetic effects of small-scale breeding populations?

Some of the questions were more troubling. What was happening to these people? What were their lives going to be like in the next generation? How were they being influenced by the outside world? If their way of life was coming to an end after so many thousands of years, what should the anthropologists do about it? Should they just chart the extinction of a people, or did their human and scientific responsibilities call for something more than that?

All of this was more than any two anthropologists could handle on their own. The Kalahari Research Group expanded to include medical doctors and specialists in fields ranging from population genetics to archeology. The work continued in various phases, and valuable work it was. For instance, it was established that the San have low blood pressures and low cholesterol levels and are remarkably free of degenerative heart disease. In addition, it was discovered that fertility rates were lower than in settled farming populations. However, other kinds of findings were more pertinent to the general problem of culture change.

Mathias G. Guenther investigated the San known as the "Farm San" in western Botswana. These were people who had been exposed to a lifeway far removed from that of hunters and gatherers; some of them were third and fourth generation farm laborers participating in the cash economy of non-San populations. Significantly, Guenther entitled his report *From Hunters to Squatters*.

These San had worked for European settlers for a long time. In the old days, the relationship between the two peoples had been far from ideal but not particularly harsh: The San had admired some aspects of the European way of life, and the Europeans had treated the San with a kind of paternalism that preserved social distance but admitted a concern for their well-being. This changed in time with the appearance of new Europeans who were intent on making a profit out of cattle ranching. The new Europeans preferred to hire other Bantu-speaking Africans who were more "educated" and "reliable." San laborers found themselves the victims of antiquated racial ideas, looked down upon by both Europeans and other Africans. When they could find work at all, they were paid less than half the wages given to other Africans. The San were barely tolerated on land that had once been their own.

The Farm San have carved out a niche for themselves, if that is the word for it, in this new society: the bottom rung of the social ladder, below the Europeans and below the other African peoples. It is not a happy picture. The Farm San tend to be "unemployed, underfed, and overcrowded on land that does not belong to them" (Guenther 1976:129).

As an oppressed people, the Farm San are searching for symbols of identity and hope. In traditional San culture, the healers often went into trances to communicate with the world of the spirits; here, the "trance dancers" have become the core of a religious movement that permits the people to voice their frustrations and express their feelings of unity or "Sanness." There are the beginnings of political awareness, but the Farm San are a changed people. Gone is the egalitarian emphasis so characteristic of hunters and gatherers: These people actively pursue—to the extent that they can—wealth and social status through the acquisition of cattle and money. They even look down on the "wild" San as "stupid."

The hunting and gathering San of an area called Dobe were the most isolated group that DeVore and Lee could find when they started their study. As Lee puts it:

> When we first arrived at Dobe in October 1963, the area had no stores or schools and only intermittent contact with the outside world. A government truck would come out about once a month, but its main concern was the Bantu-speaking cattle people and not the San themselves. At that time, the San planted no crops and kept no domesticated animals except for the dog. The majority of the people lived mainly by hunting and gathering. (Lee 1976:18)

Lee and DeVore soon learned that appearances could be misleading; the Dobe San were not as untouched as they had seemed. Many of the men had some experience in herding cattle for the Bantu-speaking Africans, and they had even tried planting crops from time to time.

As the work continued, the winds of change blew over the Dobe San with unexpected force. There was a voter registration drive in 1964, and in 1965 the San voted in their first election. They became citizens of the new Republic of Botswana in 1966. The border between Botswana and Namibia was fenced and patrolled, restricting the movements of the people. A trading store was built in the Dobe area, and by 1967–1968 trucks were arriving at a rate of one per week. This made emigration much easier, and some of the young San men went off to work in the gold mines of South Africa.

The San began to buy cattle and goats and donkeys; by 1973 many of them were living more as pastoralists than as hunters and gatherers. Crops were planted in wet years and then abandoned in dry years. In 1973, a primary school was opened at Dobe. New laws were introduced in Botswana, many of them dealing with questions of land ownership. Land was no longer open to all; areas were surveyed and fenced. This was a situation that was a far cry from the free-ranging requirements of a hunting and gathering society.

Lee states:

> Our research has found that many San communities *want* to maintain their identity while at the same time move forward economically. But they lack the means in terms of capital, education, and expert advice to take the necessary steps. Information on similar changes from other parts of the world is also lacking. Given their motivation, how can the San people close the gap between their aspirations and the means to fulfill them? (Lee 1976:p. 21).

Indeed, who *are* the San in today's rapidly changing world? Are they the Farm San who have been pushed off their land? Are they the surviving hunters and gatherers? Are they gold miners and cattle keepers and farmers? And how can they be helped? What are their real options, given the existence of a sympathetic Botswana government? What can anthropologists do to assist them?

Quite apart from the light they shed on problems of culture change, the San pose new questions for anthropology. It is no longer enough just to "study" a people and let it go at that.

The Kalahari Research Group has not resolved these thorny questions, but it has made a start. One member of the project, Megan Biesele, began by doing folklore studies and wound up serving as a kind of liaison between the San and the government of Botswana. A nonprofit organization, the Kalahari Peoples' Fund, has been founded in an effort to understand the development problems facing the San and other peoples like them and to provide expert assistance in the years ahead. The Kalahari Research Group has turned over royalties from its publications to the fund. Perhaps the dedication of the most recent book by Lee and DeVore tells the story best. It reads: *To future generations of San in a Free Africa.*

THE PROCESSES OF CULTURE CHANGE

My purpose in telling something of the story of the San was not simply to publicize the plight of these people, important though that is, and certainly not to suggest that anthropologists have all the answers to problems of this kind. The predicament of the San is unique only in terms of its specific circumstances; all over the world there are human populations faced with roughly similar dilemmas of cultural transformation. Anthropology is in a position to provide some guidelines toward understanding these phenomena, but no anthropologist would claim that we know everything that we need to know.

What *do* anthropologists know about culture change? The first point to remember, as we have already stressed, is that cultures have always changed to some degree. Change is a fundamental characteristic of cultural systems. Even though it may be possible at any given point in time to "freeze" a culture for purposes of analysis — which is in part what the functionalists tried to do, as was discussed in Chapter 11 — cultures in the real world do not stand still. In times past, one human generation may have been very similar to the one that preceded it, but it was not identical. Therefore, it is not the fact of culture change that is something new under the sun but only the rapidity of it.

At first glance, it would seem to be obvious that innovation (the creation of new ideas) is the key to what makes cultures change. Somebody dreams up something original, and as though by magic the culture is transformed. This is not a totally nonsensical notion, and it would be foolhardy to deny that innovation is indeed possible. However, anthropologists have had remarkably little to say about innovation except in the realm of technology, and even there they have tended to trace the courses of technological developments rather than to explain them. I suspect that this lack of attention to innovation is soundly based: Innovation does occur, but in itself it does little to account for what happens in culture change.

New ideas do not spring from a vacuum; they are conditioned by what has gone before, they are shaped by cultural constraints, their acceptance or rejection is situationally determined, and they tend to be recombinations of preexisting elements. Beyond this, the trouble with viewing innovation as the root cause of culture change is that it assumes that every culture is an isolate, a little cell of ideas with impervious walls around it. In fact, the more isolated a culture is, the fewer "innovations" it seems to produce. Moreover, complete isolation is not the norm for human societies and never has been.

It is *interaction* that seems to supply the fundamental impetus for culture change: interaction between one culture and another, and interaction between a cultural system and the ecological situation in which it exists. (These are not mutually exclusive categories, by the way. It makes a difference who your neighbors are in any ecological situation, and the ecological situation can influence who interacts with whom.)

While not denying the possibility of internal culture change — change that originates within a particular culture and is for a time confined to that culture—most anthropologists believe that the dynamics of culture change are best understood in a broader context. The four concepts that have been most utilized in the anthropological study of culture change can be summarized under the headings of diffusion, acculturation, adaptation, and evolution.

Diffusion

One of the differences between culture change and biological change is that specific cultural elements are learned rather than inherited genetically. One consequence of this, apart from the greater flexibility that is characteristic of the culture process, is that cultural traits or elements can spread from one human society to another without genetic interchange between the groups involved. In other words, parts of cultures—whether they are small discrete cultural products or large clusters of ideas—can be borrowed by other cultures.

Diffusion is the process by which aspects of culture spread from one society to another. The term is generally employed to refer to situations in which the cultural borrowing is not forced. That is, if one society conquers another and imposes an alien system of government, this would not be regarded as diffusion. If the Comanche witnessed the Kiowa Sun Dance and admired it and decided to put on a Sun Dance of their own—which they did—this would be an example of the diffusion of the Sun Dance from the Kiowa to the Comanche.

In our discussion of the San, we noted that the hunting and gathering San smoked tobacco and used metal for their knives and arrow points. It is diffusion that makes this possible. The tobacco plant is indigenous to the New World; it was first domesticated by the American Indians. Tobacco was carried to Europe by the Spanish and later by the English. From Europe, directly and indirectly, the custom of smoking tobacco was introduced into Africa by the Spanish, the Portuguese, and Arab traders. Eventually it found its way to the San, who accepted it as an integral part of their way of life. (Maize—the plant we call corn—has a similar history. When I worked with the Kamba of Kenya, maize was their most important crop. The Kamba believed that they had "always" grown maize, but maize too originated with the American Indians.) The traditional San had no smiths and no knowledge of metallurgy. However, ironworking is very old in Africa and was partially responsible for the spread of the Bantu-speaking Africans. The San simply waited until they came into contact with the Bantu and then traded for the metal they desired. Diffusion is no trivial matter. Some diffusion can be minor, of course, as when we find an Eskimo drinking a coke, but diffusion can also alter cultures in very significant ways.

The people we know as the Navaho Indians came down from the north into the American Southwest somewhere around A.D. 1000. When they arrived, they were hunters and gatherers. They soon launched their careers as what Ruth Underhill has termed "some of the outstanding learners among American Indians" (Underhill 1953:226). They picked up agriculture from the Pueblo Indians. They even borrowed the Pueblo system of clan organization. They acquired sheep from the Spanish. They took over the Pueblo loom and weaving techniques. They learned how to work silver from the Spanish, and they adopted

Navaho weavers.

clothing styles and materials from both the Spanish and the Pueblos.

There is no more familiar sight to tourists in the Southwest than a Navaho woman weaving a blanket or rug. The rugs themselves are handsome additions to many city homes, and they increase in value every year. Few people realize the history of diffusion that lies behind every rug or blanket. From the clothing of the weaver to the sheep that yields the wool to the loom itself: All came together in Navaho culture through diffusion.

The Plains Indians offer an even more dramatic example. The historic Plains Indians were mounted warriors and hunters; the picture of the Plains Indian on horseback charging into a bison (buffalo) herd has become a stereotype for all American Indians. And yet that lifeway was very recent. If white settlers had expanded into the Plains a few centuries earlier, they would have encountered no mounted Plains Indians. They would not have existed.

The horse evolved in the New World, but it became extinct in the New World about 8000 years ago. The native American horse was sometimes killed and eaten by Indians, but it was never domesticated. The horse was reintroduced into the New World by Cortez, who landed in Mexico in 1519 with 400 men and 16 horses—11 stallions and 5 mares. Without the horse, the Spanish conquest of Mexico might very well have failed.

In 1598, Spanish colonists came to New Mexico. They brought horses and sheep and goats with them. After a long period of exploitation, the Pueblo Indians revolted against the Spanish in 1680 and drove them out of New Mexico. The Spanish left in a hurry and stayed away for 12 years. The horses were left behind, and large herds of mustangs were there for the taking.

Horses spread from group to group. The Comanche got their first horses in 1690, although horses were not common among the Comanche for some years after that. The Comanche became what many army officers called the finest light cavalry in the world—and they also became shrewd horse traders. In general, the spread of horses on the American Plains was from south (where the Comanche were) to north. A northern Plains tribe like the Teton Dakota—the "Sioux"—did not acquire horses until 1775.

It goes without saying that the horse profoundly changed the cultures of the Plains peoples. It is one thing to hunt bison on horseback and quite another thing to do it on foot. The horse triggered a cultural explosion on the Plains, affecting almost every aspect of the daily lives of the Plains Indians.

There is another kind of explosion that can be triggered by diffusion, and that is an information explosion. The spread of the battery-powered transistor radio in the modern world has brought about changes that stagger the imagination. There are few places left on earth where there are no transistor radios—and people listen and learn.

Acculturation

Acculturation is the process that occurs when there is prolonged and intimate contact between two or more cultures. It is like diffusion in some ways—it involves the spread of cultural elements from one culture to another—but it is different in terms of the situation in which it takes place.

At one time, acculturation studies tended to focus on contact situations in which one population was dominant in a political sense over another. The classic example of this was colonialism. Indigenous peoples who were ruled by foreign powers gradually absorbed the ideas and the customs of the dominant group. Thus, in those parts of Africa colonized by the British, we find the Africans drinking tea, driving on the left side of the road, speaking English, and playing rugby. A somewhat similar situation developed among the North American Indians. By the time most anthropologists arrived on the scene, they found many Indians playing baseball, driving pickup trucks, and wearing blue jeans.

The San who went to work in the South African gold mines or the San who worked for generations in European households in Botswana may be said to be acculturated: Their lifeways have changed as a result of long-continued contact with an "outside" culture. It might be noted that revitalization movements, which we discussed in the preceding chapter, are a product of acculturation. For the Farm San, the "trance dancers" represent the beginnings of such a movement.

In recent years, it has become apparent that acculturation can occur in any situation of prolonged culture contact; one culture does not have to be "dominant" over another. It has also become obvious that acculturation is a two-way street. Much of the culture flow may be in one direction, but there are crosscurrents that go the other way. One need only contrast modern Mexico and Spain to appreciate the truth of this. Mexico is by no means just a "transplanted Spain." When the Spanish conquered Mexico, the Indian cultures did not simply disappear. There is much that is Indian in Mexico today, ranging from art styles to supernatural beliefs and practices. (A fusion of religious beliefs and practices from different origins is referred to as religious syncretism.)

Cultures are not pristine isolates that are somehow "contaminated" by alien ideas. Rather, culture contact and the resultant culture change are fundamental cultural processes. It should not be forgotten that there are many peoples who *want* to change — it is not always a case of having change forced upon them. We saw an example of this in the preceding chapter in connection with Margaret Mead's study of the Manus of the Admiralty Islands (Mead 1956). It is not at all unusual in the world today to encounter populations ranging from hunters and gatherers to peasant farmers who have glimpsed what they regard as a "better" life. Indeed, this is much of what many so-called development programs are all about. People want to retain their identity and the valued portions of traditional lifeways, but they also want the advantages of new ways of doing things. In large part, this is due to the alternatives that have been opened up to them by the process of acculturation.

Adaptation

All living things must adapt to the environments in which they exist; the alternative is extinction. In the broadest possible sense, *adaptation* is adjustment — designing a life form that can cope efficiently with environmental circumstances. Other animals are capable of learning and can modify their lifeways in this manner to some degree, but for most animals the primary mode of adaptation is biological. There is nothing wrong with this — it works — but it is very slow. One great advantage that the human animal has is that its major adaptive technique is cultural. This gives our lifeways a potential flexibility that is without equal on this planet. Although we are by no means free of biological constraints, we do not have to wait for genetics to do the job. We can learn new solutions to changing problems of survival.

Cultural ecology, which is the study of the interrelationships between cultural systems and their environmental settings, was discussed at length in Chapter 12. Indeed, it is a viewpoint that has permeated this book. I remind you of two points: Culture affects the environment as well as the other way around, and the environment includes other competing human societies.

Let us think back to the San. Here we have a people who have existed for thousands of years as hunters and gatherers in a near-desert environment. (The San were once more widely distributed than they are at present, and not all of them lived under semiarid conditions. Some of them did, however, and those are the ones who survived long enough to be studied.) You and I would perish in the Kalahari unless we had food and water and medical supplies sent in to us. It is not an easy place in which to live. But the San have not only managed to get by but have done very well. They are not starving, they have water when they need it, and they are a healthy population. It is their culture that has made this possible, an adaptation that is intricately attuned to the requirements of a difficult land. From their ostrich shell water containers to their richly detailed knowledge of the plant and animal resources available to them, they have worked out a lifeway that is both stable and rewarding. Their very system of values, with its emphasis on sharing, is bound up with their ecological situation.

It is not hard to see how and why cultures adapt. Survival is a stern taskmaster. The problem is in understanding that adaptation is a process of *change*. When we view a society like the San—or any other human society at one given moment in time—the tendency is to emphasize the stability that results from adaptation. A complex cultural adjustment to a particular set of ecological circumstances is a beautifully balanced thing, but the ecological situation is never static—it only looks that way. When the ecological picture is altered, the cultural adaptation must change to deal with the changing "environment." That is what is happening to the San. There are cattle herders moving into their hunting ranges. There are new land laws that restrict their seasonal movements. There are roads, trucks, schools, and cash economies that have transformed the social universe of the San. Whatever adaptation they make, it will involve fundamental changes in their lifeway.

There are other kinds of changes that can modify an ecological situation. Suppose that the horse had not been reintroduced into the American Plains. Back in the terminal Pleistocene—some 20,000 to 10,000 years ago—the Plains were very different from what they were like in historic times. It was wetter then, and the area was swarming with animals: several species of bison (including one much larger than the historic bison), wild horses, camels, ground sloths, and mammoths. People lived there then, surviving as foot hunters with spears. As the Plains grew more arid, most of the larger mammals disappeared. At the beginning of the historic period, only the small form of bison survived. The Plains peoples had to change, even if the horse had not reappeared on the scene. You cannot hunt mammoths when there are no mammoths.

This is a process that has been repeated countless times in human history and prehistory. Climates change, animals move, ice sheets flow over the terrain, crops fail, and epidemics sweep the earth. The situation that a culture must adapt to is not something that is fixed and eternal. Therefore, in the long run, adaptation has to involve change. It is a dynamic process and not an emblem that can be hoisted in triumph on some chosen date.

Cultural Evolution

As we discussed in Chapters 11 and 12, the first anthropologists—people like Lewis Henry Morgan and E. B. Tylor—operated within the theoretical framework of cultural evolution. Although many of the specific ideas of the evolutionists came under attack by Franz Boas and his followers, and despite the fact that anthropology for a time was oriented in nonevolutionary directions, the concept of cultural evolution staged a comeback under the leadership of anthropologists such as V. Gordon Childe and Leslie A. White. There were sound reasons for the revival of interest in cultural evolution, and paramount among the reasons was the fact that the cultural record does show a demonstrable modification and development through time.

As long as we focus our study on one great cultural abstraction, the culture of humankind, the facts are not open to serious dispute. There *is* a known temporal sequence of culture types. First came the hunters and gatherers, living in a kind of society that persisted literally for millions of years. Then, beginning only some 10,000 years ago, new tribal societies appeared based on farming and the herding of domesticated animals. After that, datable in terms of the archeological and the historical record, came the rise of states, the development of urban life, the industrial revolution, and all of the other changes that have profoundly affected the modern world. Stripped of its theoretical underpinnings, that is what general cultural evolution is all about—a known sequence of cultural types, each one different in some respects from its predecessor in time.

It is true that viewing the cultural record from the lofty perspective of an abstraction like "the" culture of mankind does violence to the particular adaptations undergone by specific human cultures; certainly not each and every culture has exhibited such a neat sequence. It is also true that not even its most ardent advocate would maintain that the concept of cultural evolution can explain everything about the development of culture.

Still, a theory does not have to "explain" everything. No theory ever does that, and it is enough if a theoretical framework simply increases our understanding of certain kinds of phenomena. And there is a further question that is worth asking: Bearing in mind the relatively brief span of time since the Neolithic changes transformed the Paleolithic world, in what direction do we seem to be headed? What does the future hold for the few surviving groups of hunters and gatherers? Will tribal farmers and pastoralists always be with us, or are they being absorbed into nation-states? There was a very long period in our prehistory when all human cultures were essentially of the same type: They were all hunters and gatherers, although there were certainly individual differences between them. There may again come a time when just one type of cultural system prevails—the industrialized nation-state, or whatever replaces it.

This is a gloomy thought for any anthropologist who treasures cultural diversity. It is a prospect that should give pause to all of us. Cultural uniformity is not only disheartening but also dangerous: We cannot possibly know what situations we may have to deal with in the future; and the more different cultures we have, the greater is our flexibility.

I do not believe that cultural sameness is inevitable. However, I am aware of my own likes and dislikes: We all have a tendency to see what we want to see. And there is no denying that "modernization" by whatever name is sweeping over the world at an ever accelerating rate.

Consider what is happening to the San. Viewed from the perspective of cultural evolution, this is a society being called upon to perform an almost unthinkable feat: It is moving from a hunting and gathering base to the threshold of an industrial society within a couple of generations. It has even been exposed to cattle herding and farming along the way. In other words, it has had to cope with *all* of the major economic developments of more than a million years of cultural

A tribesman in New Guinea *(upper left)* confronts an airplane. An African *(upper right)* in traditional clothing gets off a bus in Nairobi. *Bottom,* a scene in Japan.

evolution — and to do this within a century or so. The wonder is that the San culture has survived at all.

Certainly, the rapidly increasing rate of culture change has produced a strain in all cultural systems. The San have faced this problem in a particularly acute form, but they are not alone. All human cultures, including the one in which we happen to live, are experiencing a rapidity of change that has no real precedent in the human experience.

The Adequacy of Anthropological Explanations

It seems to me that the processes of culture change that we have been discussing do serve to illuminate both what has happened in the past and what is happening in the present. The analytical tools that have been worked out in the examination of a variety of cultural systems can contribute to an understanding of the modern world.

At the same time, it is apparent that anthropology does not have all the answers. We need new conceptual frameworks in order to handle the information explosion and the almost instantaneous communications that characterize the world in which we live. We need to know far more about the problems of planned or directed culture change. We need a way to come to grips with what is perhaps the cardinal fact about the modern world — the almost total interdependence of all people everywhere.

While recognizing that anthropology too must grow and develop, it would be folly to dismiss the contributions of anthropology as having no meaning in the world of today. Rather, we must learn to apply the lessons of anthropology wisely.

It cannot be stressed too often that it is not the fact of culture change that is new, but only the *rate* of culture change. One of the lessons that anthropology has to teach is that of perspective. As Melville J. Herskovits pointed out over a quarter of a century ago:

> There are few cultures where the elders do not register disapproval of the departures of the young from the traditions of an earlier generation, or where the young people do not voice their resentment at the restraints imposed on them, as they deviate in some respect from certain forms of behavior approved by the older people. "When we were young," goes the complaint of the elders, whether in literate or nonliterate societies, "things were different. Our generation knew how to respect old people, how to behave correctly, how to worship the gods properly. Today everything is changed. The young are unwilling to follow and to learn." (Herskovits 1951:479–480)

The Impact on Anthropology

Anthropology was formed at a particular time and within a specific cultural tradition. It was a product of the Western world, and it was shaped in the crucible of exploration, conquest, and colonialism. However much anthropologists may regret the fact, anthropology had its inception in the same intellectual climate that dispatched missionaries all over the world to bring "civilization" to supposedly unenlightened "savages."

It is not my intention to condemn all missionary activities, which have themselves changed through time. Certainly, many missionaries sacrificed a great deal to do what they believed to be right, and some of them made valuable contributions to the peoples among whom they worked. I simply want to point out the underlying assumption of the period: *We* were sending out representatives to *them,* and the message that was carried was that we were "right" and they were "wrong" — or at least ignorant.

Anthropology was not guilty of such blatant ethnocentrism. Nevertheless, anthropology was not untouched by the attitudes of the time. There is a certain provincialism and even arrogance attached to the traditional anthropological enterprise. To put it baldly, one went out into "the field" to study "the natives" and then reported back to "science" the results of the research.

Insensitivity characterized a good deal of early anthropological investigation, and some of the reports do not make pleasant reading today. It is a fact that must be faced, but I do not think that it requires brooding about "guilt" or indulging in a disciplinary orgy of self-flagellation. It amounts to a recognition that the anthropologists were human beings and were not immune from cultural conditioning. (The same holds true for modern anthropologists, a point that is sometimes forgotten.) To the extent that they freed themselves from many of the prejudices and insular ideas of their cultures, they merit our respect. After all, they were speaking up for the values of other cultures and the rights of powerless peoples long before it was either fashionable or comfortable to do so.

That insensitivity — *we* study *them* — was perhaps understandable in a different world, and it can be argued that the information that was obtained can transcend some of the attitudes that produced it. However, that point of view will not work — and should not work — in the world of today and the world of tomorrow.

There are no "natives" who are "out there" patiently waiting to be "studied" — unless we are all natives and *out there* is also *right here.* This is a world of human beings who are following lifeways that have become increasingly intertangled. Many peoples resent being "investigated" when they receive no resultant benefits except an increase in scientific knowledge: They view it as a form of exploitation. Vine Deloria, an American Indian lawyer, expressed this idea in his popular book, *Custer Died for Your Sins: An Indian Manifesto* (Deloria, 1969). It is not necessary to agree with everything Deloria says in order to appreciate his indignation.

There is an increasing awareness by anthropologists that they have a moral responsibility to assist the peoples with whom they work. The Kalahari Peoples' Fund, established by anthropologists to help the San, is an example of this sort of undertaking. There is also a growing conviction that anthropologists should participate in projects that the people want, such as programs of planned development, rather than concentrate exclusively on problems that happen to be of interest to anthropologists.

There are real dangers here that should not be minimized. Ultimately, scientific knowledge is of value to all humanity, and there can be no science without some degree of objectivity. It is sometimes a thin line to tread between participation and mindless advocacy. Certainly, the solution is not to abandon the quest for a scientific understanding of the human animal. Once we realize that we are all in the same boat—one people, one world—science is one of the firmest hopes that we have.

Perhaps the anthropologist John A. Price put it best when he wrote:

One dilemma of the scientist is that the development of science requires disinterested objectivity while society cries out for personal involvement in humane solutions. The answer seems to be that we must try to do both simultaneously; we must try to create a humanistic science. (Price 1978:viii)

SUMMARY

There is nothing new about the fact of culture change. Cultures have always changed through time, and the idea of the totally isolated and static "primitive" culture is a myth. What is novel about the modern world is the *rate* of culture change. Cultures are now undergoing change with a rapidity that is probably unique in human experience.

The San ("Bushmen") of the Kalahari in Southern Africa provide an illustration of the kinds of changes that are taking place and also show the impact of this changing world on anthropology. Traditional hunters and gatherers, the San are now having to cope with farming, cattle herding, wage work, alienation from the land, and incorporation within the nation of Botswana. The Kalahari Research Group began by studying the hunting and gathering lifeway and eventually found itself involved in communicating the needs of the San to the government of Botswana and establishing the Kalahari Peoples' Fund to assist the San in the difficult transitions they are making.

By and large, anthropology interprets culture change primarily as an interaction process. The four concepts that have been employed most extensively are diffusion, acculturation, adaptation, and evolution. *Diffusion* is the process by which cultural elements spread from one culture to another; it is cultural borrowing when the cultures concerned remain largely separate from each other. When cultures are in prolonged and intimate contact with one another, as for example in a colonial situation, the process by which one culture acquires the characteristics of the other is referred to as *acculturation*. *Adaptation* involves the adjustment of a cultural system to its total ecological environment. When the ecological situation changes, the effective adaptation must also change. *Cultural evolution* in its most general sense refers to the growth and development of culture through time: the changes that have occurred as the human animal has moved from local groups of hunters and gatherers through tribal farmers and herders to industrialized states.

Anthropology, too, has changed. It is going through a period of self-examination in which new kinds of questions are being asked. What is the responsibility of the anthropologist to the peoples being studied? Should anthropologists work on the problems of concern to the peoples themselves? To what degree should anthropologists become actively involved in situations of culture change? Scientific understanding of human beings and their lifeways requires some degree of objectivity and in the long run will benefit all humanity. The solution is not to abandon scientific investigation but rather to develop a more humane and sensitive science that is in tune with the times.

References

Deloria, Vine, Jr. 1969. *Custer Died for Your Sins: An Indian Manifesto.* New York: Macmillan.

Guenther, Mathias G. 1976. "From Hunters to Squatters: Social and Cultural Change among the Farm San of Ghanzi, Botswana," in Richard B. Lee and Irven DeVore (eds.), *Kalahari Hunter-Gatherers.* Cambridge, Mass.: Harvard University Press.

Herskovits, Melville J. 1951. *Man and His Works.* New York: Knopf.

Lee, Richard B. 1976. "Introduction," in Richard B. Lee and Irven DeVore (eds.), *Kalahari Hunter-Gatherers.* Cambridge, Mass.: Harvard University Press.

Lee, Richard B., and Irven DeVore (eds.). 1968. *Man the Hunter.* Chicago: Aldine.

Mead, Margaret. 1956. *New Lives for Old.* New York: Morrow.

Price, John A. 1978. *Native Studies: American and Canadian Indians.* Toronto: McGraw-Hill Ryerson.

Underhill, Ruth M. 1953. *Red Man's America.* University of Chicago Press.

Suggestions for Further Reading

Adams, Richard N. 1975. *Energy and Structure: A Theory of Social Power.* Austin: University of Texas Press. Heavily theoretical, this is of considerable interest as an attempt by an anthropologist to formulate methodological tools adequate for dealing with today's world.

Beals, Ralph. 1953. "Acculturation," in A. L. Kroeber (ed.), *Anthropology Today.* Chicago: University of Chicago Press. Somewhat dated, this remains a lucid statement of the problem. It is permeated with the sound judgement that is characteristic of Beals's work.

Cohen, Yehudi A. (ed.). 1974. *Man in Adaptation: The Cultural Present,* 2d ed. Chicago: Aldine. A collection of generally excellent essays on cultural adaptation. The subjects range from hunters and gatherers to industrialism.

Foster, George M. 1973. *Traditional Societies and Technological Change,* 2d ed. New York: Harper & Row. The title pretty well tells the story. A thoughtful analysis of the problem.

Hymes, Dell (ed.). 1972. *Reinventing Anthropology.* New York: Random House. Controversial is the word for this book, but it is a stimulating series of articles that effectively reveal the ferment and the questions that characterize today's anthropology.

Lee, Richard B., and Irven DeVore (eds.). 1976. *Kalahari Hunter-Gatherers.* Cambridge, Mass.: Harvard University Press. Several selections from this book were cited previously, but the entire book merits careful reading by anyone interested in the San.

Spier, Leslie. 1921. *The Sun Dance of the Plains Indians: Its Development and Diffusion.* American Museum of Natural History, Anthropological Papers 16 (Part 7). A bit on the specialized side, this remains a classic study of what diffusion is and how it works.

Steward, Julian H. 1955. *Theory of Culture Change,* Urbana: University of Illinois Press. The seminal papers of a pioneering figure in the study of culture change.

Thomas, Elizabeth Marshall. 1959. *The Harmless People.* New York: Knopf. A perfect gem of a book. It communicates the flavor of life with the San and provides a graphic picture of what will be lost when this lifeway vanishes.

Weaver, Thomas (ed.). 1973. *To See Ourselves: Anthropology and Modern Social Issues.* Glenview, Ill.: Scott, Foresman. A diverse collection of articles on a variety of topics ranging from anthropological ethics to the nature of poverty. It poses some difficult questions and is well worth examining.

Epilogue: Over the Hill or Over the Horizon?

We have come a very long way — from savannah apes to an animal concerned with souls and witches, from hand axes to nuclear bombs, from an ephemeral local group of hunters and gatherers to industrialized states and crowded cities. By most standards, we have been extraordinarily successful animals: successful to the point where our very existence threatens all other major life forms on this planet.

We know where we have been, at least in general terms. It is only natural to wonder where we are going; that is the kind of animal we are. We do not really know, and it is idle to pretend that we do. The problem is not fundamentally different from assembling a group of australopithecines a million or so years ago and asking them for their views on the future. They could not possibly have imagined the modern world, let alone predicted it. We do have the advantage of hindsight. We have learned a few things, but for all our computers and strings of numbers, we still tend to see the future in terms of the present. We can extrapolate from what we know, just as the australopithecines might have dreamed up a kind of super hunting and gathering culture. What we cannot anticipate with clarity are the quantum leaps that may change the whole context of human life. We can project from the known, but by definition we cannot predict the unknown.

Our current problems are grimly obvious: overpopulation, an unequal sharing of the world's resources, the lingering disease of racism, a frightful capacity for self-destruction. But perhaps our major problem is more subtle. We suffer from what can only be called a crisis of confidence, a kind of fashionable despair about the human animal itself.

It is worth looking back, now and again. We all see through the lenses of

The universe around us — stars beyond stars.

our own cultures, but as a species we have survived numberless situations when the odds were seemingly against us. We are here, after all. By any reasonable standards, we are tough and resourceful animals. We may or may not be admirable — that depends on who or what is doing the evaluating — but we are not frail and helpless animals who are likely to collapse at the first hint of adversity.

We may not make it, of course. There are no evolutionary guarantees. We may blow ourselves to bits or be consumed by the poisons of our hatreds. In time, we will probably be replaced. It takes a kind of arrogance to believe that we are the final perfected end products of evolution. However, we have several millions of years behind us. We may have many millions of years ahead of us. We will not endure forever, but even the "failed" dinosaurs managed to exist for more than 100 million years. It is not mere chauvinism to imagine that we might do as well as the dinosaurs. Indeed, as mammals and as primates we have certain advantages.

No, the problem is not that we are doomed by some sort of genetic predestination or by perpetual, lethal cultural influences. We have the capacity to adapt, to change, and to grow. The problem is that we must learn to survive long enough to reach our full potential, whatever that may be, and that our individual lives — each in its moment of time — must be worth the living.

In the long run, if we fail it will be because we failed to understand ourselves. That is the basic reason why anthropology is so critically important. Anthropology has no monopoly on the scientific investigation of the human animal — and anthropology itself will be transformed in the years to come — but the

The chimpanzee, Ham, *(upper left)* after a 420-mile test ride in the Mercury space capsule. *Upper right,* liftoff for Apollo II. One of the greatest adventures begins. *Bottom,* the first men on the moon.

The Earth — one world after all — as photographed from the moon.

problems with which anthropology is concerned are the problems that have to be solved.

So long as we remain human, we will be animals and mammals and primates. There can be no substitute for finding out as much as we can about what is built into the human animal. Whatever is innate in human behavior, we cannot begin to cope with it until we know for certain what it is.

So long as we remain human, we will be culture-bearing animals. There can be no substitute for finding out as much as we can about the possibilities and the limitations of culture.

Culture is an adaptational mechanism that has enabled us to spread into virtually every ecological niche on this planet. It will take us further.

In my judgment, we are living through a time of profound significance for the human animal. And I must say that we are doing it with a truly astounding lack of awareness. Anthropologists have been as guilty of this as anyone else. It is rather as though we were witnesses to the Neolithic revolution and responded with an ignorant shrug of indifference.

I think that there will come a time when future anthropologists — whatever names they go by and whatever they call their science — will classify *all* of us as ''primitive'' people. We are primitive because we live when the human race was confined to one planet in one solar system. We are primitive because our knowledge about ourselves is both tentative and fragmentary. We are primitive in the literal sense of the term: We are living at the beginning of the human experience.

The universe in which we find ourselves is vast beyond our comprehension. We live on a tiny island in an immense sea that washes a billion shores. There are billions of stars in our galaxy and billions of galaxies beyond our own. Our little sun is just an average star, and it is probable that stars with planetary systems are the rule rather than the exception. Even if we restrict our imaginations to planets similar to our own, the probable numbers are staggering.

If it does nothing else, anthropology should communicate some degree of perspective. Think of it. Here we are, all of us, huddled on our little island. We have only begun to poke our toes into the universe sea that surrounds us. We are living through an event that will dwarf the discovery of the New World and eclipse the cultural transformations of the Neolithic. And we are doing it for the most part with our eyes tightly closed and our minds shut.

Either we are alone in this universe of galaxy beyond galaxy, which would be incredible, or we are not alone, which is probable. Either way, the problems and prospects before us are limitless. Of course there are problems. There will be problems as long as we are human. But the problems are not insoluble. We have encountered problems before. They were never solved by throwing in the towel on the eve of the great adventure. They were solved by knowledge, understanding, effort, and compassion. If problems defeated us, we would have nothing at all to worry about. We would not be here.

We cannot know what the effects will be of living our lives in a new dimension. But there is one fact that is frequently overlooked when we try to imagine what the furure might be like. We *know* that there is one world in this solar system that is made to order for the human animal.

It is called Earth.

There is room here for many lifeways. The Earth of tomorrow need not be the Earth of today. It does not have to be a plastic anthill smothered in a uniform culture. It will be technologically possible—and the record shows that we have a considerable aptitude for dealing with technological problems—to move manufacturing centers, scientific laboratories, and urban complexes into satellites beyond the Earth. There are whole worlds within the solar system that are packed with resources and possibilities. There is a star—the sun—that can provide energy on a scale greater than any we have ever known.

We could have a green Earth again, an Earth free of pollution, an Earth that could be the setting for a thousand experimental lifeways. We could have an Earth on which we recognized our identity as a species, an Earth where racism and mad wars of self-destruction could not exist. We could have an Earth where other animals—our partners in the terrestrial drama of evolution—could have some living space again.

I am not suggesting that this is necessarily the vision of anthropology. Many of my colleagues do not share my views. I have even been accused of being an unreconstructed optimist, among other things.

I do not pretend that there is anything inevitable about the future I have outlined. (Remember the salt shaker!) I am aware of my own biases, cultural and otherwise. I know that other people have other dreams.

I do suggest, however, that this could be *one* possible future for mankind. As far as I am concerned, that is the essential point. Whatever your opinions may be, the *possibilities* for both continuity and change are there.

We are very young. It may be healthy to know our limitations, but it is foolish to scoff at our potential. The discovery of humanity is not something that is over and finished. The discovery has yet to be made.

Note: Many of these ideas were discussed in my paper, *Two Horizons of Man,* presented at the 73rd Annual Meeting of the American Anthropological Association in Mexico City, November 1974. They are also discussed in a commentary called "Afterthoughts," which is included in my book, *The Edge of Forever: Classic Anthropological Science Fiction Stories.* 1971. Los Angeles: Sherbourne Press.

Glossary

A

Absolute dating. A dating technique that gives a date in terms of specific years.

Acculturation. The process of culture change that occurs when two cultures come into prolonged and intimate contact with each other.

Acephalous society. Literally, without a head. A type of tribe that has no overall chief or leader.

Adaptation. The process by which a population adjusts itself to its total environment.

Affinal links. Relationships based on marriage.

Age grade. A group that forms primarily on the basis of relative age. A person moves from one age grade to another as an individual.

Age set. A group that forms primarily on the basis of relative age. A person advances from one age set to another as a member of a group that remains together.

Agriculture. Sophisticated farming that utilizes plows, irrigation, or other advanced techniques.

Anthropoidea. The suborder of the primates that includes monkeys, apes, and hominids.

Anthropology. The scientific or systematic study of human beings and their close relatives, living or extinct.

Ape. A member of the pongid family of the primates. Living apes include the chimpanzee, the gorilla, the orangutan, and the gibbon.

Applied anthropology. The attempt to utilize anthropological data or techniques in the solution of modern social problems.

Arboreal. Tree-dwelling.

Archeology. The branch of cultural anthropology that primarily studies prehistory by means of the excavation and analysis of the material remains of former cultures.

Artifact. A material object such as a tool or a weapon made by hominids and rarely by other primates.

Association. A human group based on special characteristics or interests.

Australopithecine. An extinct form of hominid characterized by upright posture and relatively small cranial capacity.

B

Band. A human territorial group that occurs in two primary contexts: a fairly stable local group in a hunting and gathering society or a subdivision of a tribal society that has some degree of independence. May also be called a local group.

Bilateral descent. Reckoning kinship equally through both parents or both sides of the family.

Bipedalism. Walking upright on two legs.

Bound morpheme. A part of a word that carries meaning but cannot function alone. Prefixes and suffixes are examples of bound morphemes.

Brachiation. A form of locomotion that involves swinging hand over hand through the trees.

Bride price. A payment made by a man's family to the family of the bride at or before the time of marriage. Also known as bridewealth payments.

C

Carbon 14. See radiocarbon dating.

Carnivorous. Meat-eating.

Caste. An endogamous, hierarchically ranked social group.

Catarrhine. A type of nose in which the nostrils face downward. The term is commonly used to refer to Old World Monkeys.

Ceboidea. The New World monkeys.

Cercopithecoidea. The Old World monkeys.

Chiefdom. A type of tribal society that has a paramount leader capable of coordinating social action.

Civilization. A type of culture usually characterized by urban centers, state systems, and writing.

Clan. A named, exogamous, unilineal descent group, the members of which cannot actually trace their ancestry back to a real person. Often associated with totemism.

Class. A social grouping composed of persons who share similar economic status and life-style. Classes are frequently ranked within a society.

Consanguineal links. Relationship based on descent.

Cranial capacity. The volume of the cranial vault of the skull, which gives an approximation of the size of the brain.

Cro Magnon. A population representing the earliest known modern human beings.

Cross cousin. Children of siblings of the opposite sex.

Cultural borrowing. See Diffusion.

Cultural ecology. The study of the dynamic interrelationships between sociocultural systems and the total environments within which they exist.

Cultural evolution. The theory that cultures have developed in a sequence of types through time.

Cultural relativism. The idea that cultures can only be interpreted in terms of their own values. In simplistic form, the idea that all cultures are equally "good," since there are no culture-free standards of judgment.

Cultural universal. Something that is found in all cultures everywhere.

Culture. The design for living or way of life characteristic of a hominid society. The specifics of culture are always learned.

D

Diachronic. A time-oriented approach to the study of culture. Historical studies and evolutionary studies are diachronic.

Diffusion. The process by which cultural elements spread from one culture to another. Sometimes referred to as cultural borrowing.

Dryopithecus. An extinct form of primitive anthropoid dating from Miocene times that may have been ancestral both to living apes and hominids.

E

Ecology. The study of the interrelationships between living organisms and their environment.

Ego. The designated point of reference on a kinship chart.

Enculturation. The process by which a person learns a culture.

Endogamy. The rule or custom by which a person marries within a specified group.

Ethnocentrism. The attitude that a person's own culture can serve as the standard for evaluating other cultures.

Ethnographic present. Discussing a society as it was at the time it was studied by anthropologists.

Ethnography. A descriptive account of a single human society or culture.

Ethnology. The branch of cultural anthropology that deals with interpretations or comparisons of ethnographic data.

Ethology. The study of animal behavior with particular emphasis on animals living under natural conditions.

Evolution. Descent with modification through time.

Exogamy. The rule or custom by which a person marries outside a specified group.

Extended family. A family composed of two or more nuclear or polygamous families with kin links between them that form a residence group.

F

Family. A social group consisting in its simplest form of a married couple and their dependent children.

Felt tribe. A tribal society in which there is a strong sense of tribal identity but no centralized system of political organization.

Fossil. The preserved remains of plants or animals that lived in the past.

Free morpheme. A word or a part of a word that carries meaning and can function linguistically by itself. The word "dog" is a free morpheme.

Functionalism. A theoretical approach that seeks to determine the operating contributions (functions) of the various parts of a sociocultural system on a total culture. The emphasis is on explaining how the system works.

G

Gene. A chemical unit of heredity that occupies a particular position on a chromosome.

Genotype. The actual genetic makeup of an organism.

Genus. A biological classification between a family and a species. Thus, all living human beings belong to the family Hominidae, the genus *Homo,* and the species *sapiens.* The plural of genus is genera.

Ghosts. Supernatural beings that once were human. When a person dies and the spirit or soul refuses to depart, this is a ghost. Ghosts differ from ancestral spirits in that the former are usually unwelcome.

Glottochronology. In linguistics, a method of dating the time of divergence between related groups of languages.

Gods. Remote supernatural beings that tend to be named and powerful. Gods are usually of nonhuman origin.

H

Historical reconstruction. A technique advocated by Franz Boas that is designed to reveal the unique series of historical events which were thought to explain the characteristics of particular cultures. Also called historical particularism.

Hominid. A subdivision (family) of the primate order that includes all people, living or extinct; mankind in the broadest possible sense, including not only *Homo sapiens* but also earlier forms such as the australopithecines, *Homo erectus,* and so forth.

Hominoid. A subdivision (superfamily) of the primate order that includes both hominids and apes, living or extinct.

Homo erectus. An extinct population of hominids including *Pithecanthropus erectus* and *Sinathropus pekinensis.*

Homo sapiens. Modern human beings including all women and men presently living. Also known as *Homo sapiens sapiens.*

Horticulture. Farming without sophisticated technology.

Humanity. As used in this book, equivalent to *Homo sapiens.*

Hunters and gatherers. Hominid societies that depend for food on hunting wild animals and collecting wild plant foods. Such societies practice no farming, have no domesticated animals other than the dog, and do not have access to concentrated marine resources.

I

Ideal culture. Patterns of culture that are regarded as desirable models for behavior; what people say they ought to do as opposed to what they actually do.

Incest. Mating between persons who are considered to be closely related.

Innate. Inborn as opposed to learned.

Instinctive. A behavior pattern that is determined or strongly affected by genetic factors.

Integration. As applied to culture, the tendency for all aspects of a culture to function as an interrelated whole.

J

Joint extended family. A type of extended family. In its simplest form it consists of two nuclear families that form a residence group and have one member in common.

K

Kindred. The persons considered to be near or close relatives in a society with a bilateral descent system.

Kula ring. A system of ceremonial exchange in the Trobriand Islands in which white shell armbands are traded counterclockwise between partners while red shell necklaces are traded in a clockwise direction. Made famous by Bronislaw Malinowski.

L

Language. At the present time, there is no universally accepted definition of language. In its broadest sense, it may be thought of as the total design system responsible for meaningful symbolic speaking. A particular language is a system of culturally shared symbolic meanings applied to spoken sounds or substitutes for spoken sounds.

Law. A system of social norms in a society, adherence to which may be enforced by political authorities.

Levirate. A custom or expectation according to which a man's widow is supposed to marry a brother of the deceased.

Lexicon. The total inventory of words in a language.

Lineage. A named, exogamous, unilineal descent group, the members of which can actually trace their ancestry back to a real person. Lineages are often subdivisions of clans.

Linguistics. The study of language.

Local group. See Band.

M

Magic. In anthropology, any technique designed to force the supernatural to make a desired response. The conception of the supernatural is such that it is not believed to have the power of choice.

Mankind. As used in this book, equivalent to hominids. All people, female or male, living or extinct.

Marriage. A socially approved sexual and economic union between two or more persons that serves to legitimatize offspring and establish reciprocal rights and obligations.

Matrilineal descent. A type of unilineal descent that reckons descent exclusively through the female line.

Matrilocal residence. A residence pattern in which a married couple live with or near the wife's family.

Miocene. A geological epoch (subdivision) of the Cenozoic era.

Moiety. One half of a society that is divided into two exogamous groups.

Monogamy. A form of marriage in which a person may have just one spouse at any given time.

Morpheme. In linguistics, the smallest unit of sound that carries a specific meaning or meanings. In effect, words and parts of words.

Myth. A traditional story often involving supernatural elements, which is believed to be true by the participants in a particular culture.

N

Natural selection. The basic process of evolutionary change in biology by which the best adapted individuals in a population contribute more offspring to succeeding generations, thus altering through time the characteristics of the population. The most "fit" individuals are selected for rather than against.

Neanderthal. An extinct subspecies of human beings *(Homo sapiens neanderthalensis)* that lived in the Old World from about 100,000 years ago until about 40,000 years ago.

Neolithic. The period of prehistory beginning in the Old World about 10,000 years ago during which farming was invented and economically useful animals other than the dog were domesticated. The literal meaning of the term is "New Stone Age."

Neolocal residence. A residence pattern in which a married couple establish a new residence separate from either the family of the husband or the family of the wife.

Nocturnal. Active at night.

Nuclear family. The simplest known type of family, consisting of a married couple together with their dependent offspring.

O

Omnivorous. Eating a wide variety of foods.

Order. A biological classification less inclusive than a class and more inclusive than a superfamily. Human beings belong to the order of primates in the class of mammals.

P

Paleocene. The first (earliest) subdivision (epoch) of the Cenozoic era.

Paleolithic. Literally, the "Old Stone Age." The division of prehistory, largely occurring in the Old World, that precedes the Neolithic. Beginning several millions of years ago and lasting until roughly 10,000 years ago, the Paleolithic was the crucible that shaped the human animal. All Paleolithic cultures were based on the gathering of wild plant foods and the hunting of wild animals.

Parallel cousin. Children of siblings of the same sex.

Pastoralism. An economic lifeway based on the herding of livestock.

Patrilineal descent. A type of unilineal descent that reckons descent exclusively through the male line.

Patrilocal residence. A residence pattern in which a married couple live with or near the husband's family.

Peasants. Rural farmers in a state system of political organization.

Phenotype. The observable, external, physical characteristics of a plant or an animal.

Platyrrhine. Flat-nosed. The term is commonly used to refer to the New World monkeys.

Pleistocene. The geological subdivision (epoch) of the Cenozoic era that lasted from around two million years ago until about 10,000 years ago.

Pliocene. The geological subdivision (epoch) of the Cenozoic era that immediately preceded the Pleistocene.

Polyandry. A rare form of marriage in which one woman is simultaneously married to several men.

Polygamy. A form of marriage in which a woman or a man has more than one spouse; a general term that includes both polyandry and polygyny.

Polygyny. The commonest form of polygamy in which one man is simultaneously married to several women.

Potassium-argon dating. An absolute dating technique based on the conversion of radioactive potassium 40 to argon; used to date materials found in volcanic rock or ash.

Priest. In anthropology, a person whose authority to deal with the supernatural is derived from membership in an organized religious group.

Primate. The order of mammals that includes prosimians, monkeys, apes, and hominids.

Primitive. Something that is or resembles the first form or an early stage of a developmental series. A comparative term that refers to a type of structure rather than to a value judgment such as "better" or "worse." Thus, a fish is more primitive than a mammal because fish developed before mammals in the evolution of the vertebrates.

Prosimian. A suborder within the primates. All primates that are not included in Anthropoidea are prosimians. Living prosimians include the lemurs and the tarsiers.

R

Race. A population within a species that differs in degree from other populations on the basis of genetically transmitted physical characteristics which were originally adaptive in nature.

Racism. The attribution of behavioral or cultural characteristics to people on the basis of what people look like; associated with the scientifically indefensible idea of "superior" or "inferior" races.

Radiocarbon dating. An absolute dating technique that depends on the rate of decay of a radioactive form of carbon. Limited in range to a maximum of about 40,000 years.

Ramapithecus. An early (Miocene) form of hominid that may be ancestral to the later hominids.

Religion. In anthropology, an approach to the supernatural which is based on the idea that supernatural entities have the power of choice. A system of beliefs and techniques such as prayer or sacrifice designed to influence the supernatural toward a favorable response.

Rite. A ceremonial observance.

Ritual. A ceremonial event or series of events by which people relate to the supernatural.

Role. The behaviors expected of a person occupying a particular status.

S

Shaman. A person whose authority to deal with the supernatural derives from personal characteristics or abilities. Shamans are primarily healers (doctors) who treat diseases partially on the basis of supernatural techniques.

Sibling. A general term for brother or sister that is not based on sex.

Social anthropology. A form or subdivision of cultural anthropology that concentrates on social structure rather than on the totality of a cultural system.

Society. An organized group of persons who share a common lifeway. A total society is the largest group of persons within a given cultural domain, the group that contains or includes all the other groups.

Sociocultural. A term used to refer to both the social and the cultural characteristics of a human group.

Sociolinguistics. The study of how people use language in various social contexts.

Sororate. A custom or expectation according to which a widower (a man whose wife has died) is supposed to marry a sister of the deceased.

Species. A population or populations of organisms that are sufficiently similar to permit interbreeding with the production of fertile offspring.

State. A type of political organization with a strongly centralized power structure that has a monopoly on the legal use of force. States are usually characterized by a high degree of specialization and a division of the citizens into urban and rural segments, or into food producers and administrative personnel.

Status. A social position within a group or a society.

Subculture. A distinctive cluster of ideas and behavior patterns that characterizes a portion of a larger cultural system; variations within a larger cultural system.

Superorganic. The idea that culture is totally separate from biology and that culture can only be studied in terms of itself.

Symbol. Something that stands for something else when the connection between the symbol and its referent is arbitrary.

Synchronic. An approach to the study of culture that is not time oriented. Functionalist studies aimed at understanding how sociocultural systems work ''in the present'' are synchronic studies.

Syntax. The linguistic rules or principles that govern the construction of sentences; meaningful word order.

T

Tabu. A supernatural prohibition, usually imposed with the idea of supernatural penalties if the prohibition is broken.

Technology. Artifacts, whether simple or complex, and the knowledge required to make and utilize them.

Territorial behavior. A type of animal behavior in which an animal or a group of animals seeks to defend an area and maintain it for its own use.

Totemism. A ritual relationship between a human social group and some type of plant, animal, or natural object; frequently involves the idea that the social group has descended from the totemic source.

Tribe. A type of political organization associated with a middle-range human society. If a population is not composed of hunters and gatherers and is not organized as a state or a part of a state, then it is a tribe.

U

Unilineal descent. A type of descent that is reckoned through one line only.

Universal evolution. A way of viewing cultural evolution in which hominid culture is considered as a single worldwide cultural system.

W

Witchcraft. The belief that certain persons are endowed with a supernatural ability to do evil.

Name index

Subject index